T0326462

Knowledge Governance

The Anthem Other Canon Series

Anthem Press and The Other Canon Foundation are pleased
to present **The Anthem Other Canon Series**. The Other Canon – also
described as 'reality economics' – studies the economy as a real object rather than as
the behaviour of a model economy based on core axioms, assumptions and techniques.
The series includes both classical and contemporary works in this tradition, spanning
evolutionary, institutional and Post-Keynesian economics, the history of economic
thought and economic policy, economic sociology and technology governance,
and works on the theory of uneven development and in the tradition of
the German historical school.

Other Titles in the Series

A 'Short Treatise' on the Wealth and Poverty of Nations (1613)
Antonio Serra, edited by Sophus A. Reinert

Competitiveness and Development: Myth and Realities
Mehdi Shafaeddin, with a foreword by Erik S. Reinert

*Development and Semi-periphery: Post-neoliberal Trajectories
in South America and Central Eastern Europe*
Edited by Renato Boschi and Carlos Henrique Santana

*Economists and the Powerful:
Convenient Theories, Distorted Facts, Ample Rewards*
Norbert Häring and Niall Douglas

*The Politics of Enlightenment:
Constitutionalism, Republicanism, and the Rights of Man in Gaetano Filangieri*
Vincenzo Ferrone, translated by Sophus A. Reinert

Thorstein Veblen: Economics for an Age of Crises
Edited by Erik S. Reinert and Francesca L. Viano

Knowledge Governance

Reasserting the Public Interest

Edited by
Leonardo Burlamaqui,
Ana Célia Castro and Rainer Kattel

ANTHEM PRESS
LONDON · NEW YORK · DELHI

Anthem Press
An imprint of Wimbledon Publishing Company
www.anthempress.com

This edition first published in UK and USA 2012
by ANTHEM PRESS
75-76 Blackfriars Road, London SE1 8HA, UK
or PO Box 9779, London SW19 7ZG, UK
and
244 Madison Ave. #116, New York, NY 10016, USA

British Library Cataloguing-in-Publication Data
A catalogue record for this book is available from the British Library.

Library of Congress Cataloging-in-Publication Data
A catalog record for this book has been requested.

ISBN-13: 978 0 85728 535 5 (Hbk)
ISBN-10: 0 85728 535 1 (Hbk)

This title is also available as an eBook.

CONTENTS

LIST OF ABBREVIATIONS

ABIA	Brazilian Interdisciplinary Aids Association
ABIFINA	Associação Brasileira das Industrias de Química Fina, Biotecnologia e suas Especialidades (Brazilian Association of Industries of Fine Chemistry, Biotechnology and its Specialties)
ABPI	Associação Brasileira de Propriedade Intelectual (Brazilian Association of Intellectual Property)
AGU	Advocacia Geral da União (Office of the Solicitor-General of the Union)
ALRC	Australian Law Reform Commission
AMBEV	Companhia de Bebidas das Américas (Americas' Beverage Company)
ANVISA	Agência Nacional de Vigilância Sanitária (National Health Surveillance Agency)
API	Active Pharmaceutical Ingredient
AUTM	Association of University Technology Managers
BRC	biological resource center
BTA	bilateral trade agreements
CADE	Conselho Administrativo de Defesa Econômica (Administrative Council for Economic Defense, Brazil)
CAFC	Court of Appeals for the Federal Circuit
CIPIH	Commission on Intellectual Property Rights, Innovation and Public Health
CIS	Commonwealth of Independent States
CL	Compulsory Licenses
COOPI	Coordenação de Propriedade Intelectual (Coordination of Intellectual Property)
DARPA	Defense Advanced Research Projects Agency
DI	Distributed Innovation
DNS	developmental network state
DOJ	Department of Justice

EC	European Commission
EEC	European Economic Community
ELSI	ethical, legal, and social issues
EPC	European Patent Convention
EPO	European Patent Office
FDA	Food and Drug Administration
FDI	foreign direct investments
FSA	Federal Security Agency
FTC	Federal Trade Commission
GATS	General Agreement on Trade in Services
GATT	General Agreement on Trade and Tariffs
GIN	global innovation networks
GIPI	Grupo Interministerial de Propriedade Intelectual (Interministerial Group of Intellectual Property)
HGP	Human Genome Project
ICT	information and communications technology
ICTSD	International Centre for Trade and Sustainable Development
INPI	Instituto Nacional da Propriedade Industrial (National Institute of Industrial Property)
IP	intellectual property
IPA	intellectual property assessment
IPAC	Industrial Property Advisory Committee
IPC	Intellectual Property Committee
IPD	Investment Property Databank
IPR	intellectual property rights
ITO	International Trade Organization
JPO	Japanese Patent Office
LEM	Laboratory of Economics and Management
LPC	Lei de Proteção a Cultivares (Plant Variety Protection Law)
LPI	Lei de Propriedade Industrial (Industrial Property Law)
M&A	mergers and acquisitions
MDIC	Ministério do Desenvolvimento, Indústria e Comércio Exterior (Ministry of Development, Industry and Foreign Trade)
MIHR	Centre for Management of Intellectual Property in Health Research and Development
MS	Ministério da Saúde (Ministry of Health)

NAFTA	North American Free Trade Agreement
NBER	National Bureau of Economic Research
NCBI	National Center for Biotechnology Information
NHS	National Health Service
NIH	National Institutes of Health
NIS	national innovation system
NM	new molecular entity
NSF	National Science Foundation
PDP	Productive Development Plan
PGF	Procuradoria-Geral Federal (Federal Attorney General)
PSDB	Partido da Social Democracia Brasileira (Party of Brazilian Social Democracy)
PT	Partido Trabalhista (Portuguese: Labour Party)
PTO	Patent and Trademark Office
R&D	Research and development
SACGHS	Secretary's Advisory Committee on Genetics, Health, and Society
SBIR	Small Business Innovation Research
SDE	Secretaria de Direito Econômico (Secretariat of Economic Law)
TPM	technological protection measures
TRIPS	Trade-Related Aspects of Intellectual Property
TTO	Transfer Technology Office
UNCTAD	United Nations Conference on Trade and Development
USPTO	United States Patent and Trademark Office
WDI	World Development Indicators
WHO	World Health Organization
WIPO	World Intellectual Property Organization
WTO	World Trade Organization

LIST OF TABLES AND FIGURES

Tables

Figures

FOREWORD

The remarkable improvements in living standards achieved over the last two centuries by a good portion of the world's population have been made possible by advances in knowledge – at the applications end, advances in practical know-how but with these often supported by dramatic advances in basic understandings of how the natural world works. These advances have been the result of a cumulative collective process. Inventors and scientists working today to advance the state of knowledge base what they do on the knowledge created by their forebears. The key to making technology and science systems work productively has been to establish and enforce a governance structure that on the one hand provides incentives and rewards for success to those working to advance knowledge, and on the other hand keeps both established and new knowledge largely open for those who can use and further advance it.

Over the years there have developed two quite different governance systems for doing this. One is the system of public science, which emphasizes open publication and rewards of recognition to scientists whose work is understood to have advanced knowledge significantly. The other is the system of largely private technology development, where successful inventors are rewarded by patents and other means through which they can appropriate a share of the economic benefits their work has allowed, but in which, customarily, their ability to control access is limited in time and scope. Until recently at least, the continuing advances in living standards and basic knowledge, and the widening spread of economic development and scientific capabilities, have shown a system of governance of knowledge that has been working reasonably well.

There presently are several strong threats to this system. One is the increasing propensity of participants in the public science system to patent aspects of their research findings. A second is the increasing propensity of companies doing work to advance technology to seek broad patents and to try to enforce them broadly. The relative openness of our scientific and technological knowledge is in danger of being eroded. It is urgent that we consider carefully the way the world presently governs its system of knowledge creation and use, recognize how that system is changing, and reflect on what kind of a governance structure we want.

This is what this book is all about.

Richard R. Nelson
Director, Program on Science,
Technology, and Global Development
Columbia Earth Institute

INTRODUCTION

Leonardo Burlamaqui
Ford Foundation and State University of Rio de Janeiro

Ana Célia Castro
Federal University of Rio de Janeiro

Rainer Kattel
Tallinn University of Technology

The Purpose of the Book

As we enter the second decade of the twenty-first century, the economics profession is grappling with how to better respond to an extremely deep financial-turned-fiscal crisis, and there is no end in sight to that debate. That context has forced at least part of the mainstream of the profession to seek for a new "identity," and concepts which were at the core of the mainstream theory – such as the efficient market hypothesis and markets as self-regulating entities – are under severe scrutiny, while Keynes's ideas are fully back in business and Hyman Minsky's Financial Instability Hypothesis regains prestige in academic circles as well as among policymakers and money managers. On the policy front, the identity crisis is equally profound. The once taken-for-granted benefits of financial globalization are being replaced by the urgency of better supervision and regulation of banks and other financial entities, and different modalities of capital controls are now part of the IMF's tool kit for dealing with the instability now associated with the complete openness of countries' capital accounts (Skidelsky 2009; Sheng 2010; Grabel 2010).

In the "nonfinancial" side of economics, a less strident but equally important shakeout is also starting to happen. Research on open-source innovation by Harvard and Stanford legal scholars such as Yochai Benkler and Lawrence Lessig and on consumer-based innovation by MIT economist Eric von Hippel and his research team

Leonardo Burlamaqui wishes to make clear that he is writing in his personal capacity and that the opinions expressed here do not necessary represent the Ford Foundation.

are throwing new light on matters like growth dynamics, innovation patterns and the interaction of competition and collaboration among firms and consumers.[1]

In that realm, processes involved in knowledge, learning and innovation are, in fact, being profoundly renewed.[2] These changes are not only happening in companies, universities and research institutions that forge technological innovations, but there are new forms of interaction between agents that affect knowledge generation and diffusion paths. Knowledge flows (or it is appropriated) by hybrid organizations composed of markets and networks that respond to different market and nonmarket incentives. The OECD Innovation Strategy defines "Knowledge Networks and Markets" as "arrangements which govern the transfer of various types of knowledge, such as intellectual property, know-how, software code or databases, between independent parties" (OECD 2011).[3] In these new types of organizations, knowledge is both proprietary and fragmented across multiple entities. It is also incorporated into intangibles assets, whose value they seek to seize (Teece 2002). These intangible assets are marketed under different forms and in emerging market structures.

However, not all knowledge is capable of being appropriated – the channels of knowledge can also circulate freely in cooperative research and innovation networks, such as in open databases and programming code, in "wikis," in the "creative commons" and "science commons" movements that seek to constitute alternative intellectual property regimes.[1] The results point to the necessity of rethinking patent law as well as government incentives for research and open sourcing and the way innovation policies are designed and managed.

---

1 This is not to argue that there has not been any significant collaborative or "open" R&D before in history (see Mowery 2009 on collaborative R&D efforts in US industry in the late nineteenth and early twentieth centuries).

2 The changes alluded to are the products not only of new technological regimes such as described in Coriat and Weinstein (2002), but, especially, the result of changes in institutions, organizations and governance structures that accompany them.

3 Countries are searching for new sources of growth, and knowledge and innovation are key pillars. For example, the OECD is carrying out a project on knowledge networks and markets (KNMs) to measure the impact of different channels through which knowledge is created and transferred. The OECD recognizes that ensuring a steady supply of new knowledge and its flows to those organizations and individuals who can exploit it most efficiently is a key policy priority, particularly when the dissemination of knowledge can also foster additional innovation. OECD economies can ill afford valuable ideas being left unexploited. Solutions are therefore needed to ensure that the two sides of the market – supply and demand – meet and interact with the lowest possible transaction costs. Any policy reform needs to anticipate its likely impact on incentives for knowledge creation, while creating conditions that best support the creation, dissemination and adoption of knowledge. There is genuine interest in understanding how different types of reward systems can complement traditional intellectual property (IP) and what policies can foster the emergence of an intermediary sector that increases the efficiency with which knowledge can be exchanged.

4 The return of the "commons," or the collective and/or shared property, is one of the most important tendencies nowadays in the exploration of natural resources such as fisheries and other community resources. The collective property is a shared bundle of rights: to access, to withdraw, to manage, to exclude and to alienate. See Ostrom (1990).

We submit that theoretical and empirical work understanding these changes in knowledge creation and diffusion is significantly lagging behind the developments in the way the economic system works. While it is obvious that firm-level dynamics are changing – towards networks and peer production in technologically leading companies in the developed countries, and towards increasing integration into global and regional production and innovation networks in developing countries – academic discussions as well as policy disputes in the World Trade Organization (WTO) and other international forums take place in a rather rigid and narrow perspective. This approach concentrates on tangible and codified knowledge creation and diffusion in R&D that can be protected via patents and other intellectual property rules and regulations (intellectual property rights, IPRs). In terms of global policy initiatives, it is becoming increasingly clear that especially the WTO is mostly a conflict resolution facility rather than a global governance body able to generate cooperation and steer international coordinated policy action.

From a very different angle, significant policy changes are also in order: Justin Lin, the new chief economist of the World Bank and the first citizen from a developing country to serve in that position, is proclaiming loudly and clearly in his papers and speeches that "governments must regain center stage" and that although industrial policies have failed more often than they have succeeded, "the only thing worse is not having an industrial policy" (quoted in Osnos 2010).

However, this renewed intellectual activity in both the financial and nonfinancial sides of economics is not linked so far. But this link must be established for the simple reason that recovering from the financial crisis will likely require new thinking about growth dynamics and strategies for sustaining it as well as reforming the financial system for those precise goals.

It is the new thinking emerging from this second shakeout – in the way knowledge and innovation are produced, disseminated and appropriated – and its implications for policymaking and institutional coordination that this book aims to contribute to.

As it is becoming more and more obvious that fiscal retrenchment and financial reregulation alone will not restore competitiveness in the United States and in the European periphery, industrial policy is back on the agenda. It is, however, also obvious that in policy terms, there is no going back to the post–World War II era of industry-led industrial policy. First, catch-up-oriented policies and strategies have become much more complex due to the technological revolutions in agriculture and in services and more globally constrained by the consolidation of China as the unrivalled master of "governing the global market," by the vertiginous growth of high-tech services as a major component of G8 countries' exports, and by the advent of the WTO and its agreements (especially the Trade-Related Aspects of Intellectual Property Rights (TRIPs) and the General Agreement on Trade in Services (GATS)), which leave much less space for developing and developed countries to experiment, and concoct, with various policy tools (Wade 2004).

It is, for instance, doubtful whether the United States could actually reissue a Glass–Steagall-based act under the WTO's financial services act to separate investment and depository banks. Further, most of classic industrial policy tools – tariff protection for infant industry, local content requirement, soft IP regimes, preferential interest rates, and so on – can still be used but in a highly restricted and cumbersome way requiring high policy skills and coordinated policy action (Amsden 2005; Kelsey 2008).

Accordingly, many countries willing to catch up rather blindly end up copying policies and institutions as international "best practices" that are in fact ill fitted to their domestic needs. Moreover, it is often difficult to discern what these domestic policy concerns should be. Should one promote industrial exports, agriculture or business services and tourism? Should one invest into domestic basic research, and if so, in what areas? These are but a few questions faced by today's developing countries – some of which are also pertinent to the "mature" ones. And as the WTO restricts countries' ability to experiment with various policies and their management, the policy-learning capacities evolve poorly.

At the same time, rent extraction and profits streaming from legal hyperprotection have become pervasively important for firm strategies to compete in a globalized market place. Patenting has become massively more important for both firms and academic researchers. Indeed, it can be argued, as this book does, that the US/WTO-based global IPR system that has evolved over the past three decades overemphasizes private interest and seriously hampers public interests in access to knowledge and innovation diffusion.

Furthermore, governance and public administration have similarly witnessed a sea change away from powerful Weberian bureaucracies in post–World War II Europe and, later, in East Asia, toward delegation of power and policymaking to networks of multiple agencies, often run by principles mimicking the market.[5] Again, there is no returning back to classical Weberian bureaucracy-backed industrial policy. However, we argue in this book, there is a way forward. In the increasingly knowledge-based economies of today's capitalism, the governance of knowledge should be at the forefront of both competitiveness upgrading and development strategies, as well as the linchpin of socially responsible policy reforms.

Indeed, the way we have it now, entire groups of countries, middle-income economies, are stuck in what Robert Wade (2011) labels the middle-income trap: "They cannot compete with firms producing standardized products in lower-wage countries; and they cannot compete with firms producing more technology-intensive goods and services in higher-wage countries." These countries in Southeast Asia, North Africa, Latin America and Eastern Europe are stuck between a proverbial rock and a hard place with no clear-cut policy options of how to go forward. This book offers an option by introducing a knowledge-governance framework.

Defining Knowledge Governance

Taking into account these structural changes, the new frontiers that have to be faced by industrial, technological, innovation and competition policies, as well as increasingly complex coordination problems rising among them, a major cluster of policy and

---

5 Although East Asia still relies on strong pools of "Weberian Bureaucracies" (Wade 2004; Weiss 2012).

institutional design challenges emerges. To address them, a new conceptual framework is necessary. We propose *Knowledge Governance* as the adequate framework to meet this challenge. Knowledge governance is an analytical framework which embraces different forms of public governance mechanisms such as supervision, rulemaking, regulation, policy prescriptions and institutional coordination and applies them to the realms of knowledge production, diffusion and appropriation (Burlamaqui 2009, 2010).

As a provisional definition, "'knowledge governance' is an approach that cuts across the fields of public policy, economic supervision and regulation, knowledge and organization management, and innovation, competition and competitiveness analysis. Knowledge governance deals with how the deployment of governance mechanisms influences knowledge processes, such as creating, retaining and sharing knowledge."[6] As an analytical perspective, it has its roots in evolutionary economics and economic sociology and encompasses industrial and competition policies as well as intellectual property rules and regulations, but supersedes them by trying to investigate how those areas link up, what the major conflicts are among them and especially by seeking to provide a public policy repertoire and an institutional framework within which those linkages build up coherently and their inherent conflicts are properly managed. Its major goal is to help to produce the contours of the new knowledge ecology where the public interest is front and center.

The knowledge governance approach assumes that knowledge is by nature both public (e.g., published scientific findings and commons-based research) and private (trade secrets and intangible assets such as organizational routines). It also assumes, in line with its foundations in Schumpeterian and institutional theorizing, that competition and public policy are the key drivers that steer the evolution of the public/private knowledge mix. More precisely, competition and the way it is governed is largely shaped through incentives, supervision and regulations, which forms of knowledge corporations will seek to develop, and which organizational forms they will use to produce and protect knowledge and innovations.

Thus, knowledge governance draws attention to and directs its research agenda toward the new interactions emerging between firm-level behavior and public policies in the realm of knowledge creation, diffusion and appropriation. This is not to say that there is no research looking at such interactions. The "evolutionary economics" literature emerging since the late 1970s with path-breaking works by Chris Freeman, Nathan Rosenberg, Richard Nelson and many others developed the concept of national innovation systems and explored its varieties. The "Coasian" perspective looks at how firms deal with transactions costs that result from diverse regulatory environments. This has led to the utilization of ideas such as externalities and network failures within the neoclassical framework, a body of work epitomized by Rodrik (2007). Further, a large and

---

6 In a more "micro" and economizing perspective, *which is not ours*, "It insists on clear micro (behavioral) foundations, adopts an economizing perspective and examines the links between knowledge-based units of analysis with diverse characteristics and governance mechanisms with diverse capabilities of handling these transactions. Research issues that the knowledge governance approach illuminates are sketched" (Foss 2007).

diverse body of literature tries to understand how institutions evolve and influence firm-level behavior towards managing innovation.

While all these research strands have merit in improving our understanding of the interactions between knowledge creation, diffusion and appropriation, none of them has put the need to govern knowledge, and its interactions with governance structures, at the center of their research agendas. The result is that "knowledge" has become hijacked by a rather narrowly focused community of scholars, policy analysts and professional lobbyists working on (ever extending) patents and copyrights.

Our core assumptions are different. In our view, knowledge and education are the main levers for the achievement of economic development, social justice, cultural enhancement and true democracy (Benkler 2006; Evans 2009). As we move into an increasingly knowledge intensive economy and society, where knowledge, information and organizational capabilities become the key strategic and transforming resources of society, it becomes clear that the governance of knowledge should be at the center of a proper global economic system of governance.

Knowledge is embodied in books, journals, equipment, technological and social innovations and, especially, in the human mind.[7] As argued above, however, it is also embodied in such intangibles as company routines and organizational cultures, that is, in human interaction patterns as argued by Nelson and Winter (1982).[8] It diffuses through society via investments and innovations and the result is development and structural change. As Schumpeter showed, modern capitalism has proved a remarkably powerful engine of technological progress. Yet, there is no linearity in knowledge generation and, in particular, in diffusion via new innovations. On the contrary, knowledge generation and diffusion are fundamental building blocks of what Schumpeter aptly described as creative destruction, where both path dependencies and revolutionary change play a crucial role.

Furthermore, thanks to the work done by Richard Nelson, David Mowery, Vernon Ruttan and Paul David, among others, it is now widely recognized that the power and speed of invention and innovation is increasingly dependent on the strength of the science base that they drew upon.[9] This science base is largely the product of publicly funded research, and the knowledge produced by that research used to be largely open and available for potential innovators. In other words, market dynamics used to rest on a publicly supported "scientific commons": ideas should never be privately owned.

---

7 Metcalfe (2004) stresses the restless and tacit nature of knowledge as a private process in the human mind. For this reason, it is important to distinguish between knowledge as such and knowledge assets, mainly embedded in institutions and organizations, as in entrepreneurial routines.

8 Selznick (1957) had called attention to "organization's distinctive competence" and Edith Penrose (1959) to the bundle of potential services that a unique combination of firm resources can render. These are the foundations for knowledge assets as the most important resources of a firm.

9 Giovanni Dosi (1988) should also be mentioned, as the technological paradigm approach, with its sources and procedures for learning, is consistent with the "governance approach" presented here.

However, as markets and corporations went global, a paradox developed. In total contradiction with the globalizers' ideology of "free movement of goods, capital and ideas," intellectual property rules and agreements became much more restrictive, embodied in enforcement mechanisms such as the Trade-Related Aspects of Intellectual Property agreement included in the WTO, and TRIPS-plus agreements embodied in bilateral and regional trade agreements (in the former framework, only countries can settle mutual disputes; in the latter, companies can take actions against countries, as well).[10] An increasingly restricted set of intellectual property rules and regulations – largely written by private law firms – became the center of a privately sponsored system of knowledge *management*. Those rules are the legal sinews of the information age; they affect everything from the availability and price of AIDS drugs to patterns of international development, to the communications architecture of the Internet. Those rules were also pivotal in the expansion of production networks into the developing world via outsourcing and foreign direct investments.

From a global perspective, an even more worrisome scenario can be outlined. If we think of knowledge production and innovation as cumulative processes where cutting-edge knowledge rests on previous know-how, and stronger patents and intellectual property rights are erected as "fences" to privatize and protect them, it is not difficult to see that there is an inevitable tension and trade-off between the private and public dimensions of IPR rules. The tradition of intellectual property as a thin layer of rights surrounding a carefully preserved public domain has been replaced by a reality in which the public domain should be eliminated wherever possible (cf. Boyle 2008 and Burlamaqui in this volume).

There are two parts to this process. The "defensive" part focuses on government-backed corporate strategies for intensifying the enforcement of monopoly rights to exclude others from using information that has been defined as private property. The "offensive" part involves strategies for taking information that has been considered part of "nature" or the common cultural heritage of humankind and transforming it into private property. The success of both parts of the process is leading to a global redistribution of property as well as to a deepening knowledge divide. What is emerging is a mix of global knowledge monopolies, preclusion of access to new knowledge and the privatization of traditional common knowledge.[11]

---

10 Cimoli, Coriat and Primi (2009) highlight the "industrial policy" component of IP management (asymmetrically managed by advanced and developing countries).

11 A frightening example of preclusion of access to new knowledge comes from biotech: Gene patents are now used to halt research, prevent medical testing and keep vital information from the public. Gene patents slow the pace of medical advance on deadly diseases. And they raise costs exorbitantly: a test for breast cancer that could be done for US$1,000 now costs US$3,000. Our genetic makeup represents the common heritage of all life on earth. We should not be able to patent genes, either. Yet by now, one-fifth of the genes in our bodies are privately owned. However, a counter tendency nowadays is a matter of dispute between the US Supreme Court and the biotech firms that own these patents. On the privatization of common traditional knowledge, the striking example comes from a recent US Patent and Trade Marks Office measure: it just issued 150 yoga-related copyrights, 134 patents on yoga accessories and 2,315 yoga trademarks. The Indian government is not laughing. It is building its own database on the millennium-old character of those practices in order to react. Another race to the bottom is clearly on its way.

Clearly, the ever-increasing privatization of knowledge at the expense of the public domain is not the only way forward. Alternative modes of knowledge governance like open source, open business, the creative commons and the copyleft movements are certainly models that deserve more attention and discussion. However, most of the attention in understanding the role of knowledge has focused on firms and entrepreneurs operating in a market setting who are the central actors in developing and introducing new products and processes. Very little thinking was dedicated to how it should be governed.

The outcome is that the emerging global architecture clearly lacks a knowledge governance system committed to the developmental needs of emergent and poor countries and designed to close the knowledge gap and restore the balance between public domain and private interests.

Knowledge Governance and the Public Interest: Restoring the Public Domain

While there are increasing changes in the way that, in particular, leading technology companies govern knowledge generation and diffusion, public governance of innovation and knowledge has undergone not less significant changes in the last few decades. We argue that there are three key tendencies that have *negatively* impacted the evolution of public governance in the field of knowledge and innovation.

First, the rise of the new public management (NPM) approach leading to the "marketization" of governance, using the "government failure" approach in order to shrink public interventions into markets (Drechsler 2005). This has led the way to a horizontal emphasis of one-size-fits-all prescriptions toward across-the-board privatization of public services and to regulations sponsored by private interests, such as the current one in the IPR regime. The core idea here is that while markets may fail, governments are bound to fail even more. This logic led to the prescription that the public sector needs an injection of market discipline in one form or other. This engendered innovation policies that are based on competitive bidding processes and IPR offices that operate as profit centers (Lawson 2008). In most cases these attempts lead to much more fragmented and uncoordinated policy arenas, where cost-effectiveness becomes the key steering mechanism of public policies. In other words, public interests become secondary.

Second, the internationalization of the intellectual paradigm within which policymakers and public officials function. Since the advent of the WTO, the European Union and multiple other international organizations, the merging of neoliberal policy reform prescriptions with new public management proposals for institutional redesign has exerted increasing pressure towards policymakers' and public officials' "intellectual homogenization" in the global forums. The result was an introduction of a host of policy and institutional changes, especially in emerging and poor countries, that lead to a contraction of the domestic policy space and increasing constraints to domestic democratic governance.[12]

---

12 In IPR, many developing countries use training for competence building offered by WIPO and by US and European patent offices.

During negotiations with the WTO and various bilateral and regional trade agreements, policymakers and international negotiators were often captured by narratives and rule-making proceedings that were completely foreign to their domestic interests.[13] This resulted in an increasing delinking of innovation policies, IPR regulations and financial deregulation agreements from domestic priorities and from the requisites of national development strategies (Deere 2008; Kelsey 2008).[14]

Third, the increasing difficulties to coordinate complex *and* fragmented innovation and knowledge policy arenas under an intellectual framework that *assumes* that markets alone will "solve the problems." The abovementioned changes in the public governance of knowledge engender massive challenges in coordinating various policy areas dealing with knowledge generation and diffusion (from public procurement to R&D, from trade regulations to higher education). In fact, related policy areas often might be in conflict: strong IPR in pharmaceuticals may be good for FDI but may easily hamper domestic academic research into specific diseases. The evidence we have from emerging economies, in particular from Latin America and Central and Eastern Europe, suggests that developing countries are not able to deal with this challenge precisely because (1) their policy arenas are increasingly fragmented between numerous ministries and agencies, and (2) their policy-making capabilities and "mind frame" are internationalized and delinked from domestic needs.

We argue, therefore, (1) that in the area of knowledge creation and diffusion, in order for policymaking to be effective – from a public interest point of view – an inclusionary knowledge governance approach is needed in order to supersede the exclusionary nature of the existing IP regime, and (2) that the effectiveness of such an approach requires policymakers to consciously counteract these "globally produced" and corporate-sponsored exclusionary rules and regulations with "domestically adapted" and public-interest-sponsored governance devices (supervision, regulation, institutional coordination and innovative policy mixes) that are able to more effectively steer knowledge creation towards diffusion and democratization. In our understanding, these tasks amount to rekindling the idea of the public sphere in knowledge creation, access to knowledge and innovation diffusion.

The current knowledge ecology is far from that set of normative prescriptions, but, notwithstanding, a few promising changes can already be detected, particularly in the European Union. In response to some of the challenges described above, a new Neo-Weberian governance approach is emerging (Pollitt and Bouckaert 2004). The Neo-Weberian approach is not a full return to the "classical" Weberian structures, but rather the incorporation of selected elements from the new public management and their "accommodation" under a Weberian basis (see Drechsler 2009; Pollitt and Bouckaert 2004; Pollitt et al. 2009, passim). The Neo-Weberian approach seeks to consolidate a fragmented policy landscape (i.e., dislocated and fragmented policy capacities in

---

13 As Drahos (1999) argues, referring specifically to IPRs, such communities are formed by virtue of their technical expertise and carry common values.

14 Perhaps the most striking example of this is the speed and depth with which most African states not simply adopted the TRIPS agreement, but often went beyond it.

multiple agencies and organizations) through (re)emphasizing coordination practices and the importance of a strong civil service with superb ethos and esprit de corps. The Neo-Weberian state signifies mostly a shift "from an internal orientation toward bureaucratic rules to an external orientation toward meeting citizens' needs and wishes. The primary route to achieving this is not the employment of market mechanisms (although they may occasionally come in handy) but the creation of a professional culture of quality and service" (Pollitt and Bouckaert 2004, 99–100). It also stresses the professionalization of public service and a move from an expert in laws and regulations to a professional manager oriented toward meeting citizens' needs.

In our view, to be effective it is vital for knowledge governance initiatives to be based in Neo-Weberian administrative structures.[15] Safeguarding public interest within knowledge governance is only possible on the basis of a strong and competent bureaucracy embedded in a civil service ethos, as some of the contributions in this book show. It is, however, important to note that many developing countries should first build solid "classic" Weberian public administration (clear rules and regulations, accountability and predictability, merit-based civil service, to name key Weberian characteristics), in order to *become eligible* to take advantage of Neo-Weberian ideas and reforms (Randma-Liiv 2009).

Summing up the previous discussion, we can point to three big challenges that scholars, policymakers, regulators and public officials need to grapple with in order to build up effective knowledge governance initiatives and institutions:

- Institutional coordination – which agencies to include and how to include them in the policy debates over knowledge and innovation, and what sort of priorities, strategies tactics and metrics should be applied.
- Scope and policy choices – which policy instruments should be used and to what extent (how widely) to coordinate different policy fields (e.g., economics, education and research, labor market, finance) that are key in the production, diffusion and appropriation of knowledge and innovation.
- Intrapolicy coordination and policy change – given the scope and the policies, how to design the policy mix (and when to change it) to achieve the goals of the knowledge governance reform agenda (Karo and Kattel 2011, 301).

None of these challenges are easy and the answers are far from obvious, but ignoring them will most certainly perpetuate the exclusionary regime for handling the knowledge we now have – both nationally and globally – and increase the imbalances between a hyperextended private-interests arena and a dangerously contracted public domain. To put it very bluntly, at their core these imbalances ultimately translate into a growing tradeoff between a corporate-sponsored globalization and democracy.

---

15 Patent offices, universities and other public research institutes can be seen as this kind of institution.

Overview of the Book

As this is the first book to introduce and use the concept of knowledge governance, the contributions are almost by necessity rather diverse. Furthermore, most of the contributions seek to demark research areas that have received only scant and fleeting attention in previous literature. Thus, the book is in many ways an invitation to deepen the research and to incite debates and dialogues. However, all contributions take the need to rethink the public sector's role in knowledge generation and diffusion as their starting point; all contributors follow the knowledge governance approach.

The first section of the book – building a knowledge governance framework – includes contributions by Burlamaqui, Primi, and Kattel and aims to clarify the framework of knowledge governance and its theoretical and policy implications.

Leonardo Burlamaqui's contribution lays the theoretical groundwork for the entire book. His chapter proposes a framework within which, in the field of knowledge, the dividing line between private interests and the public domain can and should be redrawn. It seeks to contribute to a better understanding of the interaction among innovation, competition and intellectual property rules and regulations, from an evolutionary perspective. As such, it tries to propose a coherent framework within which the discussions of both institution building and development-oriented policy design can take place. In order to accomplish that, the paper introduces the concept of "knowledge governance" as an analytical and policy-oriented approach that should produce a better way to understand how the interaction among the production, appropriation and diffusion of knowledge ought to be structured from a public policy/public interest point of view.

Annalisa Primi frames the debate about intellectual property and innovation on the basis of the evolutionary understanding of the process of innovation. She clarifies the role and impact of IP on innovative conducts, focusing mostly on patents, and looks at theoretical arguments, both from evolutionary and mainstream perspectives, about knowledge transferability and appropriability. She further demonstrates the mismatch between the intentional functionalities of the patent system (incentive and/or reward for innovation) and the effective use of the system by firms and other innovative agents (i.e., the use of strategic and defensive patenting and the emergence of new markets for knowledge). Her article also develops an intriguing knowledge governance framework based on different dynamics around knowledge, technology and learning.

Rainer Kattel's contribution looks at global drivers of knowledge in the catching-up context and develops a simple theoretical framework for knowledge governance regimes. The aim of knowledge governance regimes is to show that instead of traditional sector-specific industrial policy, globalized markets, production and innovation networks and international governance of trade and IPR require various new types of policy capacities and coordination. The latter is hampered by a decontextualization of economic policy through the WTO regime and the new public management reforms accompanying it.

The second section – the impact of antitrust and polity – deals with issues on the role of the state and regulation and includes contributions by Block and Keller, Possas and Leopardi, and finally, Shadlen's considerations dealing with the pharmaceutical industry.

Fred Block and Matthew R. Keller's contribution shows how startlingly important public sector funding – and governing – of key innovations in United States industry has been during postwar development. They draw on a unique data set of prize-winning innovations between 1971 and 2006 and document three key changes in the United States economy. The first is an expanding role of interorganizational collaborations in producing award-winning innovations. The second is the diminishing role of the largest corporations as sources of innovation. The third is the expanded role of public institutions and public funding in the innovation process. This leads Block and Keller to the surprising conclusion that the United States increasingly resembles a developmental network state in which government initiatives are critical in overcoming network failures and in providing critical funding for the innovation process. The paper concludes by addressing the implications of these finding for debates over the appropriate regime for intellectual property rights.

The article by Mario Luiz Possas and Maria Tereza Leopardi Mello looks more closely at the conflict between IPRs and competition policy. The authors argue that to the extent that competition policy – antitrust in particular – aims to protect and ensure the existence of competition in any given market, a latent contradiction between both legal systems might emerge. IPRs, insofar as they make it easier to appropriate the returns from innovative efforts, contribute to extend the resulting competitive advantages, which may on its turn incent such efforts and strengthen the rights owner's market power, thus restraining competition and innovation diffusion to some extent. Although socially ambiguous, such outcomes are intrinsic to the innovation system. The article concludes that competition-policy analytical tools provide an appropriate means to assess the net restrictive effects from particular appropriability legal mechanisms. The article compares IPR developments from an antitrust perspective in the United States, the European Union and Brazil.

Ken Shadlen looks in greater detail at challenges developing countries face in devising knowledge governance structures using their flexibilities under the TRIPS agreement with regard to patents, especially in pharmaceuticals, with a particular focus on measures to restrict pharmaceutical patenting. Shadlen analyzes the Brazilian experience of attempting to restrict pharmaceutical patents through examination procedures. He focuses on two sources of coalitional weakness: how divisions within the state isolate the officials responsible for executing the policy and how the changing interests of the local pharmaceutical sector generate resistance among key societal actors.

The third part of the book – the role of old and new institutions – presents some empirical material on the knowledge governance exploring patent office practices and procedures, and new common spaces to share property rights. The contributions by Castro et al. and Rossini and Wilbanks illustrate the role of old and new institutions in intellectual protection.

Ana Célia Castro, Ana María Pacón and Mônica Desidério look at how patent offices are governed and managed in Latin America, and how important the varied institutional culture is. A better definition of the criteria for novelty, inventive activity and utility are among the priorities for a possible positive agenda for patent examinations, and descriptive sufficiency can offer a tool for innovation policy. Better patents are a positive instrument to foster innovation and development. Patent examiners are civil servants concerned with the importance of their role in granting privileges and monopolist power. Capacity building, not only related to the technological frontier, but mainly rooted in an interdisciplinary approach, is a crucial dimension as far as building a solid institutional culture is concerned.

John Wilbanks and Carolina Rossini examine the relationships among funders, research institutions and the "units" of knowledge creation and local knowledge governance, which are hosted inside research institutions. The article seeks to uncover the knowledge spaces where commons-based approaches, peer production and modes of network-mediated innovation have – and have not – emerged and to examine the conditions under which these approaches either flourish or are discouraged. The authors conclude that the emergence of novel, democratized and distributed knowledge governance represents a meaningful complement to more traditional systems, with the potential to create new public-knowledge goods accessible to a global civil society and spur innovation in previously unforeseen ways.

Luigi Palombi asks perhaps the most provocative question of the entire book: Do we need patents? His answer is no, we actually do not need patents for knowledge governance to deliver innovations and its diffusion. Palombi looks both at historical trends in patenting and at theoretical alternatives to patent monopolies using chemical substances and their patenting practices throughout the last hundred years in Anglo-American systems as examples. He also shows how current patent systems lead to corporate rent extraction and in fact to less innovation.

Last but not least, we wish to thank the Ford Foundation for its generous support and the incentive that made the entire book possible in the first place. We would like to thank Annalisa Primi for her comments to this introduction and Sarah Anderson for suggesting the subtitle to the book. We would also like to thank the authors for their contribution and enthusiasm not only in writing the articles, but also in participating in the meetings held in Rio de Janeiro (2009) and Lisbon (2010) during this fruitful period. The editors would like to thank the Estonian Science Foundation (Grant no. 8418) for supporting this endeavor.

References

All web addresses last accessed August 2011.

Amsden, Alice. 2005. "Promoting Industry under WTO Law." In K. P. Gallagher (ed.), *Putting Development First: The Importance of Policy Space in the WTO and International Financial Institutions*, 216–32. London and New York: Zed books.
Benkler, Yochai. 2006. *The Wealth of Networks*. New Haven, CT and London: Yale University Press.
Boyle, James. 2008. *The Public Domain: Enclosing the Commons of the Mind*. New Haven, CT and London: Yale University Press.
Burlamaqui, Leonardo. 2009. "Innovation, Competition Policies and Intellectual Property: An Evolutionary Perspective and its Policy Implications." In Neil Netanel (ed.), *The Development Agenda: Global Intellectual Property and Developing Countries*. Oxford: Oxford University Press.

_____. 2010. "Intellectual Property, Innovation and Development." *Brazilian Journal of Political Economy* 30 (4). Available at http://www.scielo.br/scielo.php?pid=S0101-31572010000400002&script=sci_arttext

Cimoli, Mario, Benjamin Coriat and Annalisa Primi. 2009. "Intellectual Property and Industrial Development: A Critical Assessment." In M. Cimoli, G. Dosi and J. E. Stiglitz (eds), *Industrial Policy and Development: The Political Economy of Capabilities Accumulation*, 506–38. Oxford: Oxford University Press.

Coriat, B. and Olivier Weinstein. 2002. "Science-Based Innovation Regimes and Institutional Arrangements: From Science-Based '1' to Science-Based '2' Regimes. Towards a New Science-Based Regime? Industrial and Innovation." Available at http://www.druid.dk/uploads/tx_picturedb/ds2002-585.pdf

Deere, Carolyn. 2008. *The Implementation Game: The TRIPS Agreement and the Global Politics of Intellectual Property Reform in Developing Countries*. Oxford: Oxford University Press.

Dosi, Giovanni. 1988. "Sources, Procedures, and Microeconomic Effects of Innovation." *Journal of Economic Literature* 26 (3): 1120–71.

Drahos, Peter. 1999. "Biotechnology Patents, Markets And Morality." *European Intellectual Property Review* 21 (9): 441–44.

Drechsler, Wolfgang. 2009. "Towards a Neo-Weberian European Union? Lisbon Agenda and Public Administration." *Halduskultuur* 10: 6–21.

_____. 2005. "The Rise and Demise of the New Public Management." *Post-autistic Economics Review* 33 Available at http://www.paecon.net/PAEReview/issue33/Drechsler33.htm

Evans, Peter. 2009. "Constructing the 21st Century Developmental State: Potentialities and Pitfalls." Available at http://www.ideiad.com.br/seminariointernacional/

Foss, Nicolai J. 2007. "The Emerging Knowledge Governance Approach: Challenges and Characteristics." *Organization* 14 (1): 29–52.

Grabel, Ilene. 2010. "Promising Avenues, False Starts and Dead Ends: Global Governance and Development Finance in the Wake of the Crisis." PERI Working Paper Series 241, November. Available at http://www.peri.umass.edu/fileadmin/pdf/working_papers/working_papers_201-250/WP241.pdf

Hippel, Eric von. 1988. *The Sources of Innovation*. Oxford: Oxford University Press.

Karo, Erkki and Rainer Kattel. 2011. "Coordination of Innovation Policies in the Catching-up Context: A Historical Perspective on Estonia and Brazil." *International Journal of Technological Learning, Innovation and Development* 3 (4): 293–329.

Kelsey, Jane. 2008. *Serving Whose Interests? The Political Economy of Trade in Service Agreements*. London: Routledge.

Lawson, Charles. 2008. "Managerialist Influences on Granting Patents in Australia." *Australian Journal of Administrative Law* 15: 70–99.

Metcalfe, Stanley. 2004. "The Entrepreneur and the Style of Modern Economics." *Journal of Evolutionary Economics* 14 (2): 157–75.

Mowery, David. 2009. "Plus ça change: Industrial R&D in the 'Third Industrial Revolution.'" *Industrial and Corporate Change* 18 (1): 1–50.

Nelson, Richard and Sidney Winter. 1982. *An Evolutionary Theory of Economic Change*. Cambridge, MA: Harvard University Press.

OECD. 2011. *The OECD Innovation Strategy: Getting a Head Start on Tomorrow*. Paris: OECD.

Osnos, Evan. 2010. "Boom Doctor." *The New Yorker* 86 (11 October): 31.

Ostrom, Elinor. 1990. *Governing the Commons: The Evolution of Institutions for Collective Action (Political Economy of Institutions and Decisions)*. Cambridge: Cambridge University Press.

Penrose, Edith. [1959] 1995. *The Theory of the Growth of the Firm*. 3rd edn. Oxford: Oxford University Press.

Pollitt, Christopher and Geert Bouckaert. 2004. *Public Management Reform: A Comparative Analysis.* 2nd edn. Oxford: Oxford University Press.

Pollitt, Christopher, Geert Bouckaert, Tiina Randma-Liiv and Wolfgang Drechsler (eds). 2009. *A Distinctive European Model? The Neo-Weberian State: NISPAcee Journal of Public Administration and Policy* 1 (2).

Randma-Liiv, Tiina. 2009. "New Public Management versus Neo-Weberian State in Central and Eastern Europe." *NISPAcee Journal of Public Administration and Policy* 1 (2): 69–82.

Rodrik, Dani. 2007. *One Economics, Many Recipes: Globalization, Institutions, and Economic Growth.* Princeton and Oxford: Princeton University Press.

Selznick, Philip. 1957 [1984]. *Leadership in Administration.* Berkeley: University of California Press.

Sheng, Andrew. 2010. "The Arrival of a Minsky Revival." Available at http://english.caing.com/2010-12-31/100213205.html

Skidelsky, Robert. 2009. *Keynes: The Return of the Master.* New York: Public Affairs.

Teece, David J. 2002. *Managing Intellectual Capital: Organizational, Strategic, and Policy Dimension.* Oxford: Oxford University Press.

Wade, Robert. 2011. "Industrial Policy Redux." Paper given at the "Whatever Happened to North-South?" panel at International Political Science Association meeting, Sao Paolo, February 16–18, 2001.

Wade, Robert. 2004. *Governing the Market: Economic Theory and the Role of Government in East Asian Industrialization.* 2nd edn. Princeton: Princeton University Press.

Weiss, Linda. 2012. "The Myth of the Neoliberal State." In Kyung-Sup Chang, Ben Fine and Linda Weiss (eds), *Developmental Politics in Transition: The Neoliberal Era and Beyond,* 27–42. Basingstoke: Palgrave Macmillan. Forthcoming.

Part I

KNOWLEDGE GOVERNANCE:
BUILDING A FRAMEWORK

Chapter 1

KNOWLEDGE GOVERNANCE: AN ANALYTICAL APPROACH AND ITS POLICY IMPLICATIONS

Leonardo Burlamaqui
Ford Foundation and State University of Rio de Janeiro

I. Introduction

> The field of knowledge is the common property of mankind
> —Thomas Jefferson

Why did Schumpeter neglect intellectual property rights? For contemporary Schumpeterians, this question, posed by Mark Blaug in 2005, could be seen as an embarrassing one. How could the "father" of competition by means of innovations manage to miss completely the analysis and discussion of what in today's scholarship is one of the most – if not *the* most – influential incentive for corporations to innovate continuously? Blaug's own answer to that question is very direct, sharp and does not embarrass at all. It also calls attention to the central issue discussed in this chapter:

> It never occurred to anyone before, say the 1980s, that such disparate phenomena as patents for mechanical inventions, industrial products and processes (now extended to biotechnology, algorithms and even business methods), copyrights for the expression of literacy and artistic expressions in fixed form and trademarks and trade names for distinctive services, *could be generalized under the heading of property rights*, all conferred by the legal system in relation to discrete items of information resulting from some sort of appropriate intellectual activity. (Blaug 2005, 71–2; italics added)

For the purposes of the argument I will develop in this chapter, there are two crucial elements implicit in Blaug's answer. First, that at the time Schumpeter was writing

---

This chapter is an outgrowth of recent papers published by the author (Burlamaqui 2009a, 2009b and 2010). The author wishes to make clear that he is writing in his personal capacity and that the opinions expressed here do not necessary represent the Ford Foundation.

Capitalism, Socialism and Democracy, the balance between private interests and the public domain was completely different from what it has become today. Second, that what became codified, and largely accepted, as intellectual property *rights* was then seen as a set of *rules and regulations* issued by the state, granting temporary monopolies to corporations in very specific cases.

To this, I will add a conjecture on Schumpeter and property rights: it seems that the kind of "monopolistic practices" he praised in his 1942 book were the ones that *resulted from innovations and were short-lived* (not those that resulted from legal contracts issued by governments), were built to *assure their longevity* and were largely written on behalf of oligopolistic corporate interests which were already dominant market players.[1] Summing up, the core argument suggested by the reference to Schumpeter and Blaug is my conviction that in the last three decades, the boundaries of the private (or corporate) interests has been hyperexpanded while the public domain has significantly contracted (cf. Brown-Keyder 2007; Boyle 2008; Rodrik 2011 for similar lines of reasoning).

Recent history seems to back both Blaug's response and my conjuncture. Until the 1970s, United States patents were seen as monopolies (a term with distinctly negative connotations at that time), not rights. In fact, in some areas of economic activity, it would have been possible to say that upholding the validity of IP was the exception rather than the rule (Brown-Keyder 2007, 159). This was reflected in IP law as well as in competition or antitrust law. In copyrights, the term under United States law was 28 years.

The early 1970s witnessed several dramatic changes. In 1974, a trade act allowed the Federal Trade Commission to bring sanctions directly against countries whose products were seen to hurt United States interests. In 1975, copyrights were expanded to over 70 years from the death of the author, and for corporate owners, to 95 and sometimes even 120 years (Brown-Keyder 2007, 158; Boyle 2008, ch. 1). In 1979, Section 301 of the United States trade law was amended to "allow private parties to take significant and public steps to enforce international trade agreements" (Brown-Keyder 2007, 160). In 1988, the Justice Department rescinded guidelines for antitrust prohibitions on certain kinds of licensing clauses. This removed IP licensing from antitrust scrutiny. Finally, with the enactment of the WTO in 1995, the TRIPs agreement quickly became the linchpin of United States trade strategy. By then, private corporations had vastly expanded their enforcement power and global outreach, while the public domain had significantly contracted.

The aim of this chapter is to propose a framework within which, in the field of knowledge, the dividing line between private interests and the public domain can be redrawn. Its goal is to help establish an approach that should, analytically, produce a better way to understand the interaction among knowledge production, appropriation and diffusion and, from a public policy/public interest point of

---

1 He would probably see those as government-sponsored market failures. I will come back to that point later in Section III.

view,[2] to open up the space for a set of rules, regulatory redesign and institutional coordination which would favor the commitment to distribute (disseminate) over the right to exclude. We will label it a "knowledge governance" approach.[3]

As referenced in the introduction to this volume, contemporary research on open-source innovation and the shifting boundaries between intellectual property and the public domain by Harvard, Stanford and Duke legal scholars Yochai Benkler, Lawrence Lessig and James Boyle, and on consumer-based innovation by MIT economist Eric von Hippel and his research team, is throwing new light on matters like growth dynamics, innovation patterns, the interaction of competition and regulation and on new ways in which firms and consumers interact. Their new findings and insights point to the necessity of rethinking patent law as well as government incentives for research and open sourcing and, therefore, the way innovation policies are designed.

But when it comes to the way in which this "rethinking" should be done, as well as the subtleties of the interaction among law, economics and the governance of technological development, the available perspectives at hand still fail to give us a comprehensive approach to either the big picture (the "vision and theory," as Schumpeter would have put it) or how to craft *inclusive* policymaking and institution building for the way knowledge is governed.

On the dominating neoclassical front, the newest developments on "knowledge and innovation management" still depart from the premise that more protection is the best incentive for the achievement of more innovations and suggest a whole wave of claims about extending monopoly positions and market power (the right to patent generic knowledge, genetic sequences, business models, etc.) to corporations, in order

---

2   Incidentally, it should contribute, as well, to broadening the Schumpeterian research agenda by directing it into a scarcely explored (in the Schumpeterian domain) territory, that of "law and economics." But see Langlois (2001) for an interesting starting point in that direction. F. Scherer (1994 and 1996) has dealt consistently with these issues but, we argue, in a much more structure-conduct-performance approach than in a genuinely Schumpeterian one. The Neo-Schumpeterian legacy has dealt heavily with competition policies (or how to enforce competition) but has said very little on the relationship among innovation, intellectual property regimes, business cooperation and abuses of economic power.

3   Knowledge governance should be understood as a broad concept embracing different forms of governance mechanisms influencing the production, appropriability and dissemination of knowledge. As a provisional definition, the "knowledge governance approach" is characterized as a distinctive, emerging approach that cuts across the fields of knowledge management, innovation and competition policies and governance redesign. Knowledge governance deals with how the deployment of governance mechanisms influences knowledge processes, such as sharing, retaining and creating knowledge. "As an analytical perspective, it encompasses intellectual property rules and regulations but supersedes it by drawing on those aforementioned fields and disciplines in order to identify the contours of the new knowledge ecology, and to support alternative governance mechanisms for organizational and business models which are emerging as complements – or alternatives – to the instituted intellectual property regime we now have" (Burlamaqui 2009b).

to sharpen up their competitive advantages (cf. Merger, Menell and Lemley 2003; Landes and Posner 2003; Spinello and Bottis 2009).[4]

From a knowledge governance perspective, the critical question that should be asked here is: *When does extended protection cease to work for generating Schumpeterian profits and become a base for rent seeking and rent extraction?*[5] There is no good theoretical answer to this, but recent data on declining R&D expenditures correlating with the maintenance of handsome profits in Big Pharma seems to emphasize its relevance (cf. "Supply Running Low," *Financial Times*, February 10, 2011).

As an alternative to the mainstream approach, new insights and evidence are beginning to appear. Besides the already cited studies, a few papers and books are laying the ground for a very different way to understand the complex interactions among knowledge production, appropriation and diffusion. Examples include Jerome Reichmann's recent papers, the comparative and interdisciplinary research led by Richard Nelson, Akira Goto and Hiro Odagiri on intellectual property and catching-up and the collection of essays by Fred Block and Mathew Keller on the role of the US government in technology development.

Reichmann does so by suggesting new forms of institutional collaboration and underlining that we are in "a time for experimentation, and not a time to copy or codify obsolete approaches that are likely to boomerang against the long-term interests of the very developed countries that are most avidly pushing the harmonization buttons at the international level." Nelson, Goto and Odagiri do so by pointing to the fact that "The channels of knowledge flow and technology transfer used for the purpose of catch-up are diverse. Accordingly, many policies (in addition to the IPR policy…) affect the process of catch-up." Block and Keller do so by showing that governments – not corporations – were always at center stage in major technological endeavors in the United States.[6]

However, notwithstanding the valuable contributions by this emerging body of research, the main analytical question remains largely untouched: How should government-issued intellectual property rules and regulations interact with competition policies,[7] publicly funded R&D and other forms of technology policy in order to help craft and govern socially inclusive development strategies? It appears there is no coherent analytical framework to address that interaction.[8] But those links are central

---

4 How to reconcile these claims for legal protection by the state with the ideology of free and self-regulating markets is a mind-blowing enterprise that, curiously, is never addressed by its market-worshipper proponents.

5 See Arnold Plant's point below on that matter.

6 Nelson, Goto and Odagiri reinforce the same point for virtually all other development countries.

7 A much less catchy label, but one that reveals their real nature much better than "rights."

8 This does not imply a shortage of work discussing specific issues in what is called "the economics of intellectual property rights." See Menell (1999) for an excellent survey on general theories of IP. A very interesting review acknowledging the under-researched nature of the theme can be found in Dixon and Greenlalgh (2002). The shortcomings of most of that work are, from my perspective, the result of its concentration on "data," "measures" and "testing," with little attention paid to the theoretical framework within which they are conducted.

to any meaningful discussion of dynamic competition, knowledge accumulation and sustainable development in a global context today.[9]

This chapter aims to contribute to answering that question and is structured as follows: Section II lays the ground rules by linking knowledge production and dynamic competition with intellectual property issues from the perspective of the dynamic efficiencies and inefficiencies that are bound to appear. It will become clear that the existence of dynamic inefficiencies opens up a considerable space for knowledge governance. Section III broadens the discussion by interrogating the market-failures approach to guide policy and by introducing a "market features approach" within which markets are conceived first and foremost as *legal entities* where specificities such as contracts and regulatory rules – "features" – constitute the basis for their functioning, and where asymmetric information and uncertainty – "failures" in the neoclassical perspective – are the norm, not the exception. I will argue that "market features" is a more adequate analytical lens for structuring knowledge governance policies from an evolutionary perspective. Section IV further develops the previous framework by linking market features, competition and technology policies with intellectual property. Special attention is given to how competition policies should address intellectual property issues under a market features approach, as well as to the institutional design of public agencies dealing with knowledge production, appropriation and diffusion issues. Section V concludes the chapter by suggesting some broader theoretical and policy implications of that "knowledge governance" approach.

II. Knowledge Production, Dynamic Inefficiencies and the Role of Knowledge Governance

In the context of Schumpeterian competition, intellectual property rules and regulations (IPRs) – patents, trade secrets, confidentiality contracts, copyrights, trademarks and registered brand names – became powerful, strategic weapons for generating sustained competitive advantages and, especially, Ricardian rents (cf. Plant 1934).[10]

From an entrepreneurial perspective, patents and other IPRs are extremely effective means to reduce uncertainties and therefore, *can* contribute to igniting the animal spirits and long-term expectations through building temporary monopolies around products, processes, market niches and, eventually, whole markets (Nelson 1996; Burlamaqui and Proença 2003). However, the word *temporary* is crucial here because of creative

---

9 From an evolutionary perspective, evolution should not be confused with progress (a very common mistake), but as a process, it should definitely be understood as entailing increasing complexity.

10 Having said that, it is striking how little has been written about the crucial and complex connection between Schumpeterian competition and IPRs. And, of course, we include ourselves in that loophole. In that regard, legal theorists such as Landes and Posner and Benkler are clearly ahead, in the sense that they are already doing the reverse – using Schumpeterian concepts and insights to deal with IPR (cf. Landes and Posner 2003, Benkler 2006).

destruction; as Schumpeter (1942, 102) stated long ago, "a monopoly position is in general no cushion to sleep on."[11]

The Chicago Law and Economics framework claims that in the absence of robust legal protection for an invention, the inventor either will have less incentive to innovate or will try to keep his invention secret, thus reducing, in both cases, the stock of knowledge to society as a whole (Landes and Posner 2003, 294).

From a more generally legalistic perspective, patent law itself supposedly internalizes the goal of promoting the diffusion of innovation.[12] It requires, as a condition of granting a patent, that the patent application disclose the steps constituting the invention in sufficient detail to enable readers of the application, if knowledgeable about the relevant technology, to manufacture the patented product themselves. Of course, anyone who wishes to replicate a patented product or process legally will have to negotiate a license with the patentee (Jolly and Philpott 2004, pt. 1; Landes and Posner 2003, 294–5).

Significantly, moreover, any reader of the patent application will be free to "invent around" it, to achieve the technological benefits of the patent by other means without infringing on the patent. Translated to evolutionary economics jargon, the requirement of public disclosure creates a situation of "incomplete appropriability" for the patent holder which relates to Schumpeter's insight on the temporary nature of monopolies: incomplete appropriability allows for the possibility of technological inventiveness and borrowing from publicized information, both of which foster creative-destruction processes which are the main challengers of established monopolistic positions.

Thus, if carefully used, intellectual property rules *can be* sources of dynamic efficiencies that can help to *ignite* the Schumpeterian positive-sum game represented by falling costs, falling prices, positive margins (achieved through market power) and increased consumer welfare.[13]

Those are the basics, but the picture gets much more complicated as we examine the details. When we dive into them, considerable space opens up for dynamic *inefficiencies* to emerge and, therefore, for the introduction of governance considerations and for the emergence of a knowledge governance approach. Consider the following six points.

First, as Sir Arnold Plant, an almost forgotten analyst in the field, observed in the early 1930s,

In the case of physical property, the institution of private property makes for the *preservation of scarce goods*... In contrast, property rights in patents and copyrights make possible *the creation of scarcity* of the products appropriated... *the beneficiary is*

---

11 However, a strong IP regime is precisely the kind of "institutional innovation" that can help to build that cushion. Addressing this problem is one of the core issues of the knowledge governance approach.

12 Reference here is to American patent law.

13 From here on, I will label this "Schumpeterian positive-sum game" as the "Schumpeterian package."

made the owner of the entire supply of a product for which there may be no easily obtainable substitute. (Plant 1934 [1974], 65–7; emphasis added)

In sum, intellectual property regulations can easily give rise to dynamic inefficiencies such as cumulative monopoly power to extract rents from a given consumer base, notwithstanding the fact that they *can* at the same time create the conditions for the expansion of productivity and wealth and the generation of Schumpeterian profits.[14] That in itself leaves ground for knowledge governance-oriented initiatives to enter the scene,[15] as we will see shortly.

Second, the broader – and stronger – the IPRs, generally, the less the patentee's competitors will be able to benefit from the patent by "inventing around," or innovating on the shoulders of, the patent (or copyright) holder. Broad IPRs are thus bound to exacerbate the dynamic inefficiencies that Plant and others have observed. Accordingly, especially given the complexity and diversity of patents and other IPRs, a one-size-fits-all prescription seems ill advised. From an analytical point of view, the articulation between competition policies and IPRs is a much needed development,[16] especially if the former's goal is *innovation diffusion and delivering the Schumpeterian package, not innovators' protection per se.*

Third, the practice of *strategic patenting*, that is, the proliferating business strategy of applying for patents that the company has no intention of using, or exploiting, solely to prevent others from profiting from the innovation (cf. Varian, Farrel and Shapiro 2004, pt. 2; Landes and Posner 2003, ch. 11). Obviously, this is a major source of dynamic inefficiency. It has the effect of shifting resources from true innovative activity to litigation (or, from labs to courts). It drastically increases the costs of patent prosecution and litigation and, therefore, of innovation. Such strategic patenting constitutes a paradigmatic example of what Baumol has called "unproductive entrepreneurship." As Baumol notes:

…a variety of roles among which the entrepreneur's efforts can be reallocated… and some of those roles do not follow the constructive and innovative script conventionally attributed to that person. Indeed, at times the entrepreneur may even lead a parasitical existence that is actually damaging to the economy. (cf. Baumol 1993, 25; see also ch. 4)

Evidently, this task of "reallocation of entrepreneurship" (from unproductive roles to productive ones) is a *knowledge governance* matter, and one that goes far beyond the common notions associated with industrial policy.

---

14 Or, in a more technical way of saying it, the expected (negative) impact on future incentives for competitors to compete (innovate) and future consumer welfare (see Anthony 2000, sect. IV.)

15 On policy prescriptions, institutional building, institutional coordination and regulatory redesign.

16 We will use the term "competition policies" rather than "antitrust" here because of the outdated connotation of the latter. We will not discuss "trust busting," but a much more subtle and complex set of behaviors, institutions and policy tools.

Fourth, IPRs have a central role in the "new economy" (or "digitally renewed economy," as Paul David would label it).[17] In so-called "new-economy industries," intellectual property, rather than the products and processes in and of themselves, is a firm's primary output or asset. Overlapping innovations, rapidly falling average total costs, zero marginal costs, strong network externalities and, therefore, fierce "standards battles" and path dependence are the hallmarks of new-economy industries (Shapiro and Varian 1999; Best 2001; DeLong 2000; Brynjolfsson and Kahin 2002). These industry-structure characteristics might be seen as generating speeding waves of creative destruction and, thus, potentially more (not less) fiercely competitive challenges to incumbents. Although there is an element of truth in that picture, creative destruction in a world of increasing returns of scale, fast learning and "winner-take-all" markets does not mean anything close to some idealized form of "perfect competition" or perfectly contestable markets. Rather, it merely brings the replacement of one, or a few, dominant firms by others, such as the replacement of Fairchild by Intel, of Ciba and Geigy by Pfizer and Novartis, of Wang and Compaq by Dell and HP, IBM by Microsoft and Lenovo, and Microsoft by Google and Apple.

In other words, in the new economy, firms' abilities to combine first-mover advantages with trade secrets, patents, copyrights, brand loyalties and network externalities may afford them secure long-lasting monopolistic positions despite their low rate of (radical) innovations and not because of it.[18] The outcome is, once more, the danger of replacing Schumpeterian profits with rent extraction and Schumpeterian competition with zero-sum game exclusionary practices. From the perspective of delivering the Schumpeterian package, there is an obvious role for knowledge governance here in restoring the balance between private interests and the public domain (cf. Boyle 2008, chs 8–10). However, the normative policy framework within which it should take place is far from certain. We will revisit it in Section IV.

Fifth, if we think of knowledge production as a cumulative, and increasingly globalized,[19] process in which cutting-edge knowledge and know-how rest on previous innovations, and think of patents and IPRs, in general, as fences erected to protect those previous innovations, it is not difficult to perceive, depending on the institutional design within which IPRs are handled, the tension and potential trade-off between private interests and the conception of knowledge as a global public good. This is the so-called argument of the "second-enclosure movement" or "information feudalism," which is

---

17 Cf. David in Brynjolfsson and Kahin (2002, 85).

18 See Landes and Posner's (2003, 395–6) somewhat reluctant recognition of that point. The case of Microsoft itself can be used to illustrate the point. The lack of breakthroughs – technological innovations, or radical quality/price improvements – is notoriously known in Microsoft. It is well known that the "Windows" model was copied from Apple's user interface – which itself was a secondhand theft from Xerox PARC – as well as the tremendous lack of perception, by the company, of the Internet potential until the success of Netscape became obvious. It is also known that the differences between the versions of Windows and Office that I am using right now, although "new," display very pale improvements in relation to their 1998 predecessors.

19 In the sense of its increasingly geographical dispersion, but not denoting any sign of broader inclusion or democratic orientation.

now the subject of intense debate (cf. Drahos and Braithwaite 2002; Boyle 2003, 2008; Evans 2005; *Technology Review* 2005). According to Evans (discussing Boyle's ideas),

> There are really two halves to the second-enclosure movement. The defensive side focuses on intensifying the enforcement of protected monopoly rights to exclude others from using information that has been defined as private property. The offensive side of the agenda involves taking information that has been considered part of "nature," or the common, cultural and informational heritage of humankind, and transforming it into "private property." If both halves are successful, the "second-enclosure movement" would constitute a *global re-distribution of property* comparable to the eradication of the commons that ushered in agrarian capitalism in Western Europe 300 years ago. (Evans 2005, 2; emphasis added)

Once more, we encounter strong forces of *global* dynamic inefficiencies, presenting an opportunity for knowledge governance-oriented policies to step in.

Sixth, to the question "where do knowledge and innovations come from in the developed nations?" a very large part of the answer would include: publicly funded R&D, government contracting to buy things from the private sector that do not exist, and using the WTO to help open up markets for those innovations abroad (Block 2008; Weiss 2008, 2009). In the case of the United States, armed with an annual procurement budget of US$450 billion – more than 1 trillion if states are included – the United States state plays a crucial role in governing the way knowledge and innovations are produced and commercialized (Ruttan 2006; Weiss 2009).

Furthermore, according to some recent studies, the United States government played a decisive part in the development of virtually all general-purpose technology, from interchangeable parts and mass production to DARPA and biotech (cf. Ruttan 2006; Weiss 2007; Block 2008; Block and Keller in this volume).[20] Let me rephrase this point: If we conceive R&D as "turning money into knowledge" and innovation as "turning knowledge into money," why should governments (i.e., public money) heavily subsidize the former and almost completely retreat from participating in the latter? A knowledge governance approach to that broad source of dynamic inefficiency would quickly lead to the following question: Having financed the bulk of the basic R&D that enabled the emergence of champions such as Boeing, General Electric, IBM and a whole host of high-tech giants in hardware, software and biotech, would it not be reasonable for the United States government – or any other government, by the way – to have a stronger role in granting that technological achievements do not remain overly protected and scarcely diffused? The answer would be an obvious and resounding yes.

Last, the institutional structure – or institutional design – within which the knowledge-production appropriation and diffusion apparatus is enforced is central for

---

20 DARPA is the Defense Advanced Research Projects Agency, the central research organization of the United States Department of Defense. Its most radical innovation was the Internet (known first as ARPANET).

understanding its performance. We refer here not to the rules, as such, but to their legal enforcement apparatuses, the state structures by which they are supported and the sort of public bureaucracies available to administer the R&D and IP systems. It is well known in the literature on institutions and economic sociology that these are crucial elements in determining the degree of success any regulatory system (such as IPRs) can achieve (Evans 1995; Dobbin 2004, Smelster and Swedberg 2005; Nee and Swedberg 2005 offer excellent discussions on this theme). Jaffe and Lerner's (2002) thoughtful and provocative work on the recent changes in the United States patent system provides the background for our discussion, which will draw on the relationship between the institutional design of the United States patent system and the problems it creates for the promotion of innovation and "productive entrepreneurship" (see Section IV).

All six issues discussed above illustrate how the interaction between Schumpeterian competition and hyperextended intellectual property rules and regulations can give rise to dynamic inefficiencies that risk the delivery of the "Schumpeterian package" and call for knowledge governance interventions to restore the balance between private interests and the public good (or public interest). Before I turn to suggesting *how* those interventions should take place (in Section IV), let me introduce another pillar into the argument: the relationship between Schumpeterian competition and "market failures." This will allow me to proffer another concept that will help me in suggesting how knowledge governance should address dynamic inefficiencies: market features.

III. Competition, Market Failures and a Market Features Approach

Competition from an evolutionary perspective means mainly *rivalry*. But it also allows room for *cooperation*. In that realm, competition policies are the regulatory devices used to build a competition-enhancing environment and steer firms' behaviors toward procompetitive strategies, strategies that include both rivalry and cooperation. As any policy tool, competition policies must be framed against some sort of theoretical background. The most commonly used is the "market failure approach."[21] But applying that approach to public policy adds more confusion than clarity to the matter.[22] The reason for that is that market failures are defined against the perfect-competition

---

21 For a clear exposition of that approach, as well as for a public-choice-oriented critique of it, see Mitchell and Simmons (1994, pt 1). Both the Chicago School of economics and its heir, the public-choice perspective, have pioneered the criticisms to that approach by trying to show that most of what was presented by market failures turned out to be children of government failures. But their root is neoliberal in the sense that they stick to the notion of a self-regulated market and with the perfect-competition model as its "proof." Ours will be, instead, an evolutionary-institutionalist-based rejection that will leave spacious room for the "role of the state" in forging competition policies. (See Burlamaqui 2000 for a more general discussion of that matter.)

22 The paper by Nelson, Dosi, Cimoli and Stiglitz given at the IPD meeting in Rio (March 17–18, 2005) makes the same point but does not pursue, in that work, an alternative theory (Nelson et al. 2005, 2–3).

model. Therefore, if perfect competition is our metric, all markets are laden with market failures requiring correction.[23]

That, in fact, and not surprisingly, happens to be the case: markets do require supervision, regulation and enforcement mechanisms in order to function. That, in fact, is precisely the Polanyian approach that, as well as empirical reality,[24] points us to the fact that markets are first and foremost legal entities where contracts and regulatory rules constitute the basis for their functioning (cf. Polanyi 2001 and Harcourt 2011) and a locus where asymmetric information and uncertainty are the norm instead of the exception (cf. Shackle 1991). The policy prescription maze that follows from the "market failure approach" begins when the following question is asked: Assuming the failures, according to which blueprint are we to correct them? Again, the standard answer is…the perfect-competition model. But where can we find empirical evidence to support that model's relevance for public-policy usage (although there is plenty to reject it)? Or, how can we test this model in order to be assured of its efficiency? (Has anyone ever heard of an actual measurement of a Pareto optimum?)[25] It does not get us very far (for a similar rejection of the market-failure approach to inform public policy, see Nelson 2007).[26]

In place of the market failure approach, and in tune with the knowledge governance oriented perspective, I proffer a *market features approach*. By market features approach I mean an analytical perspective that takes into account markets' institutional diversity and sector specificities – in both their technological and industrial dimensions – as well as their regulatory and legal aspects and degrees of concentration (market power). Market features is a concept whose main advantage is that it does not *fight* the empirical evidence but, rather, accommodates it. It does not utilize a one-size-fits-all approach but relies instead on analytical flexibility. And, for our specific subject, it opens up space for

---

23 Obviously, the problem here is that if the model aims to claim even a minimal amount of relevance either as an analytical device or a tool for policy prescription, it cannot sustain at the same time that markets are self-correcting and that almost all markets are filled with "failures" that demand "intervention" (– read government action or regulation) to become able to self-correct.

24 Let me remind the reader that all market operations are backed by legal contracts enforced by regulatory agencies and subject to legal penalties if violated. Economists rarely pay attention to those "details," but they are the devices that allow markets to be created and to function.

25 On that, see Georgescu-Roegen's nearly forgotten, and brilliant, 1935 paper "Note on a Proposition of Pareto" (Georgescu-Roegen 1935).

26 After all, the perfect-competition model should be an ideal in the Weberian sense of the concept: a construct that accentuates certain properties found in reality and exaggerates them for purposes of organizing and making sense of the empirical data. That means that the construct should be abstract but empirically relevant. The problem is that none of the core assumptions supporting the hypothesis of the model – perfect information, product homogeneity, free entry and exit (absence of sunk costs), price-taking behavior (absence of market power), absence of increasing returns and tendency toward equilibrium – is found in reality, thus making the model useless either for positive or normative functions – something that Frank Hahn (1984), for instance, spelled out several times in his works.

sector-specific innovation and competition policies, as well as for differentiated ways to organize R&D and its relation to intellectual property rules.

The idea of a market features approach is not new. It comes from that undeservedly neglected tradition that unites scholars such as George Shackle and Ludwig Lachmann, a tradition that could very well be labeled "Austrian Keynesianism" (see Lachmann 1986 and Vaughn 1994 on that matter). The specific idea of a market's taxonomy comes from Lachmann's last book in his discussion of markets as economic processes embedded in institutions. As Vaughn explains it, Lachmann argues that

> Instead of examining the world through the lens of the "market" we need to develop ideal types *of particular kinds of markets:* assets markets versus production markets, fix-price versus flex-price markets, markets dominated by merchants versus markets dominated by salesmen. Such distinctions will make a difference as to how markets adjust to change. (Lachmann 1986, 128, in Vaughn 1994, 159; emphasis added)

This was a brilliant insight, but it was left more or less as it was first submitted. For our concerns, it offers a very promising alternative point of departure both for positive and normative purposes. To be more concrete, let us very briefly contrast the market features in the soft drink industry with the "apps" industry for electronic devices (like tablets, smart phones and computers). The first is dominated by two firms (Coca-Cola and Pepsi), and competition is over market share, using advertising, product differentiation and price discounts. The second is extremely fragmented, changes occur by the day, entry is very easy and technological capabilities play a major role in shaping competition. Both are examples of competition by means of innovation, but the role of technology, regulatory rules and the nature of contracts are completely different. Why should those two industries be subjected to the same intellectual property regime?

Recently, Cimoli and Primi (2007) advanced this insight by developing a taxonomy for mapping markets for knowledge, which presents a taxonomy of contemporary markets for knowledge according to four main categories: (1) rationale of the market, (2) prevailing patenting behavior, (3) main patent use and (4) barriers to entry. Those markets encompass what in the literature has been identified as market for technologies, plus two additional categories of markets: the market for science and secondary markets for science and technology (see Primi in this volume).

This new approach allows for a much more realistic, although possibly less elegant, assessment of differentiated market dynamics and how they are likely to adjust (or give rise) to change. That perspective still has to be properly developed, but it will help economic theory to become more relevant and useful from the point of view of understanding empirical reality and crafting policy. It is also in line, for instance, with the "sociology of markets" perspective (Fligstein 2001; Dobbin 2004; Nee and Swedberg 2005) as well as recent findings by Carlton and Gertner (2002, 30), in which they state that "Only detailed study of the industry of concern has the possibility of uncovering reliable relationships between innovation and industry behavior." There is clearly a very promising theoretical road to be traveled here. From a knowledge governance perspective, the market features approach should constitute a building block to crafting public policy. As the reader will find out immediately, I will be using that concept as a building block for suggesting how to structure knowledge governance interventions.

IV. Knowledge Governance: Bringing the Public Domain Back In

The market features approach has as its policy counterpart a *market-shaping policy perspective that is the linchpin for the governance of knowledge*. Its core principle is that it is possible, through institution building, legal change and policy guidance to redesign markets as well as regulatory mechanisms and proceedings in order to pursue the major public policy goal of delivering the Schumpeterian package. Within that approach, the general rule should be the promotion of innovation plus the assurance of its widest diffusion, and this implies, simultaneously, promoting and regulating entrepreneurial success. Promoting *and* regulating is a crucial link here. Together, they address both the private (profit seeking) and the public (innovation diffusion and technological upgrading) sides of competition policies and their respective institutional designs.

This policy and institutional design package was, in fact, the core of the Asian state-centered developmental strategy. Nowadays, it remains alive and well in East Asia and especially in Singapore and China. In Singapore, it is evident in the country's twin, government sponsored, initiatives, on "biomedical sciences" and on "work restructuring," where market shaping and institutional coordination are core elements (Pereira 2008). In China, it is clearly present in the 12th five-year plan for 2011 to 2015, finalized last April. The plan highlights the importance of the "magic seven" industries: (1) energy saving and environmental protection, (2) next-generation information technology, (3) biotechnology, (4) high-end manufacturing, (5) new energy, (6) new materials and (7) clean-energy vehicles. The plan's objective is to "shape" them in order to raise their share from 3 percent to 15 percent of the economy by 2020.

None of those countries phrase their government-sponsored initiatives as knowledge governance, but it is quite clear that this is what they really are: going much beyond "industrial policy" or "intellectual property," they reach the key interactions between knowledge and markets…and shape them from a public policy/public interest perspective.

From a normative perspective, knowledge governance policies should take the market features approach as their point of departure and use market-shaping devices in order to design policies to manage creative destruction processes. These policies would seek to shape markets in order to reduce dynamic inefficiencies and increase dynamic efficiencies coming from Schumpeterian competition, a form of competition that, now, overuses intellectual property rules as one of its core weapons. From the perspective of firms, knowledge governance policies should not be about preventing "market power" but about curbing its excesses: "unproductive entrepreneurship" and "rent extraction."

Within a knowledge governance framework, the main policy concerns should be to mitigate structural inefficiencies and to increase access. Plant argued that patents can make the beneficiary "the owner of the entire supply of a product for which there may be no easily obtainable substitute," (1934, 30) a troubling claim. A clever, but not radical, innovation (for instance, market-niche dominance by Post-it notes from 3M) should not raise major concerns among policymakers dealing with competition issues. But what if a proprietary general-purpose technology corners the market (for instance, a new genetic engineering research tool or a particular DNA sequence)? Then Plant's point would hold completely, and the granting of a patent would create a substantial monopoly for the owner – and potentially prevent others from exploiting it – thus slowing the diffusion of a new innovation.

More concretely, knowledge governance policies should shape markets and drive firms toward establishing research coordination and patent pools, pushing common standards, preserving multiple sources of experimentation, establishing differentiated patent and copyrights terms and severely punishing both "unproductive patenting" behavior and attempts by firms to seize markets through creating their own proprietary closed systems (see Carlton and Gertner 2002 for a similar line of reasoning).

Those examples highlight the importance of the market-shaping approach. In cases like those involving general-purpose technologies, IP rules and regulations should be much more rigorously examined and carefully constructed. A possible "tool" for dealing with that would be for the government to claim a *golden share* in the IPR system (especially patents and copyrights), by which it would be able to convert a property right previously granted into a general public license,[27] should the owner refuse, after establishing his first-mover advantage,[28] to behave cooperatively and to license broadly and fairly.

In sum, radical innovations – and, especially, general-purpose technologies – should be subjected to a special IPR regime in which the government's golden share should be able, if needed, to "shape" the market toward a more competitive institutional design (away from too secure – or broad – monopolies).[29] A legitimate, and fair, reason to

---

27 That is, a legally enforced temporary monopoly.

28 Meaning the ability to recover his costs, establish a robust competitive advantage and enjoy a sizable profit stream, but not the ability to exclude others from using and inventing around his innovation or protecting its diffusion. Taking as an example the Microsoft case, the battle should not be about "breaking" the company. The golden share would allow the government to force Microsoft to publish its source code. An open code would quickly get cleaned up and improved, consumers would benefit and new entrants would probably arise helping ignite the innovation race and dislodging Microsoft from its monopoly position while preserving the company's market power and ability to innovate.

29 As a clever reader, you should, at this point, be asking "How can an innovation – or innovation cluster –be defined as radical before it 'matures' though a process that evidently takes time?" The answer is simple: it cannot. The proposal here is for public sources of funding and regulatory bodies, through the golden share or via special provisions similar to those behind the rationale for issuing compulsory licenses, to retain the option to classify an innovation cluster as a strategic general-purpose technology for potentially delivering "massive wealth creation." As such, those technologies would be treated similarly to weapons of mass destruction, but for inverse reasons. And that placement would happen ex-post, not ex-ante.

do so is that, as already mentioned above, according to some recent studies, the US government played a decisive part in the development of virtually all general-purpose technology, from interchangeable parts and mass production to DARPA and biotech (cf. Ruttan 2006; Weiss 2007; Block 2008). Having financed the bulk of the basic R&D that enabled the emergence of champions such as Boeing, General Electric, IBM and a whole host of high-tech giants in hardware, software and biotech, it would not be unreasonable for the US government – or any other government, by the way – to have a stronger role in granting that technological achievements do not remain overly protected and scarcely diffused (cf. Fong 2001).

In fact, this is already on the EU Competition Commission's radar. Its former chief, Neelie Kroes, has recently argued in a speech that

> [I]ndustry standards for technology could be based on either proprietary or non-proprietary technologies, but when a market developed so that a proprietary technology became a *de facto* standard and the owner of that technology exploited that market power, *competition authorities might have to intervene.* One remedy would be to require disclosing of information at 'fair rates' so that other companies could design compatible products and systems." (*Financial Times,* June 11, 2008; emphasis added)

Given both the complexity and diversity of knowledge-production regimes, and R&D funding, a one-size-fits-all prescription for knowledge appropriation (IPR rules) is certainly not the best way to handle the matter. The 20-year length of a patent (or the terms of copyrights and registrations) is not a "scientifically established outcome" (Landes and Posner 2003). It is, rather, a convention – that is, a (lobbying-based) institutional–legal construct that, as such, can very well be questioned and changed.[30] Conversely, as Jaffe and Lerner (2002, 203) adduce (very much in line with the market features approach), "In the world of theoretical patent analysis, it is easy to show that the attributes of patent protection should vary depending on the characteristics of the technology."

But Jaffe and Lerner (2002, 203–5) then expose several reasons why this differential-treatment approach would not work in practical terms. The difficulties of dealing with technologies – classifying and quantifying their impact empirically – plus the political lobbying by firms to get special treatment are the main arguments submitted by the authors. We are in partial agreement with them as to having pure technological considerations serving as the basis for policy, as well as to the rent-seeking dangers surrounding any sort of differential treatment. But note, again, that if we look to the development histories of Japan, South Korea, Singapore, China, Ireland or the United States, differential treatment

---

30 As a matter of fact, a century ago, copyrights lasted for 14 years – and could be extended another 14 if the copyright holder petitioned for an extension. Today, corporate copyrights last for 95 years, and individuals retain copyrights for 70 years after their deaths. There was nothing "scientific" to back these changes but rather the powerful lobby of the entertainment industry. As for patents, mind the reader that both in Switzerland (between 1850 and 1907) and in the Netherlands (between 1868 and 1912), industrialization occurred without enforcement of patent laws (cf. Schiff 1971).

lay at the core of both their technological and industrial policies. That is, it *can* work, *has* worked and *still works* (cf. Chang 2002; Reinert 2007; Austin 2009).

To be less abstract on the matter, let us propose this broad guideline for knowledge governance policies: the length and breadth of patent protection, as well as innovations protected by copyrights, such as software, should be directly linked to the expenditures in R&D, made by applicants in the development of a technology and inversely correlated with their market power.[31] Thus, big research budgets (in terms relative to the firm's size) would, in principle, qualify better than "historical accidents" to earn legitimate protection. Conversely, "global players" would enjoy less legal protection than "garage outfits," given that the same legal contract would grant cumulative and increasing returns in the former case – reinforcing dominance – and, often, the ability to serve debt in the latter. Instead of one size fitting all, we would have something like – paraphrasing Rodrik – "many recipes under the same rule."[32]

As for the source of dynamic inefficiencies referred to above as *strategic patenting*, it should be dealt with in the same way Ricardo suggested landlords should be addressed:[33] earned but unused patents should be classified like fertile but uncultivated pieces of land in an environment structurally constrained by scarcity. They should be taxed, and progressively so. After an initial "launching period," each year of idleness in the commercialization of the patent should give rise to a severe fine, the exact amount of which should be figured out by specialists in the field but could very well be an increasing percentage of the patentee's sales or assets. Sounds rigorous? Yes, it is, but patents and IPRs, in general, are legally conceded monopolies and matters of public interest.[34] They are too important to be left to markets and lawyers to craft.[35] Additionally, the kind of

---

31 R&D expenses as a percentage of the applicant's sales or assets could become a metric. That would require a close monitoring of R&D evolution within firms. Assuming that those R&D-intensive industries are also the ones bearing more fixed and sunk costs, plus near-future planned expenses tied to the "birth" of an innovation or technology, should be in the contract granting the rights and their actual production of the enabling mechanism to conclude the exam. Otherwise, patent pending would be a sort of "reasonable doubt" proviso.

32 A very difficult emerging theme here is the protection to be given to traditional knowledge: DOC (Denominacione de Origine Controllata certifications that grant monopolies based on regional know-how and capabilities, like champagne versus sparkling wines) issues and related others. We acknowledge its importance but do not deal with that in this paper.

33 The parallel here would be between the example given by David Ricardo of the unique fertility of a piece of privately owned land, which would generate increasing revenues to its owner, regardless of efforts to improve the land's productivity, and the stream of revenue generated from a patent regardless of whether its owner keeps innovating.

34 In that sense, they are very similar to the financial industry, and especially to the banking sector.

35 Google offers a striking example on that matter: it has just bid US$900 million for the patent portfolio of Nortel Networks 2, the Canadian telecom equipment maker, as part of a strategy to defend itself against patent litigation. The amount of money involved signals how fierce the patent wars have become, particularly in Silicon Valley, where even the largest and most powerful companies, like Google, are besieged by dozens of patent infringement suits. It also underscores Google's frustration with the state of the patent-reform legislation in Congress.

approach to the governance of knowledge we are suggesting should have as its core principle the discouragement of the sort of unproductive entrepreneurship that Baumol has been talking about for more than a decade, a type of legal entrepreneurship that turns law firms into very big and profitable corporations but with zero impact on the economy's real productivity. It would, in sum, help to trigger the "relocation of entrepreneurship" – from courts back to labs – as claimed by Baumol (1993 and 2002).

Another key point outlined in Section II above relates to the relationship between the "digitally renewed economy" and intellectual property issues, and particularly to the risk of winner-take-all market outcomes or, from the point of view of firms, to locking out competitors via the combination of increasing returns, network externalities, path dependency and stronger IPRs protection (cf. Varian et al. 2004; Carlton and Gertner 2002). Knowledge governance policies here should pursue, very aggressively if needed, public enforcement of standards development, cooperative standards setting, stimulus of (instead of restriction on) joint research ventures and other forms of research coordination and venture capital financing to multiple sources of experimentation (Bartzokas and Mani 2004; Block and Keller 2012 in this volume). The aim should be a "less kind, less gentle patent system," as Jaffe and Lerner (2002) put it, in which patents are much harder to acquire and easier to share.

Also of concern is the recent wave of IPR expansion and its connection to a potential "information feudalism" or "second enclosure movement." This movement is seen by the so-called "progressive IP lawyers," software programmers and a sizable number of social and natural scientists of various extractions as a recipe for global monopoly, one that is likely to stifle innovation at the same time as it concentrates wealth (see Moglen 2003; Benkler 2003; Evans 2005). A number of commentators have called for an alternative to this second enclosure, an alternative they term "the new commons."[36] As Evan (2005, 3) has aptly put it, this alternative is "attractive both because of its distributional implications and because of its potential for raising the rate of innovation and value creation." From a knowledge governance perspective, the basis of the new commons comes from a redefinition of "ownership": from the focus on the right to exclude to the focus on the commitment to distribute (disseminate).

The key idea here is that once property rights are redefined along the lines pioneered by the open-source software movement, a much more egalitarian redistribution of

Though Google could potentially use some of the technology in the Nortel patents in future research, the company said it wanted to buy them to defend itself against patent litigation. By building a large portfolio of patents, Google keeps them out of competitors' hands. It also hopes to dissuade other companies from suing it, either because Google holds similar patents to the ones they might sue over or as deterrence – if you sue me, I will sue you (New York Times, April 5, 2011).

36 A "commons" is a piece of land over which people can exercise certain traditional rights in common, such as allowing their livestock to graze upon it. Older texts use the word "common" to denote any such right, but more modern usage is to refer to particular rights of common and to reserve the name "common" for the land over which the rights are exercised. By extension, the term "commons" has come to be applied to other resources that a community has rights or access to.

intangible assets and a more powerful rationale to foster innovations will be able to emerge. This rationale is one that unfolds from the characteristics of the networked information economy – an economy of information, knowledge and culture that flows over a ubiquitous, decentralized network.

In that environment, as Benkler remarks, productivity and growth can be sustained in a pattern that differs fundamentally from the industrial information economy of the twentieth century in two crucial characteristics. First, nonmarket production can play a much more important role than it could in the physical economy. Individuals working alongside firms can make a real difference in the creation of innovative solutions and productivity gains (Benkler 2003, 1, and 2006).[37] Second, radically decentralized production and distribution, whether market based or not, can similarly play a much more important role by increasing the diversity of ways of organizing production and consumption and, therefore, by increasing the sources and possibilities for multiple forms of experimentation.

This is clearly a global issue and – because of its global scope, and also because of the under theorized relationship between innovation, competition policies and intellectual property rights – a very difficult one to handle. It will certainly require the active involvement of governments in encouraging and assisting the development of open-source systems to move society toward more general-public-licenses-oriented IPR regimes. It will also require international cooperation – both very turbulent matters from a power politics perspective. Nevertheless, the recent decisions by IBM and Nokia, for example, to put part of their patents into the public domain suggests that there is perhaps more room to maneuver than the skeptical analyst might expect.

Finally, the crucial role of the institutional structure – or institutional design – within which the IPRs are enforced must be examined. This brings us to Jaffe and Lerner's (2002) discussion of the recent institutional design changes in the US patent system and its deleterious effects on innovation.[38] Their story unfolds around two fundamental changes in the legal–institutional foundations of the system. The first, in 1982, was a change in the process by which patent cases were handled. From then on, instead of the 12 regional courts of appeal, one single, specialized appeals court began to process all appeals in patent cases: the Court of Appeals for the Federal Circuit (CAFC). Consolidating patent appeals in one court had the salutary effect of injecting homogeneity into a fragmented system.

However, because the CAFC's formative years coincided with the "Japanese challenge," "America's lost competitiveness" and the Reagan administration's extreme pro-business policies, the new homogeneity took the form of interpreting patent law

---

37 And, he adds, one can clearly observe this behavior by noticing that most of what we do on the Internet runs on software produced by tens of thousands of volunteers, working together in a way that is fundamentally more closely related to a community than to a hierarchical big corporation standing alone.

38 Why do we want to illustrate that point with the US system? Simply because it is the most powerful patent system in the world, and also the most likely to be mimicked by "emergent economies."

"to make it easier to get, easier to enforce patents against others, easier to get large financial awards from such enforcement, and harder for those accused of infringing patents to challenge the patents' validity" (Jaffe and Lerner 2002; Weiss 2008).

The second change dates from the early 1990s, when Congress modified the Patent and Trademark Office's (PTO) financial basis, turning it into a profit center, a service agency whose costs of operation should be covered by the fees paid by patent applicants – or by its clients (Jaffe and Lerner 2002). According to Jaffe and Lerner, these two changes transformed a regime that had been committed to fostering and protecting innovation, into a lawyers' paradise. The patent system then became a very powerful generator of unproductive entrepreneurship and, hence, a severely dysfunctional institution. In order to be "efficient," the PTO started to examine – and grant – as many patents as it could, regardless of the quality and reliability of the examination process. Between 1983 and 2006, the patents granted increased from about 62,000 to 196,000 per year. The number of patent applications also ballooned to 452,633 in 2006 (from 112,040 in 1983).[39]

In analytical terms, what happened was the replacement of a qualified bureaucracy committed to public service with a business-oriented "new public management" cadre that was given the task of regulating a crucially important part of the knowledge creation system of the new economy.[40] The results were dismal in that they incentivized strategic patenting and patent litigation (which consumes literally billions of dollars) without any clear impact in terms of innovation inducement or on the rate of innovation (see Noll 2004 on this issue). In sum, the economic benefits of stronger patent protection and increased room for strategic patenting have failed to materialize – except in the big patent portfolio holders' licensing revenues and on the dedicated law firms' balance sheets. On the sort of detailed institutional redesign that ought to be done in order to improve patent quality in the United States, I direct the reader to the excellent discussion by Jaffe and Lerner (2002).

Patents and intellectual property in general are too important to be left to lawyers, juries and a single PTO. They should be institutionally restructured, in the form of a cross-cutting knowledge governance agency in charge of coordinating publicly funded R&D with innovation policies, competition policies and IPRs.[41] A rekindled competition authority should become the "pilot agency" for that type of institutional

---

39 Cf. http://www.uspto.gov/go/taf/us_stat.htm

40 As Drechsler (cf. 2005, 1) aptly sums it up, NPM is the transfer of business and market principles and management techniques from the private into the public sector, symbiotic with and based on a neoliberal understanding of state and economy. The goal, therefore, is a slim, reduced, minimal state in which any public activity is decreased and, if at all, exercised according to business principles of efficiency. NPM is based on the understanding that all human behavior is motivated by self-interest and, specifically, profit maximization.

41 Note that in the field of technology procurement, the network of US agencies already includes, today, the Department of Defense, the CIA, NASA, the Department of Energy, the National Institutes of Health and the Department of Agriculture (Weiss 2009). The fact that they are not properly coordinated does not mean that the potential for a crosscutting agency is not there. On the contrary, the US is already halfway there.

coordination, and dedicated judges and courts (but not juries) should be the "last resort" in those matters, not the first.

Additionally, this agency should be structured along "Weberian lines" – a set of offices in which appointed civil servants operate under the principles of merit selection, expertise, hierarchy, the division of labor, exclusive employment, career advancement and legality. This type of rationality – Weber's key term – would increase speed, scope, predictability and cost-effectiveness (Weber 1922, 124–30; Drechsler 2005).

V. Conclusion

The knowledge-governance-oriented policy-institutions framework I have proposed should be flexible and pragmatic and should have creative-destruction management and maximum expansion of access to knowledge as its main goals. In its innovation and competition policies dimension, it should *not* be anticonsolidation but antiunproductive entrepreneurship (Baumol 1993 and 2002); proefficiency but not libertarian (in the "Chicago School" sense of letting the market, almost always, take care of its own problems); and, especially, pro-cooperation, leaving room for business networks to thrive and for state-sponsored administrative-guidance initiatives. It should also engineer policies toward the development of multiple sources of experimentation and allow room for industrial and technology policies without jeopardizing its own core theoretical foundations.

In its intellectual property dimension, it should *not* point to a one-size-fits-all institutional design,[42] and should *not* pursue the maximum protection of monopolistic rents as both the US PTO and the WTO seem to be doing. It should, rather, search for the minimal common denominator, allowing for institutional and technological diversity and for distinctive developmental strategies (Boyle 2004, 2008; Rodrik 2011). It should take into account the asymmetries in the distance to the "development frontier" among countries and regions, echoing Joseph Stiglitz's recent, and wise, remark that "Intellectual property is certainly important, but the appropriate IPR system for an emerging country is different than the IPR system best fitting already developed nations" (Stiglitz 2005).[13]

---

42 It should not, therefore, be framed, as Coriat, Cimoli and Primi indicate in a just-released paper, as an American "export": it is essential to note that recent (dramatic) changes in IP law have been strongly embedded in the specificities of an American patent law that is predicated on a common-law regime wherein the essential criterion for patentability is the "utility" the invention is deemed to have. Utility, a property that refers to products of "useful arts," basically involves industrial and commercial advances enabled by this invention. Under these conditions, in my opinion, the aforementioned change was, in fact, that suddenly it was enough to relax or change the meaning of the word "utility" for nonpatentable areas to become patentable (Coriat et al. 2005, 4).

43 One of the main reasons for that, although certainly not the only one, is that the big pharmaceutical companies perform obscene price discrimination among nations (cf. Varian et al. 2004, 52) and almost always refuse to engage in poor and emerging countries' public policies oriented toward health care.

From an evolutionary policy perspective, the key issue to deal with is how to separate innovation-rooted profits, which should be rewarded but understood as windfalls (dependent on continuous innovation), from legal monopoly-granted rents, which should be eliminated or, at least, closely monitored and curtailed.

None of these policy prescriptions will be achieved without a huge dose of "strategic state action," and most of them will require a high degree of international institutional redesign. This is an uneasy task; nonetheless, the expected result, to which this paper intends to make a small contribution, would be a theory/policy framework linking, conceptually, market features to innovation and Schumpeterian competition and competition policies to intellectual property rights management, which will allow room for catching-up initiatives and for the (re)construction of development strategies.

Acknowledgments

I would like to thank Fred Block, Yochai Benkler, Rainer Kattel and Richard Nelson for suggestions concerning both form and content for a previous version of this paper. The paper represents my own personal views and does not reflect those of the Ford Foundation.

References

All web addresses last accessed August 2011.

Anthony, S. 2000. "Antitrust and Intellectual Property Law: From Adversaries to Partners." *AIPLA Quarterly Review* 28 (1). Available at http://www.econ.jhu.edu/People/Hamilton/antitrust/ftcip.doc

Austin, I. 2009. *Common Foundations of American and East Asian Modernization: From Alexander Hamilton to Junichero Koizumi.* Singapore: Select Publishing.

Bartokas, A. and S. Mani (eds). 2004. *Financial Systems: Corporate Investment in Innovation and Venture Capital.* Cheltenham: E. Elgar.

Baumol, W. 2002. *The Free-Market Innovation Machine.* Princeton: Princeton University Press.

_____. 1993. *Entrepreneurship, Management and the Nature of Payoffs.* Cambridge, MA: MIT Press.

Benkler, Y. 2006. *The Wealth of Networks.* New Haven, CT: Yale University Press.

_____. 2003. "Freedom in the Commons: Towards a Political Economy of Information." *Duke Law Journal* 52: 1245–76.

Best, M. 2001. *The New Competitive Advantage.* Oxford: Oxford University Press.

Blaug, M. 2005. "Why Did Schumpeter Neglect Intellectual Property Rights?" *Review of Economic Research on Copyright Issues* 2: 69–74.

Block, F. 2008. "Where Do Innovations Come From? Transformations in the U.S. national innovation system – 1970–2006." Research paper for The Ford Foundation, Grant #1075–1307.

Block, F. and M. Keller. 2012. "Where Do Innovations Come From? Implications for Intellectual Property." Chapter in this volume.

Bork, R. 1993. *The Antitrust Paradox.* New York: Free Press.

Boyle, J. 2008. *The Public Domain.* New Haven, CT: Yale University Press.

_____. 2004. "Manifesto on the Future of WIPO." Available at http://www.law.duke.edu/boylesite/

_____. 2003. "The Second Enclosure Movement and the Construction of the Public Domain." Available at http://www.law.duke.edu/boylesite/

Brown-Keyder, V. 2007. "Intellectual Property: Commodification and Its Discontents." In A. Bugra and K. Agartan (eds), *Reading Karl Polanyi for the Twenty-First Century. Market Economy as a Political Project*, 155–70. New York: Palgrave Macmillan.

Brynjolfsson, E. and B. Kahin (eds). 2002. *Understanding the Digital Economy*. Cambridge, MA: MIT Press.

Burlamaqui L. 2009a. "Innovation, Competition Policies and Intellectual Property: An Evolutionary Perspective and its Policy Implications." In N. Netanel (ed.), *The Development Agenda: Global Intellectual Property and Developing Countries*. Oxford: Oxford University Press.

————. 2009b. "Notes on Knowledge Governance." The Ford Foundation (unpublished).

————. 2010. "Intellectual Property, Innovation and Development." *Brazilian Journal of Political Economy* 30 (4). Available at http://www.scielo.br/scielo.php?pid=S0101-31572010000400002&script=sci_arttext

————. 2000. "Evolutionary Economics and the Role of State." In L. Burlamaqui, A. Castro and H.-J. Chang (eds), *Institutions and the Role of the State: New Horizons in Institutional and Evolutionary Economics*. Cheltenham: E. Elgar.

Burlamaqui, L. and A. Proença. 2003. "Inovação, Recursos e Comprometimento: Em Direção a uma Teoria Estratégica da Firma." *Revista Brasileira de Inovação* 1 (3): 4–35.

Carlton, D. and R. Gertner. 2002. "Intellectual Property, Antitrust and Strategic Behavior." NBER Working Paper 8976. Available at http://www.nber.org/papers/w8976

Chang, H.-J. 2002. *Kicking Away the Ladder*. London: Anthem Press.

Cimoli, M., G. Dosi, R. Nelson and J. Stiglitz. 2005. "A Note on the Institutions and Policies Shaping Industrial Development." Paper presented at the IPD meeting, Rio de Janeiro, March 17–18.

Cimoli, M. and A. Primi. 2007. "Technology and Intellectual Property: A Taxonomy of Contemporary Markets for Knowledge and their Implications for Development." CEPAL. Unpublished manuscript.

Coriat, B., M. Cimoli and A. Primi. 2005. "Intellectual Property Right Regimes: Incentives and Constraints for Technological and Industrial Development." Paper presented at the IPD meeting, Rio de Janeiro, March 17–18.

DeLong, J. B. 2000. *The Dilemma of Antitrust: A Short History*. Available at http://econ161.berkeley.edu/

Dixon, P. and C. Greenlalgh. 2002: *The Economics of Intellectual Property: A Review to Identify Themes for Future Research*. Manchester: CRIC.

Dobbin, F. (ed.) *The Sociology of the Economy*. New York: Russell Sage Foundation.

Drahos, P. and J. Braithwaite. 2002. *Information Feudalism*. New York: The New Press.

Drechsler, W. 2005. "The Rise and Demise of the New Public Management." *Post-autistic Economics Review* 33 (14 September): 17–28. Available at http://www.paecon.net/PAEReview/issue33/Drechsler33.htm

Ellig, J. (ed.) 2001. *Dynamic Competition and Public Policy: Technology, Innovation, and Antitrust Issues*. Cambridge: Cambridge University Press.

Evans, P. B. 2005. "The New Commons vs. the Second Enclosure Movement: Comments on an Emerging Agenda for Development Research." *Studies in Comparative International Development* 40 (2): 85–94.

————. 1995. *Embedded Autonomy: States and Industrial Transformation*. Princeton: Princeton University Press.

Fligstein, N. 2001. *The Architecture of Markets: An Economic Sociology of Twenty-First-Century Capitalist Societies*. Princeton: Princeton University Press.

Fong, G. 2001. "Arpa Does Windows: The Defense Underpinning of the PC Revolution." *Business & Politics* 3 (3): 213–37.

Hahn, F. 1984. *Equilibrium and Macroeconomics*. Cambridge, MA: MIT Press.

Harcourt, B. 2011. *The Illusion of Free Markets: Punishment and the Myth of Natural Order.* Cambridge, MA: Harvard University Press.

Hovenkamp, H. 1999. *Federal Antitrust Policy.* Minnesota: West.

Jaffe, A. and J. Lerner. 2002. *Innovation and Its Discontents: How Our Broken Patent System Is Endangering Innovation and Progress, and What to Do About It.* Princeton: Princeton University Press.

Jolly, A. and J. Philpott (eds). 2004. *A Handbook of Intellectual Property Management.* London: Kogan Page.

Kelsey, J. 2008. *Serving Whose Interests?: The Political Economy of Trade in Services.* London: Routledge.

Kwoka, J. Jr and L. White (eds). 1999. *The Antitrust Revolution.* Oxford: Oxford University Press.

Lachmann, L. 1986. *The Market as an Economic Process.* Oxford: Blackwell.

Landes, W. and R. Posner. 2003. *The Economic Structure of Intellectual Property Law.* Cambridge, MA: Belknap Press.

Langlois, R. 2001. "Technological Standards, Innovation and Essential Facilities: Towards a Schumpeterian Approach." In J. Ellig (ed.), *Dynamic Competition and Public Policy: Technology, Innovation, and Antitrust Issues.* Cambridge: Cambridge University Press.

Mazzoleni, R. and R. Nelson. 1998. "The Benefits and Costs of Strong Patent Protection: A Contribution to the Current Debate." *Research Policy* 27 (3): 273–84.

McCraw, T. 1984. *Prophets of Regulation.* Cambridge, MA: Harvard University Press.

Menell, P. 1999. "Intellectual Property: General Theories." Working paper, Berkeley Center for Law and Technology.

Merger, R. P., P. S. Menell and M. A. Lemley. 2003. *Intellectual Property in the New Technological Age.* New York: Aspen Publishers.

Mitchell, W. and R. Simmons. 1994. *Beyond Politics: Markets, Welfare and the Failure of Bureaucracy.* Boulder, CO: Westview Press.

Moglen, E. 2003. *"Freeing the Mind: Free Software and the Death of Proprietary Culture."* Fourth Annual Technology and Law Conference, University of Maine Law School, Portland, June 29.

Mowery, D. C., R. R. Nelson, B. N. Sampat and A. A. Ziedonis. 2004. *Ivory Tower and Industrial Innovation: University-Industry Technology Transfer before and after the Bayh-Dole Act.* Stanford, CA: Stanford University Press.

Nee, V. and R. Swedberg (eds). 2005. *The Economic Sociology of Capitalism.* Princeton: Princeton University Press.

Nelson, R. 2007. "Building Effective Innovation Systems versus Dealing with Market Failures as Ways of Thinking About Technology Policy." Unpublished draft.

———. 1996. *The Sources of Economic Growth.* Cambridge, MA: Harvard University Press.

Nelson, R., R. Mazzoleni et al. 2005. *A Program of Study of the Processes Involved in Technological and Economic Catch Up.* New York: The Earth Institute/Columbia University.

Noll, R. 2004. "The Conflict over Vertical Foreclosure in Competition Policy and in Intellectual Property Law." Stanford Institute for Economic Policy Research, Working Paper 03-22.

Pereira, A. 2008. "Whither the Developmental State? Explaining Singapore's continued Developmentalism." *Third World Quarterly* 29 (6): 1189–1203.

Plant, A. 1934. *Selected Economic Essays and Addresses.* London: Institute of Economic Affairs.

Polanyi, K. 2001. *The Great Transformation.* New Edition. Beacon Press. New York.

Posner, R. 1976 [2002]. *The Economic Analysis of Law.* New York: Aspen Publishers.

Reinert, E. 2007. *How Rich Countries Got Rich …and Why Poor Countries Stay Poor.* London: Constable Books.

Rodrik, D. 2011. *The Globalization Paradox: Democracy and the Future of the World Economy.* New York: W. W. Norton & Company.

Georgescu-Roegen, N. 1935. "Note on a Proposition of Pareto." *Quarterly Journal of Economics* 49: 706–14.

Roland, A. 1983–1993. *Strategic Computing: DARPA and the Quest for Machine Intelligence*. Cambridge, MA: MIT Press.

Ruttan, V. 2006. *Is War Necessary for Economic Growth?* Oxford: Oxford University Press.

Scherer, F. 1996. *Industry Structure, Strategy and Public Policy*. New York: Harper Collins.

———. 1994. *Competition Policies for an Integrated World Economy*. Washington DC: The Brookings Institution.

Schiff, E. 1971. *Industrialization without National Patents*. Princeton: Princeton University Press.

Schumpeter, J. 1934 [1997]. *The Theory of Economic Development*. New York: Transaction Publishers.

———. 1942 [1994]. *Capitalism, Socialism and Democracy*. London: Routledge.

Shapiro, C. and H. Varian. 1999. *Information Rules*. Boston: HBS Press.

Shackle, G. 1991. *Epistemics and Economics: A Critique of Economic Doctrines*. New York: Transaction Publishers.

Shelby, H. 2000. *A General Theory of Competition*. Thousand Oaks, CA: Sage Books.

Smelster, N. and R. Swedberg (eds). 2005. *The Handbook of Economic Sociology*. Princeton: Princeton University Press.

Spinello, R. A. and M. Bottis. 2009. *A Defense of Intellectual Property Rights*. Cheltenham: E. Elgar.

Stiglitz, J. 2005. "Erros e acertos da propriedade intelectual." *O Globo*, August 29.

Technology Review. 2005. *Intellectual Property Issue*, June. Cambridge, MA: MIT Press.

Teece, D. 2000. *Managing Intellectual Capital*. Oxford: Oxford University Press.

Teece, D. and T. Jorde (eds). 1992. *Antitrust, Innovation and Competitiveness*. Oxford: Oxford University Press.

Varian, H., J. Farrel and C. Shapiro. 2004. *The Economics of Information Technology*. Cambridge: Cambridge University Press.

Vaughn, K. 1994. *Austrian Economics in America: The Migration of a Tradition*. Cambridge: Cambridge University Press.

Weber, M. 1922 [1976]. *Economy and Society*. Berkeley: Berkeley University Press.

Weiss, L. 2009. "The State in the Economy: Neoliberal or Neoactivist?" Paper presented at the workshop "Innovation Policies in Hard Times", Rio de Janeiro, September.

———. 2008. "Crossing the Divide: From the Military-Industrial Complex to the Development-Procurement Complex." Paper presented at the Berkeley Workshop on "The U.S. as a Hidden Developmental State," UC Berkeley, June 19–21.

———. 2007. "Governing the Market for America." Research paper for The Ford Foundation, Grant #1075-1307.

Wells, W. 2002. *Antitrust & the Formation of the Postwar World*. New York: Columbia University Press.

Wu, L. (ed.) 2004. *Economics of Antitrust: New Issues, Questions, and Insights*. White Planes, NY: NERA Economic Consulting.

Chapter 2

FROM INTELLECTUAL PROPERTY TO KNOWLEDGE GOVERNANCE: A MICRO-FOUNDED EVOLUTIONARY EXPLANATION

Annalisa Primi
OECD Development Centre

1. Introduction

Intellectual property has been, for a long time, outside the radar of modern mainstream economic analysis. It was a domain of lawyers and legal specialists that had little to do with "economic" analysis. And when it did, it was mostly a framework condition that needed to be "in place" and "right" in order not to hamper innovative entrepreneurial activity.

Patents have been seen as mechanisms to guarantee excludability in the use of knowledge, and hence appropriability in intangibles. In theory, patents confer a temporary monopoly on the exploitation of the patented technology, in exchange for the disclosure of the relevant information necessary to replicate the technology, which will become freely available for production use to others than the patent owner when the patent expires.

As always, reality is much more complex than that.

Since the end of the 1990s, several changes contributed to making "intellectual property" an issue of rising concern for a growing number of stakeholders, such as economists, policymakers and civil society.

Globalization and rising trade openness revealed the persistency in the asymmetries between advanced, emerging and lagging economies and put pressure on the issues of knowledge generation, access and transfer. The new technological paradigms, such as information and communications technology (ICT), biotech and nanotech reshaped the ways of doing business and research, highlighting the relevance of the mechanisms that regulate access and transfer of knowledge and technology. Several international and national reforms in IP regimes reshuffled the incentives towards protection and openness of newly generated products and processes inducing changes in the attitude of agents regarding the "use" of patents (think, for example, about strategic and defensive patenting).

The opinions expressed in this paper are those of the author and do not necessarily reflect those of the OECD.

In the era of "knowledge" economies, the sets of rules that define the conditions for excludability and diffusion of "knowledge" become an issue of concern for the society as a whole. However, as it usually happens, the "popularization" of the issue (which is evident not only in the rising number of academic articles and official reports on the topic, but also in the rising attention given by the press to IP issues) went hand in hand with a "polarization" between points of view: IP, or stronger IP protection, is "good" or "bad" for innovation and industrial development.

The polarized controversy has not helped much in advancing towards better IP regimes. The complexity and the multidimensionality of the challenges of contemporary global knowledge economies require a more sophisticated approach.

The creation of institutions and mechanisms that take into account, at the same time, the need to support investment in the generation of new knowledge, to guarantee the appropriability of "intangibles" and to secure access and diffusion of knowledge and technologies is still a goal to be accomplished in contemporary global knowledge economies. Given the rising relevance of knowledge and intangibles for growth and competitiveness, this issue is not only a crucial point, but also a pressing need. A need that is complex to address, considering the different related powers and interests, not only between countries, but within countries themselves.

This chapter frames the debate about intellectual property and innovation on the basis of the evolutionary understanding of the process of innovation to clarify the role and impact of IP on innovative conducts, focusing mostly on patents.

After this introduction, the second section will briefly present what innovation theory infers about knowledge transferability and appropriability. The third section will hence revisit the traditional appropriability and disclosure function of the patent system in light of the properties of knowledge, technology and learning. The fourth section will clarify the mismatch between the intentional functionalities of the patent system (incentive and/or reward for innovation) and the effective use of the system by firms and other innovative agents (i.e., the use of strategic and defensive patenting and the emergence of new markets for knowledge). The fifth section concludes the chapter, calling for the need to nest the analysis of IP regimes and patent policy in the broader "knowledge governance" domain.

2. What Innovation Theory Says About Knowledge Transferability and Appropriability

Reexamining the rationale and role of IP protection by looking at the contributions of economic and innovation theories might be of help. We might have been looking at the IP debate through opaque (or even wrong) glasses. Taking into account the properties of knowledge, innovation and technical change might help better define the rationale and role for IP. Actually, clarifying why we need a set of rules and norms to establish property rights in the domain of intangibles and linking this with the impact of those rights on the actual behavior of the agents involved in the innovation process could help to clarify what we can expect (and what we cannot) from intellectual property systems.

The origins of the protection of intellectual property can be traced back to medieval times, when guilds used to grant exclusive property rights.[1] "Patent" literally means open letter, emphasizing the disclosure function of the special privilege of exclusive exploitation that was granted to specific producers. The British monarchy used patents as a reward mechanism by conferring an exclusive right to commerce-specific commodities; patents were explicitly considered mechanisms for creating artificial monopolies. The English Statute of Monopolies of 1623 allowed a monopoly only to the "true and first inventor" of a new "method of manufacture."

Context, legislation and economic theory around patents evolved sensibly since those times.

The specificities of the intellectual property regime are rooted in the recognition of the difference between knowledge and information, and standard tangible commodities. A certain degree of "appropriation" of knowledge, information and novelty needs to be guaranteed in order to support the generation of innovations. In his pioneer study, Arrow (1962) addresses the problematic of appropriability in the frame of the (optimal) allocation of resources for invention. The hypothesis of nonrivalry and the partial excludability in consumption of knowledge would lead to an underinvestment in knowledge production (i.e., in innovative activities). Hence, mechanisms to guarantee the appropriability of the returns deriving from innovative efforts were needed in order for innovation to take place. The argument follows the logic that in the absence of given appropriability mechanisms, the incentive to invest in the generation of innovation would be inadequate from a social welfare point of view, and the amount of innovation introduced would be less than optimal due to the eventuality of free-rider behaviors and to the potential erosion of the advantages of innovation induced by imitation.

The rationale for protection derives from the need to introduce some discretional excludability in order to create incentives for agents to engage in efforts that would lead to the generation of "conceptual" and "intangible," – that is, intellectual – products, that otherwise would easily be appropriated by competitors. Intellectual property rights, and especially patents, respond, in principle, to the tension between the necessity of rewarding innovators, thus guaranteeing exclusive rights on intangibles, and favoring the diffusion of innovation, by disclosing technical knowledge and know-how embodied in innovations. In other words, IPRs aim at balancing the interests of those who innovate and those who would benefit from innovation (see, among others, Machlup 1958; Kitch 1977; Besen and Raskind 1991; Besen 1998).

However, the balance between disclosure and appropriability is difficult to establish. What are the characteristics of an intellectual property regime that allow it to maximize the rate of innovation, thus balancing the reward to inventors with the need to foster knowledge diffusion? The economic literature extensively debated on patent subject

---

1 The first patent law is said to be the Venetian one of 1474.

matter, patent quality, patent duration and breadth, and so forth, but consensus is far from being reached. A look at the properties of knowledge, technology and learning and at the behavior of innovative agents regarding the need for appropriation and diffusion of knowledge might help in reshaping the IP debate.

2.1. The properties of knowledge, technology and learning

Evolutionary theory offers an interpretation of how novelty is generated, produced and diffused, which derives from a set of specific properties of knowledge, technology and learning (Pavitt 1987; Dosi et al. 1988; Cimoli and Dosi 1995; Metcalfe 1995).

1. In this framework, *knowledge* encompasses tacit components and it is both codifiable and noncodifiable (Arrow 1962; Polany 1967). Knowledge is nonrival, but it is excludable. And excludability might derive from regulations (for example, patent law) and from the capacities of agents to access, decodify and use knowledge, beyond the legal mechanisms that define its accessibility. Assimilating knowledge to a public good stresses its nonrivalry and nonexcludability, meaning that once it is available in the system – for example, after patent expiration – it can be freely "used" – or referred to – by different agents at the same time. For certain types of knowledge, this is certainly the desired status and it should be preserved, as in the case of the output of basic research. However, the capabilities of agents affect the capacity to access and use knowledge, even more than its legal availability. Knowledge can be assimilated to a club good (nonrival but excludable) – highlighting that only those who have certain capacities (positioning in network hierarchies, scientific base, production capacities, etc.) will be able to decode it and use it productively.

2. *Technology*, as defined in standard economics textbooks, is identified with a set of blueprints – that is, techniques – required or used to produce artifacts. The choice of production techniques rests mainly on relative prices, given that information regarding the existence of such alternative blueprints is assumed to be available – and equally decodifiable – by all agents. However, an appreciative glance at reality shows that this is hardly the case. Firms do not always adopt frontier technologies, and asymmetries in technological capacities (between firms and countries) are likely to persist over long spans of time (Atkinson and Stiglitz 1969; Freeman 1982, 1994; Dosi 1982, 1988; Nelson and Winter 1982; Dosi, Pavitt and Soete 1990; Cimoli et al. 2006). Technology cannot be reduced to the standard view of a set of well-defined blueprints (Dosi 1982; Pavitt 1987). Rather, it can be defined as the means, the methods and the know-how through which agents "do things." It concerns problem-solving activities also involving – to varying degrees – tacit forms of knowledge embodied in individuals and organizational procedures, the means and the interfaces through which knowledge is produced, codified or transformed in "transferable" artifacts (Rosenberg 1976, 1982; Dosi 1988; Freeman 1982, 1994; Freeman and Soete 1997). At the micro level, technologies are to a fair extent incorporated into particular institutions, and the firms whose capabilities

are fundamental in shaping the rates and directions of technological advance. But firms are not the sole repositories of technologies. More ample socioeconomic and institutional settings shape the availability of existing technologies, such as universities and public institutions supporting technological development and innovation (Nelson 1993).

3. *Learning* is local, cumulative and embedded in organizations and their routines. Local means that the exploration and development of new techniques is likely to occur in the "neighborhood" of the techniques already in use (Atkinson and Stiglitz 1969; Antonelli 1995). Cumulative means that current technological development – at least at the level of individual business units – often builds upon past experiences of production and innovation, and it proceeds via sequences of specific problem-solving junctures (Arthur 1989; David 1985). The evolutionary path of technological learning is enhanceable through collective experiences, and it is fostered – or jeopardized – by socioeconomic frameworks. But at the same time, it requires nonsubstitutable individual efforts and processes.

This synthetic overview of the properties of knowledge, technology and learning leads to the recognition of a set of constraints regarding their transferability (and hence their appropriability):

1. The transferability of knowledge is segmented, according to its nature of public, private or club good; it is limited by its tacit and noncodifiable nature and enhanced by the proximity of capacities and capabilities of firms, systems and even countries. In a parallel way, the appropriability of knowledge overcomes the set of legal and strategic appropriability measures available to firms. Likewise, the tacit, noncodifiable and nontransferable component of knowledge embedded in procedures, routines and organizations guarantees its appropriability beyond any direct legal effort to protect it.

2. Transferability of technologies is constrained (or enhanced) by "technological proximity" of producers and users, by their absorptive capacity and by networks, partnerships, routines etc. There is no guarantee of automatic substitutability between obsolete or less efficient technologies and improved ones. The choice of techniques is far from being an allocative choice between available sets of blueprints. Technology transfer and licensing are effective means of transferring technology, but the effectiveness and the "demand" for this transfer is shaped by the specific characteristics and capacities of agents (firms, universities etc.).

3. The transferability of learning is limited and requires a sequence of adaptive trial-and-error processes that constitute the basis of learning itself. Transferability in terms of expertise and reverse engineering is possible (through networks, cooperation, interchange of personnel etc.). However, it is constrained by the structural capacities and capabilities of agents. Learning is to a great extent completely appropriable due to its inner nature of being a process embedded in organizations and routines.

2.2. Beyond IP: The appropriability problem

In addition to the clarification of the limited transferability of knowledge deriving from the comprehension of its tacit and noncodifiable components, innovation theory also helps to nest the analysis of the use of IP in broader firm strategies.

The term "appropriability" refers to the capacity of innovating agents (individuals, firms, institutions) to capture the value generated by innovations. It relates to the different mechanisms used by firms to secure their ownership of intangibles. Firms use a set of complex (and sometimes complementary) mechanisms to appropriate the rents deriving from innovations. Industrial secrets, lead-time advantages, complementary manufacturing or technological capacities, branding and costumer fidelization are different means, among others, that firms might use to appropriate rents deriving from intangibles (see Nelson 1959; Arrow 1962; Teece 1986; Dosi et al. 2006a, 2006b; Winter 2006; among others).

The appropriability problem is influenced by the recognition that the generation of new (valuable) knowledge suffers from indivisibilities in production and uncertainty regarding outcomes. The time lag between the innovative effort and the generation of rents through the sale of the innovation augments the costs of innovation and pushes firms to develop and use mechanisms to protect the results of the innovative effort all along the various innovation phases.

There is a high level of uncertainty associated with innovation. On the one hand, the outcome of innovative effort is not granted; on the other hand, the costs for innovation are sustained in a given moment in time, while benefits from innovation could accrue to the firm as a flow of resources for an undetermined period of time. This transforms the "prize" for innovation into an issue which suffers from a double uncertainty, both in terms of "profitability" and in terms of the "amount" of that profitability.

While firms deploy various strategies to secure their innovative efforts, the analysis of appropriability strategies has been biased towards patenting. A series of concurring factors contributes to explaining this issue. On the one hand, there has been a tendency to focus on R&D efforts and technological innovations, which are the forms of innovation most subject to patenting. On the other hand, the deep institutional changes in global patent regimes also contributed to shifting the attention towards patenting, too often forgetting the relevance of other appropriability mechanisms.

The fact that firms rely on a combination of mechanisms to protect their innovative efforts is quite obvious. The different appropriability mechanisms address different aspects of the intangible value created by the firm. They are based on diverse requirements, and they respond to different strategic functions. Patents, for example, are legal mechanisms granting the inventor a temporary monopoly for use of the patented innovation in exchange of the disclosure of the procedure to obtain or realize the innovation. The national law defines the patentable subject matter, which, in general, should include a non-obvious inventive step with industrial applicability. Trademarks, in turn, are meant to protect names and signs indicating a product, a process or a service, and the like.

The choice between using one – or a combination – of those appropriability mechanisms rests upon different structural factors that include, among other issues, the kind of innovation or technology the firm is willing to protect, the stage of the innovation process to which the new product or process refers to, the capabilities of the innovative firm in terms of legal, financial and human resources dedicated to the enforcement of the entitled property rights, and the strategic management of the firm's technological assets (Levin et al. 1987; Cockburn and Grilliches 1988; Cohen et al. 2000; Dosi et al. 2006a; Winter 2006).

Two major works contributed to shifting the focus from patent to the broader appropriability approach: one (Levin et al. 1987) analyzes the results of the Yale Survey, and the other (Cohen, Nelson and Walsh (2000) is based on the results of the so-called "Carnegie Mellon Survey."

The "Yale survey" (Levin et al. 1987) "describes the results of an inquiry into appropriability conditions in more than one hundred manufacturing industries" (1987, 785). The study aimed at contributing to the ongoing discussion in the United States regarding potential reform in patent law, antitrust and trade policy. The premise of that study was the realization that "because technological advance is often an interactive, cumulative process, strong protection of individual achievements may slow the general advance" (Levin et al. 1987, 788). The document advocated that "it should not be taken for granted that more appropriability is better [and that] better protection necessarily leads to more innovation" (Levin et al. 1987, 787). The Yale survey gathered empirical evidence on the basis of interviews with high-level R&D managers of firms in the US manufacturing industry. The study collected information regarding the effectiveness of alternative methods to protect the introduction of new products and processes, and results confirmed the starting hypothesis of limited effectiveness of patents with respect to other mechanisms as a means to secure appropriability. The only exception was the drug industry, in which the majority of respondents considered patents to be the most effective appropriability mechanism.

The Carnegie Mellon Survey collected information regarding the use of different appropriability mechanisms on a sample of 1,478 R&D labs in the US manufacturing industry in 1994 (Cohen, Nelson and Walsh 2000). Starting from the realization that in practice, patents were not considered an effective protection mechanism for innovation, the survey aimed at gathering information regarding why firms do or do not patent their innovations, considering the sustained increase in patent applications and grants. Even though the results of the Carnegie Mellon Survey are not strictly comparable to those of the Yale survey, the study confirms on the one hand that patents are not the primary source of appropriability by firms in the US manufacturing industry, and on the other hand that there are strong sectoral differences in preferences and effectiveness of different appropriability mechanisms.[2]

---

2 Recently, the literature on appropriability and patenting behavior has been enriched by firm-level analyses based on data from national innovation surveys (for additional references, see Arundel and Kabla 1998; Arundel 2001; Laursen and Salter 2005; López and Orliki 2006).

The available body of evidence on patenting behavior shows that:

1. Patents are not the preferred mechanism for protecting product and process innovation, even though the preference for patents varies substantially across sectors and by firm size;
2. There are some innovations which are technically easier to protect by means of patents, while others are more easily securable through secrets or through other mechanisms, and this depends both on the kind of innovation itself and of its codificability, and on the strategy of the firm;
3. Firms generally use a combination of appropriability mechanisms, which are then more complementary than substitutes.

3. Revisiting the Appropriability and Disclosure Function of the Patent System

The evolutionary theoretical framework recognizes the persistency of the nonsubstitutability of technologies and techniques, both in the short run and in the long run, beyond legal appropriability mechanisms. There are components of technology that are the exclusive domain of the repository – like some forms of tacit or noncodified knowledge, cumulated learning effects, and so on – the appropriability of which does not derive from specific efforts tailored to that (patents, trade marks, etc.), but from the fact that technology and "know-how" are associated with certain bodies of knowledge that are embedded in the procedures and routines of the repository organization.

Standard IP analysis is primarily molded on the theory of choices of techniques; the availability of information and relative prices determines firms' choices, and intellectual property protection is justified on the basis of the nonrivalry of information and knowledge as opposed to physical artifacts. The assumption that changes in relative prices and the availability of information primarily affect innovative behavior is not entirely consistent with the innovation theory framework. Actually, the rate and direction of innovative search and imitation are shaped by a set of different factors beyond legal regimes, such as:

- Technological capabilities of agents (which rest on the accumulated knowledge and necessary resources for the generation and management of technical change);
- Production capacities (which concern the stocks of resources, the nature of capital-embodied technologies, labor skills, product and input specification and organizational routines in use);
- The sectoral specificities of the technology in question;
- Path-dependent trajectories of firms – or countries – (which shape the collective knowledge shared by agents in each socioeconomic system and that define the *entourage* where firms – or countries – are likely to move in their search for innovation);
- The (nonrational) perception of innovative opportunities, irrespective of whether relative prices change or not, which might lead to the discovery of intended and unintended new techniques.

In fact, according to innovation theory, even if all patent information was freely available and disclosed, the direction of innovative search and the resulting innovative and imitative trajectories of firms and countries would remain bounded within some relatively narrow paths. The knowledge base and the technological capabilities of agents, the structural characteristics of systems in which every particular activity is embodied, as well as market forces, shape innovation trajectories beyond information availability. There is no automatic, linear or deterministic relationship between innovative and imitative search and patent protection (David 1993; Heller and Eisenberg 1998; Mazzoleni and Nelson 1998; Dosi et al. 2006a, 2006b; Eisenberg 2006; Gosh and Soete 2006).[3]

It is recognized that (1) that technology is highly specific and embedded in routines and procedures, (2) that knowledge has a strong tacit component and that (3) learning is a trial-and-error process which entails nonsubstitutable experiences. These considerations lead to a controversy over blaming or blessing patents for their effect on innovative conducts in developing countries, losing most of its relevance.

The approach of the paradigm-based theory of innovation leads us to include the intellectual property discourse within the more extensive debate on appropriability and mechanisms for knowledge governance and to revisit the scope of the two primary standard functions of the patent system: the appropriability and disclosure functions.

3.1. The appropriability function

The capacity of agents to appropriate the advantages and the rents deriving from innovation goes beyond the regulatory framework and the set of established (intellectual) property rights. Firms, and in a wider perspective countries, use a set of complex (sometimes complementary) appropriability mechanisms in order to guarantee the capturing of rents stemming from innovation efforts (Levin et al. 1987; Cockburn and Grilliches 1988; Cohen et al. 2000; Dosi et al. 2006a, 2006b). The choice between using one – or a combination – of those mechanisms rests upon different structural factors which include the kind of innovation or technology the firm is willing to protect, the size of the firm which influences the legal, financial and human resources the firm can dedicate to the enforcement of the entitled rights and the strategic management of the firm's technological and intangible assets.

At the same time, patents play different roles according to structural characteristics of firms.[4] The asymmetry in patent propensity, that is, in the share of patented inventions,

---

3 On the discussion regarding the appropriability of knowledge and its effect on the rate and direction of technical change, see Plant (1934), Kitch (1977), Machlup and Penrose (1950), Arrow (1962), Scherer (1977) and, for a critical review of recent stances, see Dosi et al. (2006b).

4 There have been many attempts to empirically investigate the patent propensity of firms. Some studies look at the proportion of patented innovation on total innovations; others consider the number of patents in relation to the prevailing R&D outlay and moreover, additional studies analyze the determinants of patenting according to firms' characteristics (Scherer 1965, 1983; Mansfield 1986; Arundel, Van de Paal and Soete 1995; Cincera 1997; Arundel and Kabla 1998; Brower and Kleinknecht 1999; Arundel 2001; Hall and Ziedonis 2001; López and Orliki 2006).

between different technological fields derives, on the one hand, from the different appropriability strategies of firms according to the specificities of the concerned technology and innovation, which in general have a high-sector-specific component (Scherer 1965, 1983; Mansfield 1986; Levin et al. 1987; Cockburn and Griliches 1988). On the other hand, patent propensity is affected by the size of firms and the differences in the value assigned to the disclosure of information to users or consumers, features which, again, have a strong sectoral component related to the replicabilty, decidability and usability of disclosed information for agents others than the "inventor" (Scherer 1965, 1983; Mansfield 1986; Horstman et al. 1985; Levin et al. 1987; Harter 1993; Harabi 1995; Arundel and Kabla 1998; Cohen et al. 2000). Thus, patents appear as one, but not the unique appropriability mechanism, whose relevance is indeed highly sector-specific and influenced by a set of structural characteristics of firms.[5]

In addition to that, it has to be noted that the legal recognition of the intellectual property right conferred by the patent is not automatically translated into effective capacity of guaranteeing the control over technologies. Patents confer the right to defend a temporary exclusive right through legal action. Effective appropriability is a function of the capacity and the willingness of the owner of the right to enforce the right, hence following Shapiro (2003) and Lemely and Shapiro (2005), patents can be defined as probabilistic rights. Litigation costs, the expertise of legal advisors, the bargaining power, the capacity of monitoring the market and the competitors are some of the factors that influence the possibility of the "legal entitlement" to be converted into "effective entitlement." In order to allow patents to act as effective appropriability mechanisms, the legal entitlement should be matched by the capacity – and the willingness – to enforce the right.[6]

3.2. The disclosure function

Certain interpretations tend to emphasize the role of patents in favoring incremental innovation and technical change through the increase in the amount of knowledge available in the public domain. Patents are seen as a mechanism to disseminate (relevant) information into the economic system. Actually, a patent should incent the disclosure of technical information so that any person skilled in the art would be able to reduce the invention to practice, in exchange for a limited exlusive right of exploitation.

However, here again, the translation of the potential disclosure function into practice is constrained by the nature of technology and learning and by the structural characteristics of agents.

---

5 Chapter 5 will present an analysis of the determinants of patenting in the Brazilian manufacturing industry, on the basis of the National innovation survey (PINTEC).

6 It is not uncommon for firms to avoid engaging in legal action in cases of infringement of their intellectual property rights. In an analysis of the patenting behavior of small and medium enterprises in the US, Koen (1991) finds that 55 percent of firms do not take action against infringement of their patents due to high litigation costs and the excessive length of trials.

The disclosure function assumes that patents allow diffusing information that would have otherwise been secret. However, it is quite common that the information disclosed in patents is inadequate or opaque. And even assuming that the disclosed information does not suffer from any limitation – which is quite a strong assumption – given that technology and learning involve organizational and tacit knowledge embedded in routines and procedures, the simple disclosure of information does not guarantee the disclosure of what is needed in order to reverse engineer, copy or reproduce the technology in question.

Think, for example, about generics in the pharmaceutical industry: Why do not all firms in every country produce them? Because most firms are simply not able to do it. Even if they are informed about the existence of a certain technique or technology, they might not have the capabilities for developing or using it. Pushing the argument further leads us to affirm that even if firms were given all the blueprints of technique, that is, assuming the perfect disclosure of patent information (and supposing in an extreme case also the availability of equal production capacities, basically capital inputs), performances, and thus the revealed input coefficients, might still differ widely. Following R. Nelson:

[It] is easy to illustrate this by means of a gastronomical metaphor: despite readily available cooking blueprints and codified rules on technical procedures, outcomes in terms of standards of food quality are unequivocally asymmetrical. This applies to comparisons among individual agents and also to institutionally differentiated groups of them: for example, we are ready to bet that most eaters randomly extracted from the world population would systematically rank samples of English cooks to be "worse" than French, Chinese, Italian, Indian…ones, even when performing on identical recipes!!! (Cimoli and Dosi 1995)

This should apply, much more so, to circumstances whereby performances result from more complex and opaque organizational routines.

The disclosure function of patents is also generally assumed to increase efficiency in the search for novelty and innovation in economic systems, allowing it to prevent the duplication of R&D efforts. Following our critical stance, it is quite easy to derive that this is hardly the case. Firms might engage in competitive R&D trajectories. And patent races are a clear example of this behavior. On the other hand, the duplication of R&D efforts is not necessarily to be seen as a systemic inefficiency. Since technology and knowledge are clearly more than a set of blueprints and entail organizational capacities, routines and tacit codes, firms might well have to follow a certain learning path in order to be able to decode technical information. To profit from the availability of technical information deriving from external sources, firms need to posses a certain degree of capabilities that allows them to identify potential opportunities related to the technique or the technical information in question, and then they need to dispose of the technical capacities of profiting from the technological interchange. Actually, firms' absorptive capacity explains the potential complementarities between in-house R&D efforts and external sourcing (Cohen and Levinthal 1989, 1990).

4. Patenting Behavior: From Incentives to Strategic Assets

The arguments presented in the previous sections restrict the domain of influence of IP regimes on innovative conducts and call for nesting the analysis into a broader framework that takes into account the strategic approach of agents towards innovation. However, even though IP regimes are not the unique determinants of innovative conducts, they do impact innovation trajectories. Patents, and the whole set of issues like patent subject matter, patent length and breadth, as well as patent quality, and the capacities to enforce the rights conferred, affect entrepreneurial behavior in diverse ways.

Beyond acting as an incentive to innovate or to transfer technology, patents might influence the perception of what is public or freely available and what is proprietary in given fields of science and knowledge. Patents might shape R&D trajectories of firms – favoring or discouraging the entrance in given research fields – and can influence mergers and acquisitions within firms. At the same time, patents can act as reputation signals between firms, and they might perform as negotiation instruments in legal settlements. In addition, patents might become "assets" in a firm's portfolio that assume a value beyond the value of the patented technology (Cimoli, Primi and Coriat 2010).

In fact, the rationale behind patenting goes beyond the logic provided by the standard markets-for-technologies approach, that is, patent licensing for production. Patents have been transformed into peculiar strategic assets whose relevance is increasingly disentangled from the subjacent technology, being more and more dependent on nonrational expectations regarding possible future technological scenarios.

The transformation of patents from incentives and rewards for innovation into strategic assets for rent management can be explained by the concurrence of two major phenomena:

1. *The emergence of new technological paradigms* entails a redefinition of what innovation is, how it is generated and through what means it can be diffused and appropriated. In new technological paradigms, mainly ICT, biotech and nanotech, innovation is, each time, more incremental and cumulative in character, intensive in interrelations between firms (countries and institutions), and it entails an increasing relevance of science. The concepts of replicabilty, usability and copying are constantly redefined, the potential technological interrelations are multiple, and uncertainty regarding future possible outcomes is even higher than in past technological paradigms.
2. *The reshaping of world intellectual property systems.*[7] IP systems are institutional and regulatory infrastructures embodied in an evolving socioeconomic system; hence,

---

7 See Cimoli, Coriat and Primi (2010) for an analysis of the reshaping of global IP systems.

they naturally entail change and transformation. IP systems have been subject to various transformations according to the development of modern economies (Machlup and Penrose 1950; David 1993). From regulation of national scope at the beginning of industrial development and during the phase of inward industrialization, which characterized the take-off of first comers, IP systems evolved to supranational regimes. This transformation went hand in hand with the increase in relevance of international trade and interactions between countries and according to the rising articulation and diversification of production processes which lead to an increase in the role of technical information and know-how and in its appropriability (Dasgupta and David 1994; Mazzoleni and Nelson 1998; Mowery et al. 2004).[8]

The contemporary reshaping of IP happened in a context characterized by increased trade liberalization and integration pointed to an (upward) harmonization of standards. It entails two major aspects: First, the changes and the increasing pro-protection attitude within the United States, which to different extents molded subsequent changes in foreign countries, and the inclusion of IP issues within the trade-negotiation agenda. The United States assisted in a progressive expansion of the patenting frontier, especially through a series of court rulings that reverted previous doctrines in favor of a more lax interpretation of patent subject matter and a transition to a more proprietary and commercialization-oriented science model that departed from the more traditional open science stance, sustained by the adoption of the Bayh–Dole Act.[9] Second, in response to a proactive competitiveness strategy, IP issues have been included within the trade-negotiation agenda. The ratification of the Trade-Related Aspects of Intellectual Property Rights (TRIPS) agreement in 1994 within the General Agreement on Trades and Tariffs (GATT) represented the baseline for calling for a worldwide harmonization of IP laws. Requirements, exceptions to rights conferred and policy spaces are currently being redefined by the wave of bilateral agreements and treaties (Fink and Reichenmiler 2005; Moncayo 2006).

The changes in patent regimes and in innovative behavior of agents contributed to generating additional markets to the traditional markets for technologies. In the new markets for knowledge, the value of the patent is increasingly independent of the subjacent technology and the effective utilization of the patented technology in production. The value of patents is increasingly associated with expectations about (1) the possibility that the patent becomes relevant for production in the future,

---

8 The Paris Convention of 1883 on industrial property protection, and the Berne Convention of 1886 that regulates the protection of original forms of expression like artistic or literary works, represented the first phases of the internationalization of the protection of intellectual property rights.

9 Adelman (1987); Merges (1992); Mazzoleni and Nelson (1998); Mowery et al. (2004); Jaffe (2000); Cohen and Lemely (2001); Hunt (2001); Hall and Ziedonis (2001); Gallini (2002); Graham and Mowery (2003); Hall (2003); Bessen and Hunt (2004).

(2) the fact that it might be determinant in M&A, in legal settlements and in company negotiations and (3) the potential value of other patents to which the patent might be associated, as in patent pools or patent portfolios. The new sets of rules and the new technological scenario transform patents into "simple" legal mechanisms of potential and temporary exlcusive rights into strategic assets for firms. Additional "markets" are created in which patents are "traded" not because they are the carrier of a technology that is needed in production today or potentially tomorrow, but because they might be a source of revenues without implying the need to carry out production. This changes the rules of the game, the barriers to entry, the rationale and the characteristics of participants and transactions of markets for knowledge as they were intended in their primary technology licensing function. And this new setting calls for increased understanding and interpretation to derive policy implications, both for advanced and for developing countries.

The new markets for knowledge include markets for science, especially in the areas in which scientific output is closer to business application such as ICT and biotech and "derivative" markets for knowledge in which firms carry out transactions of patent valutation beyond the effective industrial utility of the patented technology, as in mergers and acquisitions (M&A) and in litigations (Cimoli and Primi 2006; Cimoli, Coriat and Primi 2010).

5. Conclusions: Beyond Patent Policy, Toward Knowledge Governance

The role of patents in shaping innovation trajectories is an extensively studied phenomenon in the economic literature. However, several changes occurred in the last few decades that modified the behavior of agents and the role of patents in firms' competitive strategies. As knowledge and innovation become a more and more relevant source of growth for contemporary dynamics in global open economies, there is a need to increase our understanding and implications of intellectual property regimes (and patents) and to identify ways to improve the relevant policy and legal framework in the light of current challenges (Burlamaqui in this volume).

A first contribution that innovation theory might bring to this debate is that any satisfactory attempt to analyze the role of IP regimes in influencing the rate of generation, adoption and diffusion of knowledge should start by recognizing "what technology is" and "what innovation is." Technology, as well as innovation, cannot be reduced to the standard view of a set of well-defined new blueprints. Rather, it should encompass the means, the methods, the know-how and the problem-solving activities through which agents "do things." This helps to explain why firms do not always adopt frontier technologies, that is, it is far more complicated than replicating blueprints. It is precisely because knowledge is partly tacit and embodied in complex organizational practices that technological lags and leads within and between firms, industries and even countries may be persistent beyond the opportunities and limits established by legal appropriation mechanisms, like intellectual property rights. In fact, asymmetries in technological capacities (between firms and countries) are likely to persist over rather long spans of time, beyond the legal mechanisms defying the appropriability and transferability conditions of technologies because of the capacities of agents. But the opposite also holds true: if firms show similar technological capabilities, imitation might occur very quickly, patent protection notwithstanding, by means of "inventing around."

This leads to a call for a broader approach to the innovation and intellectual property debate. IP regimes influence behavioral choices of innovative agents, but isolating their effect is not possible, and not desirable. The search for and diffusion of novelty are influenced by a series of factors beyond IP, such as direct incentives to innovation, regulations, market structure, competition policy, firms' strategic choices, among others. Nesting the analysis of patent policies into a broader "knowledge governance" perspective seems the relevant approach.

The challenge for contemporary economies is to define the conditions for knowledge generation, diffusion and exploitation (i.e., the conditions for knowledge governance), and this requires a comprehensive approach which looks at all the differences and interactions between different policy fields (see Table 2.1).

The evolutionary perspective helps to nuance the effective appropriability and transferability of knowledge, and it highlights the impact of appropriability and transferability on the generation of new knowledge, technology and learning.

The mechanisms for knowledge appropiability and transferability (1) are only in part shaped by policies; they are also strongly influenced by the business and institutional strategy of the firm or institution in question, (2) are influenced by several policy leverages beyond IPRs policy, including competition policy, labor market regulations, science and technology policies, industrial policies, and (3) impact the rate and direction of the generation of new knowledge, which is shaped by the circulation of available knowledge and influenced by several policies, like science and technology policy, education policy, industrial policy, and the like.

The "knowledge governance" approach is skeptical about the reduction of the behavioral foundations of innovative and imitative conducts to linear and deliberate profit-maximizing choices, and it leads to recognize that:

1. "Getting the IPRs right" is far from being the solution. Also because there is too much uncertainty about what "right" might mean in terms of intellectual-property regimes across firms and countries with profound differences in technological and production capacities. Legal appropriability mechanisms, that is, prevailing intellectual property norms, are classified as second-order effect factors with respect to production capacities and technological capabilities embodied in socioinstitutional systems in shaping innovative and imitative conducts of firms and countries.

2. A wide set of inducements bind or incent firms in their imitative and innovative search. Firms (and hence countries) may appropriate innovation rents beyond any legal attempt to do it, simply through the complexity and the embeddedness

Table 2.1. An evolutionary framework for knowledge governance

	Generation	Appropriability	Transferability	Mechanisms for knowledge and technology		
				Generation	Appropriability	Transferability/circulation
KNOWLEDGE (Public, private or club good)	Requires absorptive capacities, original individual and collective effort and builds up on the available existing stock	High due to the tacit dimension of K. Influenced by the regimes which define the nature of K as a public or private good (ex. open science)	High for codified K. Low for tacit knowledge/know-how. Limited by the absorptive capacities of agents	Policies: – Education, training and human capital – STI policies (R&D and fiscal incentives, infrastructure for S&T, etc.). – Industrial policy	Corporate/institutional strategy: – Lead time advantage – Trade secrecy – Exclusive clause for managers/workers Policies Industrial policy **IPRs**	Corporate/institutional strategy: – Fairs/exhibitions – Talent mobility Policies Human capital (training/mobility of talent) Competition policies (M&A) Labor market (mobility) Science and technology policy (networks, collaboration) **IPRs** (licensing, patent pools)
TECHNOLOGY (Embedded or disembodied)		Varied. Shaped by institutional/business strategies and by regulations (IPR regimes, competition policy, standard setting)	Varied. Constrained (or enhanced) by "technological/cognitive" proximity of agents	Corporate/institutional strategy: – Investment in R&D; training, organization of production etc.	Corporate/institutional strategy: – Complementary manufacturing capacities/bundling – Lead time advantage – Trade secrecy Policies **IPRs**	Corporate/institutional strategy: Reverse engineering Inventing around Technology transfer Policies Competition policies (M&A) **IPRs** (licensing, patent pools)
LEARNING		Very high. Embedded in individual/institutional routines	Limited. It can be enhanced by sharing processes	-----	-----	-----

of technology and knowledge in their organizational procedures and technical know-how, or through lead-time advantages. The availability of a set of diverse appropriability conditions and of a given knowledge base is not irrelevant in shaping the search for novelty and entrepreneurial endeavors in innovation. However, explanations about the willingness of firms (and to a broader extent, of countries) to explore new paradigms, to carry out experimental research or to engage in reverse-engineering or imitative efforts, and about differences in the rate of the introduction of new products, processes or start-up firms, require a comprehensive understanding of specific social, institutional and corporate characteristics, which go beyond the prevailing legal framework governing the access and transferability of knowledge.

3. Innovativeness, beyond being partly the result of a random process naturally concerning something new and not expected, entails a degree of stickiness shaped by accumulated scientific, technological and production capabilities. Firms and countries do not depart from the same line. They suffer deep asymmetries in terms of production capacity and technological capabilities. And it is reasonable to assume that these asymmetries will tend to persist over rather long spans of time, unless tailored and sustained efforts (mainly industrial and innovation policies) are taken in order to foster structural change and to induce transformations in production structures and allocation of inputs. Hence, patent policy should be defined, taking into account industrial and innovation policy objectives.

The existence of unexploited technological opportunities, together with the relevant knowledge base and the set of appropriability conditions, concurs to define the boundaries of the set of potential innovations: those which are actually explored might depend on socioeconomic traits of production, organizational and institutional systems. Hence, it is not about "getting the IP right," but about clarifying the required conditions and incentives for the creation of new knowledge and for the diffusion and transfer of existing ones. This requires defining the conditions that operate at several levels (science, competition, industrial, technology policy, etc.) and that shape the governance of knowledge creation, diffusion and exploitation in any given socioeconomic system.

Going forward in this debate requires a broader approach that includes the intellectual property debate within the more extensive discussion of knowledge governance and public policies for the creation and strengthening of scientific, technological and production capacities. It also requires imagining a governance structure for IP policies nested in the broader industrial and technology policy strategy (Burlamaqui in this volume). This governance structure needs to take into account the policy complementarities with other relevant policy domains (such as competition policy, trade policy, science policy, just to name a few) and needs to allow defining IP policies on the basis of local and global scientific and production development challenges.

References

Adelman, M. J. 1987. "The New World of Patents Created by the Court of Appeals for the Federal Circuit." *Journal of Law Reform* 20: 979–1007.

Antonelli, C. 1995. *The Economics of Localized Technological Change and Industrial Dynamics.* Dordrecht, Boston, London: Kluwer Academic Publishers.

Arora, A., A. Fosfuri, and A. Gambardella (eds). 2001. *Markets for Technology: The Economics of Innovation and Corporate Strategy.* Cambridge, MA: MIT Press.

Arrow, K. 1962. "Economic Welfare and Allocation of Resources for Inventions." In R. R. Nelson (ed.), *The Rate and Direction of Inventive Activity*, 609–25. Princeton, Princeton University Press.

Arthur, B. 1989. "Competing Technologies, Increasing Returns and Lock-in by Historical Events." *Economic Journal* 99 (394): 116–31.

Arundel, A. 2001. "The relative effectiveness of patents and secrecy for appropriation." *Research Policy* 30 (4): 611–24.

Arundel, A. and I. Kabla. 1998. "What Percentage of Innovations Are Patented? Empirical Estimates for European Firms." *Research Policy* 27: 127–41.

Arundel, A., G. van de Paal and L. Soete. 1995. "Innovation strategies of Europe's largest industrial firms: Results of the PACE survey for information sources." Public Research Protection of Innovations and Government Programmes, Directorate General XIII, European Commission EIMS Publication 23.

Atkinson A. B. and J. E. Stiglitz. 1969. "A New View of Technological Change." *Economic Journal* 79 (315): 573–8.

Besen, S. M. 1998. "Intellectual Property." In P. Newman (ed.), *The New Palgrave Dictionary of Economics and the Law*, vol. 2, 348–52. London: Macmillan.

Besen, S. M. and L. J. Raskind. 1991. "An Introduction to the Law and Economics of Intellectual Property." *Journal of Economic Perspectives* 5 (1): 3–27.

Bessen, J. and R. H. Hunt. 2004. "An Empirical Look at Software Patents." WP 03/17R, Federal Reserve Bank of Philadelphia.

Brouwer, E. and A. Kleinknecht. 1999. "Innovative output and a firms' propensity to patent, an exploration of CIS micro data." *Research Policy* 28: 615–24.

Cesaroni, F. and P. Giuri. 2005. "Intellectual Property Rights and Market Dynamics." LEM Working Paper Series 2005/10.

Cimoli, M., B. Coriat and A. Primi. 2010. "Intellectual property and industrial development: a critical assessment." In M. Cimoli, G. Dosi and J. Stiglitz (eds), *Industrial Policy and Development, The Political Economy of Capabilities Accumulation*, 506–40. Oxford: Oxford University Press.

Cimoli, M. and G. Dosi. 1995. "Technological Paradigms, Pattern of Learning and Development: An Introductory Roadmap." *Journal of Evolutionary Economics* 5 (3): 243–68.

Cimoli, M., G. Dosi, R. R. Nelson and J. Stiglitz. 2006. "Institutions and Policies Shaping Industrial Development: An Introductory Note." LEM Working Paper Series 2006/02.

Cimoli, M., M. Holland, G. Porcile, A. Primi and S. Vergara. 2006. "Growth, Structural Change and Technological Capabilities Latina America in a Comparative Perspective." LEM Working Paper Series 2006/11.

Cimoli M. and A. Primi. 2008. "Technology and intellectual property: A taxonomy of contemporary markets for knowledge and their implications for development." LEM Papers Series 2008/06, Laboratory of Economics and Management (LEM), Sant'Anna School of Advanced Studies, Pisa, Italy.

Cincera, M. 1997. "Patents, R&D and technological spillovers at the firm level: Some evidence from econometric count models for panel data." *Journal of Applied Econometrics* 12: 265–80.

Cohen, J. E. and M. A. Lemely. 2001. "Patent Scope and Innovation in the Software Industry." *Columbia Law Review* 89 (1): 1–57.

Cohen, W. and D. Levinthal. 1990. "Absorptive Capacity: A New Perspective on Learning and Innovation." *Administrative Science Quarterly* 35: 128–52.

_____. 1989. "Innovation and Learning: The Two Faces of R&D." *Economic Journal* 99: 569–96.

Cohen, W. M., R. R. Nelson and J. P. Walsh. 2000. "Protecting their Intellectual Assets: Appropriability Conditions and why US Manufacturing Firms Patent (or not)." NBER Working Paper No. 7552. Available at http://www.nber.org/papers/w7552

Cockburn, I. and Z. Griliches. 1988. "Industry Effects and Appropriability Measures in the Stock Market's Valuation of R&D and Patents." *American Economic Review* 78 (2): 419–23.

Dasgupta, P. and P. David. 1994. "Toward a New Economics of Science." *Research Policy* 23 (5): 487–521.

David, P. A. 1985. "Clio and the Economics of QWERTY." *American Economic Review* 75: 332–7.

_____. 1993. "Intellectual Property Institutions and the Panda's Thumb: Patents, Copyrights and Trade Secrets in Economic Theory and History." In M. B. Wallerstein, M. E. Mogee and R. A. Schoen (eds), *Global Dimensions of Intellectual Property Rights in Science and Technology*, 19–61. Washington DC: National Academy Press.

Dosi, G. 1988. "Sources, Procedures and Microeconomic Effects of Innovation." *Journal of Economic Literature* 26: 1120–71.

_____. 1982. "Technological Paradigms and Technological Trajectories: A Suggested Interpretation of the Determinant and Direction of Technological Change." *Research Policy* 11: 147–62.

Dosi, G., C. Freeman, R. Nelson, G. Silverberg and L. Soete (eds). 1988. *Technical Change and Economic Theory*. Pinter: London.

Dosi, G., F. Malerba, G. B. Ramello and F. Silva. 2006a. "Information, Appropriability and the Generation of Innovative Knowledge Four Decades after Arrow and Nelson: An Introduction." *Industrial and Corporate Change* 15 (6): 891–901.

Dosi, G., L. Marengo and C. Pasquali. 2006b. "How Much Should Society Fuel the Greed of Innovators? On the Relations between Appropriability, Opportunities and the Rates of Innovation." *Research Policy* 35 (8): 1110–21.

Dosi, G., K. Pavitt and L. Soete. 1990. *The Economics of Technical Change and International Trade*. London: Harvester Wheatsheaf Press.

Eaton, J. and S. Kortum. 1996. "Trade in Ideas: Patenting and Productivity in the OECD." *Journal of International Economics* 40: 251–78.

Eisenberg, R. S. 2006. "Patents and Data Sharing in Public Science." *Industrial and Corporate Change* 15 (6): 1013–31.

Fink, C. and P. Reichenmiler. 2005. "Tightening TRIPS: The Intellectual Property Provisions of Recent US Free Trade Agreements." World Bank Trade Note 20 (February).

Freeman, C. 1994. "The Economics of Technical Change: A Critical Survey." *Cambridge Journal of Economics* 18: 1–50.

_____. 1982. *The Economics of Industrial Innovation*. London: Francis Pinter.

Freeman, C., and L. Soete. 1997. *The Economics of Industrial Innovation*. 3rd edn. Cambridge, MA: MIT Press.

Gallini, N. 2002. "The Economics of Patents: Lessons from the Recent US Patent Reform." *Journal of Economic Perspectives* 16: 131–54.

Gosh, R. and L. Soete. 2006. "Information and Intellectual Property: The Global Challenges." *Industrial and Corporate Change* 15 (6): 919–35.

Graham, S. and D. C. Mowery. 2003. "Intellectual Property Protection in the US Software Industry." In W. M. Cohen and S. Merrill (eds), *Patents in the Knowledge-Based Economy*. Washington DC: National Academic Press.

Hall, B. H. 2003. "Business Methods Patents, Innovation and Policy." Economics Department, University of California Berkeley, Working Paper E03-331.

Hall, B. H. and R. H. Ziedonis. 2001. "The Patent Paradox Revisited: An Empirical Study of Patenting in the US Semiconductor Industry, 1979–1995." *RAND Journal of Economics* 32: 101–28.

Harabi, N. 1995. "Appropriability of Technical Innovations: An Empirical Analysis." *Research Policy* 24: 981–92.

Harter, J. F. R. 1993. "The Propensity to Patent with Differentiated Products." *Southern Economic Journal* 61: 195–200.

Heller, M. A. and R. S. Eisenberg. 1998. "Can patents deter innovation? The anticommons in biomedical research." *Science* 280 (5364): 698–701.

Horstman, I., G. M. MacDonald and A. Slivinski. 1985. "Patents as Information Transfer Mechanisms: To Patent or (Maybe) Not to Patent." *Journal of Political Economy* 93: 837–58.

Hunt, R. M. 2001. "You Can Patent that? Are Patents on Computer Programs and Business Methods Good for the New Economy?" *Business Review* Q1: 5–15.

Jaffe, A. B. 2000. "The US Patent System in Transition: Policy Innovation and the Innovation Process." *Research Policy* 29: 532–57.

Kitch, E. W. 1977. "The Nature and Function of the Patent System." *Journal of Law and Economics* 20 (1): 265–90.

Koen, M. S. 1991. *Survey of Small Business Use of Intellectual Property Protection.* Missouri: MO-SCI Corp.

Laursen, K. and Salter, A. 2005. "My precious: the role of appropriability strategies in shaping innovative performance." DRUID Working Paper 05-02.

Lemely, M. A. and C. Shapiro. 2005. "Probabilistic Patents." *Journal of Economic Perspectives* 19 (2): 75–98.

Levin, R. C., A. K. Klevorick, R. R. Nelson and S. G. Winter. 1987. "Appropriating the Returns from Industrial Research and Development." Brookings Papers on Economic Activity 3: 242–79.

López, A. and E. Orlicki. 2006. "Innovación y mecanismos de apropiabilidad en el sector privado en América Latina." Document elaborated in the frame of the WIPO-ECLAC Project on Intellectual Property for Development.

Machlup, F. 1958. "An Economic Review of the Patent System." Study of the Subcommittee on Patents, Trademarks and Copyrights of the Committee on the Judiaciary, US Senate, 85th Congress, Second Session, Study 15, Washington, US Government Printing Office, 1–86.

Machlup, F. and E. Penrose. 1950. "The Patent Controversy in the Nineteenth Century." *Journal of Economic History* 10 (1): 1–29.

Mansfield, E. 1986. "Patents and Innovation: An Empirical Study." *Management Science* 32: 173–81.

Mazzoleni R. and R. R. Nelson. 1998. "The Benefits and Costs of Strong Patent Protection: A Contribution to the Current Debate." *Research Policy* 27: 273–84.

Merges, R. P. 1992. *Patent Law and Policy.* Charlottesville: Michie.

Metcalfe, J. S. 1995. "Technology Systems and Technology Policy in an Evolutionary Framework." *Cambridge Journal of Economics* 19: 25–46.

Moncayo, A. 2006. "Bilateralismo y multilateralismo en materia de patentes de invención: Una interacción compleja." Document elaborated in the frame of the WIPO-ECLAC Project on Intellectual Property for Development, ECLAC Santiago, Chile.

Mowery, D. C., R. R. Nelson, B. N. Sampat and A. A. Ziedonis. 2004. *Ivory Tower and Industrial Innovation: University-Industry Technology Transfer before and after the Bayh-Dole Act.* Stanford, CA: Stanford University Press.

Mowery, D. C. and B. N. Sampat. 2005. "Universities in national innovation systems." In J. Fagerberg, D. C. Mowery and R. R. Nelson (eds), *The Oxford Handbook of Innovation*, 209–39. Oxford: Oxford University Press.

Nelson, R. R. 1959. "The simple economics of basic scientific research." *Journal of Political Economy* 67 (3): 297–306.

Nelson, R. R. (ed.) 1993. *national innovation systems, a Comparative Analysis*. New York: Oxford University Press.

Nelson, R. R. and S. Winter. 1985. *An Evolutionary Theory of Economic Change*. Cambridge, MA: Belknap Press of Harvard University Press.

Pavitt, K. 1987. "The Objectives of Technology Policy." *Science and Public Policy* 14: 182–8.

_____. 1984. "Sectoral Patterns of Technological Change: Towards a Taxonomy and a Theory." *Research Policy* 13: 343–75.

Plant, A. 1934. "The Economic Theory concerning Patents for Inventions." In *Selected Economic Essays and Addresses*, 35–56. London: Routledge and Kegan Paul.

Polanyi, M. 1967. *The Tacit Dimension*. New York: Doubleday Anchor.

Rai, A. K. 2001. "Fostering Cumulative Innovation in Biopharmaceutical Industry: The Role of Patents and Antitrust." *Berkeley Technology Law Journal* 16 (2): 813–53.

Rosenberg, N. 1982. *Inside the Black Box*. Cambridge: Cambridge University Press.

_____. 1976. *Perspectives on Technology*. Cambridge: Cambridge University Press.

Scherer, F. M. 2001. "The Innovation Lottery." In Rochelle Dreyfuss et al. (eds), *Expanding the Boundaries of Intellectual Property*, 3–21. Oxford: Oxford University Press.

Scherer, F. M. 1983. "The Propensity to Patent." *International Journal of Industrial Organization* 1: 107–28.

_____. 1977. *The Economic Effects of Compulsory Patent Licensing*. New York: Graduate School of Business Administration, New York University.

_____. 1965. "Firm Size, Market Structure, Opportunity, and the Output of Patented Inventions." *American Economic Review* 57: 1097–1125.

Shapiro, C. 2003. "Antitrust Limits to Patent Settlements." *RAND Journal of Economics* 34 (2): 391–411.

Teece, D. 1986. "Profiting from technological innovation: implications for integration, collaboration, licensing and public policy." *Research Policy* 15 (6): 285–305.

Winter, Sidney G., 2006. "The logic of appropriability: From Schumpeter to Arrow to Teece." *Research Policy* 35 (8): 1100–1106.

Chapter 3

CATCHING UP AND
KNOWLEDGE GOVERNANCE

Rainer Kattel
Tallinn University of Technology

Introduction

"There are general Maxims in Trade which are assented to by every body." So starts *British Merchant*, published in 1721 by Charles King. He continues, "That a Trade may be of Benefit to the Merchant and Injurious to the Body of the Nation, is one of these Maxims" (King 1721, 1). King proceeds to list varieties of trade that are either "good or bad" and thus he exemplifies perhaps the key feature of pre-Smithian economics: a taxonomic understanding of the economic world of production.[1] The pre-Smithian taxonomy of "good" and "bad" trade was based on the observation of the obvious urban bias of economic development that was found everywhere in Europe. Somewhat ironically, the current debate about international trade is coming back not only to a similar understanding, but also images and words are reminiscent of pre-Smithian taxonomies.[2] In essence, recent discussions about trade policy and globalization seem to come to the consensus that it is not simply the scale and scope of trade that is conducive to economic growth (as the classical post-Smithian Ricardian theory assumes), but rather the nature of trade and, more specifically, how much technological content (i.e., increasing returns activities) is traded with whom and how. That is, there is a growing understanding that trade policy is, or rather should be, a natural part of technology

This paper was originally presented at the MINDS international seminar on "Promoting Strategic Responses to Globalization," November 3–6, 2009, in Rio de Janeiro. I would like to thank Leonardo Burlamaqui, Erkki Karo, Jan Kregel, Mario Possas, Ringa Raudla and Ken Shadlen for their comments on earlier versions of this paper. Email: rainer.kattel@ttu.ee.

1 See Reinert (2007) for an excellent discussion.
2 Gomory and Baumol (2000) use, for instance, "the good, the bad and the mediocre" to denote various equilibria possible under globalization if one figures in the existence of increasing returns into comparative advantage models (20–21).

policies and vice versa.[3] Perhaps the key conclusion is that trade models and policies that do not figure in technology and increasing returns (such as the Washington Consensus trade policies and the accompanying international governance system embodied by the World Trade Organization create an environment that undermines both developed and developing countries' attempts at sustainable growth. Thus, the emerging consensus admits not only to theoretical shortcomings, but also to the fact that the global trade system under currently existing conditions makes catching up a rare occasion.[4]

Interestingly, in parallel to the above-mentioned developments in international trade theory, evolutionary economics in general and national-innovation-systems literature in particular is reaching a similarly widespread consensus that innovation systems theory has largely failed to take into account the impact of vastly changed macroeconomic conditions for developing countries under the Washington Consensus and WTO policies.[5] Indeed, a lack of macroeconomic theorizing can be seen as one of the major weaknesses of evolutionary economics.[6] In essence, innovation systems literature, either in its narrow scope (focusing on codified knowledge, such as scientific and R&D output in terms of patents, publications, etc.) or its broad scope (focusing on tacit and experience-based knowledge such as routines, networks, etc.) have had precious little to say about development and poor countries on the theoretical level (Lundvall et al. 2009).

Trade policy and innovation systems discourses seem to converge towards a mutual understanding even if it takes place at a relatively slow pace. To simplify: both discourses agree that knowledge, in codified and tacit forms (leading to increasing returns in whatever activity), is essential for growth.

Yet, there is also a common blind spot. Neither trade theory nor innovation systems literature is particularly good at explaining the financing of growth and development. While in theory, both trade and innovation systems theorists can agree that diversification of domestic economy is key for sustained growth and catching up, the financing of that growth seems to be a secondary and even independent issue. Or rather, financial liberalization is taken as a given and, consequently, developing countries can and should rely on foreign savings. Yet, financial globalization has not brought growth (Rodrik and Subramanian 2008), and on the other hand, capital management seems to work well for growth (Ocampo and Stiglitz 2008). Increased vulnerability to financial flows via the footloose nature of portfolio investments and also of FDI, transformation of domestic banking and many other features of financing of growth in developing countries suggests that the nature of

---

3 See discussions by Samuelson (2004), Krugman (2008 and 2009), Gomory and Baumol (2000 and 2004), and Palley (2006).
4 For a discussion of state failure in this context, see Wade (2005) and Reinert and Kattel (2010).
5 See discussons by Cimoli, Dosi and Stiglitz (2009), Lundvall et al. (2009 and 2010), Chaminade et al. (2009). There are number of interesting discussions from this viewpoint in the Latin American (more or less) structuralist tradition; see, for instance, Cimoli (2000), Palma (2005), and Cimoli, Ferraz and Primi (2005); Primi (2009) provides a recent summary of this tradition.
6 See Kattel, Drechsler and Reinert (2009) for a brief discussion; further Kregel and Burlamaqui (2005 and 2006).

the financing of demand is a substantial and systemic feature of knowledge creation and evolution. Thus, it is safe to assume that any successful catching-up strategy would need to be based on strategic policymaking in which trade, finance and innovation form pieces of the same puzzle. While there are ample historical examples how this has been done,[7] it is equally safe to assume that there are no one-size-fits-all solutions that can easily be copied into the twentieth century. The specific policy mix that worked for East Asia in the 1960s and 1970s, or that is working for China as we speak, is not necessarily a model to be emulated. In particular, the international governance of global economy has changed drastically in the last two decades. The emergence of TRIPS and other global governance mechanisms of innovation, finance and trade change the context for today's catching-up strategies. So does, naturally, the ongoing change in the technoeconomic paradigm and incessant slicing of production, services and, more recently, also of R&D value chains (see Perez 2002 and 2006). Clearly, there are also bound to be massive sectoral and country differences – manufacturing car parts in the Slovak Republic is different from cardboard manufacturing in Bangladesh or financial services in Mexico. What is lacking, though, is a more or less unified theoretical framework to capture all these changes and policy needs. Following recent work by Burlamaqui (in this volume) and others, this chapter denotes such theoretical framework as *knowledge governance* in order to capture both codified and tacit aspects of innovation, the impact of macroeconomic environment, international specialization, financing of demand and the role various governance structures (company level, public policies, international agreements) play in it. This chapter intends to widen and substantiate the concept of knowledge governance through a unified theoretical framework.[8] In other words, this chapter aims to show that global trade and financial environments play such a crucial role in the ways private sector organizational capabilities and routines (tacit knowledge) evolve, that in many ways companies in developing countries are very far removed from even starting to contemplate IPR and lobbying local politicians for enhanced IPR regimes or using WTO and TRIPS policy space for themselves (Reichman 2009). The chapter attempts to provide a theoretical framework to understand these challenges; most importantly, such a framework makes it possible to create a taxonomy of knowledge governance regimes, each a mix of trade, finance, IPR rules and forms of embedment of public- and private-sector actors. The taxonomy should illuminate what kind of policy space and tools are needed for successful catching-up strategies in the ICT-based paradigm with globalized trade and finance. In other words, while many development economists argue for widening the policy space under WTO and are particularly critical of TRIPS, few would argue for the return of the developmental state of East Asian blend. This article attempts to offer tools for delineating the developing-country agenda under the WTO global regime.

What follows is structured somewhat counterintuitively: instead of building theory first that is then followed by empirics, the chapter briefly summarizes key features and

---

7 East Asian experience being the most recent (see Wade 2004).

8 In this chapter, knowledge is understood in a very wide sense to also include technology and learning; the latter two are incorporated into tacit and intangible knowledge (for differentiation and discussion, see Primi in this volume).

challenges in global economy for developing countries, and only then does it proceed
to construct theoretical premises that make it possible to understand the challenges in
a single framework. While developing countries as a group differ greatly from Latin
America to Africa to Eastern Europe – and also within these large regions, there are
enormous differences (see Basheer and Primi 2009) – this chapter treats them as a
group insofar as the challenges they face originate from the same sources. Precisely
these sources are discussed next. This is done in order to understand what actually
drives knowledge creation and dissemination in the catching-up context.

Part I: Global Drivers of Knowledge Creation and Dissemination in Developing Countries

The discussion that follows is not meant to be exhaustive in describing trends in global
economy, nor is it based on solely original research; instead, it focuses on key features
that influence innovation and technological change in developing countries and are
global in nature. Following a broadly Neo-Schumpeterian approach, the chapter
assumes that companies innovate in order to gain competitive advantages (see OECD
and Eurostat 2005 for a classic definition). In doing so, companies rely on skills and
routines they have developed, or as Alfred Chandler observed, companies rely on
"learned organizational capabilities" that include technical know-how, management
and marketing skills, established networks, and so on (Chandler 2005; Nelson and
Winter 1982). In other words, in innovating, companies rely, use, create and reuse
both codified and tacit knowledge and in doing so, they interact with the wider
socioeconomic context or governance structures.[9] Hence, firms innovate at least in part
in reaction to and in interplay with the knowledge governance structures surrounding
them. Thus, the trends listed subsequently deal with governance structures in the
global economy that impact innovation and knowledge creation and dissemination in
firms in developing countries, in both *tacit and codified forms*.

Canvassing the existing literature, the following key trends in innovation and
knowledge creation in developing countries can be brought out first, by the impact of
Foreign Direct Investment (FDI) and global financial flows; second, by the emergence
of global production and innovation networks; and third, by the impact of global
governance of trade and intellectual property rights. The first two features have a huge
impact mostly (but not only) on tacit knowledge creation, the latter on the codified
knowledge creation in developing countries.

Impact of FDI and global financial flows

Spurred by financial liberalization in most developing countries, the global financial
flows (FDI, portfolio investments, etc.) have been increasing, particularly during the

---

9 The latter is typically denoted as national innovation system (see, in particular, Freeman
   1974 and 1987).

Figure 3.1. Growth rate of GDP per capita of selected world regions; regional average in selected periods between 1820 and 2001; annual average compound growth rate

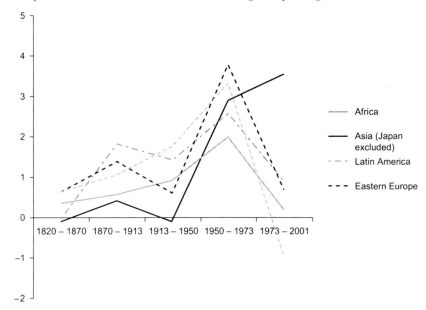

Source: Original data extracted from Maddison (2003); see also Kattel, Kregel and Reinert (2009b) and Wade (2005).

1990s, yet this seems to have little impact on development (with the exception of East Asia and China – countries heavily using various capital management techniques from capital account controls to sector specific FDI policies). On the contrary, as is shown on Figure 3.1.[10]

As foreseen by early development theorists, foreign-financing- and liberalization-led growth strategies tend to worsen the terms of trade for poorer countries (raising costs of imports and lowering costs of exports) and to lock these countries into lower value-added activities (undiversified economic structure). Moreover, typically negative externalities abound; for instance, in the form of price externalities with both capital inflows and outflows (via exchange rate appreciation and depreciation respectively); or in the form of quantity externalities (reduced credit availability following capital flight), or accumulation of large currency reserves as self-insurance against capital flight (Ocampo, Spiegel and Stiglitz 2008, 8–10). One can further add maturity mismatch problems (long-term investments are financed with short-term borrowing, engendering interest rate risk), dollarization/euroization of domestic borrowing, exposing borrowers to currency risks (on the latter, see, for instance, Becker and Weissenbacher 2007). In sum, "in international capital markets, developing countries bear the brunt of exchange

10 For discussion and various data, see Wade (2005); Ocampo, Kregel and Griffith-Jones (2007); Ocampo and Stiglitz (2008); Rodrik and Subramanian (2008).

rate and interest rate risk even when the source of the fluctuations lies outside the country" (Ocampo, Spiegel and Stiglitz 2008, 14). While FDI tends to be more stable than portfolio investments,[11] both have strongly pro-cyclical character. This is often married in developing countries with a general macroeconomic policy environment that is already pro-cyclical (targeting inflation and fiscal balance, for instance). Thus, financial liberalization and macroeconomic liberalization tend to enforce each other (see also Epstein, Grabel and Jomo 2008).

Trade liberalization and increasing financial inflows have been accompanied by financial sector liberalization in terms of growing foreign ownership of the banking sector in developing countries (Chandrasekhar 2009, 36–9). Particularly, Latin American and Eastern European banking systems have seen transformative changes with, for instance, Mexico's banking sector having 82 percent of foreign ownership by 2002 (Chandrasekhar 2009). This figure is surpassed by Estonia, where virtually all of the banking sector is foreign-owned (Kattel 2010). However, this has not led to significantly increased investment and lending to the domestic productive sector. Rather, consumption, real estate and retail have seen growing lending during the last ten years. In essence, the domestic banking sector that used to be best equipped to assess local industry risk levels and that played a key role in intermediating domestic and foreign savings to productive investments, is now much less inclined and even less competent to do so.[12] On the contrary, the increased internationalization of the domestic banking sector has led to increasing financing of consumption-led booms in the real estate and retail sectors; a particularly drastic example is Eastern Europe and the Baltics, where the reversal of capital inflows in the aftermath of global crises has brought declines in GDP growth rates in double digits (with Lithuania topping the list in 2009 with a drop of almost 19 percent (see BIS 2009, 85). In addition, both in the history of the now developed countries and some of the catching-up countries, public development banks have played an important role in development via priority-sector lending and other forms of guarantees. This also has decreased dramatically. Indeed, it can be argued that financial liberalization has brought to many developing countries what can be called a monoculture banking that excels in consumption financing and securitization, but not at assessing risks of, and lending to, the domestic productive sector. This type of banking sector has little interest in cooperating with local productive and public sectors in working towards long-term development goals; it has a much stronger allegiance to its own shareholders.

The impact of such financialization of the economy and its increasing fragility on tacit innovation capabilities is enormous. Coupled with the change of the technoeconomic paradigm towards ICT-based production that enables an increasing modularity of

---

11 However, see the discussion by Kregel (1997) on how FDI is one of the most expensive forms of borrowing capital for financing growth. FDI risks are more difficult to hedge as such investments are less easily standardized and consequently, lenders' risk premiums tend to be high.

12 See, in particular, Kregel and Burlamaqui (2006); also Dore (2000) on German and Japanese relational banking.

products and tasks, the Washington Consensus policies emphasizing FDI- and export-led growth have created a truly toxic situation for many developing countries, especially in Latin America and Eastern Europe, where liability destruction was initially strong and quick in the 1990s, but was then followed by slow asset creation. This has left many developing countries with an almost completely changed economic and industrial structure that is deeply different from and much less skill- and technology-intensive than the previous structure. This explains the fast growth, but also why they do not catch up with the Asian economies in terms of productivity and income growth.

Specializing in lower-end production or services (also in sectors like ICT) virtually traps developing countries into low-wage jobs and, at the same time, lures the high-wage middle-class jobs away from the developed nations. Thus, while the global production grows, not all countries necessarily benefit from it. And, consequently, "firms maximize global output but do not necessarily maximize national income" (Palley 2006, 16). Perversely, this encourages "overspecialization" in developed countries towards high value-added activities and in developing countries towards industrialized production activities with low value added and linkages.

Emergence of global production and innovation networks

While global free trade and financial flows encourage the stickiness of knowledge creation in developed countries and the stickiness of production in developing countries – both are forms of geographic agglomerations or clustering that tends to be regional as well (Wade 2005 and 2008) – there is a trend towards global innovation networks (GIN), particularly so in ICT-intense production such as electronics. As Ernst (2009, viii) argues about the latter, "the offshoring of research and development through GIN creates handful of new – yet diverse and intensely competing – innovation offshoring hubs in Asia." The examples are Cisco, Intel and other multinationals that have research labs in Asia and, to a lesser degree, in other catching-up regions such Russia and Eastern Europe; but Asian companies can also create and manage such networks (see Table 3.1 for an example).

In fact, such global networks are also emerging on a much smaller scale; for example, Modesat, a small ICT company that sources R&D from Belarus, has headquarters in Estonia and sales in the United States. Similar to geographic dispersion of production, the major drivers of innovation offshoring and global networking are the seemingly endless possibilities to modularize tasks, particularly so in ICT-based or ICT-related industries (see Perez 2006 generally). The modularization of design enables the disintegration of value chains where standards become increasingly important for interoperability and compatibility. However, while intraindustry standards have become key for networking, patents and patent families are still highly important for electronics and ICT industry development. For instance, while for the second generation of GSM technology 140 key patents were claimed, "for the current third-generation mobile standards, the number of essential patents has substantially increased. For example, W-CDMA (one of the three competing 3G standards) is protected by more than 2,000 patent families comprising more than 6,000 individual patents from some 50 companies

Table 3.1. Global innovation network: Handsets

Telecom service provider defines system architecture (China Mobile)

- Supplier of handsets and components (Taiwan, Korea, China)
- Suppliers of design platform (integrated device manufacturer: US, EU Korea; design houses: US, Taiwan, China)
- IP providers (UK, Taiwan)
- Software providers: OS/MMI/GUI* (India, Taiwan, US)
- Foundries (Taiwan, Singapore, China)
- Tool vendors for design automation and testing (US)
- Design support service providers (various Asian countries)

*OS = operating system; MMI = a special technique of printed circuit design; GUI = graphic designer interface

Source: Ernst (2009, 25).

and consortia" (Ernst 2009, 43). Such an enormous rise in networking makes, first, further networking both in R&D and production increasingly likely, but second, it also increases standardization within global networks. The standardization acts both as a barrier to entry for competitors and as a means to increase competition within the network. In effect, while knowledge sharing – opening up the innovation process to outside companies – becomes more and more the norm within global networks, this sharing is still highly asymmetric (multinational companies remain in the key role). Thus, developing-country hubs may experience diminishing returns to network integration: in electronics, for instance, "Asian labs remain focused primarily on repetitive detailed engineering and product development tasks" (Ernst 2009, 20; see Abrol 2004 on India's pharmaceutical industry). Developing-country innovation hubs may, in other words, experience a commodification of R&D similar to the commodification of production in the 1990s (see Ernst and Hart 2008, 28–9). This also means that statistics may easily not catch these trends (Krugman 2008). Indeed, developing countries might seem both to industrialize (measured by, e.g., the rising share of industry in GDP) and catch up technologically (measured by, e.g., the raising share of high technology exports), yet either trend is not necessarily indicating increased capacity for development, as domestic linkages remain weak and intense competition within global production and innovation networks keeps wages and profits low. On the contrary, there seems to be evidence of emerging high-tech enclaves around developing-country innovation hubs that form relatively low-intensity linkages and synergies with domestic actors within industry, research labs and the public sector.

Thus, while China has become the world's second largest R&D investor after the United States and ahead of Japan, and while South Korea graduates nearly the same number of engineers as the United States (with only one-sixth of the population) (Ernst and Hart 2008), the patenting activity shows that

> [F]irms and organizations from the top ten developed countries account for more than ninety percent of all patents granted [in USPTO]... the US, Japan, and

Figure 3.2. The knowledge ladder: industry value added and trade in knowledge, 1990–2008

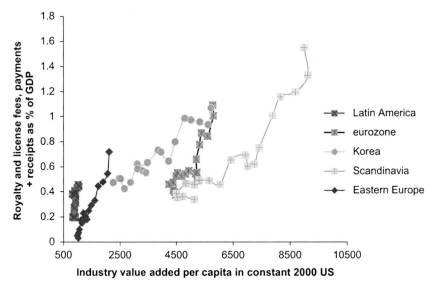

Source: World Bank WDI online database; calculations by the author.[13]

Germany alone account for nearly eighty percent... the firms and organizations from the top ten developing and transition economies account for less than seven percent, with greater than five percent coming from Taiwan and South Korea. (Shadlen 2005, 4)

In 2005,

developing countries paid net US$17 billion in royalty and licensing fees, mostly to IP rights holders in developed countries. Also, in 2005, the United States alone earned US$33 billion from developed and developing countries through the global IP system, more than its total development assistance budget of US$27 billion for that year. (Deere 2008, 10)

Combined with the above-mentioned impact of FDI and global financial flows, developing countries are decidedly behind the "knowledge curve" (Cimoli and Primi 2008; also Cimoli, Coriat and Primi 2009), as Figure 3.2 shows.

Thus, very few developing countries have the capacity and capability to rise to global innovation hubs, and even those that do face dangers of diminishing returns

13 Data for royalties and licenses includes both payments and receipts. Royalties and license fees includes international payments and receipts for the authorized use of intangible, nonproduced, nonfinancial assets and proprietary rights (such as patents, copyrights and industrial processes and designs). Hungary is excluded from Eastern European calculations, as it had a very high level of royalty and licensing fees in GDP in the late 2000s.

Figure 3.3. Knowledge creation and trade balance in knowledge

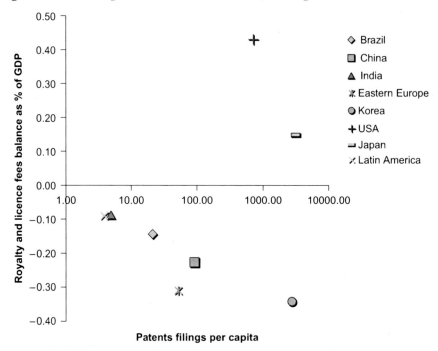

Source: WIPO, World Bank WDI Online database; calculations by the author.[14]

from network integration. While in terms of patents, South Korea is able to keep up with the United States and Japan, its trade in knowledge has a decidedly negative balance as shown in Figure 3.3.

This does not bode very well for the rest of the developing countries. Indeed, if we compare Latin America and Central and Eastern Europe to East Asian economies,[15] we can see clear differences emerging during the last two decades. The former can be said to lag further behind the developed countries, not to catch up (Figure 3.4).

This is also clearly visible in the generation of codified knowledge. Figures 3.5–3.7 show trends in patent applications, scientific and technical articles and in the number of researchers in the last two decades in three catching-up regions.[16] Eastern Europe,

---

14 Data for patents is for 2006 and includes all filings around the world; data for royalties and licenses is for 2008 and includes both payments and receipts. Royalties and license fees includes international payments and receipts for the authorized use of intangible, nonproduced, nonfinancial assets and proprietary rights (such as patents, copyrights and industrial processes and designs). Hungary is excluded from Eastern European calculations as it has a very high level of royalty and licensing fees in GDP (1.99 percent).

15 For an overview of East Asian innovation clusters, see Chaminade and Vang (2006).

16 In order to simplify, one country from each region is shown as a "proxy" for regional trends; in addition, all three countries have relatively strong similarities in terms of high rates of FDI inflow and growth of exports, including high-tech exports; choosing other countries from the respective regions does not change the trends significantly.

Figure 3.4. GDP per capita in selected developing countries, 1950–2001 (in 1990 international Geary-Khamis dollars); UK = 100

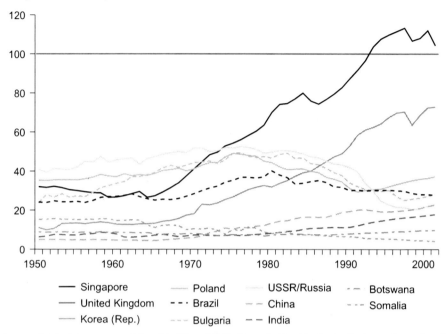

Source: Original data extracted from Maddison (2003). Countries listed in the key in descending order of GDP (2001).

Figure 3.5. Patent applications at European, US and Japanese patent offices, 1990–2005; 1990 = 100

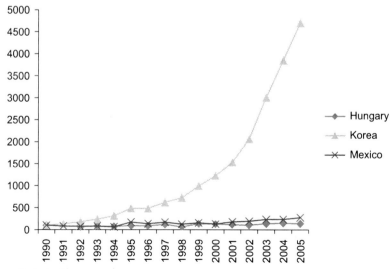

Source: OECD database.

Figure 3.6. Scientific and technical articles, 1985–2005; 1985 = 100

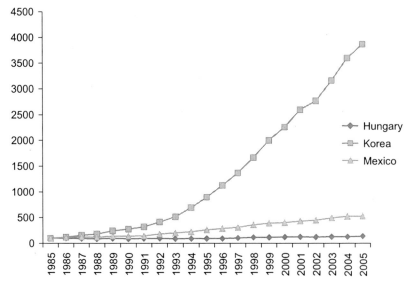

Source: World Bank WDI Online database.

Figure 3.7. Researchers per million inhabitants

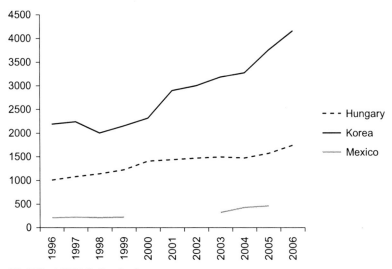

Source: World Bank WDI Online database.

positioned by many to become one of the key areas for global innovation networks from electronics to automobile manufacturing to biotechnology, does not exhibit dynamics similar to East Asia.

In other words, while both Eastern Europe and Latin America pay increasing attention to innovation and innovation policy, and are indeed creating a myriad of policies and in fact investing more and more into these and related fields, these two regions seem unable to match East Asia's dynamics.

And while it is noticeable that in many areas, the starting points of South Korea and East Asia, respectively, were very low, the dynamics of its trends are simply breathtaking: for instance, according to World Bank data, in 1981 South Korea had only 168 hits in scientific and technical publications compared to Hungary's 2,107; but by 2005, South Korea had 16,396 hits compared to Hungary's 2,614 (same data is used in Figure 3.6).

It is more than telling that even on the back of such dynamic changes, East Asian companies face serious challenges in reaping the economies of network integration (notably in electronics), as argued above.

The best explanation is probably the enormous agglomeration effect that the developed countries enjoy despite the growth of East Asian innovation hubs. In fact, as argued above, a liberalized trade environment only enforces agglomeration effects in a sense predicted by Ricardian comparative advantage theory.

If it is more or less true that agglomeration effects only get stronger towards the developed countries with global markets and finance, then one has to draw two conclusions. First, open innovation, peer production and other similar ideas showing the benefits from non-IPR-based R&D can only have a limited positive impact in developing countries (notwithstanding all the positive externalities in the rich countries).

Indeed, heavy patenting and standardization in R&D and production bear witness to almost opposite trends in many industries. Second, the emergence of global IPR governance is very much in the interest of developed countries; the stronger the governance system and the more stringent the rules are, the better it should be for the developed countries. In essence, globalized and liberalized free trade necessitates the rise of global IPR regulation (see next section).

To sum up, without engendering diversified domestic demand and linkages, developing countries may end up having a comparative advantage in simple low-value-added production and R&D activities and in low-cost, low-impact innovation (see Chaminade and Vang 2008; Rodrik 2007). Standardization of production and R&D activities has an enormous impact on the tacit organizational capabilities of developing-country companies as this essentially creates "rules of the game," and thus, domestic linkages may be significantly less important for many companies. As Evans (1995, 16) has already argued, "The new alliance of local entrepreneurs and transnational corporations make it harder to sustain the old alliance between local capital and the state."

In terms of codified knowledge creation, the rich countries still have an enormous advantage, with many developing regions actually falling behind. As codified knowledge (patents, copyrights, scientific publications, etc.) paves the way for standardization and is highly helpful in defining technology trajectories, increasing IPR is fundamental to the emerging business models of many companies (see Cimoli and Primi 2008). While there are highly publicized cases of companies such as IBM giving some of their patents to the public domain, there is also increasing evidence of a growing IPR (over)importance in many industries (see, e.g., Jaffe and Lerner 2004;

Heller 2008).[17] Similarly, as with increased trade and production, such tendencies increase global codified knowledge without necessarily helping global wealth and growth.

Impact of global governance of trade and intellectual property rights

For much of the twentieth century, countries discussed how to regulate international trade. However, while these debates were strongly colored by the developmental agenda from the Havana Charter of 1948 to attempts in UNCTAD during the late 1970s and early 1980s to establish a code of conduct for technology transfer (Roffe 1985; UNCTAD 2001),[18] during the 1980s and 1990s, both the United States and the European countries successfully managed to turn the agenda upside down (Deere 2008). Moreover, the earlier developmental agenda relied on what Reinert (2009) calls emulation: successful cases of development during the 500 years of capitalism have mostly been based on unrestrained copying from other successful countries, past and present. In essence, successful development has been historically based on policy creation using history as a toolbox. While the latter includes basic principles such as infant-industry protection, policy bias towards increasing returns activities, and so forth, the application of these principles has been based on context-specific amendments – that is emulation, not simply copying. It can be argued that international development debate sought to agree more or less on the rules for emulation up to the 1980s and that the Uruguay Round initiated the exact opposite. The WTO and its descendants (e.g., bilateral agreements) assume universal rules and institutions that should be more or less precisely copied by developing countries in order to widen markets and allow access for technological and market leaders whose activity should then lead to various spillovers and positive externalities. Thus, while emulation assumed high levels of capacity to choose from a heterogeneous set of policy options, the WTO policy

---

17 However, pooling of patents between different companies to form networks or new companies to reap the benefits from networking is not, strictly speaking, a novel approach or specific only to our times. Thus, for instance, the US radio and electronics industry was created via pooling patents into RCA in the post–World War I era (Chandler 2005). Further, the role of industry associations and similar forms of knowledge sharing and standardization is widely known to have been highly conducive to development, at least since Colbert's reign in France in the seventeenth century (Cole 1964). Indeed, the idea of embedded autonomy developed by Evans (1995) and others is based on the assumption of both tacit and codified knowledge "traveling" along local linkages between various actors, both public and private (see Hirschman 1958). Such successful processes are not tied to high-tech sectors, where knowledge is so important. McDermott's (2005) study of Mendoza and San Juan wine regions in Argentina shows how and why such embedded linkages are successful in terms of knowledge generation and innovation also in traditional sectors.

18 This was partly inspired by the Japanese success at technology transfer, partly by the so-called Andean Code of 1970 that attempted to regulate foreign investment, technology transfer and trade for the six Andean economies (Abbott 1975).

space assumes decontextualization of policymaking (e.g., in what field and for how long to grant patents and to whom vs. patents being granted in all fields anywhere in the world for 20 years). The former assumes an institutional framework for policy learning, the latter in turn assumes the capacity to implement agreed policies. Policy learning is usually associated with high levels of policy competence, strong bureaucratic autonomy and coordination, high levels of embeddedness between economic actors and the state, exemplified by the Weberian state described by Evans and others. Policy implementation and copying in the 1990s, in turn, became associated with decentralization and market-like discipline within the public sector, exemplified by new public management reforms (see Drechsler 2005). Consequently, the WTO is based not only on a very different set of economic ideas and ideals, but also on a substantially different view on policy capacity and governance.

Accordingly, the establishment of the WTO in 1994 and its accompanying treaties such as GATS, TRIPS, TRIMS and a host of other multilateral and bilateral agreements regulating trade, IPRs and investment is seen by many heterodox economists as severely limiting the policy space available for developing countries.[19]

Particularly, TRIPS have come to epitomize the significantly changed international landscape of trade and IPR governance. In general,

> [T]he changes in intellectual property regimes concern two different, although related, domains: (1) the modification of prevailing norm and the generation of a new set of incentives deriving from jurisprudential rulings within the US system, and (2) the increasing relevance of intellectual property in multilateral and bilateral trade negotiations and in international disputes between countries. (Cimoli, Coriat and Primi 2009, 508; see also 509–13)

Yet, as Wade (2003, 622) succinctly argues, these international regulations "are not about limiting *companies'* options, as 'regulation' normally connotes; rather, they are about limiting the options of developing country governments to constrain the options of companies operating or hoping to operate within their borders." This is consistent with the assumption shared by most Washington institutions in the last decades that government failures are usually worse than market failures and thus disciplining governments should bring more return in terms of developmental intervention. Further, this view is hardened by the perceived lack of policy capacity in developing countries, but "ironically, the world is proceeding on the assumption, in the TRIPS agreement, that developing countries do have a considerable capacity to enforce patents and copyrights" (Wade 2003, 634).

While up to the 1990s, much IPR regulation and governance was national and based on late nineteenth-century conventions, TRIPS "places significantly greater limitations on how countries configure their patent regimes" (Shadlen 2003). TRIPS

---

19 Wade (2003), Gallagher (2005), Shadlen (2003 and 2005), Correa (2000), Li and Correa (2009) and Thrasher and Gallagher (2008) offer summaries and discussions of such arguments.

makes it easier to establish private rights over knowledge, these rights are more absolute and tend to last longer (20 years):

> Whereas countries could previously deny patents to certain types of inventions so as to encourage reverse-engineering and lower the barriers to entry in technologically-intensive sectors, now countries must offer patents in virtually all fields... Whereas countries could make the enjoyment of the monopoly rights conferred by patents conditional upon local production or licensing and transferring technology to local users, TRIPS limits how governments regulate patent-holders.[20] (Shadlen 2005; also Wade 2003, 625–7)

Similarly, TRIMS (Trade-Related Investment Measures), "bans performance requirements related to local content, trade balancing, export requirements, and it also bans requirements on public agencies to procure goods from local suppliers" (Wade 2003, 627; Kattel and Lember 2010 on procurement and the WTO). GATS (General Agreement on Trade in Services), another result of the Uruguay Round, has a similar objective to liberalize and deregulate trade in services. In addition, GATS also includes Financial Services Agreement (FSA; second and fifth protocols to GATS) that came into force in 1999 and that is bound to make the above-described tendencies in financial liberalization only more pronounced (Raghavan 2009). Perhaps ironically, the liberalization of financial services, undertaken under US leadership, also led to the repeal of the Glass-Steagall act (segmentation of investment and commercial banking) in the United States that is seen by many as one of the main culprits in the financial meltdown of 2008/2009 (see, e.g., Kregel 2008a). The situation is probably even more ironic given that it is not by any means certain whether under FSA, the reintroduction of Glass-Steagall would be even legitimate (Raghavan 2009, 11).

However, there is particularly strong agreement among researchers that in many cases, bilateral trade agreements (BTA) apply much more stringent IPR regulations, trade liberalization measures and investment requirements than various WTO agreements proper. While some researchers argue that WTO agreements are asymmetrical ("developing countries' rights and developed countries' obligations are unenforceable" (see Wade 2003, 624), others go on to argue that developing countries should in fact cooperate in the WTO to try to enforce the agreements on the developed countries also (and not dismantle TRIPS; see Shadlen 2003).[21] The agreement on BTAs is much more equivocal: they should be avoided by developing countries.[22]

---

20 In particular, the pharmaceuticals were outside of patent coverage in many countries prior to TRIPS (Shadlen 2003).

21 See also Dreyfuss (2009); further also Cimoli, Coriat and Primi (2009, 514–18) on flexibilities within TRIPS; an even wider discussion is provided by Rodrik (2007, 123–47), and by Thrasher and Gallagher (2008); the latter also discuss South-South agreements.

22 In addition to global IPR and trade regulations, there are over 200 regional free-trade agreements that again focus on IPRs, investments, services and similar issues.

In addition to IPR and trade regulations, BTAs tend to also preclude usage of capital management techniques and in many cases force changes in the banking system as well (Thrasher and Gallagher 2008).

All these agreements – GATS, TRIPS, TRIMS and BTAs – internationally regulate areas that were previously typically left to countries themselves to govern and, moreover, in many ways, the agreements preclude or at any rate make classical industrial policy tools difficult to use.

There is also one more problem, particularly with TRIPS: it has failed to deliver growth and innovation: "contrary to the argument championed by the TRIPS' advocates, stronger and homogenous patent regimes have not accelerated the pace of innovation in developing countries" (Cimoli, Coriat and Primi 2009, 521; see also Hu and Jaffe 2007; Laforgia, Montobbio and Orsenigo 2009).

Summary of global trends

Summarizing the above-mentioned three drivers (nature of global innovation and production networks, impact of foreign owned banking on domestic producers, and changed in international governance), it can be argued that financial liberalization has brought not only increasing investment into developing countries, but also increasing fragility both in the form of vulnerability through openness and in the form of underdiversified domestic economies. Simply put, increased FDI and financial flows, transformation of domestic banking and increasing integration into global production and innovation networks crowd out diversification. For firms in the catching-up context, this means that they are often trapped in activities where barriers to acquire new knowledge or imitate and use the existing products and processes are relatively high. At the same time, knowledge, particularly in its codified form, is still and even increasingly so, being produced in developed countries in the North. This makes for a peculiar world where rich countries are increasing their share in knowledge and innovation while poorer countries are increasing their share in producing rapidly commodifying industrial goods. Such a world motivates and justifies both the neomercantilistic behavior of rich countries (increasing patenting) as well as the beggar-thy-neighbor policies of developing countries (increasing production through, e.g., exchange rate depreciation; see also Wade 2003, 633). The problem is that such a behavior neither induces global growth nor is it available to most countries caught in the middle that fall under international governance institutions. For these countries, most governance tools remain out of reach as they lack the policy capacities to maneuver with the space allowed by the WTO, and they are forced to operate in a world where international governance essentially means a nongovernable economic sphere that precludes these countries from developing the required policy capacities. In essence, for most developing countries, infant-industry protection and reaping economies of network integration via upgrading is increasingly difficult due to global forces of trade and specialization as well as the tightened policy space available for policy selection. It is, however, relatively clear, first, that to change international governance of IPR and trade makes sense only when done in unison with changes in the financing of growth; second, different countries and different sectors within countries need to have different policy regimes. This is, of course, what the traditional industry policy used to be about: sectoral (vertical) policies. Yet, it seems relatively safe to assume that both global trade and finance, and global production and innovation networks are here to stay. The question is how to find policy regimes and tools that fit the needs and context of developing countries under these circumstances.

While the East Asian developmental state relied on what can be called bilateral embeddedness with policymakers and industry leaders, today we arguably need something that can be termed multilateral embeddedness with various knowledge poles and actors (see Evans 2009, and Jayasuriya 2005 from the public-policy side). For instance, the capacity and institutional learning required for negotiating with international financial institutions and local R&D labs tends to be increasingly different and separated from each other as well. As Evans argues,

> In the twentieth-century developmental state, embeddedness was important both as a source of information and because implementation of shared projects depended on private actors. Insofar as embeddedness aimed at industrialization, the logic of constructing it was comparatively straightforward. The key information involved figuring out which industrial projects were feasible and what kind of incentives would be required to engage the energy of the relevant firms. The "culture" of leading firms had to be reshaped so that competition was seen more in terms of innovation and risk taking. The primary cast of partners was a small set of industrial elites with relatively well-defined interests. Building ties on the basis of personal networks and administrative structure was a feasible project. (Evans 2009)

As argued earlier, global trends and in particular the changing technoeconomic paradigm make it necessary to significantly upgrade this; now "the need for information and engagement from societal partners is even greater, but the interlocutors and the character of the networks are more complicated. Information must be gathered from constituencies that are more numerous and less organized" (Evans 2009). For this, we need a theoretical framework that enables us to unify key aspects in global economy – innovation, trade and financial aspects – into one systematic setting.

Part II: Towards a Taxonomy of Knowledge Governance Regimes

What follows is a simple exercise that should enable us to create taxonomies of knowledge-governance regimes that, in turn, should clarify why catching up has become relatively rare and why developing countries need to rethink most of all their policymaking structures.

The framework

As argued in the introduction, in a Schumpeterian framework, companies innovate in order to gain competitive advantages. Or, to express it in financial terms, we can understand innovations as ways that companies use to hedge their balance sheets. Thus, innovations are the connection between macroeconomic financial stability and microeconomic firm behavior.[23] However, as shown by Arthur (1994) and others working in the Schumpeterian tradition, innovations and technological change often follow self-enforcing mechanisms that are highly path dependent and act as natural barriers of entry for competitors. Path dependency follows what is called a life cycle of a technology or a product (Abernathy and Utterback 1978): most innovations develop through three main phases from undefined and experimental, through rapid growth and transformational, to maturity. The first phase is characterized by high market risks and research and development costs for an entrepreneur. This is usually a highly experimental period, often involving customers in testing innovative solutions. Once the technology enters the transitional phase, the entrepreneur benefits from economies of scale/scope and possible exports to other regions and countries, increases in companies' employment levels and real wages, and so forth. In a final phase, the sales volume declines or stabilizes, prices as well as profitability diminish and entrepreneurs often seek either to retain market positions by patents and other forms of protection (or rent-seeking) or innovating again.

However, to understand knowledge creation and dissemination dynamics involved along the technology/product life cycle where firms try to hedge their balance sheets via innovation, it is useful to look at the transaction-cost dynamics involved in knowledge creation along the life cycle. We can make three observations: First, the nature of knowledge changes along the life cycle: while in its early experimental phases, codified knowledge in the form of scientific findings, inventions, and so on, plays a crucial role, in the transformational growth phase, as shown by Arthur (1994), increasing returns generate powerful learning effects via feedback from the market and accordingly, tacit knowledge is more fundamental here. In the maturity phase, in turn, the role of codified knowledge generally declines as process innovations to lower costs are prominent. In sum, along the life cycle, the balance between tacit and codified knowledge changes and this in turn impacts other market participants via competition.

Second, the lowering of transaction costs involved in knowledge creation can be done, as the original Coasean idea suggests (Coase 1988), in two ways: either via the market or within the firm. In the Coase framework, markets are bundles of rules and regulations (either enforced by private agreements or by governments) and accordingly,

---

23 This is loosely based on Hyman Minsky's work. In Minsky's (1982, 22–9) terms, there are three distinct financing positions for business units (and households and governments) in a free-market system: hedge, speculative and Ponzi finance. All positions are defined according to the ability of a business unit to meet its financial commitments. At any given point in time, any economy consists of businesses, households and eventually, government finances that are a mix of all three positions. Innovation in industry (coupled with competition) can create all of the above-described financing positions (e.g., failed product development can engender speculative or Ponzi positions; the same results from successful innovations by competitors). Equally, these financing positions can impact business units' incentives to innovate in order to create a hedged financing position.

firms exist as reactions to these. And as firms seek to hedge their financing positions via innovations, the latter are in turn made possible by applying knowledge that is available on the market or has to be developed in-house, or both, depending on the phase of the particular product life in which the company happens to be.

Third, it is relatively obvious that tacit knowledge such as routines, company culture, and the like, cannot be acquired or licensed in the same way that patents or other forms of codified knowledge can be. The former are, in essence, nonmarket ways of knowledge generation that then, if successful, hugely influence competitors via enforcing the latter away from hedged financing positions which forces a new cycle of innovations or at least attempts at innovating and acquiring or generating knowledge for innovation.

In such a framework, it becomes clear that knowledge creation and dissemination is an arena inherently structured by both technological dynamics and company behavior in reaction to existing diverse governance structures, both within the company and created by the public sector (either domestically or internationally). Or, to put it differently, transaction costs are in large part influenced by governance structures that in turn influence the way companies *can* innovate in order to hedge their positions – or fail to do so. Such a framework offers a relatively simple matrix to differentiate knowledge governance regimes.

Taxonomy of knowledge governance regimes

There are highly interesting attempts to categorize knowledge markets. In addition to Burlamaqui's (2006) market features approach, Cimoli and Primi (2008) have created a taxonomy of how companies can capitalize on intellectual property. However, both the market features approach and the knowledge markets taxonomy concentrate more on codified knowledge and leave out tacit capabilities influenced by macroeconomic environment, financial structure and other knowledge governance features. In addition, the knowledge markets taxonomy reflects knowledge markets viewed from the developed-country perspective and their impact in the developing world.

To simplify the above-described framework further, one can think of it in two dimensions. First, knowledge governance structures have formed various policies, institutions and their impact in terms of levels of diversification of domestic economy, banking sector activities, origins of financing, knowledge rules (IPR and competition policies), macroeconomic variables (interests, exchange rates, trade treaties) and the like. This dimension reaches from domestic to international. Second, innovation and technological change can be captured in a dynamic sense through technological and product maturity and life cycles described above. This dimension covers the typical life-cycle range from the undefined product/technology to maturity. It is important to note that the latter assume the existence of increasing returns during the life cycle.

However, both dimensions need to be understood context-specifically: while biotechnology is in many ways in early stages in rich countries, car production would be in a similar position in the poorest economies where the lack of skills and other

Figure 3.8. Knowledge markets and ideal types of strategies to hedge financing positions through innovations[24]

Mature stage. Hedging financing positions through securing market power/share through barriers of entry, cartel agreements, domestic and international M&A, regulatory capture and/or expanding exports. Financing through domestic and international capital markets. Orientation towards domestic and export markets.

Dynamic stage. Hedging financing positions through innovations that engender barriers of entry, path dependencies, technological standards. Financing through domestic commercial banks, also mergers and acquisitions. Orientation mostly towards domestic markets.

Commons stage. Hedging financing positions through innovations that tap into variety of public goods such as scientific commons, research/education networks and collaboration. Financing through domestic VCs, development banks and agencies. Orientation towards domestic markets.

(vertical axis) Knowledge governance structures from domestic to international

(horizontal axis) Context specific technological and/or product maturity from early experimental stage towards maturity

framework conditions make car production an early-stage activity, albeit with a very short life cycle, as internationally, car markets are well developed.

Such a categorization into two dimensions makes it possible to come up with a taxonomy that consists of three ideal-typical stages. For simplicity's sake, these can be called commons, dynamic and mature stages. As depicted in Figure 3.8, each stage represents an ideal-typical scenario for entrepreneurs to hedge their financing positions through innovations where regulatory and policy bundles influence transaction costs in knowledge acquisition, usage and generation. Thus, these stages represent types of knowledge markets in the sense that each stage offers distinctly different opportunities for innovation and profit-making and is characterized by different types of competition and financing and regulatory environment in terms of trade agreements, safety standards, and so on. In sum, each stage offers a relatively unique nature of demand that in turn is structured by national and international institutions, rules and agreements.

While the stages in Figure 3.8 refer to theoretical and ideal-typical private-sector strategies at hedging innovation in various knowledge markets, these can be

24 See also Primi's taxonomy in this volume; instead of technology life cycle, she uses the knowledge-technology-learning continuum.

supplemented with historically successful development strategies and policies described briefly above. Figure 3.9 structures the historically successful development experiences into ideal-typical successive policy cycles that in real economies took place not only in succession (as technologies/products mature), but also in parallel in different sectors.

Now each stage from Figure 3.8 represents its own variety of knowledge governance regime that enables hedging through respective innovations that in turn are influenced by knowledge governance structures that enable or disable innovations. The idea of a regime is directed towards the question which kind of organizational capabilities and knowledge dynamics the policy regime should induce in private-sector actors, that is what kind of transactions costs should be lowered by public interventions, and, on the other hand, what kind of public-sector capacities (institutions and policies) are needed for this, whether more hierarchical (e.g., creating state-owned companies, dealing with the companies directly from a ministry) or network-based (e.g., developing industry association, cooperation between various actors). In other words, each stage reflects a different type of embeddedness that is a combination of organizational capabilities (private), including tacit and codified knowledge, and capacities (public). The framework developed above makes it possible, essentially, to map the need for different regimes and to catalogue them, and thus to overcome the limits of traditional sector-specific industrial policies, as sectors themselves are often sliced in different value chains, different sectors utilize university research, and so on. Figure 3.9 lists all three stages and regimes with exemplary keywords in innovation, finance, trade and policies, based on historical experience with industrial, technology and innovation policies and development financing. The regimes are ideal-typical in nature and essentially represent normative lessons from the development history within the theoretical framework developed above.[25]

Each regime thus represents a combination of activities and actors that have institutionalized interaction and learning mechanisms. The key lesson from Part I, however, was that global challenges make it difficult to generate relatively straightforward institutional responses typical of twentieth-century developmental states with clear apex or nodal agencies at the top of development-guiding companies, universities and indeed, politicians through various stages and industries during the development processes. Indeed, global networks and trade make it highly likely that once developing countries embark on enhancing scientific commons, they may easily end up subsidizing international innovation and R&D networks and reap very low benefits of their own. Equally significantly, developing-country policymakers have decreasing bargaining power with multinational corporations as the latter can be footloose and, moreover, can rely on WTO rules and lobby their own governments for WTO-plus type of bilateral agreements. Indeed, this is what both the United States and the European Union are increasingly doing (see Deere 2008). Further, actors from different regimes may easily

---

25 In many ways, such regimes could be found in Japan during its development decades after World War II, when it deployed a mix of competition, industrial and investment policies reminiscent of the dynamic regime described here (see Singh 2002).

Figure 3.9. Knowledge governance regimes in the historical perspective[26]

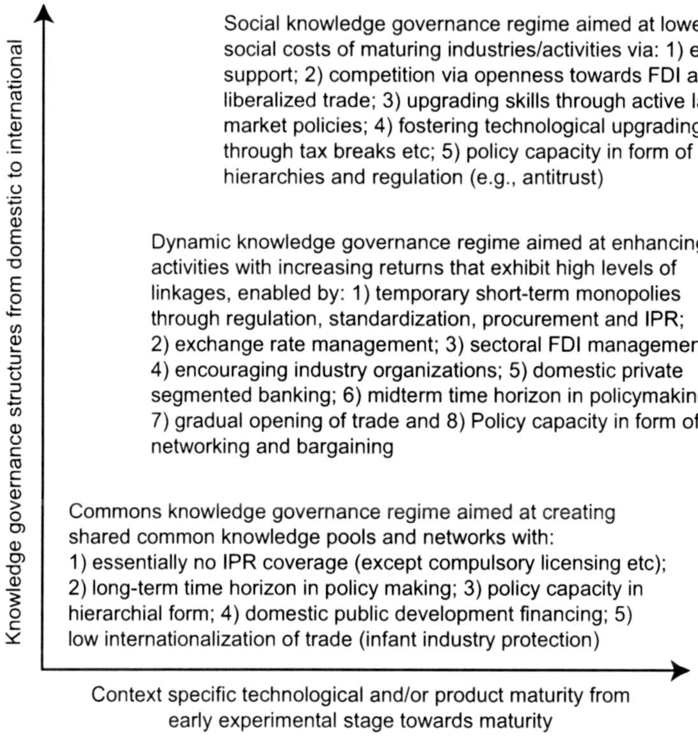

Knowledge governance structures from domestic to international →

Social knowledge governance regime aimed at lowering social costs of maturing industries/activities via: 1) export support; 2) competition via openness towards FDI and liberalized trade; 3) upgrading skills through active labour market policies; 4) fostering technological upgrading through tax breaks etc; 5) policy capacity in form of hierarchies and regulation (e.g., antitrust)

Dynamic knowledge governance regime aimed at enhancing activities with increasing returns that exhibit high levels of linkages, enabled by: 1) temporary short-term monopolies through regulation, standardization, procurement and IPR; 2) exchange rate management; 3) sectoral FDI management; 4) encouraging industry organizations; 5) domestic private segmented banking; 6) midterm time horizon in policymaking; 7) gradual opening of trade and 8) Policy capacity in form of networking and bargaining

Commons knowledge governance regime aimed at creating shared common knowledge pools and networks with: 1) essentially no IPR coverage (except compulsory licensing etc); 2) long-term time horizon in policy making; 3) policy capacity in hierarchial form; 4) domestic public development financing; 5) low internationalization of trade (infant industry protection)

Context specific technological and/or product maturity from early experimental stage towards maturity →

have strongly conflicting needs and values (think, for instance, of needs and values of scientific communities and those of large production or agricultural companies). In addition, as said earlier, these stages are different in different contexts. Indeed, it is important to keep in mind that developing countries also exhibit high levels of differences between themselves in terms of technological capabilities (Basheer and Primi 2009).

However, the taxonomy of regimes also helps to analyze developing-country problems with knowledge creation and innovation. As argued in Part I, many developed countries are squeezed into the mature stage in various activities without significant policy capacities to manage the exit or upgrading of these activities. At the same time, many catching-up economies emphasize innovation policies aimed at collaboration between universities and industry, hoping to engender a higher rate of commercialization activities, thus, in terms of knowledge governance regimes, these countries attempt to facilitate the move from

26 Kumar and Gallagher (2007) and Thrasher and Gallagher (2008) build policy regimes around market failures and also connect the respective domestic regimes with international treaties that cover these (see, in particular, Kumar and Gallagher 2007, 8). Thus, for instance, for alleviating market failures in scale economies and technological dynamisms, the policy regime includes tariff sequencing, technology-transfer requirements, joint ventures, public research and development, compulsory licensing, selective permission for patents, government procurement.

commons to a dynamic regime (Kattel and Primi 2009). Yet, most catching-up economies lack both dynamic private-sector actors (as they are squeezed to maturing activities and hence send "wrong" signals to policymakers in the form of keeping wages and safety standards low, etc.) and, as we saw earlier, their policy capacity has been hollowed by an increased application of universalistic rules emanating form WTO regimes and new public management reforms that make coordination exceedingly difficult. Shadlen's analysis of Brazil's difficulties in trying to differentiate between incremental and radical innovations through a law that enforced cooperation between the intellectual property agency and health authorities is a good example of how management issues have become pivotal in using the policy space available under the WTO as well as pushing innovation as a development-policy tool (Shadlen in this volume). Indeed, the impact of increasing decentralization (e.g., in the form of developmental agencies and regional innovation initiatives) of innovation management in developing countries seems largely underresearched and yet, in light of the above, it seems fair to argue that understanding deficiencies in policy management holds the key to developing countries' chances in using available policy spaces to develop context-specific knowledge governance regimes. Developing countries thus face not only complex policy choices (e.g., to support strong basic research or more applied research) but these are necessarily accompanied by choices of governance and management structures (e.g., centralized versus decentralized policy arenas). And, on top of it, as already argued, conflicts are bound to be strong between different knowledge markets/stages/regimes compounding governance and prioritization even further. The idea of knowledge governance regimes thus suggests that developing countries should work toward being able to coordinate different regimes. Consequently, the move from creative emulation towards international harmonization of universal rules is not simply a decisive "tightening" of policy space often discussed in heterodox literature, but moreover, a process towards complexity and, even more importantly, of weakened policy capacity by developing countries. The latter is mainly due to a blockage of learning processes that is generated through, first, complexity and conflicts between various knowledge markets and, second, because of harmonization pressures to global WTO regimes that motivate direct and quick coping instead of slow experimentation and resulting learning.

Thus, the idea of a variety of knowledge governance regimes strongly implies that developing countries should build their policy capacity with three rather large policy arenas in mind with often differing and even conflicting needs and actors. This speaks for increased efforts both in capacity building and, as importantly, in policy coordination. These efforts should pay attention not only to technical knowledge, domestic institution building and networks, but also to the public-sector structure and the nature of public service, and to international coalition building among like-minded countries.

It is, however, a somewhat one-sided argument to say that developing countries should build strategic policy capacities and alliances to utilize the existing policy space.[27] The logic

---

27 See, however, Reichman (2009) for an excellent discussion how this is possible, especially for large dynamic economies such as India and China; also see Jones, Deere-Birbeck and Woods (2010) on how small states can collaborate within WTO rules.

of global economy also says that much of the responsibility rests with the rich countries: BTAs are key to narrowing the policy space available to poorer countries. In many ways, the development agenda has to be turned upside down: financial flows need to be curbed and managed, and knowledge flows need to be reversed. Yet, both seem highly unlikely within the current international governance and global trade liberalization.

Conclusion

This chapter argues that, simply put, increased FDI and international financial flows, transformation of domestic banking and increasing integration into global production and innovation networks crowds out diversification of domestic economy in many developing countries. At the same time, knowledge, particularly in its codified form, is still, and even increasingly, being produced in developed countries in the North. In essence, for most developing countries, infant-industry protection and the reaping economies of network integration via upgrading is increasingly difficult due to global forces of trade and specialization as well as the tightened policy space available for policy selection.

The chapter then develops a simple theoretical framework for knowledge markets and knowledge governance regimes. These allow it to show what are three ideal-typical knowledge governance regimes. For simplicity's sake, these can be called commons, dynamic and mature stages. Each stage has its own variety of knowledge governance regime. The aim of regimes is to show that instead of traditional sector-specific industrial policy, globalized markets and international governance require various types of policy capacity (institutions and policies), that is, different types of organizational capabilities (in the private sector) and capacities (in the public sector). It is possible to use some of the aspects of knowledge governance regimes under current global rules (as shown by East Asia, China, India and increasingly, also by Brazil), yet for most countries the policy space and domestic capacities remain very limited.

References

All web addresses last accessed November 2009.

Abbott, Frederick M. 1975. "Bargaining Power and Strategy in the Foreign Investment Process: A Current Andean Code Analysis." *Syracuse Journal of International Law and Commerce* 3: 319–58.
Abernathy, W. J. and J. M. Utterback. 1978. "Patterns of Innovation in Industry." *Technology Review* 80 (7): 40–47.
Abrol, Dinesh. 2004. "Post-TRIPs Technological Behaviour of the Pharmaceutical Industry in India." *Science Technology & Society* 9 (2): 243–71.
Arthur, B. W. 1994. *Increasing Returns and Path Dependence in the Economy.* Ann Arbor: University of Michigan Press.
Basheer, Shamnad and Annalisa Primi. 2009. "The WIPO Development Agenda: Factoring in the 'Technological Proficient' Developing Countries." In Jeremy de Beer (ed.), *Implementing the World Intellectual Property Organization's Development Agenda*, 100–117 Ottawa: Wilfried Laurier University Press.

Becker, Joachim and Rudy Weissenbacher (eds). 2007. *Dollarization, Euroization and Financial Instability: Central and Eastern European Countries between Stagnation and Financial Crisis?* Marburg: Metropolis.

BIS (Bank for International Settlements). 2009. *Annual Report.* Available at http://www.bis.org/publ/arpdf/ar2009e.htm

Burlamaqui, Leonardo. 2006. "How Should Competition Policies and Intellectual Property Issues Interact in a Globalised World? A Schumpeterian Perspective." The Other Canon Foundation and Tallinn University of Technology Working Papers in Technology Governance and Economic Dynamics 6. Available at www.technologygovernance.eu.

Chaminade, Cristina, Bengt-Åke Lundvall, Jan Vang and K. J. Joseph. 2009. "Innovation Policies for Development: Towards a Systemic Experimentation-Based Approach." Paper presented at 7th Globelics conference, Senegal, 2009. Available at www.globelics.org.

Chaminade, Cristina, and Jan Vang. 2008. "Globalisation of Knowledge Production and Regional Innovation Policy: Supporting Specialized Hubs in the Bangalore Software Industry." *Research Policy* 37: 1684–96.

_____. 2006. "Innovation Policies for Asian SMEs: An Innovation System Perspective." Available at http://www.globelics.org/downloads/BRICS+workshop06/chaminade_vang_paper.pdf

Chandler, Alfred. 2005. *Inventing the Electronic Century. The Epic Story of the Consumer Electronics and Computer Industries*, Cambridge, MA: Harvard University Press.

Chandrasekhar, C. P. 2009. "Continuity or Change? Finance Capital in Developing Countries a Decade after the Asian Crises." In Jayati Ghosh and C. P. Chandrasekhar (eds), *After Crisis: Adjustment, Recovery and Fragility in East Asia*, 32–52. Delhi: Tulika.

Cimoli, Mario (ed.) 2000. *Developing Innovation Systems: Mexico in the Global Context.* New York: Continuum-Pinter Publishers.

Cimoli, Mario, Benjamin Coriat and Annalisa Primi. 2009. "Intellectual Property and Industrial Development: A Critical Assessment." In Mario Cimoli, Giovanni Dosi and Joseph E. Stiglitz (eds), *Industrial Policy and Development: The Political Economy of Capabilities Accumulation*, 506–38. Oxford: Oxford University Press.

Cimoli, Mario, Giovanni Dosi and Joseph E. Stiglitz (eds). 2009. *Industrial Policy and Development: The Political Economy of Capabilities Accumulation.* Oxford: Oxford University Press.

Cimoli, Mario, J. C. Ferraz and Annalisa Primi. 2005. *Science and Technology Policies in Open Economies: The Case of Latin America and the Caribbean.* Santiago: ECLAC.

Cimoli, Mario and Annalisa Primi. 2008. "Technology and Intellectual Property: A Taxonomy of Contemporary Markets for Knowledge and their Implications for Development." LEM Working Papers Series 2008/06.

Coase, Ronald. 1988. *The Firm, the Market and the Law.* Chicago: University of Chicago Press.

Cole, Charles Woolsey. 1964. *Colbert and a Century of French Mercantilism*, vols 1–2. New York: Columbia University Press.

Correa, Carlos M. 2000. *Intellectual Property Rights, the WTO and Developing Countries: The TRIPS Agreement and Policy Options.* London and New York: Zed Books.

Deere, Carolyn. 2008. *The Implementation Game: The TRIPS Agreement and the Global Politics of Intellectual Property Reform in Developing Countries.* Oxford: Oxford University Press.

Dore, Ronald. 2000. *Stock Market Capitalism: Welfare Capitalism. Japan and Germany vs the Anglo-Saxons.* Oxford: Oxford University Press.

Drechsler, Wolfgang. 2005. "The Rise and Demise of the New Public Management." *Post-autistic Economics Review* 33. Available at http://www.paecon.net/PAEReview/issue33/Drechsler33.htm

Dreyfuss, Rochelle D. 2009. "The Role of India, China, Brazil and Other Emerging Economies in Establishing Access Norms for Intellectual Property and Intellectual Property Lawmaking." IILJ Working Paper 2009/5.

Epstein, Gerald, Ilene Grabel and K. S. Jomo. 2008. "Capital Management Techniques in Developing Countries: Managing Capital Flows in Malaysia, India, and China." In José Antonio Ocampo and Joseph E. Stiglitz (eds), *Capital Market Liberalization and Development*, 139–69. Oxford: Oxford University Press.

Ernst, Dieter. 2009. *A New Geography of Knowledge in the Electronics Industry? Asia's Role in Global Innovation Networks*. East West Center, Policy Studies 54.

Ernst, Dieter and David M. Hart. 2008. "Governing the Global Knowledge Economy: Mind the Gap!" East-West Center Working Papers, Economic Series 93.

Evans, Peter. 2009. "Constructing the 21st Century Developmental State: Potentialities and Pitfalls." Available at http://www.ideiad.com.br/seminariointernacional/

Evans, Peter. 1995. *Embedded Autonomy: States and Industrial Transformation*. Princeton: Princeton University Press.

Freeman, Chris. 1987. *Technology Policy and Economic Performance: Lessons from Japan*. London: Pinter.

———. 1974. *The Economics of Industrial Innovation*. London: Routledge.

Gallagher, Kevin P. (ed.) 2005. *Putting Development First: The Importance of Policy Space in the WTO and International Financial Institutions*. London and New York: Zed Books.

Gomory, Ralph E. and William J. Baumol. 2004. "Globalization: Prospects, Promise and Problems." *Journal of Policy Modeling* 26 (4): 425–38.

———. 2000. *Global Trade and Conflicting National Interests*. Cambridge, MA and London: MIT Press.

Heller, Michael. 2008. *The Gridlock Economy: How Too Much Ownership Wrecks Markets, Stops Innovation, and Costs Lives*. New York: Basic Books.

Hirschmann, Albert O. 1958. *The Strategy of Economic Development*. New Haven, CT: Yale University Press.

Hu, Albert G. Z. and Adam B. Jaffe. 2007. "IPR, Innovation, Economic Growth and Development." Available at http://www0.gsb.columbia.edu/ipd/pub/Hu_Jaffe.pdf

Jaffe, Adam B. and Josh Lerner. 2004. *Innovation and Its Discontents: How our Broken Patent System is Endangering Innovation and Progress, and What to do About It*. Princeton and Oxford: Princeton University Press.

Jayasuriya, K. 2005. "Capacity Beyond the Boundary: New Regulatory State, Fragmentation, and Relational Capacity." In M. Pinter and J. Pierre (eds), *Challenges to State Policy Capacity: Global Trends and Comparative Perspectives*, 19–37. Basingstoke: Palgrave Macmillan.

Jones, Emily, Carolyn Deere-Birkbeck and Ngaire Woods. 2010. *Manoeuvring at the Margins: Constraints Faces by Small States in International Trade Negotiations*. London: Commonwealth Secretariat.

Karo, Erkki and Rainer Kattel. 2010. "The Copying Paradox: Why Converging Policies but Diverging Capacities for Development in Eastern European Innovation Systems?" *International Journal of Institutions and Economies* 2 (2): 167–206.

Kattel, Rainer. 2010. "Financial and Economic Crisis in Eastern Europe." *Journal of Post Keynesian Economics* 33 (1): 41–60.

Kattel, Rainer, Wolfgang Drechsler and Erik S. Reinert. 2009. "Introduction: Carlota Perez and Evolutionary Economics." In Rainer Kattel, Wolfang Drechsler and Erik S. Reinert (eds), *Techno-Economic Paradigms: Essays in Honour of Carlota Perez*, 1–18. London: Anthem.

Kattel, Rainer, Jan A. Kregel and Erik S. Reinert (eds). 2009a. *Ragnar Nurkse: Trade and Development*. London: Anthem.

———. 2009b. "The Relevance of Ragnar Nurkse and Classical Development Economics." In Rainer Kattel, Jan A. Kregel and Erik S. Reinert (eds), *Ragnar Nurkse (1907–2007): Classical Development Economics and its Relevance for Today*, 1–28. London: Anthem.

Kattel, Rainer and Veiko Lember. 2010. "Public Procurement as an Industrial Policy Tool: An Option for Developing Countries?" *Journal of Public Procurement* 10 (3): 368–404.

Kattel, Rainer and Annalisa Primi. 2009. "The Periphery Paradox in Innovation Policy: Latin America and Eastern Europe Compared." Paper presented at FIRB-RISC conference, Milan, 2009. Available at http://portale.unibocconi.it/wps/allegatiCTP/Kattel.pdf

King, Charles. 1721. *The British Merchant or Commerce Preserv'd*. 3 vols. London: John Darby.

Kregel, Jan A. 2008a. "Changes in the U.S. Financial System and the Subprime Crisis." Levy Economics Institute of Bard College Working Paper 530. Available at http://www.levy.org/pubs/wp_530.pdf

———. 2008b. "The Discrete Charm of the Washington Consensus." Levy Economics Institute of Bard College Working Paper 533. Available at http://www.levy.org/pubs/wp_533.pdf

———. 2004. "External Financing for Development and International Financial Instability." G-24 Discussion Paper Series, United Nations. Available at http://www.unctad.org/en/docs/gdsmdpbg2420048_en.pdf

———. 2003. "The Perils of Globalization." Available at http://www.cfeps.org/pubs/sp-pdf/SP13-Jan.pdf

———. 1997. "Some Risks and Implications of Financial Globalization for National Policy Autonomy." *UNCTAD Review 1996*: 55–62.

Kregel, Jan A. and Leonardo Burlamaqui. 2006. "Finance, Competition, Instability, and Development Microfoundations and Financial Scaffolding of the Economy." The Other Canon Foundation and Tallinn University of Technology Working Papers in Technology Governance and Economic Dynamics 4. Available at www.technologygovernance.eu.

———. 2005. "Innovation, Competition and Financial Vulnerability in Economic Development." *Revista de Economia Política* 25 (2): 5–22.

Krugman, Paul. 2009. "Increasing Returns in a Comparative Advantage World." Available at http://www.princeton.edu/~pkrugman/deardorff.pdf

———. 2008. "Trade and Wages, Reconsidered." Available at http://www.princeton.edu/~pkrugman/pk-bpea-draft.pdf

Kumar, Nagesh and Kevin P. Gallagher. 2007. "Relevance of 'Policy Space' for Development: Implications for Multiltateral Trade Negotiations." RIS Discussion Papers 120.

Laforgia, Francesco, Fabio Montobbio and Luigi Orsenigo. 2009. "IPRs and Technological Development in Pharmaceuticals: Who Is Patenting what in Brazil after TRIPS?" Available at http://www0.gsb.columbia.edu/ipd/pub/Laforgia_Montobbio_and_Orsenigo.pdf

Li, Xuan and Carlos M. Correa (eds). 2009. *Intellectual Property Enforcement: International Perspectives*. Cheltenham: E. Elgar.

Lundvall, Bengt-Åke, Jan Vang, K. J. Joseph and Cristina Chaminade. 2009. "Bridging Innovation Systems Research and Development Studies: Challenges and Research Opportunities." Paper presented at 7th Globelics conference, Senegal, 2009. Available at www.globelics.org

———. 2010. *Handbook Of Innovation Systems and Developing Countries: Building Domestic Capabilities in a Global Setting*. Cheltenham: E. Elgar.

Maddison, Angus. 2003. *The World Economy: Historical Statistics*. Paris: OECD.

McDermott, Gerald A. 2005. "The Politics of Institutional Renovation and Economic Upgrading: Lessons from the Argentine Wine Industry." Available at http://www-management.wharton.upenn.edu/mcdermott/files/McDermott-PS-10-06.pdf

Minsky, Hyman. 1982. *Can 'It' Happen Again? Essays on Instability and Finance*. New York: Sharpe.

Nelson, Richard and Sidney Winter. 1982. *An Evolutionary Theory of Economic Change*. Cambridge, MA: Harvard University Press.

Ocampo, José Antonio, Jan Kregel and Stephany Griffith-Jones (eds). 2007. *International Finance and Development*. New York: United Nations.

Ocampo, José Antonio, Shari Spiegel and Joseph E. Stiglitz. 2008. "Capital Market Liberalization and Development." In José Antonio Ocampo and Joseph E. Stiglitz (eds), *Capital Market Liberalization and Development*, 1–47. Oxford: Oxford University Press.

Ocampo, José Antonio and Joseph E. Stiglitz (eds). 2008. *Capital Market Liberalization and Development*. Oxford: Oxford University Press.

OECD and Eurostat. 2005. *Guidelines for Collecting and Interpreting Innovation Data*. Oslo Manual. 3rd edn. Paris: OECD Publishing.

Palley, Thomas. 2006. "Rethinking Trade and Trade Policy: Gomory, Baumol, and Samuelson on Comparative Advantage." Levy Economics Institute of Bard College Working Papers 86.

Palma, H. G. 2005. "The Seven Main 'Stylized Facts' of the Mexican Economy Since Trade Liberalization and NAFTA." *Industrial and Corporate Change* 14 (6): 941–91.

Perez, Carlota. 2006. "Respecialisation and the Deployment of the ICT Paradigm: An Essay on the Present Challenges of Globalization." In R. Compañó, C. Pascu, A. Bianchi, J.-C. Burgelman, S. Barrios, M. Ulbrich and I. Maghiros (eds), *The Future of the Information Society in Europe: Contributions to the Debate*. Seville: European Commission, Directorate General Joint Research Centre.

_____. 2002. *Technological Revolutions and Financial Capital: The Dynamics of Bubbles and Golden Ages*. Cheltenham: E. Elgar.

Primi, Annalisa. 2009. "Nurkse and the Early Latin American Structuralists: A Reflection on Development Theory, Industrialization and their Relevance Today." In Rainer Kattel, Jan A. Kregel and Erik S. Reinert (eds), *Ragnar Nurkse (1907–2007): Classical Development Economics and its Relevance for Today*, 119–45. London: Anthem.

Raghavan, Chakravarthi. 2009. *Financial Services, the WTO and Initiatives for Global Financial Reform*. Intergovernmental Group of 25. Available at http://www.g24.org/cr0909.pdf

Reichman, Jerome H. 2009. "Intellectual Property in the Twenty-First Century: Will the Developing Countries Lead or Follow?" Available at www.ideiad.com.b/seminariointernacional.

Reinert, Erik S. 2009. "Emulation versus Comparative Advantage: Competing and Complementary Principles in the History of Economic Policy." In Mario Cimoli, Giovanni Dosi and Joseph E. Stiglitz (eds), *Industrial Policy and Development: The Political Economy of Capabilities Accumulation*, 79–106. Oxford: Oxford University Press.

_____. 2007. *How Rich Countries Got Rich and Why Poor Countries Stay Poor*. London: Constable & Robinson.

Reinert, Erik S. and Rainer Kattel. 2010. "The Economics of Failed, Failing, and Fragile States: Productive Structure as the Missing Link." In Khan Shahrukh and Jens Christiansen (eds), *Towards New Developmentalism: Markets as Means rather than Master*, 59–68. London: Routledge.

Rodrik, Dani. 2007. *One Economics, Many Recipes: Globalization, Institutions, and Economic Growth*. Princeton and Oxford: Princeton University Press.

Rodrik, Dani, and Arvind Subramanian. 2008. "Why Did Financial Globalization Disappoint?" Available at http://ksghome.harvard.edu/~drodrik/Why_Did_FG_Disappoint_March_24_2008.pdf

Roffe, Pedro. 1985. "Transfer of Technology: UNCTAD's Draft International Code of Conduct." *International Lawyer* 19: 689–707.

Samuelson, Paul. 2004. "Where Ricardo and Mill Rebut and Confirm Arguments of Mainstream Economists Supporting Globalization." *Journal of Economic Perspectives* 18 (3): 135–46.

Shadlen, Kenneth. 2012. "The Politics of Pharmaceutical Patent Examination: Lessons from Brazil." In this volume.

_____. 2005. "Policy Space for Development in the WTO and Beyond: The Case of Intellectual Property Rights." Global Development and Environment Institute Working Paper 05-06.

_____. 2003. "Patents and Pills, Power and Procedure: The North-South Politics of Public Health in the WTO." Development Studies Institute, Working Paper 03-42.

Singh, Ajit. 2002. "Competition and Competition Policy in Emerging Markets: International and Developmental Dimensions." G-24 Discussion Paper Series, 18.

Thrasher, Rachel Denae and Kevin P. Gallagher. 2008. "21st Century Trade Agreements: Implications for Long-Run Development Policy." *The Pardee Papers* 2.

UNCTAD. 2001. *Transfer of Technology*. New York and Geneva: United Nations.

Wade, Robert. 2008. "Financial Regime Change?" *New Left Review* 53 (September–October). Available at www.newleftreview.org.

_____. 2005. "Failing States and Cumulative Causation in the World System." *International Political Science Review / Revue internationale de science politique* 26 (1): 17–36.

_____. 2004. *Governing the Market: Economic Theory and the Role of Government in East Asian Industrialization*. 2nd edn. Princeton: Princeton University Press.

_____. 2003. "What Strategies Are Viable for Developing Countries today? The World Trade Organization and the Shrinking of 'Development Space.'" *Review of International Political Economy* 10 (4): 621–44.

Part II

INNOVATION, COMPETITION
POLICIES AND INTELLECTUAL
PROPERTY: INSTITUTIONAL
FRAGMENTATION AND THE CASE
FOR BETTER COORDINATION

Chapter 4

WHERE DO INNOVATIONS COME FROM? TRANSFORMATIONS IN THE US ECONOMY, 1970–2006

Fred Block
University of California, Davis

Matthew R. Keller
Southern Methodist University

Introduction

There is a growing international realization that nations that develop more effective national systems of innovation will have a significant advantage in the global economy. And that realization, in turn, has led to intense debates over which rules for governing intellectual property are most consistent with a strong innovation system. The problem, however, is that most of the empirical work on this question has focused on the analysis of data on patenting rates across countries and by different types of firms. But patent rates are a problematic proxy for effective innovation, and there is a danger that reliance on this proxy is producing a distorted understanding of the circumstances under which innovation occurs and the intellectual property regimes that might best facilitate such innovation.

This chapter brings a quite different data source to bear on understanding changes in the US innovation system over the last four decades. The data set is a sample of key innovations in the US economy drawn from an annual awards competition for innovative products organized by *R&D Magazine*. By looking not at patent data but at actual new products that are admired by prize juries, we hope to illuminate the changing sources of innovation in the US economy.[1]

---

1 For another analysis of this data source, see Roberto Fontana, Alessandro Nuvolari, Hiroshi Shimitzu and Andrea Vezzulli. "Schumpeterian Patterns of Innovation and the Sources of Breakthrough Inventions: Evidence from a Data-Set of R&D Awards." Unpublished paper, October 2010.

Reviewing the Literature

In *The Coming of Post-Industrial Society*, the late sociologist Daniel Bell provided the most systematic elaboration of the postindustrial concept. In his analysis, postindustrial change is driven by the systematic harnessing by both business and government of science and technology to expand and continuously update the production of goods and services. For Bell, the rise of the computer industry in the 1950s and 1960s with its armies of skilled technologists was a paradigmatic case of this broader process of transformation. Bell anticipated that the growing dependence of business on scientists, engineers and technicians would necessitate larger shifts in business organization and in the role of government.

Bell also anticipated that scientists and engineers would transform both products and processes across the full range of industries in much the same way that industrial technologies diffused across all sectors of the economy over the nineteenth century. Craft knowledge and traditional production techniques would give way to sophisticated science-based approaches that enhanced efficiency and created a cornucopia of new goods and services. "This new fusion of science with innovation, and the possibility of systematic and organized technological growth, is one of the underpinnings of the post-industrial society" (Bell 1973, 197).

Bell foresaw significant changes in the corporation as scientists, engineers and other members of a "new intelligentsia" rose in importance.

> If the dominant figures of the past hundred years have been the entrepreneur, the businessman, and the industrial executive, the "new men" are the scientists, the mathematicians, the economists, and the engineers of the new intellectual technology. (Bell 1973, 344)

The argument pointed both to the growing role that technical experts would play in top management positions and to structural changes in the organization of firms. While Bell did not address the issue explicitly, his argument paralleled those of Burns and Stalker (1961) and Bennis and Slater (1968), who argued that the growing centrality of technological expertise would push organizations to be both less authoritarian and less hierarchical, moving from steeper to flatter organizations with a greater emphasis on coordination by multidisciplinary teams.

Bell was even bolder in arguing that postindustrial change would transform the relationship between business and government. On the one hand, government's dominant role in financing scientific and technological research greatly enhanced its role in the economy. On the other, Bell argued that corporations would have to move beyond narrow profit-maximizing strategies if they were to take full advantage of the new technological possibilities. Hence, he foresaw a new balance of power between business and government:

> It seems clear to me that, today, we in America are moving away from a society based on a private-enterprise market system toward one in which the most

important economic decisions will be made at the political level, in terms of consciously defined "goals" and "priorities." (Bell 1973, 297–8)

Although Bell's framework is now infrequently referenced (see, however, Block 1990, Brick 2006), several currents of research have followed up on these arguments. A growing body of scholarly work over the last two decades focuses on "national systems of innovation" to track how different societies organize the complex task of linking scientific research with product and process innovations (Collins 2004; Lundvall 1992; Nelson 1993). This literature rests on the idea that innovation capacity is centrally important as nations seek to gain advantage in the world economy.

Many of these studies of innovation systems focus on the interface between the public and private sectors, looking particularly at public funding of research and higher education, the growth of the scientific and technical labor force, the systems for establishing and protecting intellectual property rights for innovators and the mechanisms that facilitate the movement of ideas from the research lab to the market. The great strength of this literature is that it looks simultaneously at the role of government and the role of business and raises important questions about the interaction between the two. Nevertheless, this work has identified an important focus of inquiry, but it has not yet identified systematic and causally significant variations in the organization of innovation systems across nations.

A second relevant body of work consists of studies that analyze the shift of business firms, particularly in the United States, towards networked forms of organization. This shift represents a reversal of a pattern of corporate development that started in the last years of the nineteenth century. Back then, successful US firms aspired to a high level of vertical integration that meant controlling many different stages of the production process under one corporate roof (Fligstein 1990). Some of these firms attained high levels of self-sufficiency, often financing their growth with retained profits and drawing much of their technology from their own research laboratories. However, with gathering speed over the last half century, there has been a significant shift in the dominant business model away from vertical integration (Castells 1996; Powell 2001).

Many firms have shifted key parts of the production process to supplier firms. The trend is exemplified both by Nike, which has outsourced the production of its athletic shoes, and the increased reliance of Detroit automakers on subcontractors to produce many key parts of their automobiles (Whitford 2005). But the pattern also extends to the research-and-development function where many firms are less reliant on their own laboratories and more involved in complex webs of collaboration with other firms, universities and government laboratories (Hounshell 1996; Mowery 2009; Powell 2001).

Implicit in much of the literature on networked firms is the idea that there will be much more fluidity than in a world of vertically integrated firms. New firms will continue to form as a result of spin-offs from existing firms and from university and government laboratories. Moreover, some of these newcomers will be able to exploit their initial role as subcontractors to establish superiority in important new technologies in the way that Microsoft gained strategic control over the operating system for IBM's personal computers. Similarly, large established firms are at risk of precipitous decline if they fail to remain at the frontier of innovation. This gives us our first research question: Over the last four decades, has there been a decline in the role of the largest firms as developers of innovative new technologies, or have the largest firms continued to serve as the central nodes of innovation networks?

The rise of a networked industrial structure is particularly obvious in the computer industry and in biotechnology (Powell et al. 2005; Saxenian 1994). In both industries, small and large firms are involved in elaborate collaborative networks, and it is widely recognized that innovation grows out of processes of cooperation that cross organizational lines. But research to date has been unclear as to whether this pattern of interorganizational collaboration is characteristic of the entire economy or confined to the most technologically dynamic sectors. Our second research question is whether or not the shift towards interorganizational collaboration in the innovation process has been a general trend across the entire economy.

A final body of literature has documented the emergence of a triple helix of intertwined efforts by government, universities and corporations to produce more rapid innovation. Extending Bell's analysis, this body of work shows how tightly university-based science efforts are now linked to industry, but it also shows that government agencies play an increasingly central role in managing and facilitating the process of technological development (Block 2008; Etzkowitz 2003; Geiger and Sa 2008; Kenney 1986). In cases such as the Human Genome Project, organized by the National Institutes of Health (NIH) and the Department of Energy, and the Strategic Computing Initiative organized by the Defense Advanced Research Projects Agency (DARPA), government officials have played a central role in both setting technological goals and providing the funding to facilitate joint efforts by university-based researchers and business (Kevles 1992; McCray 2009; Roland 2002).

These targeted government programs have been combined with a highly decentralized system for encouraging innovation. Starting in the 1980s, new incentives were created for publicly funded researchers at universities and government laboratories to pursue commercial applications of their discoveries. Such efforts have been supported by funding programs, such as the Small Business Innovation Research (SBIR) program through which government agencies set aside a small percentage of their R&D budgets for projects proposed by small firms, many of which are newly created spin-offs from university or federal laboratories (Wessner 2008). Other programs have been created to encourage joint ventures between researchers in university and federal laboratories and business firms (Block 2008; Geiger and Sa 2008). This provides us with our third research question: Has there been a marked increase in the public sector's role in funding and facilitating innovation efforts?

Exploring each of these questions requires finding some way to measure innovative activities. However, the measurement of innovation has been a longstanding problem for social scientists. It is not adequate to count the dollars spent on research and development or the number of scientists and technologists at work, since these are simply inputs to the innovation process. Many studies have used patent statistics as a proxy, but these are a problematic indicator because the rate of successful patenting does not necessarily track changes in useful innovations.

The quality of patents can vary significantly over time as a consequence of shifts in policy that govern patent offices and changes in the incentives of different economic actors (Sciberras 1986, Taylor 2004). For example, one study showed that many universities in the United States significantly increased the quantity of their patent filings in the aftermath of the Bayh–Dole legislation. However, the quality of the resulting patents, as reflected in subsequent citations, also fell substantially (Mowery et al. 2004; Thursby and Thursby 2002). Similarly, there has been an increase in "strategic patenting" by corporations and other actors in recent years.

Strategic patenting refers to the acquisition of a patent without any serious interest in developing products that use the patent. An individual or firm that acquires a portfolio of such strategic patents can sometimes make a significant return by suing other firms for infringement of those patents. There is some debate about the size of the problem posed by these "patent trolls," but the phenomenon has received a lot of attention. Probably the more serious problem is that large corporations have been aggressive in acquiring substantial portfolios of strategic patents as a defensive maneuver. If they are sued by another firm for infringing an existing patent, they might use some of the patents in their portfolio to mount a countersuit against the other firm. If the suits have somewhat similar levels of plausibility, the chances of negotiating a settlement increase significantly.

In short, an increase over time in the amount of strategic patenting could easily alter the relationship between patents and actual usable new products or processes. For this reason, we use a data set of award-winning innovations to illuminate structural shifts in the US economy that have occurred over the last four decades. This data set shows much more substantial changes over time than those revealed in patenting data.

Introducing the Data

For more than forty years, *R&D Magazine* has annually recognized 100 innovations that are incorporated into actual commercial products. These awards are comparable to the Oscars for the motion picture industry; they carry considerable prestige within the community of research-and-development professionals. Organizations nominate their own innovations, and a changing jury that includes representatives from business, government, and universities, in collaboration with the magazine's editors, decide upon the final list of awards (the nomination and selection procedures are described on the magazine's website).[2] The awards go to commercial products that were introduced into the marketplace during the previous year. The entry forms require evidence of the

2 http://www.rdmag.com/Awards/RD-100-Awards/R-D-100-Awards/

availability of the product and its price. With 100 innovations that can be recognized, juries are able to cover the full diversity of innovative products, not just to focus on dynamic sectors such as electronics or biotechnology.

We coded all of the winning innovations for three randomly chosen years in each of the last four decades to identify the types of organizations that were responsible for nurturing the award winners (full data is provided in Appendix 1). Since 1971, somewhere between five and thirteen of the awards each year went to foreign firms that had no US partners.[3] We excluded those cases and focused our analysis on the roughly ninety award winners each year that involved US-based firms.

While the awards recognize innovations in a wide range of different industries, there are some biases in the process. The awards are tilted towards product innovations rather than process innovations – those that are designed to raise the efficiency of the production process for goods and services. Some process innovations, such as a new type of machine tool or a more advanced computer program for managing inventories, are recognized, but many important process innovations are not considered because they involve complex combinations of new equipment and new organizational practices. Many military innovations are also excluded, since cutting-edge weapons are usually shrouded in secrecy and unavailable for purchase. Since the great bulk of federal R&D dollars are still directed towards weapons systems, many government-funded innovations lie outside of this competition.

Furthermore, the awards are structured to recognize just the tip of the proverbial iceberg – the last steps in the innovation process. The many earlier steps are submerged and out of sight. This bias means that the awards understate the role of university-based research, since detailed case studies suggest that many key innovations can be traced back to scientific breakthroughs in university laboratories (Roessner et al. 1997).

What other biases might enter the awards process? Questionable decisions and politics will always be a factor as jury members seek to reward friends and deny recognition to enemies. But for our purposes, it is not necessary that these awards recognize *the very best* innovations of any particular year. All that is necessary is that the awardees represent a reasonable cross section of innovative products and that there is not a consistent bias that favors awardees of a particular type.

The different resources that organizations have at their disposal to prepare their nomination materials are another potential source of bias in competitions. Big architectural firms, for example, can hire the best photographers and devote considerable resources to a nomination, while the hard-pressed solo practitioner might throw the application form together in a few hours (Larson 1993, 1994). There is probably a similar bias in these awards with larger organizations having more expertise at putting together persuasive nomination packets.

However, there are reasons to think that the magnitude of this bias would be limited. For one thing, the universe of applicants is limited to organizations that have actually

---

3 The only exceptions occur when a foreign firm owns a large, established US business, such as when Chrysler was owned by Daimler Benz. In such cases, we code the firm as a Fortune 500 firm.

developed a commercial product, and since winning the award is a powerful form of advertising, even the tiniest firms have strong incentives to devote resources to an effective application. For another, the quality of "coolness" that engineers and technologists admire in a product is substantially easier to convey in words than the more abstract, aesthetic qualities that architectural or film juries might be rewarding. Finally, over the years, there have been many one-time winners, which reinforces the impression that it is the quality of the product and not the quality of the nomination packet that wins awards.

There are, however, two distinct biases in the awards that are important for interpreting our results. First, it is very rare for the *R&D 100* awards to recognize new pharmaceutical products. While there are many awards for medical devices and equipment, there seems to be a deliberate decision to avoid medications of all kinds. Our assumption is that this reflects an abundance of caution by the magazine, which does not want the bad publicity or legal liability of recognizing a product that might later be found to have negative side effects.

A second exclusion is more surprising. There have been few awards over the last twenty years for products – either hardware or software – developed by the largest computer firms. Apple did not win an award for the iPod, Microsoft has received only one R&D award since its inauguration, and firms such as Intel, Sun Microsystems and Cisco have each won only once, as well. Many of the products of this industry represent incremental improvements such as new versions of software packages or slightly improved notebook computers, and it is logical that the jurors ignore these. But it also seems likely that even when they produce a more dramatic innovation, jurors hold them to higher standards than those used for other organizations.

While these two exclusions indicate the need for caution in interpreting the results, they are analytically fortuitous. Since the data largely leave out big firms in the two industries – biotechnology and computing – that are generally seen as paradigmatic examples of science-based production, strong network ties among firms and substantial governmental involvement in the innovation process, the awards data allows us to take a broader view of the innovation economy. To what degree are the same trends effecting sectors that have not been as strongly associated with science-based production?

Coding

It would be ideal to code both the organizational auspices and the funding sources for every innovation awarded in the 12 competitions that we analyze. But while the organizational auspices can be established with a reasonable amount of research, uncovering the funding sources for almost 1,200 different innovations is an almost impossible task. The primary difficulty is that tracking flows of federal support to businesses is laborious and complicated. In our data, we coded the organizational auspices as completely as possible for the roughly 1,200 innovations. Our approach to establishing the funding sources of the recognized innovations represents a compromise. We performed a detailed analysis of federal funding to award-winning firms and innovations for the years 1975 and 2006 to maximize the contrast across time.

In organizational terms, the data revealed seven distinct loci from which the award-winning innovations originated. They are:

Private

1. Fortune 500 firms operating alone.
2. Other firms operating on their own; this is a residual category that includes small- and medium-sized firms.
3. Collaborations among two or more private firms with no listed public sector or nonprofit partner. Industrial consortia are included in this category.[1]

Public or mixed

4. Supported spin-offs. These are recently established (less than 10 years from founding) firms started by technologists at universities or government labs who have been supported by federal research funds.
5. Government laboratories – working by themselves or in collaboration. Most of these innovations come from the federal laboratories run by the Department of Energy, but some come from NIH, military laboratories and labs run by other agencies. If a university is a partner in one of these collaborations with a laboratory, it will be reported here and not under universities.
6. Universities – working by themselves or in collaboration with entities other than federal labs.
7. Other public sector and nonprofit agencies – working by themselves or in collaboration with private firms.

Analyzing the Data

The R&D awards data provide powerful evidence on all three research questions. We start with the second question – whether the shift towards collaboration has become a general trend. Analysts of the networked firm have argued that innovation increasingly results from collaborations between two or more organizations (Hargadon 2003; Lester and Piore 2004). The connections between the knowledge embodied in one organization and the knowledge embodied in other organizations are critical for the innovation process. The sparks generated when these different approaches are combined facilitate

---

4 We list any innovation as public as long as there is a collaborator that is public or a supported spin-off. We avoid double counting by listing collaborative winners under just one of these categories. If a government laboratory is a participant in a collaboration, the innovation is attributed to the laboratory regardless of other participants. If no government lab is involved, but there is a university, then the innovation is attributed to the university. If there is another public or nonprofit participant, the innovation is attributed to that participant. If there are multiple private participants, then it is coded in category 3 – private collaboration. Table 1 in the Appendix provides sufficient detail to show that this particular coding scheme does not bias our results.

Figure 4.1. R&D 100 Awards to interorganizational collaborations

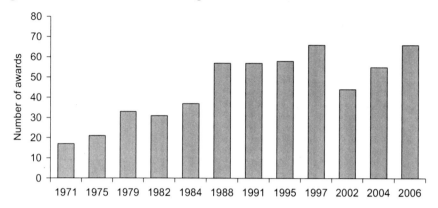

the discovery of effective new approaches (Hargadon 2003). Our data provide support for this claim. Figure 4.1 shows a dramatic rise in the number of domestic award-winning innovations that involve interorganizational collaborations. The number of innovations attributed to a single private-sector firm operating alone averaged 67 in the 1970s, but has dropped to an average of only 27 in the current decade.

In part, this shift reflects the growing importance of public-sector agencies as award winners, since we code all public agencies as engaging in collaboration since they invariably employ private partners to market their innovative products. But it is also the case that even among the dwindling number of private-sector winners, the frequency of formal collaborations rose from 7.8 percent in the 1970s to 17.5 percent in the current decade.

An equally striking finding addresses the first research question – the role of large corporations in the innovation process. Figure 4.2 shows the dramatic decline in both solo and collaborative winners from the Fortune 500 firms. While these firms were the largest single winner of awards in the 1970s, by the current decade, solo winners from the Fortune 500 could be counted on the fingers of one hand. Even with collaborators, they averaged only ten awards per year.

Figure 4.2. R&D 100 Award winners from the Fortune 500

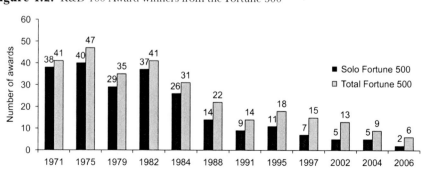

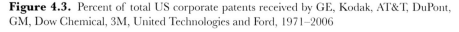

Figure 4.3. Percent of total US corporate patents received by GE, Kodak, AT&T, DuPont, GM, Dow Chemical, 3M, United Technologies and Ford, 1971–2006

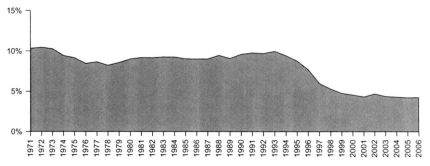

To be sure, this is the place where the almost total exclusion of large computer-industry firms and pharmaceutical firms impacts the data. Data on US patent applications shows that firms such as IBM, Microsoft, Intel and Sun rank among the most prolific US firms in the number of patents received (United States Patent and Trademark Office).[5] They also represent important exceptions to the tendency for big firms to reduce their outlays for R&D over the past twenty years. So the fact that their R&D effort is only rarely recognized in the *R&D 100* means that Figure 4.2 overstates the declining innovative capacity of Fortune 500 firms. But even if the large computer industry firms collectively received ten of these awards per year, Figure 4.2 would still show a significant downward trend.

The situation with pharmaceutical firms is more complicated. While the established large firms, such as Merck and Pfizer, and the most successful biotech firms, such as Genentech and Amgen, continue to fund significant research efforts, the number of innovative drugs they have brought to the market in recent years has been quite limited. The drug industry has its own awards for innovation published by *Prescrire International*.[6] Their highest award, the Golden Pill, recognizes new drugs that represent a major breakthrough. But between 1997 and 2006, only two drugs received this recognition, and there were only 12 others that received second-place recognition as a clear advance over existing therapies. This suggests that if the *R&D 100* competition had recognized prescription drugs, the results in Figure 4.2 would not have changed much at all.

The real significance of Figure 4.2 is the decline in awards won by general-purpose manufacturing firms such as General Electric, General Motors and 3M. Firms like these dominated the awards in the 1970s, but they have won only rarely in recent years. This decline parallels the trend in their patenting activity, strongly suggesting diminished innovative efforts. Figure 4.3 shows a dramatic decline in the percentage of US corporate patents won by nine of these manufacturing firms that have been in continuous existence and are outside the computer industry.

---

5 http://www.uspto.gov/web/offices/ac/ido/oeip/taf/reports.htm

6 We are grateful to Donald Light for bringing these awards to our attention.

These declines can be traced to the priorities of corporate executives faced with continuing pressure over the last several decades to improve the quarterly financial results of their firms. Many firms have cut back their R&D efforts or shifted funds towards product development. After all, research is expensive and its contribution to the bottom line is likely to come long after the current CEO's tenure in office. At the same time, the financial orientation of top executives means that they see new technologies as simply another asset that can be acquired rather than produced internally. They are confident that when the time comes, they can either license the technologies they need or buy up the firms that produce innovations (Estrin 2009; Tassey 2007).

The magnitude of this shift is indicated by employment trends among scientists and engineers working for private firms. According to data collected by the National Science Foundation (NSF), in 1971 7.6 percent percent of R&D scientists and engineers working for industry, or 28,200 individuals, were employed by firms with fewer than 1,000 employees. By 2004, this percentage had risen to 32 percent, while the actual number of people had grown to 365,000. NSF data also indicate that PhD scientists and engineers have become even more concentrated in small firms; in 2003, 24 percent of those working for industry were employed at firms with fewer than ten employees and more than half were at firms with under 500 employees.[7] It is, of course, impossible to know how much of this shift reflected push factors that led technologists to leave large firms and how much was the attraction of working in smaller firms. Either way, the trend in the awards away from big firms follows the trend of the technologists who create the innovations.

As the role of large corporations declined, there has been a corresponding gain in awards for public and mixed entities. This provides answers to the third research question – whether the public sector is playing an expanding role in the innovation system. As Figure 4.4 shows, the majority of awards are now won either by federal laboratories, universities or by firms that we have categorized as supported spin-offs. In the last two decades, the federal laboratories have become the dominant organizational locus for winning these awards. They now have about the same weight in the overall awards as the Fortune 500 firms did in the 1970s – averaging about 35 awards per year.[8] This is a surprising finding because many observers hold federal laboratories in low esteem and doubt their capacity to contribute to innovation. Most of the winning innovations originate in the Department of Energy laboratories that were initially

---

7 "Number of Full-Time-Equivalent (FTE) R&D Scientists and Engineers in R&D-Performing Companies, by Industry and by Size of Company" is available at http://www.nsf.gov/statistics/iris/search_hist.cfm?indx=24 and http://www.nsf.gov/statistics/nsf07314/pdf/tab41.pdf. These figures should be taken as approximations due to changes in NSF's procedures for collecting and estimating this data over time. Data on PhD employees are provided in Figure 3.18 in *Science and Engineering Indicators, 2008* at http://www.nsf.gov/statistics/seind08/figures.htm.

8 In the cases that we have coded as solo, the innovation award went solely to a federal lab or a university. This presumably indicates that the partner enlisted to commercialize the product had no ownership of the intellectual property involved in the innovation.

Figure 4.4. Awards to federal labs, supported spinoffs and other public entities

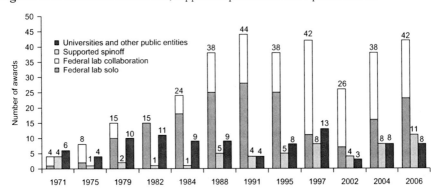

created to develop atomic weapons in the early years of the Cold War. The sinister image of PhD physicists and chemists working assiduously to develop ever more destructive weaponry has certainly colored the public image of these facilities.[9]

After the Federal laboratories, the next most important public or mixed entities are the supported spin-offs. These entities – on their own – averaged close to eight awards per year in the current decade, and they also win some additional awards in partnership with government laboratories or universities. Moreover, as we will see later, firms that began as supported spin-offs but have been in existence for more than ten years are coded as "other firms" – part of the private category – and their weight in the awards has also increased over time.

The typical pattern of a supported spin-off is that a professor or a scientist at a university or federal laboratory makes an important discovery and consults with university or lab officials as to how best to protect the resulting intellectual property. In many cases, the organization encourages the innovator to start his or her own firm to develop and ultimately market the new product. The more entrepreneurial universities and laboratories function almost as venture capitalists by helping the individual find investors and experienced managers who could guide the new firm (Geiger and Sa 2008).

The final category in Figure 4.4 encompasses awards won by universities and other public-sector agencies and nonprofit firms. Surprisingly, the direct weight of universities among award winners is relatively modest. There are several reasons for this: First, some innovations that originate in university laboratories show up in the supported-spin-offs category because the researcher started his or her own firm. Second, university-based researchers are increasingly part of collaborations with federal laboratories and our coding system attributes those innovations to the labs. In 2006, for example, universities received two awards in partnership with other firms and seven in partnership with federal

---

9 Even in the scholarly literature, it is rare to find recognition of the innovation productivity of the labs. For an overview of the labs, see Crow and Bozeman (1998). One of the rare sources that recognizes the increased commercial productivity of the labs is Jaffe and Lerner (2001).

Figure 4.5. Awards to SBIR-funded firms

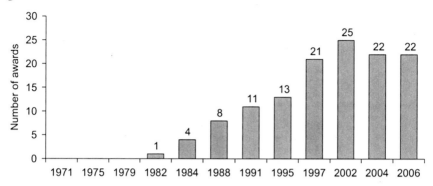

laboratories. In short, even though the importance of scientific discoveries at universities has become ever more central to the innovation process, most of the transition into commercial products is mediated through spin-offs and the activities at federal laboratories.[10]

Yet, a focus on organizational auspices alone does not capture the full extent of US government financing of the innovation process. Figure 4.5 shows the role of one of the most important – but little known – federal programs: the Small Business Innovation Research (SBIR) program. Firms that had previously received one or more SBIR awards represent a very large share of winners in the current decade. SBIR is a set-aside program that requires federal agencies with large research budgets to devote 2.5 percent of their R&D budgets to support firms with 500 employees or less. It is also a program that provided initial funding for many of the supported spin-offs. The program awards up to US$100,000 in no-strings support for projects in Phase I and up to US$750,000 for Phase II projects that have shown significant progress in meeting the initial objectives.[11] In 2004, the SBIR program gave out more than US$2 billion for some 6,300 separate research projects. As the figure shows, current and past SBIR award winners have come to constitute roughly 25 percent of domestic winners each year.

In Figure 4.6, we try to provide a more comprehensive measure of the role of federal financing over time by looking in greater detail at funding for award winners in 1975 and 2006. The bottom part of each graph shows the various public-sector winners that rely heavily on federal funding. As indicated earlier, this shows a dramatic rise from 14 to 61 of the awardees. But the top part of the graph shows the number of "other" and Fortune 500 firms that received at least 1 percent of their revenues from the federal government.[12] This 1 percent screen picks up both large

---

10 Even if we recode collaborations that involve both a federal lab and a university as "university," the number of award-winning innovations involving federal labs still substantially outweighs those involving universities.

11 The NIH has applied for and received a waiver that enables it to exceed these caps.

12 The logic of using a 1 percent-of-revenue screen is that it is common among large firms to devote only 3 percent to 4 percent of revenues to R&D expenditures. Hence, federal awards or contracts of that magnitude could help fund a significant increase in R&D effort.

Figure 4.6. Federal involvement with award-winning innovations, 1975 and 2006

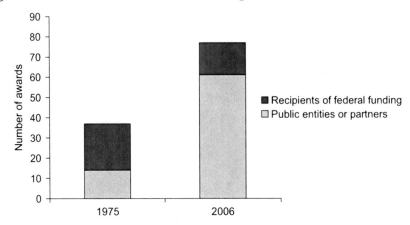

defense contractors and firms that have received substantial federal grants to support their R&D efforts. In 1975, there were 23 awards won by private firms that received at least 1 percent of their revenues from federal support. Prominent among these was General Electric, which in that year was responsible for nine award-winning innovations.[13]

In 2006, we found that of five private collaborations, the federal government directly funded three. Of the 20 "other firms" that won awards, 13 had federal support above the 1 percent threshold, *and* we were able to link the federal money directly to the specific innovation that received the award. Hence, 16 of these "private" innovations count as federally funded. The overall result in Figure 4.6 is that the number of federally funded innovations rises from 36 in 1975 to 77 in 2006.

In 2006, literally only 11 of the domestic award winners were *not* beneficiaries of federal funding. Two winning firms – Brion Tech and MMR Technologies – were recent spin-offs from Stanford University, but they had not received federal funding after their launch. In short, Figure 4.6 probably understates the magnitude of the expansion in federal funding for innovations between 1975 and 2006. After all, in 1975 we count innovations as federally funded even if support was not going to the specific unit of the firm that was working on a particular innovation. For 2006, however, a demonstration of federal support required showing that the federal funds were going to the same unit that was responsible for the particular technology that won the award.

Even in the period when Fortune 500 corporations dominated the innovation process, they drew heavily on federal funding support. If one is looking for a golden age in which the private sector did most of the innovating on its own without

---

13 There were five additional awards that went to Fortune 500 companies that had contracts to manage government laboratories in 1975 – two each for Union Carbide and DuPont and one for Monsanto.

federal help, one has to go back to the era before World War II (Hounshell 1996). Nevertheless, over the last 40 years, the awards indicate a dramatic increase in the federal government's centrality to the innovation economy. In the earlier period, US industrial and technology policies were almost entirely monopolized by the military and space programs (Alic 2007; Hooks 1990). More recently, a wide range of nondefense agencies have been involved in supporting private-sector research-and-development initiatives. Key agencies now include Commerce, Energy, NIH, Agriculture, NSF and Homeland Security.

Discussion

Our data set provides evidence of three interrelated changes in the US economy over the past generation. These are (1) the declining centrality of the largest corporations to the innovation process in the United States, (2) the growing importance of interorganizational collaboration and small start-up firms in the innovation process and (3) the expanded role of public-sector institutions as both participants in and funders of the innovation process.

It is the last of these shifts that is the most surprising since this change coincided with the period in which market fundamentalist ideas dominated public-policy debates. But it is important to recognize how different the federal role is from models of centrally planned technological change. In Chalmers Johnson's (1982) classic account of the Japanese model of industrial policy, he shows how government officials, working at the Ministry of Trade and Industry, operated as both coordinators and financiers for the conquest of new markets by Japanese firms. The key was that the government officials were implementing a shared plan that linked investments in particular technologies with specific business strategies to win in particular markets – both domestically and internationally.

In the US case, there is no unified plan, and different government agencies engage in support for new technologies, often in direct competition with other agencies. The approach is more like Mao's "let a hundred flowers bloom": the United States has created a decentralized network of publicly funded laboratories where technologists have strong incentives to work with private firms and find ways to turn their discoveries into commercial products. Moreover, an alphabet soup of different programs provides agencies with opportunities to fund some of these more compelling technological possibilities.

Alongside this "build it and they will come" approach, there are also targeted government programs that are designed to accelerate progress across specific technological barriers. However, these programs are also implemented in a decentralized fashion by small agencies. The model developed by DARPA of setting technological goals and working closely with researchers to accelerate breakthroughs has now diffused across the federal system (Block 2008).

But because these programs contradict the market-fundamentalist ideology that celebrates private enterprise and denigrates the public sector, they have remained largely unknown to the public. Journalists rarely write about government-technology initiatives; for example, the *New York Times* has mentioned the SBIR program in its news coverage fewer than ten times over the last 27 years. To be sure, Congress periodically debates the design and funding for these programs, but reports on these discussions are rarely covered in the *Wall Street Journal* or general-purpose business publications. Since the programs are largely unknown, they simply do not figure in public-policy debates (Block 2008).

Ironically, the parameters of these little known state programs fit the model of a developmental network state (DNS) that Sean Ó Riain (2004) elaborated in his study of the Irish government's efforts to encourage high-tech growth in that nation (see also Breznitz 2007). Just as in Ó Riain's case, government efforts are highly decentralized, rely on strengthening technological networks that cut across the public/private divide and require public-sector officials to play a multiplicity of roles in supporting entrepreneurial efforts.

Recently, Whitford and Schrank (2011) have usefully conceptualized these government programs as efforts to overcome failures that are endemic in networked forms of economic organization. In contrast to market failures, network failures occur when economic actors are unable to find appropriate network partners that are both competent and trustworthy.

The programs of a developmental network state (DNS) help to stitch together networks and work to improve and validate the competence of potential network partners. Furthermore, the federal laboratories, industry/university research centers sponsored by the NSF and informal meetings sponsored by agencies such as DARPA create "collaborative public spaces" (Lester and Piore 2004) where network participants are able to share key ideas.

But this revised understanding of how innovation is organized in the US economy has important implications for the regime governing intellectual property rights. The growing interdependence between private firms and researchers at university and government laboratories make it imperative to rethink the assumptions on which intellectual property rules rest. The existing rules rest on the old distinction between basic science and applied science. With basic science, researchers are supposed to publish their findings so they can be replicated and everyone understands the need for openness and the sharing of information. But with applied science, where there are clear commercial applications, it is simply assumed that researchers should be able to protect the intellectual property they generate.

While the divide between basic and applied science has always been problematic (Stokes 1997), it now no longer makes any sense at all. Basic scientific discoveries such as breakthroughs in molecular biology rapidly generate commercial applications, and work on such applied problems as conquering particular diseases routinely generate basic scientific discoveries. The growing interdependence between university and federal laboratory scientists and private firms is a manifestation of the obsolescence of this distinction.

One response to the disappearance of this boundary is to redefine all scientific inquiry as potentially having commercial applications so that all practitioners are urged to establish and protect their discoveries as valuable intellectual property. This is the direction that was signaled by the Supreme Court in its 1980 *Diamond v. Chakrabarty* decision approving a patent for a genetically modified organism. But this path threatens the very survival of the scientific project which is built on creating shared knowledge and prioritizing publication as the key to individual scientific careers.

The opposite and far more constructive response is to stretch the scientific norms that include the free flow of information and knowledge more deeply into the realm of applied science. This could be done by substantially raising the bar on what kinds of innovations are patentable – a move that would simultaneously address the chronic problem of backlog with which patent offices now struggle. One reason that patent applications have proliferated so rapidly is that they have become extremely narrow – they can cover a single tiny step in a complex process or a single microscopic component in a complex mechanism. With nanotechnology, this quickly reaches a *reductio ad absurdum* because it is conceivable that there would be separate patents for each of the thousands of layers of atoms laid down for the construction of a new material.

In the United States, in the first half of the nineteenth century, innovators had to provide a physical model of their new idea. The idea then was that patents were limited to something holistic and close to a commercial product, not to the dozens of small components and processes that were combined into a finished product. Obviously, that nineteenth century model is now impractical, but some movement in the direction of making patents broader should be possible. The biggest difficulty would be delineating the size or importance of a component that would be substantial enough to merit a patent, but one possible rule of thumb would be whether that particular component could operate effectively in a different context.

A move to require patentable ideas to be broader fits with our findings about the networked nature of contemporary innovation. As we have seen, collaboration among firms is now essential to the innovation process, but firms have to worry that collaborators might steal the valuable intellectual property that their researchers have already produced. The resulting distrust is a major source of network failure. This is precisely why the collaborative public spaces provided by federal and university laboratories loom so large in our study of the *R&D 100* awards. These settings provide a safe place where scientists and engineers – including those working at private firms – can work together with a much-reduced danger that their ideas will be unfairly appropriated by others. But shifting the patent regime to protect only broader concepts would mean that many of the small solutions required to develop an effective new product would not reach the threshold of a patentable idea. This could help encourage collaboration and reduce distrust.

Conclusion

The current systems of intellectual property protection were developed for a very different innovation environment than that which currently exists. In an era where most innovations were produced by corporate laboratories or individual inventors, the existing patent system made sense. But since innovation now occurs in collaborative networks, often linking the public and private sectors, the existing patent system has often become a significant barrier to scientific and technological advance. In the computer industry, patents are widely considered to be simply a nuisance that large firms manage by acquiring large portfolios of patents that they use defensively when they are accused of infringement. In the biomedical area, university-based researchers sometimes find themselves restricted from pursuing a line of research because some other entity has proprietary rights in a particular organism or genetic sequence. And business firms must be constantly alert to the danger that their collaborators might appropriate their intellectual property and get to the patent office first.

The situation is further complicated by the growing role of the public sector in financing much of the research that produces commercially valuable intellectual property. A study by Vallas, Kleinman and Biscotti (2011) shows that many of the highest-selling biotechnology drugs were developed with substantial research financing by the US government. Pharmaceutical firms often sell these products at extremely high prices and generate large profits, but there is no specific payback to the government for its earlier contribution. This problem now exists in milder forms across much of the economy.

All this suggests the need for seriously rethinking the current framework for the protection of intellectual property. A new regime of knowledge governance is necessary to recognize the important role of the public sector in facilitating innovation and to minimize the negative consequences on technological advance of the current restrictive regime of intellectual property rights. To be sure, there is still a need to protect and provide proper incentives for those who help to develop innovative new products, but this could be done within a very different set of rules from those that have been inherited from the recent past.

Acknowledgments

This paper was supported with funding from the Ford Foundation. An early version of this paper was published as a working paper by the Information Technology and Innovation Foundation in Washington DC. Another version was published in *Socio-Economic Review* and reprinted as a chapter in Fred Block and Matthew R. Keller (eds) *State of Innovation: The U.S. Government's Role in Technology Development.* Jason Logan, John Kincaid, and Chris Knight provided valuable research assistance, and we are grateful for comments received in several different settings where we presented the findings, including the Power and Inequality Workshop at UC, Davis and the American Sociological Association meetings, August 2008.

Appendix 1

Composition of *R&D 100* award winners

	1971	1975	1979	1982	1984	1988	1991	1995	1997	2002	2004	2006
Total awards	**102**	**98**	**100**	**100**	**100**	**100**	**98**	**101**	**100**	**97**	**94**	**100**
Total foreign	5	12	10	14	14	11	13	12	12	14	10	12
Total domestic	97	86	90	86	86	89	85	89	88	83	84	88
Of domestic award winners												
Private												
1. Fortune 500 alone	38	40	29	37	26	14	9	11	7	5	5	2
2. Other firms alone	42	25	28	18	23	18	20	20	15	34	24	20
3. Private consortia	3	8	6	4	3	5	4	7	3	11	1	5
Includes F-500 firm	1	2	4	3	1	4	1	4	1	7	1	0
Subtotal	**83**	**73**	**63**	**59**	**52**	**37**	**33**	**38**	**25**	**50**	**30**	**27**
Public or quasi-public												
4. Supported spin-offs	4	1	2	1	1	5	4	5	8	4	8	11

(Continued)

Continued

	1971	1975	1979	1982	1984	1988	1991	1995	1997	2002	2004	2006
5. Government labs	4	8	15	15	24	38	44	38	42	26	38	42
Solo credit	*1*	*2*	*10*	*15*	*18*	*25*	*28*	*25*	*11*	*7*	*16*	*23*
w/F-500	*1*	*5*	*2*	*0*	*3*	*4*	*4*	*3*	*5*	*1*	*2*	*3*
w/university	*0*	*0*	*0*	*0*	*1*	*2*	*4*	*2*	*3*	*2*	*5*	*7*
w/others	*2*	*1*	*3*	*0*	*2*	*7*	*9*	*8*	*23*	*16*	*15*	*9*
6. Universities	3	0	4	4	1	1	1	5	6	2	4	2
Solo credit	*1*	*0*	*4*	*1*	*1*	*1*	*1*	*1*	*2*	*0*	*1*	*0*
w/F-500	*1*	*0*	*0*	*0*	*0*	*0*	*0*	*0*	*0*	*0*	*0*	*0*
w/others	*1*	*0*	*0*	*3*	*0*	*0*	*0*	*4*	*4*	*2*	*3*	*2*
7. Other public	3	4	6	7	8	8	3	3	7	1	4	6
w/F-500	*0*	*0*	*0*	*1*	*1*	*0*	*0*	*0*	*2*	*0*	*1*	*1*
Subtotal	**14**	**13**	**27**	**27**	**34**	**52**	**52**	**51**	**63**	**33**	**54**	**61**
Total F-500	41	47	35	41	31	22	14	18	15	13	9	6

References

Alic, John. 2007. *Trillions for Military Technology.* New York: Palgrave.

Arrighi, Giovanni. 2007. *Adam Smith in Beijing: Lineages of the 21st Century.* London: Verso.

Bell, Daniel. 1973. *The Coming of Post-Industrial Society.* New York: Basic Books.

Bennis, Warren and Philip Slater. 1968. *The Temporary Society.* New York: Harper & Row.

Block, Fred. 2008. "Swimming Against the Current: The Rise of a Hidden Developmental State in the United States." *Politics & Society* 36 (2): 169–206.

———. 1990. *Postindustrial Possibilities.* Berkeley: University of California Press.

Breznitz, Dan. 2007. *Innovation and the State: Political Choice and Strategies for Growth in Israel, Taiwan, and Ireland.* New Haven, CT: Yale University Press.

Brick, Howard. 2006. *Transcending Capitalism: Visions of a New Society in Modern American Thought.* Ithaca, NY: Cornell University Press.

Burns, Tom and G. M. Stalker. 1961. *The Management of Innovation.* London: Tavistock.

Castells, Manuel. 1996. *The Rise of the Network Society.* Oxford: Blackwell.

Collins, Steven. 2004. *The Race to Commercialize Biotechnology.* New York: Routledge Curzon.

Crow, Michael and Barry Bozeman. 1998. *Limited by Design: R&D Laboratories in the U.S. National Innovation System.* New York: Columbia University Press.

Estrin, Judy. 2009. *Closing the Innovation Gap: Reigniting the Spark of Creativity in a Global Economy.* New York: McGraw Hill.

Etzkowitz, Henry. 2003. "Innovation in Innovation: The Triple Helix of University-Industry-Government Relations." *Social Science Information* 42: 293–337.

Fligstein, Neil. 1990. *The Transformation of Corporate Control.* Cambridge, MA: Harvard University Press.

Fong, Glenn R. 2000. "Breaking New Ground or Breaking the Rules: Strategic Reorientation in U.S. Industrial Policy." *International Security* 25 (2): 152–86.

Geiger, Roger and Creso Sa. 2008. *Tapping the Riches of Science: Universities and the Promise of Economic Growth.* Cambridge, MA: Harvard University Press.

Gordon, David, Richard Edwards and Michael Reich. 1982. *Segmented Work, Divided Workers: The Historical Transformation of Labor in the United States.* New York: Cambridge University Press.

Hargadon, Andrew. 2003. *How Breakthroughs Happen: The Surprising Truth About How Corporations Innovate.* Boston: Harvard Business School Press.

Hooks, Gregory. 1990. "The Rise of the Pentagon and U.S. State Building: The Defense Program as Industrial Policy." *American Journal of Sociology* 96 (2): 358–404.

Hounshell, David. 1996. "The Evolution of Industrial Research in the United States." In Richard Rosenbloom and William J. Spencer (eds), *Engines of Innovation: US Industrial Research at the End of an Era,* 13–85. Boston: Harvard Business School Press.

Jaffe, Adam and Josh Lerner. 2001. "Reinventing Public R&D: Patent Policy and the Commercialization of National Laboratory Technologies." *Rand Journal of Economics* (March): 167–98.

Johnson, Chalmers. 1982. *MITI and the Japanese Miracle.* Stanford, CA: Stanford University Press.

Kenney, Martin. 1986. *Biotechnology: The University-Industrial Complex.* New Haven, CT: Yale University Press.

Kevles, Daniel. 1992. "Out of Genetics: The Historical Politics of the Human Genome." In Daniel Kevles and Leroy Hood (eds), *The Code of Codes: Scientific and Social Issues in the Human Genome Project,* 3–36. Cambridge, MA: Harvard University Press.

Kotz, David M., Terence McDonough and Michael Reich (eds). 1994. *Social Structures of Accumulation: The Political Economy of Growth and Crisis.* New York: Cambridge University Press.

Larson, Magali Sarfatti. 1994. "Architectural Competitions as Discursive Events." *Theory and Society* 23 (4): 469–504.

Larson, Magali Sarfatti. 1993. *Behind the Postmodern Façade.* Berkeley: University of California Press.

Lerner, Josh. 1999. "When Bureaucrats Meet Entrepreneurs: The Design of Effective 'Public Venture Capital' Programmes." *Economic Journal* 112 (477): 73–84.

Lester, Richard and Michael J. Piore. 2004. *Innovation: The Missing Dimension.* Cambridge, MA: Harvard University Press.

Lundvall, B.-A. 1992. *National Systems of Innovation: Towards a Theory of Innovation and Interactive Learning.* London: Pinter.

McCray, W. Patrick. 2009. "From Lab to iPod: A Story of Discovery and Commercialization in the Post-Cold War Era." *Technology and Culture* 50 (1): 58–81.

Mowery, David C. 2009. "*Plus ça Change:* Industrial R&D in the 'Third Industrial Revolution.'" *Industrial and Corporate Change* 18 (1): 1–50.

Mowery, David C., Richard Nelson, Bhaven Sampat and Arvids Ziedonis. 2004. *Ivory Tower and Industrial Innovation: University-Industry Technology Transfer before and after the Bayh-Dole Act.* Stanford, CA: Stanford University Press.

Nelson, Richard (ed.) 1993. *National Innovation Systems: A Comparative Analysis.* New York: Oxford University Press.

Newfield, Christopher. 2008. *Unmaking the Public University: The Forty-Year Assault on the Middle Class.* Cambridge, MA: Harvard University Press.

Ó Riain, Sean. 2004. *The Politics of High-Tech Growth: Developmental Network States in the Global Economy.* Cambridge: Cambridge University Press.

Powell, Walter. 2001. "The Capitalist Firm in the Twenty-First Century: Emerging Patterns in Western Enterprise." In Paul DiMaggio (ed.), *The Twenty-First Century Firm,* 33–68. Princeton: Princeton University Press.

Powell, Walter, Douglas White, Kenneth Koput and Jason Owen-Smith. 2005. "Network Dynamics and Field Evolution: The Growth of Interorganizational Collaboration in the Life Sciences." *American Journal of Sociology* 110: 1132–1205.

Prescrire International. 2007. "Prescrire Awards." 16 (88) (April): 76.

Roessner, David, Barry Bozeman, Irwin Feller, Christopher Hill and Nils Newman. 1997. *The Role of NSF Support of Engineering in Enabling Technological Innovation.* Stanford, CA: SRI Policy Division.

Roland, Alex, with Philip Shiman. 2002. *Strategic Computing: DARPA and the Quest for Machine Intelligence 1983–1993.* Cambridge, MA: MIT Press.

Rosenbloom, Richard, and William J. Spencer (eds). 1996. *Engines of Innovation: U.S. Industrial Research at the End of an Era.* Boston: Harvard Business School Press.

Saxenian, AnnaLee. 1994. *Regional Advantage: Culture and Competition in Silicon Valley and Route 128.* Cambridge, MA: Harvard University Press.

Sciberras, E. 1986. "Indicators of Technical Intensity and International Competitiveness: A Case for Supplementing Quantitative Data with Qualitative Studies in Research." *R&D Management* 16 (1): 3–14.

Slaughter, Sheila and Gary Rhoades. 2002. "The Emergence of a Competitiveness Research and Development Policy Coalition and the Commercialization of Academic Science and Technology." In Philip Mirowski and Esther Mirjam Sent (eds), *Science Bought and Sold: Essays in the Economics of Science,* 69–108. Chicago: University of Chicago Press.

Stokes, Donald. 1997. *Pasteur's Quadrant: Basic Science and Technological Innovation.* Washington DC: Brookings.

Tassey, Gregory. 2007. *The Technology Imperative.* Cheltenham: E. Elgar.

Taylor, Mark Zachary. 2004. "Empirical Evidence Against Variety of Capitalism's Theory of Technological Innovation." *International Organization* 58 (Summer): 601–31.

Thursby, J. G. and M. C. Thursby. 2002. "Who is Selling the Ivory Tower? Sources of Growth in University Licensing." *Management Science* 48 (1): 123–44.

Vallas, Steven P., Daniel Lee Kleinman and Dina Biscotti. 2011. "Political Structures and the Making of U.S. Biotechnology." In Fred Block and Matthew R. Keller (eds), *State of Innovation: The U.S. Government's Role in Technology Development*, 57–76. Boulder: Paradigm.

Weiss, Linda and Elizabeth Thurbon. 2006. "The Business of Buying American: Public Procurement as Trade Strategy in the United States." *Review of International Political Economy* 13 (5): 701–24.

Wessner, Charles W. (ed.) 2008. *An Assessment of the Small Business Innovation Program*. Washington DC: National Academies Press.

Whitford, Josh. 2005. *The New Old Economy: Networks, Institutions, and the Organizational Transformation of American Manufacturing*. New York: Oxford University Press.

Whitford, Josh and Andrew Schrank. 2011. "The Paradox of the Weak State Revisited; Industrial Policy, Network Governance, and Political Decentralization." In Fred Block and Matthew R. Keller (eds), *State of Innovation: The U.S. Government's Role in Technology Development*, 261–81. Boulder, CO: Paradigm Publishers.

Chapter 5

ANTITRUST AND INTELLECTUAL PROPERTY: CONFLICTS AND CONVERGENCES

Mario Luiz Possas and Maria Tereza Leopardi Mello
Federal University of Rio de Janeiro

Introduction

In general, even though the relation between intellectual property rights (IPRs) and competition policies – particularly antitrust – may be regarded as essentially compatible, it tends to present tensions and conflict zones. That is because intellectual property rights were created mainly to deter free imitation, which by definition constrains competition to some degree. Therefore, the economic function of intellectual property intrinsically restricts rights or freedoms at some level; and if such restraint is exercised in an anticompetitive way, it may be deemed an antitrust offence.

However, the actual problem arising from the application of antitrust law to the exercise of an intellectual property right does not involve an unsolvable conflict between both normative fields, but rather a systematic analysis – employing the antitrust method and the rule of reason – directed at identifying, in each specific case, the particularly abusive nature of the exercise of such a right, from the standpoint of the competition.

This chapter seeks to examine the relation between the two fields under this perspective, in which zones of tension or conflict permeate the affinities or even convergence of general goals. Such a view is largely supported by the Schumpeterian theory of competition, summarized in Section 1, which states that innovation and its resulting appropriation of profits play a leading role in the process of competition and the dynamics of the economy. In Section 2, IPR protection will be examined in relation to the appropriability of profits from innovation and competitive strategies of innovative companies. Section 3 will address the main subject of this essay: the fundamental relations between IPRs and antitrust, the main intersecting and potentially conflicting points and possible solutions. It also includes a preliminary study on how the United States and the European Union handle this relation. The fourth and final section will examine the Brazilian law and its application. A conclusion follows.

1. The Schumpeterian Perspective on Intellectual Property and Competition

The relation between intellectual property protection and competition is not naturally convergent, but neither should it be antithetical. Although there certainly are conflictive dimensions, the common sense of scholars, professionals and IP policymakers tends to underline these, influenced by the static approach of mainstream economic science concerning the nature and normative implications of competition. The Schumpeterian theoretical perspective we adopt allows a better assessment of this relation, showing how inevitable policy conflicts may be straightened out and subordinated to a broader normative convergence, one in which both subjects may complement each other as a means to a higher end – the incentive of innovation as the main goal to be pursued by the competitive process in a capitalist economy.

The following two subsections address, respectively, how this essential normative convergence, notwithstanding topic areas of conflict, is supported by the Schumpeterian theory of competition, pinpointing its most distinctive elements; and how appropriability and its protection, a crucial matter to this subject, emerges from such convergence.

1.1. An outline of the Schumpeterian theory of competition

Unlike neoclassical theory, which accounts for the mainstream of economic science, Schumpeter's theory regards competition as a *process*, and not as a state, particularly a state of *equilibrium*.[1] The key idea – associated with a distinctive view on how the capitalist economy works – is that in principle, *there is not* (unless otherwise proven, which will never occur as a general rule, but rather in particular cases) a state that could sufficiently represent such process – that is, a terminal state of equilibrium. Therefore, this dynamic process must be analyzed by itself, and not by means of some hypothetical static "representative state."

This implies, among other relevant and unconventional features, an approach focused on the dynamics of the economy, forsaking the mainstream's signature paradigm of static equilibrium. Furthermore, analytically, this theoretical perspective revolves around the pursuit of a nonequilibrium dynamic to understand how the capitalist economy works.

Some of the cardinal concepts to understand and analyze this mechanism gain entirely distinctive features when reexamined through this perspective. As for our main concern here – firms and their interaction with the market (competition) – the first crucial distinctive point is that the process of competition is based on, and continually reproduces, competitive asymmetries of a productive and technological nature, and others, among companies. And it is the companies' own initiatives that produce this phenomenon, not

---

1 The main reference is Schumpeter (1943, chs 7 and 8). A compact view, including the Neo-Schumpeterian approach, may be found in Possas (2002, ch. 17).

exogenous "shocks" or market failures. On the contrary, the continuous generation and diffusion of variety – an essential evolutionary aspect – occurs endogenously by means of innovations in a broad sense, as Schumpeter defined it, and constitutes the *essence* of the market mechanism, and of the competition thereof, in a capitalist economy.

A second essential aspect, a corollary of the first, is that not only is competition a process of adjustment through which differences among agents are eliminated (the "passive," traditional, dimension of competition), but also, and most importantly, of maladjustment, better yet, of creation of new lucrative opportunities by means of innovations (the "active" dimension, which conventional theories fail to perceive or approach). And it is the latter that responds to the production or reproduction of differentiation among agents typical of capitalist industries and markets. In brief, Schumpeterian competition involves both the elimination and the creation of differences, with a higher emphasis on the latter.

Other relevant analytical aspects of Schumpeter's theory, corollary of his concept of competition, are:

1. The inexistence of "normal" profits, or of a tendency towards a uniform profit rate, since competition is not subordinated to a theoretical rule or predetermined trend. Profits are simply the result – of a theoretically undetermined magnitude – of a successful innovation.
2. Profit has a temporary and (to a certain extent) circumstantial nature, similarly to quasi-rent or monopoly profit, deriving from a successful competitive effort towards differentiation (*lato sensu* innovation) that has not been sufficiently spread through the market and imitated by competitors.
3. For the same reason, monopoly is not the opposite of competition, as stated by the static (neoclassic) tradition, but the motivation and the result of competition – when the latter succeeds!
4. For the same reason as well, the question of appropriability of the benefits from innovation – of profits, in brief – is theoretically crucial for economic analysis in general, and not just some specialized matter pertaining to innovation or IPR economics.

1.2. Appropriability

As mentioned above, our choice of Schumpeter's theory is crucially important for its ability to regard competition and IPR protection as convergent in terms of fundamentals, and not as essentially antagonistic. The notion of appropriability is particularly emphasized: due to general theoretical reasons – its relation with monopoly (temporary) profits – and not to a special focus, it assumes a leading role as one of the main attributes of competitive advantages yielded by innovative agents in the capitalist economy.

Since profits are temporary monopolistic gains derived from successful innovations, by their very own nature and not due to exceptional circumstances, their appropriation – both in terms of magnitude and time – becomes a matter of strategic interest for innovative firms as well as innovation policymakers. In practical terms, it is about extending the period in which innovators are the only ones to appropriate the fruits of competitive advantage yielded by a successful innovation. For innovators, such extension should be as long as possible; for policymakers, just the adequate length for policy effectiveness.

In short, the degree of appropriability of profits deriving from a competitive advantage obtained through a *lato sensu* innovation (differentiation) depends upon factors that constrain or hinder its immediate diffusion or dilution. Among those, imitation time and cost stand out (elimination of differences): the lower they are, the lower the degree of appropriability, so that the pioneer innovator cannot retain all benefits of the innovation.

Therefore, appropriation effectiveness – be it through IPRs, industrial secrets or other means – should be evaluated through its capacity to affect the relative cost and time of imitation, creating or strengthening appropriability conditions. The legal mechanism of protection through IPRs, in particular, is an instrument of competition and must be analyzed as such. The economic importance of IP derives from its effectiveness as a means to appropriate (creating or strengthening the "natural" appropriability) differential gains resulting from competitive strategies focused on innovations and, thus, from its impact on these same strategies.

Interestingly, IPRs are a condition neither necessary nor sufficient for the appropriation of innovative effort profits. For this microeconomic goal, the degree of their effectiveness depends upon several factors, summarized in the next section. Their impacts over the competitive environment and the legal means to mitigate anticompetitive effects shall be discussed in Section 3.

2. Intellectual Property as a Means of Appropriability

The theoretical framework outlined above helps to adequately place the economic relevance of IPRs, arising from their effectiveness as a means of appropriability (creating or strengthening it), which turns them into a strategic instrument in the process of competition. The relevant question in evaluating this effectiveness is whether and under what circumstances an IPR is capable of influencing an innovation's imitation cost and time (so as to increase them), knowing that between total and zero effectiveness, there is a *continuum* of intermediate situations.

Several empirical studies show the need to consider market features (including institutional,[2] technological, and innovative agents' characteristics[3]) that privilege legal

---

2 Levin et al. (1987); Taylor and Silberston (1973); Mansfield et al. (1981); Mansfield (1986); Angelmar (1989); Bertin and Wyatt (1988); Ordover (1991); Hippel (1982); Lerner (2002); Branstetter (2005); Branstetter et al. (2005); Arora et al. (2005); Giuri et al. (2007). See Mello (1995, 2009) for a critical review of several studies that discuss the effects of intellectual property.

3 The approach applied herein may be seen as somewhat similar to that proposed by Burlamaqui (2008) – a *market-feature approach*, understood as "…an analytical perspective that takes into account institutional diversity, sector specificities, distinctive dynamics – in both their technological and industrial dimensions – as well as the regulatory and legal aspects of differentiated degrees of market power" (Burlamaqui 2008, 15). To discuss the factors that affect the possible effectiveness of intellectual property as a means of appropriability, see Mello (2009).

instruments in determined industries and not in others – because they represent the most effective means of appropriability, or because there are no alternatives.

Some of these conclusions are particularly interesting for our discussion on the competition effects of IPRs: (1) IP is a condition neither necessary nor sufficient for the appropriation of innovative effort results: it is not the only appropriability instrument used,[4] seldom is it the main one, and nor is it absolutely effective;[5] (2) the strategic use of IP varies a great deal among sectors, and not always is it used so as to eliminate competitors: even in industries where patents are not regarded as the most effective instrument, they may be used to other strategic ends (e.g., to measure the value of technological assets or propagate a dominant standard); (3) R&D cooperation or technology-transfer agreements seem to benefit from patent protection to the extent that patents provide parameters to evaluate the economic value of the technology under negotiation, as well as reduce the risks connected to opportunistic behavior. A strong protection may promote the development of technology markets, allowing for specialization gains.[6]

From another standpoint, Teece (1986) relates intellectual property to agents' strategies, in a conceptual-analytic framework useful for systematizing the perception of the (limited) importance of intellectual property in determining who profits from innovation, and thus of the (small and indirect) effects that legal protection has on the market power pursued by innovative agents. According to the author, the innovator's possibility of appropriating most innovation-deriving gains, vis-à-vis imitators, competitors and claimants, depends primarily upon three elements: the regime of appropriability, the dominant design stage and the access to complementary assets.

1. *The regime of appropriability* comprises two elements: the degree to which the knowledge involved in an innovation is tacit or codifiable and the effectiveness

---

4 Secret, a well-known name in the market (through trademarks or otherwise), pioneering in high-cumulativeness technologies, learning, scale and scope economies, the presence of tacit knowledge, among others, are elements that, depending on technical and economical conditions of the industry, are as effective (or even more so) as legal tools, in the sense of ensuring appropriability conditions. The possibility of privileging the employment of one or the other – or, as often done, combining them all – strongly depends on sector and/or technology characteristics.

5 Although IP protection encumbers imitation and reduces the possibility of bypassing the protected technology, empirical studies show that most patented innovations are imitated within a shorter period than the patent term.

6 Arora et al. (2005). An analysis on European patent data investigated how companies use their patents – why some are not commercially exploited, others are licensed and others are not even used – concluding that the most significant factor is the size of the company: small companies license a relatively greater share of their patents, while large companies keep a substantial part unused. The data also show that the greatest percentage of unused patents is found in the chemical and pharmaceutical industries, with patents being used as a means to block competitors (Giuri et al. 2007, 1.118). The concentration of licenses among small companies is consistent with the literature, which suggests that firms with limited downstream assets tend to exploit their inventions through technology transfer, a strategy that is facilitated by an effective patent-protection system. The role of patents on the foundation of new companies should also be noted (Giuri et al. 2007, 1.118).

of IP protection (including rulings and enforcement). The regime may be "tighter" or "weaker" depending on the degree to which these elements are present.

2. *The state of dominant design* refers to whether or not the innovation brings about a dominant standard or paradigm: an imitation is more likely to take over the market if the dominant standard is not the one adopted by the innovator.

3. *The innovator's access to complementary assets*: firms very often lack the assets and capabilities needed for the commercial exploitation of an innovation. If the firm does not control such assets, it risks losing a great share of innovation-derived gains to competitors who may otherwise have them. If these are specialized assets, granting access to the market may involve transaction costs, which justify the search for solutions to minimize such costs: contracts, vertical integration, strategic alliances, and so on.

By combining the regime of appropriability with the control of complementary assets, Teece identifies the best strategies for the firms involved – contracting or integrating – in an approach similar to that of Williamson (1985). In a *tight* appropriability regime, the innovative firm may specialize without worrying so much about complementary assets and vice versa.

Pisano (2006) explores other aspects of the relation between appropriability regimes and strategy, noting that this regime may be a *product* of the strategies. There is a causal inversion: in many cases, firms take their complementary asset positions as given and seek to influence the appropriability regime so as to optimize the use of their assets (Pisano 2006, 128). From this hypothesis, the author remarks that private interests may be associated with a weak appropriability regime, depending on the firm's complementary asset position; there are cases, for example, in which firms share their research results as a rent-seeking strategy. A weak appropriability regime may also be positive for imitators.

The focus of IPRs on the context of business strategies suggests, in brief, that a weak protection is not necessarily the best choice for public interest, nor is it necessarily negative for private interests. Teece's contribution allows us to conclude that a patent is neither a synonym for monopoly, nor necessarily conducive to monopoly, nor does it grant market power to its owner, which brings about clear implications when analyzing intellectual property and its effects on competition.

From the innovator's standpoint, the possibility of retaining gains from innovation depends upon several contextual conditions and strategic choices – institutional and structural aspects, market and technology features, decisions of the agents involved – and the weight that IPRs bestow on the final result is too restricted. Hence the need to analyze each case individually. A combination of these factors results in (variable) effects as to the market power of the intellectual property rights owners. A synthesis of these factors is presented in Table 5.1, which may be used as a reference for analyzing IP's restrictive effects, indicating whether it is able to create or strengthen the market power of the rights owners.

Table 5.1. Factors affecting the degree of intellectual property possible effectiveness as a means of appropriability

Technological characteristics	Factors affecting relative imitation cost and time	Ease to imitate once R&D results are known		(+)
		Knowledge nature	Tacit knowledge	(−)
			Codifiable knowledge	(+)
		Possibility of replication		(+)
		Possibility of inventing around	Low	(+)
			High	(−)
	Factors affecting the rights' lifetime	Possibility of improving or surpassing	Low	(+)
			High	(−)
Market characteristics	Related to the type of innovation	Preponderance of process innovations		(−)
		Preponderance of product innovations		(+)
	Related to the characteristics of the actual or potential competing firms	Competitors have equal or higher technological capabilities than the innovator		(−)
	Innovator's position regarding complementary assets	Innovator does not have access to complementary assets		(+)
		Innovator has access to specialized or cospecialized complementary assets		(−)
Legal and institutional factors	Related to normative statements of rights	Clear definition of rights		(+)
		Wide scope of rights		(+)
		Existence of limits as to exercising the rights		(−)
	Related to the enforcement of rights	Tight requirements for granting rights		(+)(−) *
		Tight requirements for invention's description		(−)
		Ease to prove counterfeiting		(+)
		High costs of litigation in courts		(−)

Notes:
(+) means that the IPRs may be a good appropriability means for the innovator;
(−) means that the IPRs are not an effective appropriability means for the innovator.
(+) and (−) may be regarded as opposite extremes between which there is a continuum of intermediate situations. The signs indicate the orientation, not the intensity, of the effects.
* The orientation of the influence is ambivalent: a higher rigorousness may hinder patent granting, but once obtained, it also hinders imitation, inventing around, improvement and surpassing the patented technology.
Source: Mello (2009).

In short, in some industries, patent protection is actually regarded as one of the main appropriability means; in these cases, the restrictive effects of protection may be significant (e.g., pharmaceutical industry), and vice versa: when innovation incent effects are small (implying little social benefit for the protection), the restrictive effects are also generally diluted. The protection of IPR, thus, carries ambiguous effects over firms, according to the agent's strategy and position in the competitive process: a high level, in theory, would render the innovator a positive effect; but it may also be negative for firms that adopt imitative strategies. Ambiguous as well are the social effects of protection: they may be positive, for stimulating innovation, or negative, if leading to excessive restraint to competition and the diffusion of innovations.

This ambiguity is important, for it implies that it is not possible to entirely dissociate IPR effects: the conditions that determine the intensity of the restrictive effects also determine the intensity of the incentive effects – and vice versa. These are inseparable and inherent effects of profit-appropriability protection in general and of the IP system in particular.

At this analytical level, there is no basis to corroborate the existence of a general relation between the degrees of intellectual-property protection and restraint of knowledge and the diffusion of technical progress. Nor is there a clear logical or theoretical prevalence of one or the other orientation of protection effects.

3. Intellectual Property and Antitrust

Conflict zones notwithstanding, the ultimate goals of both antitrust and IPR protection are convergent, and not contradictory: they both aim to promote competitive and innovative conditions in the economical environment capable of increasing its efficiency, thus producing positive effects for the social welfare, either through cost and price reduction and product-quality increase or the diffusion of new products, processes and organizational methods. For this purpose, as Schumpeter noted in his formulations on the importance of innovation-based competition, patent restraints and the like avoid the premature dissipation of gains and private incentives to innovation, which, in principle, represents an advantage: granting rights is an incentive *because* of the restraints implied.

Therefore, some level of competition restraint will always be intrinsic to the very purpose of the IPR institution. The key is discerning to what extent – and in exchange for what – such restraints should be accepted, which requires a policy tool that is capable of handling the ambivalent, inseparable and inherent effects of IP: incentive and restraint. Sensibly applying antitrust rules to such rights, instead of hampering the generation of intended incentives, will help to channel these rights toward a socially desirable procompetitive direction.

We believe that the analytical tools adopted in antitrust not only are applicable to IPRs, but are also consistent with the analysis that we have developed over its ambiguous effects, thus offering adequate means to identify the restrictive effects on competition that may arise from exercising such rights. There are three main reasons underpinning this compatibility:

1. First, the antitrust approach only allows questioning IPRs insofar as they generate market power and competition restraints. In other words, one should not assume that the effects are always restrictive and contrary to social interests, but they may become so.
2. Second, the antitrust law is applied according to the anticompetitive effects of any kind of practice. This shifts the analytical focus to the market conditions in which the exercise

of market power is more likely, allowing all economic, technological and institutional aspects that affect the protection effectiveness to be incorporated into the analysis.

3. Finally, for acknowledging that certain conducts or competition-restricting mergers may also generate efficiency gains that compensate for their negative effects, the antitrust analytical tools ensure that they are able to handle the aforementioned ambiguous effects of intellectual property. Each case is pondered individually to verify which effect prevails, in order to object only to those situations that generate net anticompetitive effects.

In other words, it is commonly said that the antitrust analytical focus is on how market power is conquered and maintained by agents. Market power may be acquired and maintained through the competitive capacity of its owner, but may also be acquired through anticompetitive means (e.g., cartels) and/or maintained through anticompetitive means (by imposing restrictive conditions on the competition).

Almost every antitrust analysis revolves around distinguishing these two situations, which implies the development of the notions of *use* and *abuse* of dominant position, as well as an analytical method capable of handling the aforementioned ambiguities of the effects of competition-restricting practices (we here refer to the rule of reason – developed by US jurisprudence).

The idea that it is possible to distinguish the "normal" exercise of a dominant position/market power (its socially acceptable *use*) from the abusive exercise of such a position explains why antitrust analysis focuses rather on the effects that actions/conducts exert on competition, for it is the effects, and not conducts as such, that make the (abusive) use of a dominant position illegal. Complementarily, the US rule of reason approach has allowed the development of analytical methods to evaluate net effects, acknowledging that some competition-restricting practices may as well generate efficiency gains that counterbalance the restraints.

The antitrust field has reached a consensus establishing that mergers or conducts should not be forbidden when their incidental restrictive effects are duly compensated by the efficiency generated; otherwise, applying the law would cause markets to be inefficient, delivering results contrary to social interests. Consequently, the possible positive effects of IP protection – as a tool of appropriability, incentive to technological development, productivity boost, transaction costs reduction, and so forth – may be explicitly considered in an antitrust analysis. This is a fundamental aspect that ultimately makes the antitrust approach consistent with the Schumpeterian view outlined before. In general, both from a legal and an economic antitrust perspective, the acquisition of monopolistic positions is not per se illegal, as long as acquired and maintained through the competitive process – that is, when an agent earnestly seeks to be more efficient than its competitors.[7] This implies acknowledging that market

---

7 The Brazilian Law, for instance, explicitly states that "a conquista de mercado resultante de processo natural fundado na maior eficiência de agente econômico em relação a seus competidores." [the achievement of market control as a result of competitive efficiency does not entail the occurrence of an illicit action] (Law 8884/94, Art. 20, § 1).

power is often generated by the very process of competition, which does not constitute a competition offense.

Applying this approach with normative purposes depends upon national legislations. Nonetheless, many countries already have it outlined in their law, including Brazil. Both in the United States and Europe, the jurisprudence tends to analyze the effects of the allegedly anticompetitive practices without establishing a predefined set of rules (Cueva 2009, 125). As we shall see, US and European guidelines are very clear on this matter.

In brief, we may state that the antitrust policy is sufficiently adequate to handle the complexity, diversity and ambivalence of IPR effects and is able to bypass, with great advantage over alternative policies, the "one-size-fits-all" problem, frequently mentioned by scholars of the field.[8]

This is not to say that such analysis is free of operational problems. The greater difficulty is related to the possibility of comparing and balancing positive and negative effects, since these effects are perceptible on different levels of analysis:[9] while restrictive aspects of intellectual property are directly associated with its exercise in some concrete case, social gains – arising from greater market efficiency – on the other hand, are sometimes generic, being regarded as a result of the institution's own existence rather than an effect of a specific conduct. This crucial matter represents a great analytical challenge, because it makes pondering net efficiency effects much more complex (for most situations in which IPR protection is capable of restraining competition) than typical situations in the antitrust field.

However, our purpose here is not to go further into that matter, but to discuss and present evidences that this kind of analysis is indeed adequate and has been successfully applied in concrete cases by antitrust authorities from several countries, including Brazil.

We must also warn that our argument on the consistence of antitrust analytical tools with the Schumpeterian approach on competition implies that we find these tools adequate – and sufficient – to handle the economic (market) effects of IP; which is not to say that there are no other socially relevant aspects. Public-health matters, for instance, may generate problems that would not be considered anticompetitive from an antitrust standpoint, but still justify types of intervention from public policies other than the anticompetitive concerns. Nonetheless, these incidental problems are specific, so they do not admit generalizations over the social effects of IP protection.

---

8 Burlamaqui, for example, defends a system where the degree of protection – the extension and duration of IPRs – is subject to a different treatment according to the sector or technology, or even to the R&D expenditure of the firm. The author acknowledges that there should be operational and political difficulties in instituting such a system, starting with the choice of technologies or groups that should receive more or less protection, and with the possibility of different groups lobbying for their own interests (Burlamaqui 2008, 20–21).

9 Besides requiring different analytical tools to comparatively measure such effects, which is rarely made satisfactorily.

In other words, if on one hand competition policy does not have the monopoly of public interest, on the other, problems of another nature do not authorize generalizations over the effects of IP protection, and, according to our argument, the economic effects of IP – which almost always involve impacts on the market – should be handled from the perspective, and with the tools, of antitrust analysis.

In the next section, we will discuss the intersecting points – and differences – between these antitrust fundamentals on the abuse of dominant position and the notion of misuse of rights in the context of intellectual property.

3.1. Misuse of IP rights and competition

The misuse of IPRs may be characterized both as a *purpose deviation* and a *power excess*. In both hypotheses, the abuse may (but not necessarily *will*) lead to anticompetitive effects and allow for the application of antitrust remedies (exclusively or cumulatively).[10]

Abuse as a power excess is characterized by the attempt to exercise exclusive powers beyond the scope of the granted right.

In US jurisprudence, for example, this patent misuse (patent-misuse doctrine) is of the exclusivity extension kind,[11] and is characterized by the patent-rights owner's attempt to extend its exclusivity powers beyond the borders of the right (Barbosa 2005, 61). It is typified by the exercise of actions not covered by the patent's scope, in both technical and legal terms. The first corresponds to the technological content, being limited by the extent of the claims listed in the application. As for the legal aspect, limitations depend upon the normative definition of the exclusivity rights granted to the patent owner – using, selling, licensing, and so on[12] (Carvalho 1994, 61).

In counterfeit lawsuits, this notion of misuse can be used as an affirmative defense by an alleged infringer – if the claims of the rights owner are beyond the scope of granted rights, the imitator's right of use is acknowledged (Carvalho 1994, 61).

---

10 The works of Carvalho (1994) and Barbosa (2005) analyze different notions of abuse that may be applied to IPRs and their relations with abuse of economic power.

11 Which originated in the case *Morton Salt Co. v. Suppiger Co.*, ruled by the Supreme Court in 1942 (Hoerner 2002, 670). In the United States, proving the abuse does not nullify the right, but while an abusive practice remains in force, there is a temporary nonopposability: patent rights cannot be opposed against third parties, implying that anyone charged with a patent violation may use the abuse in his defense, regardless of whether the abusive practice has actually caused him any harm (Carvalho 1994, 46–7).

12 This notion is similar to the one identified by Barbosa as an *excess of power*: the exercise of the right beyond legal power limits – beyond the scope of protection (Barbosa 2005, 64); when characterizing the excess of power, the extension refers to the exclusive powers that the right grants to the owner. Carvalho identifies yet another meaning for the criterion in the ambit of patents, which stems from the economic functions that patents should fulfill. For him, the ambit of patents "…confines the owner's exercise of rights to the limits bounded by law, whereas such limits are defined by the economic functions that the law intends to perform" (Carvalho 1994, 61 – free translation). This meaning is closer to the notion of abuse as a purpose deviation, to be discussed soon.

Since it represents a restraint that the legal system does not authorize, this abuse hypothesis may be characterized irrespective of the rights owner's display of market power or any other anticompetitive effect in relevant markets. The very conduct of the rights owner – extending granted powers – could be considered illegal regardless *of its* effects, once the grounds for repressing this kind of conduct may not be the protection of competition.[13]

However, this kind of misuse may also cause anticompetitive effects, thus becoming – cumulatively – subject to antitrust law repression. In this case, proving the attempt to unduly extend exclusive rights may even suffice to apply the legal consequences of abuse – make a patent unenforceable – regardless of any discussion of anticompetitive effects in relevant markets; nonetheless, legal consequences in the antitrust sphere should, at least in theory, depend upon these analysis items.

This seems to be the orientation underlying a great number of US court rulings, affirming that monopoly-extending practices in general may violate the antitrust law, even though the application of the patent-misuse doctrine does not require proof of damage to competition (it is illegal per se).[14] Hoerner (2002), however, notes that this inclination has been altered by recent rulings of the Federal Circuit, which has demanded proof of anticompetitive effects in order to invoke the patent-misuse doctrine. To the author, such decisions point towards a tendency terminating with abuse of the monopoly-extension kind, so that it only survives when fitting antitrust violation requirements.

Another way to characterize misuse consists in regarding it as a *social purpose deviation* from a law-granted right, distinguishing misuse from an illegal action or fraud. The exercise of a property right within law-bounded limits may be found abusive if it perverts the economic and social purposes upon which the institution of such a right was founded.

In this case, repressing abusive acts is the cornerstone of the search for a solution of the conflict between individual and diffuse interests, in favor of the latter, that is, of society in general, to whom preserving the purpose grounding such a right is interesting (Scisinio 1998, 60). The conflict may also be seen from the standpoint of means and ends relationship, in the terms of Carvalho (1994, 48) – "...when the means (patent exclusivity rights defined by law) is used for another end...different from that which it was created for" [free translation].

Therefore, discussing abuse requires clarifying the purpose of IPRs from a social point of view, which is no simple task. The literature usually points towards different

---

13 For Carvalho (1994), regarding this as abuse would even be improper, for technical or legal criteria only indicate if the patent owner acted within or outside the power sphere granted by law (legal boundaries of law-granted rights); if the actions were carried beyond such a sphere, then the owner would not have exclusive rights, consequently there would be no abuse of rights.

14 For instance: "although an antitrust violation involving a patent comes clearly within the patent-misuse doctrine, a showing of such violation and actual lessening of competition is not required" – Northern Discrict of California, *Sonobond Corp. v. Uthe Tech., Inc., 314 F. Supp. 878, 880 (N.D. Cal. 1970)* – (in Hoerner 2002, 672).

reasons for society to institute a property title over an immaterial object and warrant the exclusive use of this object – from a generic justification highlighting the economic importance of a good and clear definition of property rights to very specific functions of the patent system: stimulating the publication of the knowledge generated by the innovator, compensating research investments or stimulating future investments, and so forth. For each of these possible purposes, there is a different notion of misuse according to the characterization of the deviation, but almost all of them involve operational difficulties.

If the purpose of the right is defined as the incentive to private innovative activity, a deviation would be the use of the right to restrain the continuity of the very innovative activity being stimulated – either because the owner of a patent ceases to prosecute it or precludes others from doing so. Still, as the incentive effect of a patent depends essentially upon restricting the diffusion of the innovation that originated it, this restrictive effect is inherent; therefore, it is necessary to define to what degree restraint is tolerable, and beyond which it should be repressed.

If the purpose is the publication of the protected innovation, for example, a deviation would be an insufficient description of the invention in the patent application. If it is to compensate for the investment in R&D, the establishment of deviation would require measuring these expenses and estimating the rate of return on investment.

Carvalho proposes considering that the purpose of establishing IPRs is the reduction of transaction costs – which would comprise the costs of valuating the object of an innovation and the enforcement of rights. Instituting the exclusive use of an innovation would allow society to measure the value of inventions more precisely than if they were kept in secret or financed by public resources; this patent function is possible exactly because (and when) inventions are subjected to the competitive forces of the market (Carvalho 1994, 51). The conduct of a patent owner who is able to prevent the invention from being exposed to the market, thus disregarding the measurement function, would be considered deviant or abusive: "As patents play their social role because they expose inventions to the effects of the market's competitive forces, the abuse consists in eliminating such forces (or attempting to do so) so as to increase the value of the patented inventions (thus causing inaccurate measurement)" (Carvalho 1994, 79 – free translation). From this perspective, patent misuse is equivalent to an action with anticompetitive effects, from the antitrust point of view.

3.2. Misuse in the antitrust sphere

The notions of "purpose deviation" and "conflict between individual and collective interests" are applied by Ferraz Jr to the analysis of misuse of economic power, characterized as a seemingly legal act which actually violates the economic purpose of the social institution of the market (Ferraz 1995, 24). Such a purpose, on a more abstract level, may be taken as the ideal welfare potentially generated by the adequate operation of competition mechanisms. In this sense, the behavior of the economic power controller implies the duty to direct its exercise towards the production of the "purposes ideally presumed by law," which is more concretely translated in the duty of not creating restraints to the competitive process (Schuartz 1998).

There is, however, a significant difference between the concepts of misuse of *rights* and of *economic power*, for one, the latter does not constitute a property right – someone does not have the *right* to exercise economic power. First and foremost, it is a situation indeed allowed "…to the extent that it is not forbidden (but not positively allowed, that is, authorized by explicitly expressed rules)" (Ferraz 1995, 24 – free translation).

There are also differences as to protected interests, since the misuse of rights contemplates hypotheses that may refer uniquely to the relations between private agents, protecting their respective interests. Additionally, even if the misuse of an IPR refers to a social interest (from the standpoint of purpose deviation), it may be one other than competition.[15]

As for the notion of misuse of economic power, it is found within the scope of antitrust policy, whose protected interest is, by definition, a diffuse interest. An action is abusive because it generates net anticompetitive effects, regardless of whether such an act affects interests or causes private damages. In order to evaluate these effects, it is necessary to analyze the conditions of the market, for which the agent's hold of market power is a logical precondition.

Even the misuse of economic power through IPR does not completely absorb the concept of abuse of IPR. The former may comprise hypotheses that are also characterized as abuse of rights, but it is not completely comprehended by the latter – that is, the misuse of rights does not necessarily imply the misuse of economic power through intellectual property, since: (1) the rights do not necessarily ensure market power and (2) even if they generate market power, the exercise of rights may not damage the competitive process.

In short, there might be a misuse of economic power without the characterization of antitrust infringement, because purpose deviation or the attempt to unduly extend a right may affect spheres other than competition and vice versa – there may be an antitrust infringement without a misuse of IPRs. They are two distinct sets with a possible intersection.

The hypothesis that there might be a misuse of economic power through patents, for instance, without a corresponding misuse of rights, brings to light the compatibility between the goals of the two legal systems, since the power of restraint intrinsic to the exercise of a patent right may always be regarded as suspiciously anticompetitive from the antitrust standpoint. After all, could there be some sort of restraint to competition that should be tolerated simply for the fact that it is the result of an IPR?

---

15 In a case of public health interest, for example, in spite of competition (and the nonapplicability of antitrust analysis parameters – market power is not characterized, etc.), there might a case of use contrary to the social purpose of the right that justifies an intervention, depending on the legal system in force (i.e., these possibilities may be contemplated depending on legal and political decisions that define cases in which the use of intellectual property rights conflicts with social interests).

In other words, if the exercise of a patent right – without any sort of misuse and without being an attempt to extend monopoly – causes competition restraints, ascertained in accordance with antitrust standards, would the existence of rights be enough of a condition to withdraw illicitness from the antitrust scope? Should patents be considered in some way exempt from the antitrust law application?

Like any right – be it a property or obligational right, or a legally guaranteed freedom – the exercise of an IPR is subject to the restraints imposed by several regulations that condition private activity in general, and business in particular, including restraints imposed by antitrust law, with a view to forbidding anticompetitive practices.

It is rather common that the application of antitrust law ends up restricting a private freedom – for instance, of a company to freely dispose of its assets (a well-known example is that of essential facilities). Therefore, incidental antitrust restraints to the exercise of IPRs cannot be distinguished, in their core, from restraints imposed on any other rights or legally warranted freedoms. As in any case, if sensibly applied, they do not imply any conflict or any legal or administrative deadlock.

On the other hand, we must not forget that IPRs, particularly patents, are institutions created with the specific purpose of preventing imitation, which always restricts, at some level, competition – one of the aspects intrinsic to their economic function, discussed earlier. Hence, the necessity to admit that the restrictive effect is natural to the essential elements of exclusive rights, and the conclusion that such restrictive aspect could never be considered illegal per se. The antitrust law should challenge only those exercises of rights that produce more anticompetitive effects than what is reasonable, or than the necessary extent to achieve their goals, or than those intrinsic to the exercise of exclusivity. It may be hard to define such a limit in a practicable way, but the European and US jurisprudences have been long dedicated to establishing criteria for the application of antitrust sanctions to IPRs.

But the reasons for tolerating restrictive practices may be the same which antitrust analysis admits as compensatory – the efficiencies or other social gains generated by the same restrictive practices, whether deriving from IPRs or not. In this sense, intellectual property could be treated as any other power of disposition and control, right or freedom that may be exercised anticompetitively, subject to being considered illicit under antitrust law.

3.3. The guidelines to analyze IPR licensing in the United States and in Europe and some trends in jurisprudence

In the United States, the principles put forward by the "Antitrust Guidelines for the Licensing of I.P." (FTC/DOJ, US, 1995)[16] coincide essentially with the propositions we made before. Thus, as to the basic principles: "The intellectual property laws and the antitrust laws share the common purpose of promoting innovation and enhancing consumer welfare" (2).

---

16 Hereinafter *Guidelines*. References to pages of this document are included parenthetically in the text.

The three general principles that, according to the *Guidelines*, guide their orientation are also worth citing:

1. For the purpose of antitrust analysis, the Agencies [FTC and DOJ] regard intellectual property as being essentially comparable to any other form of property;
2. The Agencies do not presume that intellectual property creates market power in the antitrust context; and
3. The Agencies recognize that intellectual property licensing allows firms to combine complementary factors of production and is generally procompetitive. (2)

Next, the text presents a few details of the application of these principles. As they carry important implications for the Brazilian context, we have summarized some comments (3) developed by the *Guidelines* on the principle number 1:

a. "The Agencies apply the same general antitrust principles to conduct involving intellectual property that they apply to conduct involving any other form of tangible or intangible property." Some distinctive characteristics of these conducts, as misappropriation, "...can be taken into account by standard antitrust analysis ... and do not require the application of fundamentally different principles."
b. "Although there are clear and important differences in the purpose, extent, and duration of protection provided under the intellectual property regimes... the governing antitrust principles are the same. Antitrust analysis takes [these differences] into account in evaluating the specific market circumstances in which transactions occur, just as it does with other particular market circumstances."
c. "Intellectual property law bestows on the owners of intellectual property certain rights to exclude others...[which] are similar to the rights enjoyed by owners of other forms of private property. As with other forms of private property, certain types of conduct with respect to intellectual property may have anticompetitive effects against which the antitrust laws can and do protect. Intellectual property is thus neither particularly free from scrutiny under the antitrust laws, nor particularly suspect under them."

Most of what follows describes the possible restraints associated with IPR licensing and their compliance with antitrust laws, wherein the vast majority of cases may be evaluated under the rule of reason (6–21). As our approach here is general, it suffices to add that the *Guidelines* expressly admit – in accordance with the comments above, with regard to the uniformity of criteria for different types of property – that restraints associated with intellectual property with possible anticompetitive effects may be considered as

reasonably necessary to achieve procompetitive efficiencies. If the restraint is reasonably necessary, the Agencies will balance the procompetitive efficiencies and the anticompetitive effects to determine the probable net effect on competition in each relevant market. (21)

In the same sense, it may also be interesting to consider the stances of R. Gilbert,[17] one of the authors of these *Guidelines*, in his statement to the US government's Antitrust Modernization Commission. The author dedicates most of his testimony to the most innovative and state-of-the-art technology sectors, but some core aspects of his arguments refer to the general relation between innovative activity and corresponding IPRs, irrespective of the corresponding sector's being particularly innovative or not.

The first basic stance worth mentioning is that antitrust policy must take dynamic competition into account – understood as the development of new products and the improvement of existing ones that may have more impact on consumers' welfare than static competition over prices – but without having to "rewrite antitrust laws."

> Although the new economy has a number of distinct characteristics that should be taken into account…antitrust enforcement is sufficiently flexible to account for these features and preserve competition when it benefits consumers. (1)

This stance is essentially aligned with the principles established in the *Guidelines* – which is no surprise, since the deponent is one of its authors (2), and, in his opinions, "the policies described [there] have held up well since their publication ten years ago" (3).

> The antitrust laws are not limited to static economic efficiency concerns and nothing prevents their application to dynamic industries. The courts have clearly noted that market dominance attained through innovation is not a violation of the antitrust laws. (4)

Specifically with regard to the relation between antitrust regulations and IPRs, the author is as explicit as the *Guidelines*: although "tensions sometimes exist between the antitrust laws, which promote competition, and intellectual property laws, which grant exclusive property rights, the antitrust laws and the courts recognize that consumers benefit from conduct and arrangements that promote innovation" (4). To exemplify, he quotes an absolutely explicit decision by the Federal Courts of Appeal in evaluating the potential conflict between antitrust and intellectual property laws:

> …the two bodies of law are actually complementary, as both are aimed at encouraging innovation, industry and competition.[18]

In his testimony, the author also lingers on a series of specific technical aspects of the antitrust-IPR interface. However, in spite of the acknowledged convergence of principles and compatibility of analytical tools, the author highlights some specificities of the antitrust law application in the case of innovation-driven industries. The author

---

17 "New Antiturst Laws for the 'New Economy'?" Testimony before the Antitrust Modernization Commission. Washington DC. November 8, 2005. Available at http://www.amc.gov/commission_hearings/pdf/Statement_Gilbert.pdf

18 *Atari Games v. Nintendo*, 897, 1990.

makes a somewhat detailed reference to the fact that the DOJ and the FTC have challenged mergers over the last few years, manifesting their concern with possible adverse innovation effects, when the sectors and firms at stake are innovation-driven (expressed, for example, in a large proportion of R&D expenditure to sales). He shows that, between 2000 and 2003, the DOJ and FTC together challenged 38 percent of the mergers alleging concerns over the possible innovative effort decrease of the merged companies; this percentage had been only 3 percent in the period of 1990–1994 and 17.5 percent in 1995–1999 (19).

In 2004, the European Community established the "Guidelines on the application of Article 81 of the EC Treaty to technology transfer agreements" (2004/C 101/02), which, similar to the American *Guidelines*, explicitly assume that IPRs do not, per se, confer market power or create problems for the competitive process. Therefore, technology transfer agreements involving IPRs should be analyzed in light of their effects (a somewhat similar approach to the US rule of reason):

> The assessment of whether a license agreement restricts competition must be made within the actual context in which competition would occur in the absence of the agreement with its alleged restrictions. In making this assessment it is necessary to take account of the likely impact of the agreement on inter-technology competition (i.e., competition between undertakings using competing technologies) and on intra-technology competition (i.e., competition between undertakings using the same technology). (*Guidelines*, item 11, in Cueva 2009, 126)

The European guidelines even admit that not only may licensing give rise to efficiency gains, they indeed often do so:

> Most license agreements do not restrict competition and create pro-competitive efficiencies. Indeed, licensing as such is pro-competitive as it leads to dissemination of technology and promotes innovation. In addition, even license agreements that do restrict competition may often give rise to pro-competitive efficiencies, which must be considered under Article 81(3) and balanced against the negative effects on competition. (*Guidelines*, item 9, in Cueva 2009, 125)

The analysis made by Cueva (2009) shows that there is a clear convergence between the stances of the US and EU jurisprudences, besides their respective guidelines. Considerations over companies' innovative activity in the antitrust context are particularly important, as is evidenced by the concern over restrictive effects of agreements (they should not excessively restrain research and innovation activities of licensees and competitors) as well as by the possible compensating efficiencies. In our opinion, it demonstrates that antitrust analytical tools have been considered so plastic and flexible that they may be adapted to peculiar concerns of the IP system – in which the incentive of technological innovation plays a leading role.

A few examples are shown here:

- In the United States, there are simplified procedures to create patent pools, considering that they may be procompetitive because they avoid the obstruction of certain technological areas, dilute innovative activity risks, and make it more likely for the inventor to receive a share of the royalties (Cueva 2009, 126).
- Also in the United States, a patent quality assessment and a challenge of obvious, fragile or invalid patents are admitted:[19] In a recent case, the US Supreme Court ruled that patents protecting inventions obtained through the combination of preexisting elements should be made void "sob pena de se permitir impacto substancial sobre os custos das empresas e sobre a inovação tecnológica" (under the penalty of allowing substantial impact on business costs and on technological innovation) (Cueva 2009, 127).
- The European Commission has discussed the criteria by which refusing to license an IPR-protected product/service should be deemed unjustifiable (mainly due to the Microsoft case), admitting that such a refusal is not an abuse of a dominant position per se, unless under the following circumstances: (1) the product/service in point is indispensable for the exercise of an activity in a derived market; (2) the refusal is capable of excluding all effective competition from the derived market; (3) the refusal hinders the issuing of a new product with a potential demand (Cueva 2009, 130).
- The practice known as "evergreening" – which seeks to extend for as long as possible the period of patent protection – has also been discussed, and criticized, in Europe, as in the attempts to block the entry of generic medicines into the market: in the AstraZeneca case (still under appeal) the court considered abusive the practice of making inaccurate statements to obtain additional protection, to which the company was aware of not being entitled, for a patented medicine. In Cueva's analysis, "se a conduta exclusionária não se funda na concorrência quanto ao mérito – ou seja, se não cria eficiências e se presta, antes, a criar barreiras à concorrência – presume-se que é abusiva" (if the content of the exclusionary conduct is not based upon competition – that is, if instead of efficiencies, it attempts to block competition – it is presumed abusive) (2009, 131).

4. Intellectual Property and Antitrust Under Brazilian Law

IPRs – in several legal systems and also in the international system of the Paris Convention and TRIPS agreement[20] – may suffer limitations; legally admissible reasons to do so are varied. Competition concerns may be one of them, but they certainly are not the only one.

---

19 *KSR v. Teleflex* (US 550, 2007); *MedImmune, Inc. v. Genentech, Inc.* (US 549, 2007); *eBay. Inc. v. MercExchange LLC* (US 547, 2006), in Cueva (2009, 127).

20 The Paris Convention for the Protection of Industrial Property, in the version of Stockholm, 1967; Agreement on Trade-Related Aspects of Intellectual Property Rights, negotiated at the Uruguay Round of multilateral commercial negotiations of GATT (TRIPs Agreement), 1994.

Internationally, the treatment dispensed to these limits has evolved so as to decrease the degree of national legislations autonomy in order to establish restraints, such as demanding that the object of the patent should be manufactured locally or excluding certain areas from legal protection. On the contrary, harmonizing tended to strengthen the rights, extending protection to new areas (such as biotechnology, integrated circuits, etc.), increasing the reach of exclusive rights and terminating with restraints used for protectionist and nationalist purposes (Mello 1995).

Even so, international treaties unanimously acknowledge the possibility of restraints due to abuse of rights or damage threats to the process of competition. The Paris Convention allows contracting states to adopt laws that contemplate granting compulsory licenses to "prevent the abuses which might result from the exercise of the exclusive rights conferred by the patent, for example" and uses as an example the traditional anticompetitive practice of production restraint – failure to work (Paris Convention, Art. 5, A.2).

The TRIPs agreement narrowed the possibilities for national legislations to contemplate patent compulsory licensing, but allows it in cases of anticompetitive practices, determined after administrative or judicial process (Art. 31, k). In the same sense, it allows the control of licensing conditions that may "constitute an abuse of intellectual property rights having an adverse effect on competition in the relevant market," which allows measures to prevent competition-restraining clauses in license agreements, such as "exclusive grant-back conditions, conditions preventing challenges to validity and coercive package licensing" (Art. 40, 1 and 2).

Brazilian law provisions that somehow limit the exercise of intellectual rights contemplate restraints to the free exercise of rights, as well as possibilities of licensing somewhat directly related to controlling and preventing anticompetitive practices. We will see how these limits are contemplated in the law of patents and trademarks (Law 9279/96) and protection of plant varieties (Law 9456/97) so that, afterwards, we may analyze the possibilities of abusive situations applying the concepts of abuse discussed in the previous section.

4.1. Voluntary and compulsory licensing in Law 9279/96

Law 9279/96 (Lei de Propriedade Industrial – LPI / Industrial Property Law) contemplates the grant of patents on invention and utility models (new shapes of tools or objects with utilitarian or commercial result), the registration of industrial designs and the registration of trademarks. Patents and registrations may be the object of assignment (ownership transfer) or license agreements, both subject to registration by the Instituto Nacional de Propriedade Industrial – INPI (National Industrial Property Institute), not a validity requirement, but rather an instrument to ensure that such actions will be effective in relation to third parties.

Additions made to inventions/models that are the subject matter of licensed patents will be owned by whoever has created them, while the other party has the first right to license such improvements, which may even be the subject matter of a new patent (Art. 63).

Table 5.2. Hypotheses of patent compulsory licensing and forfeiture in Law 9279

	Characterization of the hypothesis	Conditions
a	Abusive exercise of rights (Art. 68, caput), duly proven (Art. 73, § 2)	Depends upon request from a person with legitimate interest and technical and economical capabilities for the exploitation (Art. 68, § 2)
b	Abuse of economic power *through patents*, as per previous administrative or judicial ruling (Art. 68, caput), duly proven (Art. 73, § 2)	Depends upon request from a person with legitimate interest and technical and economical capabilities for the exploitation (Art. 68, § 2) Requires an administrative ruling by the antitrust office (CADE)
c	Failure to exploit the subject matter in Brazilian territory (failure to manufacture the product or employ the process), except in cases of: – Economic impossibility (Art. 68, §1, I) – Failure to use due to *legitimate reasons* or *legal obstacle* (Art. 69) – Proof that serious and effective preparations for exploitation have been made (Art. 69)	Depends upon request from a person with legitimate interest and technical and economical capabilities for the exploitation (Art. 68, § 2) May only be requested after 3 years from the patent granting (Art. 68, § 5)
d	Commercialization that does not satisfy the needs of the market (Art. 68, §1, II)	Depends upon request from a person with legitimate interest and technical and economical capabilities for the exploitation (Art. 68, § 2) May only be requested after 3 years from the patent granting (Art. 68, § 5)
e	Dependent patents that constitute substantial progress in relation to the original one (Art. 70)	Depends upon a request from an interested party, owner of the dependent patent
f	National emergency or public interest, so declared in a statement from the Presidency of the country, as long as the patent holder does not meet these needs (Art. 71)	May be granted *ex officio* (regardless of a request from an interested party)
g	Forfeiture (Art. 80), which is equivalent to the termination of the right, so that its subject matter falls into public domain	Depends on a compulsory license issued at least two years before on grounds of abuse or disuse, insofar as that period has not been sufficient to remedy the problems that led to the license issuing in the first place May be granted *ex officio* or at the request from an interested party

In trademark licensing, the licensor retains the right to exercise effective control over the specifications, nature and quality of the respective products/services identified by it (Art. 139).[21] Besides voluntary licenses, the Brazilian law also contemplates hypotheses of nonexclusive compulsory patent licensing, as summarized in the Table 5.2.

In the first five cases, the licensor's exploitation of the subject matter should be directed towards the internal market (Art. 68, § 2).

At the caput of article 68, the law seems to admit two distinct hypotheses for compulsory licensing: that of abusive exercise of patent right and that of misuse of economic power through patent. The first contemplates situations of abuse of rights that do not presume the existence of a dominant position, as per antitrust standards: these are abuses of patent rights that do not impair competition, being irrelevant from the antitrust standpoint. On the other hand, the second hypothesis necessarily presumes a dominant position (or economic power), whose exercise through the use of a patent is abusive.

Hypotheses *b* (expressly) and *d* (implicitly) may be related to antitrust; Law 9279 assigns the competence to rule over these cases to INPI, but demands proof of the misuse of economic power (*b*) through an administrative or judicial ruling (Art. 68, caput). Thus, we may infer that before an application for a compulsory license may be submitted, there must have been either a lawsuit or an administrative proceeding by Conselho Administrativo de Defesa Econômica (Administrative Council for Economic Defense, Brazil) (CADE), the office in charge of analyzing such matters. On the other hand, compulsory licensing based on cases of commercialization that does not satisfy the needs of the market – *c* (Art. 68, § 1, II) – may also characterize a traditional anticompetitive practice (refusal to sell, unjustified restraint of production), but apparently, for this hypothesis, no previous administrative rulings are demanded.

One should also notice that hypothesis *c* (failure to exploit in Brazilian territory) does not have any relation with antitrust, since the concerns and criteria therein applied do not characterize anticompetitive effects. Therefore, they are not relevant arguments for an antitrust procedure against a conduct.

4.2. Licensing in the plant variety protection system

The Plant Variety Protection Certificate (or breeder's rights) is a title created by Law 9456/97 (Lei de Proteção a Cultivares – LPC / Plant Variety Protection Law) aiming

---

21 It is worth mentioning that the previous regulation of technology licensing was far stricter as to the possible content of agreements, forbidding restraints to commercialization and exportation of licensed products, as well as importation of inputs used in their manufacture (Law 5772/71, Art. 29, § 2). The law also assigned to INPI the competence to take measures to speed up and regulate technology transfer and establish better grounds for negotiations and use of patents, aiming at the economic development of the country (Law 5648/70). Nevertheless, this system was not designed as a tool of competition defense, so it did not control anticompetitive practices, for it was actually designed to protect national companies from foreign technology suppliers, in an attempt to help them relinquish any kind of foreign aid as quickly as possible. Currently, INPI can no longer interfere in the content of contracts, nor can it assess possible competition-restricting practices involving technology transfer agreements (patented, registered or otherwise).

at the protection of new plant varieties obtained through genetic improvement.[22] The system contemplates exclusivity over commercial breeding only, so that seeds may be multiplied for personal use with neither the rights owner's permission nor the payment of royalties; it is possible to freely use protected plant varieties for purposes of research and as original source of new varieties (free access principle).[23]

Rights arising from the Plant Variety Protection Certificate, like the others, may as well be assigned or licensed (Art. 23 of Law 9456/97), and are also subject to a declaration of compulsory license or restricted public use. Compulsory licensing depends upon a request from an interested party who is able to prove both having the technical and financial capability to exploit and breed the protected variety and having tried, unsuccessfully, to obtain a voluntary license from the rights owner. The law does not establish a clear list of reasons for its application, but one may infer that they would be those which characterize an unjustified restraint to competition (Art. 28, sole paragraph), which encompasses situations in which the rights owner unduly hinders the maintenance of a regular supply, as described in Article 28, I.

The mentioned restraints to competition must be assessed on the basis of Article 21 of Law 8884/94 (Law 9456/97, Art. 28, sole paragraph), which indicates that restrictive conducts involving IPRs of plant varieties are the same as those of the antitrust law, for the criteria used to analyze them are the same. Article 31 of Law 9456/97 determines that the Ministry of Agriculture should receive the requests for compulsory licenses, adding its own expert opinion to each case and forwarding it to CADE for ruling.

A compulsory license may only be requested after three years have elapsed since the protection certificate was granted, except in cases of abuse of economic power (Art. 35); this article may lead us to believe that there are other hypotheses for compulsory licensing besides abuse of economic power, although the law fails to clarify the matter.

Article 34 refers to Law 9279/96, stating that its provisions should be implemented, where applicable, to the compulsory licensing of protection certificates. However, it is not clear whether such application refers only to the licensing procedures or to the patent law's hypotheses for compulsory license granting. As Barbosa (1998) sees it, this article implies that in addition to abuse of economic power, the hypotheses for granting patent-compulsory licenses are also contemplated, which are: failure to exploit in Brazilian territory and patent dependency.[24]

---

22 Protection usually expires after 15 years, or 18 years for vines and trees. To be protected, the variety must fulfill the requisites of *distinctness* (the variety must differ from others in one or more relevant characteristics), homogeneity (individuals from a variety must present minimally uniform features) and stability (maintenance of genetic features throughout successive generations). Additionally, the noncommercialization in national territory is required until the date of the application's filing (or even a year before), or in any other territory for more than 4 years (or 6 years for vines and trees).

23 These features turn this kind of protection more procompetitive in principle than the patent system.

24 In the Patent Law, situations of national emergency or public interest that compel for compulsory licensing are contemplated by the Plant Variety Protection Law as hypotheses for the declaration of restricted public use, which will be discussed soon.

The dependent patent is similar, in the field of plant protection, to the essentially derived variety,[25] whose commercial exploitation is conditioned on an authorization from the owner of rights over the plant that originated it (Art. 10, § 2, II). Such authorization is also needed when the production of a variety on a commercial scale requires the repeated use of the other protected variety. Thus, these two hypotheses in which the exploitation of a variety depends on a license are cases in which compulsory licensing replaces an otherwise voluntary license agreement between the parties involved.

But curiously, according to LPC's provisions, requests for compulsory licensing are always ruled by CADE (Art. 31). Therefore, there is a risk of a very extravagant situation in which CADE may be required to rule over a matter that cannot be characterized as a violation of the economic order, or whose parties do not possess market power.

As already mentioned, LPC also contemplates the declaration of restricted public use in the following hypotheses: (1) to meet the needs of agricultural policy, (2) national emergency, (3) abuse of economic power, (4) other circumstances of extreme urgency, (e) cases of noncommercial public use (Art. 36). The Ministry of Agriculture is in charge of issuing such declarations, in ex-officio decisions, which make a protected variety subject to being directly exploited by the federal government or any other third parties assigned by it, always on a nonexclusivity basis, for a three-year term that may be extended. However, even in that event, the law ensures that the title owner should receive some form of remuneration, in accordance with criteria to be defined by regulation (Art. 36, § 1).

The range of possibilities for a declaration of restricted public use is not an exhaustive one, so other situations of *extreme urgency* are also admitted. The hypothesis of misuse of economic power nearly repeats that of compulsory licensing; the difference lies in the office in charge of ruling over the matter (the Ministry of Agriculture in cases of restricted public use, CADE in cases of compulsory license requests), and in the possibility of ex-officio ruling (only possible for restricted public use, not for compulsory licenses, which depend on a request from an interested party).

4.3. Provisions of the antitrust law with regard to intellectual property

The antitrust law (Law 8884/94), in its Art. 21, presents a series of examples of potentially anticompetitive conducts, among which is one that expressly mentions intellectual property: "to take possession of or bar the use of industrial or intellectual

---

25 The essentially derived variety is distinguished from the other by a minimum margin of descriptors, but it predominantly derives from the initial variety, from which it maintains the expression of essential characteristics that arise from the genotype or the combination of genotypes (Law 9456, Art. 3, IX). In the field of plant breeding, the continuous practice of improvement makes it easy to obtain a new variety sufficiently distinct from another one so as to fulfill the *distinctness* requisite, and thus, being entitled to a new – autonomous – protection certificate. This could make the legal protection of plant varieties "weak," because "cosmetic" variations could be created only to bypass legal protection. So, the law states that the protected variety may be freely used in the creation of new ones, but their commercialization, when essentially derived, depends upon a license from the protected variety's title owner.

property rights or technology" (Art. 21, XVI). The terms used to define the conduct are rather obscure: after all, "[barring] the use of industrial or intellectual property rights" constitutes the exercise of the right's core. The exploitation of such a right, by definition, is never free, and its owner is not required to allow competitors to use the protected invention.

But what really matters on this level of analysis is identifying the possible effects of a conduct, both restrictive ones and efficiency gains. Given how illegality is characterized (by the effects of any kind of practice, as per Art. 20), one may say that almost every kind of restrictive practice, be it individual or common, horizontal or vertical, may be committed by means of intellectual property rights, in the same way that a merger may create or strengthen market power due to IPRs.

Nevertheless, the presence of these rights may originate practices somewhat defined in the antitrust literature, with which certain patterns of anticompetitive effects and efficiency gains are associated. Antitrust cases typically include restrictive clauses of IPR licensing agreements, such as noncompetition clauses for effectively or potentially competing firms in relevant markets, market-sharing agreements or standardization of prices among licensed competitors (resale price maintenance agreements); restraint of competition among substitute technologies; barring new technologies from the market.[26]

With regard to horizontal practices, CADE's Normative Ruling 20/99 highlights those restraints that involve "…esforços conjuntos temporários voltados à busca de maior eficiência, especialmente produtiva e tecnológica" (provisional common efforts aiming at greater efficiency, especially in terms of production and technology) which demand a careful assessment of possible benefits, for they present smaller restrictive effects than cartels.[27] Typical cases include joint ventures for R&D projects, agreements to regulate the exchange of information among research teams or to regulate how research results will be shared, and so on, which usually involves IPRs.

With regard to merger reviews of intellectual-property-holding companies, the analysis also presents specific items. If the parties own competing invention rights, the operation may propitiate the end of competition for that innovation, but, on the other hand, it may also lead to joint efforts for its development. Specificities may also be expected at the circumscription of the relevant market(s), since some cases may require the establishment of an innovation or future product market, or an R&D market (Azcuenaga 1995).

4.4. Misuse hypotheses

In an attempt to make a general balance of Brazilian legal provisions applicable to the intersection of the antitrust and intellectual property systems, we may say that

---

26 An OECD (1989) study discusses several types of restrictive clauses in IPR licenses that may be used to cartelize an industry or increase the market power of the rights owner, although licensing per se benefits the competitive process as it propagates the innovation. The very definition of IPRs allows the transmission costs of the innovation to be reduced.

27 A sort of simplified *Guidelines*, which establishes assessment procedures and criteria of the most relevant types of anticompetitive conducts.

Table 5.3. Misuse of rights and/or economic power hypotheses, grounds for objecting and applicable analysis criteria

Effects on competition / Exercise of right	With no anticompetitive effects	With anticompetitive effects
With attempt to extend legal exclusivity	**A.** Exercise of unauthorized restraint. Analysis criteria should be based on the technical and/or legal definition of the right.	**B.** Exercise of unauthorized restraint *and* anticompetitive effects. Analysis criteria of legal scope of rights *and* antitrust. Legal consequences may be cumulative.
With no attempt to extend legal exclusivity	**C.** (Allowed conduct.)	**D.** Exercise of an authorized restraint, with anticompetitive effects. Antitrust analysis criteria. Should there be antitrust exemptions for restrictive conducts?
With no attempt to extend, but with purpose deviation (conflict between social and private interests)	**E.** Contrariness to other socially relevant interests (other than competition). Analysis criteria depend on the *social* purpose to be considered.	**F.** Anticompetitive effects. Analysis criterion: Social purpose related to competition (e.g. the function of 'invention value measurement', cf. Carvalho 1994).

misuse in general (of rights, of economic power through patents or plant breeder's rights) always subjects the title holder to compulsory licensing (besides the forfeiture of the patent and the declaration of restricted public use of the plant certificate), though through different institutional channels.

In the case of patent misuse, subject to compulsory licensing, the request must be filed with INPI; in cases of misuse of economic power through patents, the request is also filed with INPI, but such abuse must be previously proven before CADE (the administrative office in charge of it) or in a court of law. Besides these two, the case may simply be judged by CADE, which has the power to cease the abusive practice (though it cannot impose compulsory licenses).

As for compulsory licenses of protected plant varieties, the decision is up to CADE; in cases of declarations of restricted public use, the decision is up to the Ministry of Agriculture, even in the event of abuse of economic power.

Finally, incidental anticompetitive effects of restrictive clauses in technology transfer agreements – regardless of the right in question – can only be objected to by CADE, which has the power to order its cessation, acting on behalf of the interested party, INPI, or through a proceeding instituted by SDE (Secretaria de Direito Econômico / Secretariat of Economic Law).

In an attempt to summarize the discussion of the different types of abuse and their possible interactions, we present, in Table 5.3, the different hypotheses in which IPRs may be exercised abusively, through the improper extension of monopoly or through purpose deviation, causing (or not) anticompetitive effects (i.e., being also characterized as abuse of economic power). For each one, we indicate the possible legal grounds for objecting to the conduct and the criteria through which it should be judged.

Hypothesis A is irrelevant from the antitrust standpoint. The conduct can be objected to because the law does not contemplate its exercise, that is, it does not constitute a property right. In the Brazilian legal system, there is no such office in charge of supervising and objecting to this kind of practice; but, similar to US jurisprudence, it is possible to use it as a defense in counterfeit lawsuits: as the rights do not protect the "extended" exclusivity, one cannot demand the enforcement of a right that has never been protected by the justice system. It may also characterize an abuse of rights subject to compulsory licensing (cf. Law 9279/96, Art. 68, caput).

Article 71 of the patent law (9279/96) may be used as an example of hypothesis E, compulsory licensing due to national emergency or public interest,[28] as well as misuse of rights. As for misuse of economic power through patents or plant certificates, these should be classified as hypotheses B, D or F, always subject to compulsory licensing (or patent forfeit or declaration of restricted public use of breeder's rights).

4.5. The cases judged by CADE: A summary

Preliminarily, we should remark that CADE's decisions in matters of mergers have already tried to minimize the effects of market power associated with trademarks, imposing restrictions on use in the consent decree signed : the alternatives of licensing or withdrawing the trademark from the market, as in the Kolynos–Colgate case of 1995; the mandatory use of the medicine's active ingredient name instead of its brand name (Novalgina), in the 1997 merger review involving the laboratories Hoescht and Merrel Lepetit; the mandatory sale of the trademark Bavária, in the AMBEV case in 2003.

The antitrust office, however, has no power to impose a patent's compulsory licensing in cases of conducts; it can only recommend that INPI do so (cf. Art. 24, IV, a). As for the compulsory licensing of Plant Variety Protection Certificates, as seen, the decision is up to CADE.

CADE already has some jurisprudence, though incipient, concerning the competition effects of the exercise of IPRs, all related to cases involving patent licensing in the fields of biotechnology (genetically modified seeds) and software, comprising merger reviews and administrative proceedings to investigate presumed anticompetitive conducts. Despite the small number of judged cases, it is possible to say that they outline a consistent jurisprudence, considering the presence of at least three elements: (1) the acknowledgement, equally present at other important jurisdictions, that IPRs are not unconditional, thus being subject, among others, to restraints motivated by the possible harming impact on competition; (2) the systematic adoption of the rule of reason to assess the *net* anticompetitive effects of IPRs and (3) the adoption, as remedies to mitigate

---

28 Declared through a federal government statement, as long as the patent owner cannot meet this need, and subject to being declared ex-officio (regardless of a request from an interested party).

such anticompetitive effects, of restrictions based on the proportionality principle, that is, with the minimum intensity required to achieve the expected result.[29]

Briefly, those are the judgments CADE has made so far, subdivided into the two types of activity mentioned above (Cueva 2009):

– *In biotechnology*:

1. *Administrative proceeding*: initiated in 1998 against Monsanto do Brasil to investigate its selling of transgenic soybean conditioned to the herbicide (glyphosate) produced by the company, while at the same time hindering competitors' access to tests of the variety against other herbicides. After the two markets had been distinguished, the first charge was dismissed for lack of evidence; the second one was rejected insofar as the seed was not in the market (concluded in 2007).
2. *Merger review* (*MR*) Monsanto + Cargill, 1998: to prevent the tying sale mentioned above, it was approved with the restriction of mandatorily extending the seed's warranty to other glyphosate herbicides.
3. *MR* Monsanto + Embrapa, 2000: cooperation agreement approved without restrictions after exclusivity clauses were removed.
4. *MR* Monsanto + Syngenta, 2007: licensing approved with the restriction of exclusivity clause withdrawal, allowing the licensee to perform similar agreements so as to prevent the undue extension of IPRs into another market (pesticides).
5. *MR* Monsanto + Nidera, 2008: licensing approved with equivalent restriction (elimination of exclusivity).
6. *MR* Monsanto + Fundação Mato Grosso and Unisoja, 2003: licensing approved with the same kind of restriction, but requiring the licensor's previous approval in case of joint use of the developed variety with another technology.
7. *MR* Monsanto + Brasmax Genética, 2007: licensing approved with the same restriction above.

In all these cases, CADE's main concern was eliminating exclusivity clauses that might propitiate the undue extension of the market power generated by IPRs into other markets, with the main purpose of guaranteeing the continuance of the licensee's research and development on other technologies besides the patented one. Furthermore, in all verdicts the rule of reason and the principles of proportionality and minimum intervention were observed (Cueva 2009, 140).

– *In software*:

1. *Preliminary Investigation* (*PI*) – which precedes the administrative proceeding – started in 2000 against Microsoft to investigate accusations of tying sales, excessive margins,

---

29 See Cueva (2009, 134 ff.), for a more detailed and analytical approach on CADE's decisions. The summary here presented is based upon this text.

etc., relative to a licensing agreement of educational software with a private education entity; archived for lack of competition grounds (private litigation).

2. *AP* started in 2005 against Microsoft to investigate discrimination conduct to hinder the development of potentially competing software. Archived, but with reservations resulting from the work of experts employed in the case. Verifying the possibility of vertical extension of the defendant's market power, CADE determined that SDE's investigations should go further.

– In the field of SIM cards (subscriber-identity module):

MR Axalto + Gemplus, 2005: operation approved conditioned to a consent decree, in which the merged company vouched to license its patents filed in Brazil under reasonable and nondiscriminatory terms, in accordance with the European Commission's decision.

In brief, these decisions – though small in number – besides the mentioned application of the rule of reason and the proportionality principle, primarily aim at restricting the possibility of undue extension ("leveraging") of market power into distinct market segments through patents – including the use of a large patent portfolio to increase bargaining power.

Conclusions

Intellectual property owes its economic significance to its constituting a property right, a socially acknowledged power of disposition and control over economic opportunities, which ensures the appropriability that its object is not physically and naturally provided with. Particularly relevant is its capacity to guarantee the possibility of appropriating the profits from the innovative effort to its owner, by hindering imitation and, thus, restricting competition to some degree. For this reason, it may also stimulate private expenditure on innovation; hence, its ambiguous nature, since both socially positive and socially negative consequences may be associated with the exercise of the rights. In brief, protecting the right is an incentive *because* it is restrictive.

Intellectual property is not an antithesis of competition; it is rather a competition tool that, as others, may be used to obtain and/or maintain monopolistic positions.[30] Its incentive-with-restraint effects are not dichotomous; on the contrary, the incentive and restraint dimensions are inherent and inseparable. Both are part of the same process – competition – and it is within this sphere, including companies' competitive strategies, that they must be dealt with.

---

30 According to the Schumpeterian idea that restrictive practices should be regarded from a dynamic perspective that takes into account the long-term effects caused by the impact of innovations (Schumpeter 1943, ch. 8).

Therefore, IPRs may become a tool for market-power exercise, though it is not a necessary consequence, for it depends on a series of technological and economic features of the markets involved, as well as on business strategies. In any case, the most appropriate judicial sphere to control these restrictive effects is that of antitrust.

When one focuses on the relations between intellectual property laws and the antitrust law, however, a series of questions comes up, since the restrictive power intrinsic to the exercise of a patent right may always be regarded with some suspicion from the antitrust standpoint. After all, are the two systems' goals and legally protected interests contradictory? If, by restraining imitation and competition, the right *may* constitute a means for the exercise of market power, then, likewise, the immediate goals of both legal systems may indeed be contradictory.

On the other hand, if we consider intellectual property from a dynamic and long-term perspective, based on the Schumpeterian notion of competition, it ceases to be just a tool for profit increase at the expense of consumers and competitors, performing instead the role of a protective institution that reduces the uncertainty associated with investing in a changing environment, allowing the innovator to reap the fruits of what he has sown. In this sense, IPRs are a competition tool rather than its antithesis; their ultimate purpose – which makes them justifiable from a social point of view – is the pursuit of economic efficiency and welfare, the same purposes of the antitrust law.

In brief, intellectual property restrains competition in an immediate sense, but it is destined to promote it in the long run. The greatest difficulty in harmonizing them both – and the corresponding normative analytical challenge – lies in the perception and measurement of net effects: while restrictive aspects of intellectual property are directly associated with a practice in a concrete case, its positive effects – social gains, greater efficiency of the markets' inner workings – are generic, being attributed to the institution's own existence and performance rather than resulting from or being associated with a specific conduct.

The Brazilian legislation clearly points towards the same direction, from the perspectives of both intellectual property and competition. In the antitrust law, any anticompetitive conducts contemplated by Article 20 may, in principle, be exercised through the misuse of intellectual property. In other words, the presence of IPRs may originate several types of restrictive conducts defined by the antitrust literature and jurisprudence, with similar patterns of anticompetitive effects and possible efficiency gains.

In antitrust analyses, the application of the rule of reason to possibly anticompetitive practices based on IPRs must abide by the same principles and usual criteria: although IPRs' net effects cannot be considered restrictive or anticompetitive beforehand, that may just as well happen in particular cases; this is why such effects should be pondered against possible efficiency gains of a given practice. In each situation, only the existence of such anticompetitive net effects – which, in this case, could be characterized as a misuse of property rights – would subject these rights to an antitrust challenge. In brief, there is no apriorism or generalization in determining whether a competitive abuse of IPRs has happened; instead, each particular situation must be examined with the same usual tools of antitrust analysis, peculiarities aside, by means of the rule of reason.

As we intended to point out in this chapter, the antitrust policy is sufficiently adequate to handle the complexity, diversity and ambivalence of IPR effects, and is able to bypass, with great advantage over alternative policies, most economic problems arising from restrictive aspects of IP protection – although we acknowledge other socially relevant problems for which antitrust tools may be ineffective.

In other words, if on one hand, competition policy is clearly not the only means to protect public interest, on the other hand, the existence of other problems arising from IP protection outside the scope of competition policy does not authorize generalizations over the effects of IP protection. In our view, at least the *economic* effects of IP – which in most cases involve impacts on market competition – should be handled from the perspective, and with the tools, of antitrust analysis.

References

All web addresses last accessed July 2011.

Angelmar, R. 1989. "Brevets et Investissements en Biotechnologies: Le Cas des Grandes Societés Pharmaceutiques." *Innovation dans les Semences – Recherche et Industrie – Actes et communications* 4. Paris: INRA.

Arora, A., A. Fosfuri and A. Gambardella. 2005. "Markets for technology, intellectual property rights and development." In K. E. Maskus and J. H. Reichman (eds), *International Public Goods and Transfer of Technology Under a Globalized Intellectual Property Regime*, 321–36. Cambridge: Cambridge University Press.

Azcuenaga, Mary L. 1995. "Intellectual Property and Antitrust: A Perspective from the FTC." Remarks before the American Law Institute–American Bar Association. Available at http://www.ftc.gov/speeches/azcuenaga/ali-aba.shtm

Barbosa, Denis. 2005. "A criação de um ambiente competitivo no campo da propriedade intelectual: O caso sul americano." Geneva: International Centre for Trade and Sustainable Development (ICTSD). Available from http://www.ictsd.org

————. 1998. *Uma Introdução à Propriedade Intelectual*, vol. 2. Rio de Janeiro: Lumen Juris.

Barton, John. 2002. "Antitrust Treatment of Oligopolies with Mutually Blocking Patent Portfolios." *Antitrust Law Journal* 69 (3): 851–82.

————. 1995. "Patent Breadth and Antitrust: A Rethinking." Available at http://www.ftc.gov/opp/global/barton.shtm

Bertin, Gilles and Sally Wyatt. 1988. *Multinationals and Industrial Property*. Hemel Hempstead: Harvester-Wheatsheaf.

Branstetter, Lee, Raymond Fisman and C. Fritz Foley. 2005. "Do Stronger Intellectual Property Rights Increase International Technology Transfer? Empirical Evidence from U.S. Firm-Level Data." NBER Working Paper No. 11516. Available at http://www.nber.org/papers/w11516

Burlamaqui, Leonardo. 2008. "Innovation, Competition Policies and Intellectual Property: An Evolutionary Perspective and its Policy Implications." In Neil Netanel (ed.), *The Development Agenda: Global Intellectual Property and Developing Countries*, 429–52. Oxford and New York: Oxford University Press.

Carlton, Dennis and Robert Gertner. 2002. "Intellectual Property, Antitrust and Strategic Behavior." NBER Working Paper No. 8976. Available at http://www.nber.org/papers/w8976

Carvalho, Nuno. 1994. "Abusos dos Direitos de Patente: Um estudo do direito dos Estados Unidos com referências comparativas ao direito brasileiro." *Revista da Associação Brasileira da Propriedade Intelectual* 12: 44–105.

Carvalho, Sérgio, Sérgio Salles-Filho and Sonia Paulino. 2006. "Propriedade Intelectual e Dinâmica de Inovação na Agricultura." *Revista Brasileira de Inovação* 5 (2): 315–40.

Cohen, William. 1997. "Per se Illegality and Truncated Rule of Reason: The Search for a Foreshortened Antitrust Analysis." Available at http://www.ftc.gov/opp/jointvent/1Perse pap.shtm

Cueva, Ricardo. 2009. "A Proteção da Propriedade Intelectual de Defesa da Concorrência nas Decisões do CADE." *Revista do IBRAC* 16 (1): 121–47.

Dosi, Giovanni. 1988a. "Sources, Procedures and Microeconomic Effects of Innovation." *Journal of Economic Literature* 26, 1120–1171.

_____. 1988b. "Institutions and Markets in a Dynamic World." *Manchester School* 56 (2): 119–46.

Federal Trade Commission (FTC). 1995. *Guidelines for Antitrust Enforcement over Intellectual Property.* Available from http://www.ftc.gov

Ferraz, Tércio Jr. 1995. "Da Abusividade do Poder Econômico." *Revista de Direito Econômico* 21: 23–30.

Gilbert, Richard. 2005. "New Antitrust Laws for the 'New Economy'?" Testimony before the Antitrust Modernization Commission, Washington DC, November 8, 2005. Available at http://www.amc.gov/commission_hearings/pdf/Statement_Gilbert.pdf

Giuri, Paola, Myriam Mariani, Stefano Brusoni et al. 2007. "Inventors and Invention Processes in Europe: Results from the PatVal-EU Survey." *Research Policy* 36: 1107–27.

Gold, Bela. 1980. "On the Adoption of Technological Innovations in Industry: Superficial Models and Complex Decision Processes." *OMEGA* 8 (5): 505–16.

Grabowski, Henri and John Vernon. 1986. "Longer Patents Life for Lower Imitation Barriers: The 1984 Drug Act." *American Economic Review* 76 (2): 195–8.

Griliches, Zvi (ed.) 1984. *R&D, Patents and Productivity.* Chicago: University of Chicago Press.

Hippel, Eric von. 1982. "Appropriability of Innovation Benefit as a Predictor of the Source of Innovation." *Research Policy* 11: 95–115.

Hoerner, Robert. 2002. "The Decline (and Fall?) of the Patent Misuse Doctrine in the Federal Circuit." *Antitrust Law Journal* 69 (3): 669–85.

Lerner, Josh. 2002. Patent Protection and Innovation over 150 Years. NBER Working Paper No. 8977. Available at http://www.nber.org/papers/w7068

Levin, Richard. 1986. "A New Look at the Patent System." *American Economic Review* 76 (2): 199–202.

Levin, Richard, William Cohen and David Mowery. 1985. "R&D, Appropriability, Opportunity and Market Structure." *American Economic Review* 75 (2): 20–24.

Levin, Richard et al. 1987. "Appropriating the Returns from Industrial Research and Development." *Brookings Papers on Economic Activity* 3: 783–831.

Mansfield, Edwin. 1986. "Patents and Innovation: An Empirical Study." *Management Science* 32 (2): 173–81.

Mansfield, Edwin, Mark Schwartz and Samuel Wagner. 1981. "Imitation Costs and Patents: An Empirical Study." *Economic Journal* 91: 907–18.

Mello, Maria Tereza. 2009. "Propriedade Intelectual e Concorrência." *Revista Brasileira de Inovação* 8 (2): 445–82.

_____. 1995. "Propriedade Intelectual e Concorrência: Uma Análise Setorial" [Intellectual Property and Competition: A Sectoral Approach]. PhD dissertation, Institute of Economics, State University of Campinas.

Merges, Robert and Richard Nelson. 1993. "On Limiting or Encouraging Rivalry in Technical Progress: The Effect of Patent Scope Decisions." Mimeo.

Neale, Alan and Dan Goyder. 1962. *The Antitrust Laws of United States of America: A Study of Competition Enforced by Law.* 3rd edn. Cambridge: Cambridge University Press.

Nelson, Richard. 1992. "What Is 'Commercial' and What Is 'Public' about Technology, and What Should Be?" In Nathan Rosenberg, Ralph Landau and David Mowery (eds), *Technology and the Wealth of Nations*, 57–71. Stanford, CA: Stanford University Press.

OECD. 1989. *Competition Policy and Intellectual Property*. Paris: OECD.

Ordover, Janusz. 1991. "A Patent System for Both Diffusion and Exclusion." *Journal of Economic Perpectives* 5 (1): 43–60.

Pisano, Gary. 2006. "Profiting from innovation and the intellectual property revolution." *Research Policy* 35: 1122–30.

Possas, Mario. 2002. "Concorrência Schumpeteriana." In David Kupfer and Lia Hasenclever (eds), *Economia Industrial: Fundamentos Teóricos e Práticas no Brasil*, 415–29. Rio de Janeiro: Campus.

Scherer, Frederic. 1993. "Pricing, Profits and Technological Progress in the Pharmaceutical Industry." *Journal of Economic Perpectives* 7 (3): 97–115.

Schuartz, Luis Fernando. 1998. "Dogmática Jurídica e Lei 8.884/94." *Cadernos de Direito Tributário e Finanças Públicas* 6: 70–98.

Schumpeter, Joseph. 1943. *Capitalism, Socialism, and Democracy*. London: Allen & Unwin.

Scisinio, Alaor Eduardo. 1998. *As Maiorias Acionárias e o Abuso de Direito*. Rio de Janeiro: Forense.

Scotchmer, Suzanne. 1991. "Standing on the Shoulders of Giants: Cumulative Research and the patent law." *Journal of Economic Perspectives* 5 (1): 29–41.

Taylor, Christopher and Aubrey Silberston. 1973. *The Economic Impact of the Patent System*. Cambridge: Cambridge University Press.

Teece, David. 1992. "Strategies for Capturing the Financial Benefits from Technological Innovation." In Nathan Rosenberg, Ralph Landau and David Mowery (eds), *Technology and the Wealth of Nations*, 175–205. Stanford: Stanford University Press.

———. 1986. "Profiting from technological innovation." *Research Policy* 15: 285–305.

Williamson, Oliver. 1985. *The Economic Institutions of Capitalism*. New York: The Free Press.

Chapter 6

THE POLITICS OF PHARMACEUTICAL PATENT EXAMINATION IN BRAZIL

Kenneth C. Shadlen
London School of Economics and Political Science

The Politics of Pharmaceutical Patent Examination in Brazil

Since the 1980s, the world of intellectual property (IP) has undergone a sea change in the direction of harmonization. Reflecting a goal to universalize the high levels of IP protection common throughout the OECD, the United States and the European Union worked to replace the flexible and largely unenforceable rules that had prevailed in the policy area, with more restrictive and enforceable international rules to guide national IP practices. The most important product of this campaign was the inclusion of the Agreement on Trade-Related Aspects of Intellectual Property Rights (TRIPS) as part of the new WTO.[1]

Although TRIPS establishes universal standards for IP policy, countries retain latitude with regard to how they implement the standards. Thus, while TRIPS is part of a broader phenomenon of a movement toward regulatory harmonization, a phenomenon that imposes unprecedented constraints on areas of economic policy where countries historically had significant autonomy (Gallagher 2005; UNDP 2003), developing countries retain opportunities for policy innovation in the field of IP (Reichman 1997; Correa 2000; Watal 2000; CIPR 2002; Shadlen 2005).

This paper examines the challenges to utilizing this remaining (if limited) space, focusing on the politics of patent examination in pharmaceuticals. To be sure, yet another contribution on "policy space" may hardly seem worthwhile, considering the significant amount of attention that the topic has received. Yet most analyses of IP policy space have addressed one particular policy instrument, compulsory licenses (CLs). Patents provide private rights of exclusion over knowledge, and CLs regulate patents by establishing the conditions and terms under which actors who are not the owners can utilize the patented knowledge. Prior to regulating private rights, however,

---

1 See, among others, Drahos (1995); May (2000); Matthews (2002); Ryan (1998); Sell (2003).

comes the process of establishing the private rights in the first place. This chapter focuses on this prior aspect of IP policy, patent examination.

Patents are granted by the state only when the knowledge is judged to be novel, inventive, and industrially useful. Because these criteria for patentability are ambiguous, how each is operationalized in national patent examination guidelines and practices affects how many (and what sorts of) patents are granted. In the area of pharmaceuticals, health-oriented examination practices may entail preventing the granting of patents to some incremental innovations that effectively extend periods of market exclusivity (Correa 2007). The reason for this, simply, is that if a patent on a drug is set to expire in, say, 2012, then the granting of additional patents on small modifications of the drug, with expiration dates of, say, 2018, might mean that generic competition would not begin for another six years.

Because efforts to acquire multiple patents on the same products and thereby extend periods of exclusivity is a standard practice in the pharmaceutical industry, a number of developing countries have introduced special mechanisms to scrutinize applications for patents on incremental pharmaceutical innovations (Deere 2008, 78–80, table 3.4). The most prominent case is India, which now allows patents on pharmaceuticals, but explicitly states in Section 3d of the patent law that incremental innovations cannot be patented without the applicant demonstrating that the incremental modification yields increased "efficacy." According to Amin (2012), the Philippines adopted virtually identical legislation, and another source reports that more than ten countries in Asia-Pacific are supposedly emulating India's system for restricting incremental pharmaceutical innovations.[2] In Latin America, Argentina and the Andean Community deny patents to new uses of existing drugs (Helfer, Alter and Guerzovich 2009), while Brazil and Paraguay involve the health ministry in the examination of pharmaceutical patent applications.[3]

In this chapter, I use the case of Brazil to shed light on the difficulties of sustaining coalitions for health-oriented the examination and granting of patents. Pharmaceuticals have been eligible for patents in Brazil since 1997, and in 2001 the government introduced an additional measure that involves officials from the health ministry in the examination of pharmaceutical patent applications. The measure, referred to as "Prior Consent," has been extraordinarily conflictual, particularly as regards incremental pharmaceutical innovations. I use an analysis of the ensuing conflicts over Prior Consent in Brazil as a lens to understand the political challenges to using IP policy space in developmentally propitious ways. The case study illustrates how the isolation within the state of the actors responsible for such examination, combined with the ambivalent interests and preferences of key industrial actors, can weaken and undermine coalitions sustaining health-oriented patent examination.

---

2 "Copycats Popping Patent Law Pill." *Economic Times*, August 13, 2007. Available at http://spicyipindia.blogspot.com/2007/08/spicyip-tidbits.html. Unless otherwise stated, all web addresses in this chapter were last accessed in August 2012.

3 In Egypt the patent law invites the Health Ministry to participate in pharmaceutical patent examination. No doubt there are other examples. This is far from an exhaustive list.

This chapter has three sections. In the first section, I provide a brief overview of the constraints imposed by TRIPS and explain the particular challenges of patent examination in the case of pharmaceuticals. In the second section, I introduce the Brazilian case, explaining how the Prior Consent mechanism is designed to work and illustrating the high level of conflict. In doing so, I contrast my findings on the actual operations of this policy intervention with the way it has been depicted by many international observers. In the third section, I explain why Prior Consent has generated so much conflict, focusing on the isolation of state officials responsible for executing the policy and the ambivalent interests of key actors in the local, Brazilian pharmaceutical industry.

TRIPS, Patent Examination, Pharmaceutical Innovation

An important characteristic of patents is that the private ownership rights are not conferred automatically upon possession of knowledge. Instead, patents are granted by the state only where (1) the knowledge falls within the range of subject matter that is eligible for patents and (2) applicants demonstrate that their inventions satisfy standard patentability criteria of being novel (i.e., new), inventive (i.e., non-obvious) and have industrial utility.

With regard to determining patentable subject matter, TRIPS reduces discretion in setting the scope of patent eligibility. Article 27 requires countries to grant patents of 20 years in all fields of technology.[4] The nondiscrimination rule means that countries can no longer refuse, as a matter of policy, to issue patents to particular classes of goods. The importance of this change cannot be emphasized enough. The issue of what sorts of inventions are eligible to be patented has historically been a critical feature that differentiated national approaches toward IP. Many countries refused to grant patents to certain products, for example. In the 1800s and early 1900s many countries did not grant patents at all, and many did so only to nationals.[5]

The inability to deny patents on a sectoral basis is particularly significant in the realm of pharmaceuticals. Prior to the Uruguay Round, more than 40 countries did not provide any patent protection for pharmaceuticals and pharmo-chemicals, while many that did so issued patents only for processes and not for products (WHO 2002, 15). In many developing countries, the lack of patent protection drove the growth of local pharmaceutical industries, which specialized in making generic versions of drugs,[6] some patented in developed countries, some older drugs whose patents had

---

4 This article introduces a new definition of the term "nondiscrimination," no longer referring to countries' practices vis-à-vis other countries, but rather toward economic sectors.

5 Machlup and Penrose (1950); (Schiff (1971); Chang (2002); May (2007).

6 I use the term "generic" to refer to nonpatented versions, what the World Health Organization calls "multiple source drugs." More comprehensive definitions of "generic" would also refer to trademark status (i.e., there are plenty of drugs that are off-patent but sold under brand names and therefore not formally "generic") and bioequivalence with the patented (reference) drug (that is, in many countries alternative, nonpatented versions of drugs that have not had bioequivalence demonstrated would not be called "generics" but rather "similars"). To repeat, in this chapter I use the simplest definition of generic: a nonpatented version of a patented drug. See Homedes and Ugalde (2005) for a discussion of defining "generics."

expired. The inclusion of mandatory pharmaceutical patentability was a trophy that the transnational pharmaceutical sector, through its national governments, secured in the Uruguay Round: as of 2005 all but the least developed countries were required to grant patents on pharmaceuticals and agricultural chemicals.[7]

With regard to applying patentability criteria in the process of patent examination, countries retain latitude under TRIPS (CIPR 2002, 114–19). Quite simply, any individual patent application can be denied on the grounds of deficiency in novelty, inventiveness and utility, even if patents are available, in principle, to its technological class. After all, these three standard criteria for patentability are ambiguous terms. How novelty, inventiveness and utility are operationalized by national patent offices (and legal systems) affects what sorts of patents are granted (and upheld by courts). A country that seeks to make knowledge ownership relatively easy to obtain and to grant many patents might have relaxed standards for novelty. In contrast, a country that seeks to restrict the extent to which knowledge becomes privately owned may introduce more rigorous standards, de facto or de jure, such that fewer applications pass the test. Likewise, some countries may require greater degrees of inventiveness than others.

With regard to pharmaceuticals, denying patent applications on the grounds of insufficient novelty or inventiveness may form an important element of health-oriented patent policy (Correa 2007). To understand this better, it is important to clarify, first, what incremental innovations in pharmaceuticals consist of, and then, second, how patents on incremental pharmaceutical innovations can extend periods of exclusivity and thus prevent generic competition.

Incremental innovations in pharmaceuticals consist of the various changes that are made to existing molecules and drugs. These may include alternative molecular forms (e.g., polymorphs, salts, isomers), different formulations (pills, capsules, tablets, ointments, syrups, suspensions), diverse dosage regimens, and new uses. Despite the sector being depicted as a bastion of "radical innovation" (Hall and Soskice 2001), the pharmaceutical industry is in fact built on incremental innovation. Base molecules do not become drugs without additional innovations along the way. Some molecules perform well in laboratory tests but are less effective in the human body than alternative forms of the same base molecules. And once effective and stable molecules are settled upon, pharmaceutical innovation also consists of figuring out how to deliver them safely and effectively. The reader should simply consider any medication in the cabinet, which might include as little as 10 milligrams or as much as 500 milligrams of the active pharmaceutical ingredient (API). Delivering such miniscule amounts would be exceedingly difficult, if not impossible, were they not combined with a range of additional inert ingredients (i.e., excipients). Yet while excipients' role may ultimately be simply to consume space and to facilitate handling (again, imagine trying to store and handle 100 milligrams of something!), they must be selected and included in the

7 To be clear, developing countries' deadline for full compliance with TRIPS was 2000, but countries that did not previously grant patents on pharmaceuticals and agricultural chemicals were given until 2005 to begin doing so.

manufacturing process in such a way as to make for a deliverable and consumable medication that retains the desired effect of the API. Finally, the same molecules often affect multiple parts of the body differently; when molecules intended for one therapeutic use turn out to be more effective in ways other than intended, additional work is entailed to develop the drug for the "new uses."[8]

Taking a step back, and at the risk of being overly simplistic, the pharmaceutical research, development and production chain might be said to consist of three stages: (1) discovery of the underlying biological mechanisms that cause particular ailments, (2) creation or identification of molecules to target the relevant cells (either to cause the cells to perform more of their normal functions or to cease functioning abnormally) and (3) converting seemingly useful molecules into consumable and deliverable drugs. At each step along the chain, the propensity to patent increases exponentially: the basic knowledge revealing biological mechanisms is typically not patentable (that is for Nobel Prizes!), but the subsequent steps are – and each new molecular entity (NME, stage 2) typically yields countless more applications for drug patents (stage 3). Indeed, as the International Chamber of Commerce testified to the World Health Organization, "the vast majority [of pharmaceutical patents] cover innovations which build on inventions of others…" (ICC 2005, 4). And when we examine patent landscapes of many drugs, it is common to see one medication protected by tens and tens (in some cases upwards of a hundred) of diverse molecular forms, formulations, processes and uses (Howard 2007; Rathod 2010).

Taking out multiple patents on different aspects of a drug in order to effectively cordon off competitors and extend periods of exclusivity is standard practice in the pharmaceutical industry. Critics refer to this pejoratively as "evergreening." Although the industry vehemently rejects use of this specific term (GSK 2007), devising patenting strategies to extend periods of protection and protect market shares remains fundamentally important to the pharmaceutical industry (Schertenleib n.d.). Consider, for example, Carlos Correa's definition of evergreening as "a patenting strategy consisting of acquiring patents on minor, often trivial, modifications of existing pharmaceutical products or processes in order to indirectly extend the period of patent protection over previously patented compounds." Suppose we remove the adjectives "minor" and "trivial" and refer simply to "a patenting strategy consisting of acquiring patents on modifications of existing pharmaceutical products or processes in order to indirectly extend the period of patent protection over previously patented compounds." The new definition is hardly different from what the pharmaceutical industry (and patent lawyers) enthusiastically refer to as "patent lifecycle management."

Beyond the semantic debates, why might granting additional patents on incremental pharmaceutical innovations be worrisome from a public-health perspective? The

---

8 The last sentence sounds a lot like a description of side effects. When molecules affect additional parts of the body and biological processes in ways that detract from their targeted uses, we refer to "side effects," yet when the unexpected effects are beneficial (perhaps even better than the targeted uses) these become known as "new uses."

principal reason is that patents on incremental innovations can extend periods of exclusivity beyond the dates in which they would otherwise expire, thus postponing the entry of competition and, subsequently, the effects that generic competition ordinarily has on prices. By way of illustration, consider an imaginary pharmaceutical firm "Px" that in 1994 applied for a patent on a new molecule XYZ for treating diabetes. Through subsequent research, Px came to believe that an alternative form of the molecule, XYZ*, would work better and Px applied for a patent on XYZ* in 2000. In 2003, after completing clinical trials, Px received authorization from health authorities to place a drug based on XYZ* on the market. The patent on the base molecule XYZ expires in 2014, while the patent for the alternative form XYZ*, if granted, would not expire until 2020. Should the second patent be granted?

How countries treat applications for patents on incremental innovations of this sort is controversial. XYZ* may be an innovation, but any country that grants this patent will be extending Px's period of market exclusivity for six years beyond 2014, which will affect prices, the government's health budget, and patients' access to medicines. From a health perspective, then, a country may have an interest in minimizing patents on incremental pharmaceutical innovations. Although simply declaring that incremental innovations, per se, are not patentable may be a violation of TRIPS, a TRIPS-compatible policy instrument is to apply patentability criteria as rigorously as possible to make it very difficult for pharmaceutical firms to obtain such patents (Basheer 2005).[9] Despite Px having expended resources to undertake the research required to come up with XYZ*, examiners may nevertheless rule that the incremental innovation does not warrant a patent, determining that XYZ* is not novel (perhaps this form was revealed in the original patent or prior art) or that it is not inventive (perhaps on the basis of existing knowledge and scientific literature, any person "skilled in the art" could have obtained the molecular form XYZ*). The more rigorously countries apply these criteria, the fewer patents on incremental pharmaceutical innovations will they end up granting, with subsequent effects on the degree of competition in the provision of particular drugs and, ultimately, prices.

Suppose that patentability criteria are not applied rigorously at the time of examination and thus, more incremental innovation patents are granted. What tends to happen then is that the period between the expiration of the patent on the base molecules and the expiration of the patent on the incremental additions is witness to lawsuits, as generic firms seeking to enter the market challenge the validity of particular patents. Patentability criteria thus are essentially applied *ex post* in the course of litigation rather than *ex ante* in the course of examination. According to Drahos

---

9 There are plenty of examples of patents that lack novelty or inventiveness and clearly should never have been granted in the first place. In this example, I present a more difficult case where there does appear to be an innovation (XYZ* is an improvement on XYZ), but granting the patent on the incremental innovation will nevertheless extend Px's period of market exclusivity. In that light, it is also worth noting that not all incremental innovation patents have equal blocking effects. The extent of the blocking effect of a patent on XYZ* depends on the pharmacological usefulness of XYZ.

(2008), however, there are significant benefits to denying the patents preemptively and not relying on litigation. Most importantly, patent litigation, in addition to being risky, has the characteristics of a public good in that the challenger bears all the costs but, if successful in invalidating a patent, the benefits are available to all, since invalidation places the knowledge in the public domain. Building on Drahos's argument, one could maintain that the problems of relying on *ex post* litigation (and thus the rationale for a system of preemptive denial of weak patents) are likely to be particularly acute in developing countries for two reasons: First, the smaller size of markets means the gains of successful litigation are smaller (thus reducing the incentive to litigate). Second, the greater resource asymmetries between owners and challengers means the likelihood of succeeding in litigation may be smaller.

As indicated, developing countries are permitted under TRIPS to introduce examination procedures that are designed to minimize the granting of patents to incremental pharmaceutical innovations. A number of countries have implemented so-called "preemptive" systems designed to achieve this goal. The remainder of this chapter examines the case of Brazil.

Pharmaceutical Patent Applications in Brazil: INPI vs. ANVISA

Brazil's new, TRIPS-compliant patent law (Lei de Proprieadade Industrial, LPI) was passed in May 1996, coming into effect in May 1997. The LPI made pharmaceutical products eligible for patents. In 1999, the law was reformed, requiring all pharmaceutical patent applications that are approved by Brazil's National Institute for Industrial Property (INPI) to be sent to the Ministry of Health (MS, Ministério da Saúde) for review. The reform, which came into effect in 2001, means that pharmaceutical patents are issued only after the MS's health surveillance agency (ANVISA) issues "Prior Consent."[10]

The Prior Consent regulation is widely celebrated. Deere (2008, 213), who cites Brazil as an example of IP policymaking being successfully coordinated among relevant ministries, highlights the "formal collaborative relationship" between INPI and ANVISA. Drahos (2008, 169) lauds Prior Consent as a "model of patent office regulation in the area of pharmaceuticals that operates on the basis of prevention."

Notwithstanding the praise that Prior Consent has received from these observers, within Brazil the measure has proved to be the source of never-ending controversy. In fact, Prior Consent has been subject to strong – and growing – legal and political attacks for nearly a decade. In the early 2000s, for example, the Brazilian Intellectual Property Association (ABPI) challenged the constitutionality of the law. Specifically, ABPI maintained that INPI has sole authority for granting patents in Brazil, and thus, the government was violating the constitution by allocating examination responsibilities

---

10 ANVISA was created in 1999. Its IP division (COOPI) was established in 2001, at the time the Prior Consent rule entered into effect, and placed in the same Rio office building as INPI.

to two separate bodies. ABPI also maintained that ANVISA, as the health regulator, should be focused on health matters and only health matters, not patents. And because the clause requiring ANVISA's approval was placed in the section of the LPI addressing pipeline patents,[11] ABPI asserted that the legislative intent must have been for Prior Consent to only be required for pipeline patents,[12] and that ANVISA was overstepping its authority.[13] Although a Rio de Janeiro court upheld the legality of ANIVSA's role in 2005, the challengers continued to press their case on multiple fronts. In 2008, a deputy from the opposition Brazilian Social Democratic Party (PSDB) introduced an initiative in the Congress that would restrict ANVISA's role to pipeline patent applications, basing this call, in the bill's motivations, on precisely the same grounds as ABPI had put forward.[14]

At the same time as Prior Consent was under siege in the courts and congress, it also came under attack from within the government. The INPI, arguing that it was solely and uniquely charged with the role of examining patent applications, formally requested that the Brazilian Attorney General (PGF) strike down the Prior Consent mechanism.[15] In October 2009, the PGF published a report that supported INPI's position and called for ANVISA's role to be restricted.[16] The PGF declared that while ANVISA could continue to evaluate pharmaceutical patent applications, in doing so it must only make health-based assessments of these applications and deny its "Prior Consent" to applications strictly in instances where granting the patents would pose health risks. ANVISA would no longer be allowed to examine the novelty

---

11 Pipeline patents refer to patents on pharmaceuticals whose original priority dates precede the change to the LPI making pharmaceutical patents eligible in Brazil (and thus could not be patented when they were new) but that were still in the development stage and thus not yet on the market as of 1996. Pipeline patents are not examined, but simply revalidated, with the expiration date 20 years from the date of application in the first country where they were filed.

12 Because Prior Consent was originally introduced by executive decree (*medida provisora*, MP) in 1999, there is no legislative debate to infer intent. The 2001 law that converted the MP into a formal reform of the LPI law also lacks such debate. The little information we have to go on is the letter that the executive submitted to Congress in making the original MP, and this simply says that the purpose of the revision was to assure more competencies in examining pharmaceutical patents. Kunisawa (2009) provides more discussion of the origins of Prior Consent.

13 ABPI Resolution, October 21, 2004. See also Rosman (2004). Basso (2006) responds to these criticisms, making a legal defense of the Prior Consent mechanism, as do Beas Rodrigues and Murphy (2006, 437–8). Souza (2008, 64–6) provides details on the court cases.

14 PL 3709/08, Deputado Rafael Guerra (PSDB-MG). In early 2009, the bill's rapporteur voted to reject the PL. In order to keep the bill alive through the congressional period, however, another deputy who supported the legislation called for additional hearings, which occurred in October 2009.

15 Email from INPI to PGF, August 2008.

16 PGF (2009); Lígia Formenti. "Decisão do governo afeta autorização de novos genéricos." *O Estado de São Paulo*, November 5, 2009, 1. Available at http://www.estadao.com.br/estadaodehoje/20091105/not_imp461392,0.php

and inventiveness of claims made in pharmaceutical patent applications; that sort of evaluation would be reserved exclusively for the INPI.

The PGF's report was attacked by public health activists, who were alarmed by INPI's permissive examination guidelines and thus regarded ANVISA's participation in the formal examination process as crucial for preventing the excessive granting of patents on incremental innovations that lack novelty or are insufficiently inventive. Civil society groups launched an online petition against the PGF's position,[17] and ANVISA formally requested that the PGF's report be rejected. Yet, despite these criticisms and demands, in January 2011 the solicitor general in the government of Brazil's new president, Dilma Rousseff, upheld the PGF's ruling.[18] Confirmation on the part of the solicitor general effectively converted the PGF's report from a recommendation into a mandate that, once signed by the president, would bind all actors in the executive branch. Thus, Prior Consent, though formally part of Brazilian law, is effectively eliminated: ANVISA is no longer able to intervene in the examination process as it had done, or attempted to do in the past (as discussed below). Indeed, following the AGU's ruling and the decision of ANVISA's directorate to not resist the new arrangements, the director of the patent examination team within the health surveillance agency subsequently resigned from his position in protest.[19]

Not only has this novel and TRIPS-compatible policy instrument effectively been terminated, it is also worth noting that even when in operation, it did not achieve the outcomes it was designed to achieve. Observers who praise the Brazilian model tend to do so on the basis of how the Prior Consent mechanism was supposed to operate, not on how it actually functioned in practice. INPI has been explicit in its strategy of "completely rejecting" ANVISA's participation in patent examination: patent examination is for patent offices, not health officials, according to INPI;[20] ANVISA should dedicate itself to health affairs. Thus, INPI did not just seek to eliminate ANVISA's role in patent examination, de jure, but pending that outcome, it also worked to minimize the latter's role, de facto.

Consider two ways that the Prior Consent system required INPI and ANVISA to collaborate: communicating with applicants in the course of examination, and dealing with applications where the two agencies reach different conclusions. Upon reviewing patent applications that had been approved by INPI, ANVISA's examiners

---

17 The petition is available at http://www.petitiononline.com/gtpi2/petition.html

18 Lígia Formenti, "AGU restringe poder da Anvisa na concessão de patente de medicamento," *O Estado de São Paulo*, January 24, 2011. Available at http://www.estadao.com.br/noticias/impresso,agu-restringe-poder-da-anvisa-na-concessao-de-patente-de-medicamento,670238,0.htm

19 See William New, "Top Official Discusses Resignation From Brazil's ANVISA Over Patent Policy," *Intellectual Property Watch*, August 11, 2011. Available at http://www.ip-watch.org/weblog/2011/08/11/top-official-discusses-resignation-from-brazil%E2%80%99s-anvisa-over-patent-policy/. One of the curiosities of the PGF's and AGU's rulings is that the new arrangements may be exceptionally difficult to put into effect since it is rarely if ever possible to assess "health risks" on the basis of the sort of information included in patent applications.

20 The quotation comes from INPI's request to the attorney general (PGF 2009, 1–2).

typically made preliminary reports in which they sought additional, clarifying materials from applicants. Until June 2008 the reports and requests for information were transmitted via INPI, leaving the patent office as the sole point of contact between applicants and the state. Yet, INPI routinely refused to pass such communication along to the applicant, thus inhibiting ANVISA's subsequent evaluation of the patent application. At times, the system would work as envisioned, with ANVISA requesting more information and INPI dutifully obtaining this information from the applicant;[21] and at times, ANVISA would request more information, and INPI would reject the application on procedural or substantive grounds without referring it back to the applicant.[22] The problem, thus, was not a blanket refusal of INPI to intermediate, but rather its unpredictability and unreliability. ANVISA asking for more materials *may* have lead to INPI obtaining the materials or even rejecting the application, but it just as well may not have. INPI, not ANVISA, decided the cases where the system worked or did not work.

Another area of poor (or nonexistent) communication occurs when INPI and ANVISA reached different conclusions on applications. To be sure, most patent applications approved by INPI are also approved by ANVISA (and recall that ANVISA only receives patent applications that are already approved by INPI; if INPI rejects the application it is not passed along to ANVISA). But what happened when ANVISA denied Prior Consent to applications approved by INPI? As of August 2009 this had occurred 121 times, but only five of these applications were subsequently rejected by INPI. In the case of the others, of course, INPI cannot publish them as granted patents, as the Prior Consent clause in the LPI prohibits the granting of patents without ANVISA's approval, but INPI did not reject them either. According to INPI, its mandate is to examine patents and it is uniquely vested with that mandate, so once its examiners have approved a patent, there is no reason why INPI should change its verdict on account of the health surveillance agency's evaluation. Accordingly, INPI would freeze the applications, doing nothing, holding the applications in a state of legal limbo, neither granted nor rejected. One may interpret INPI's actions as a bet on the eventual abolition of the Prior Consent requirement: once INPI has rejected a patent, the knowledge disclosed is in the public domain, and there is no going back, but if ANVISA's role is formally removed, either by a judicial ruling or a legislative change to LPI, then any not-yet-rejected patent applications could still be granted. And it should be noted that the state of nondecision provides effective protection because of third parties' fear of retroactive damages in the case of the patent ultimately being granted.[23]

---

21 When this happened, ANVISA was often able to narrow the claims of patents before granting its Prior Consent (Silva 2008, 63).

22 This is not surprising: INPI's examiners are overwhelmed by the huge number of applications, and, operating with limited resources and under intense pressure to work through the considerable backlog, they are prone to errors. At times, even the unwanted intervention of ANVISA can have welcome effects in terms of revealing faults in examination.

23 Ironically, since the Brazilian patent law guarantees a minimum of ten years of patent protection from the time of the grant, this would effectively extend patent terms – precisely the opposite of what the regulation was designed to achieve.

From ANVISA's perspective, INPI's actions amounted to a "boycott" of the system, and in June 2008, ANVISA fought back by beginning to communicate directly with patent applicants (thus minimizing reliance on INPI's uncertain intermediation) and also publishing, in the official gazette, its final reports where Prior Consent was denied.[24] Yet, by making its application of patentability criteria explicit and more visible, ANVISA unwittingly facilitated charges of duplication and institutional redundancies that underpinned the legal and legislative measures to eliminate its role. INPI could now declare, "our job is to examine whether patents are novel, inventive, and useful; ANVISA's job is to make sure that health products are safe – and look, ANVISA is now formally and publicly announcing its rulings as to whether patent applications are new, novel, and useful." Indeed, INPI did say this, in so many words, in its request to the PGF, which concurred.[25] Thus, ironically, by attempting to improve its role in patent examination ANVISA contributed to the case for retiring its role.

The discussion of the conflict to this point may give the impression that this is a story of two government agencies squabbling over the division of labor, each fighting to protect its own turf. Indeed, when one reads accounts of the INPI–ANVISA conflict in the Brazilian press, one also gets a similar sensation that what is being reported is a rather dry case of an intragovernmental row over who should be examining patent applications. Yet, underlying this conflict is a fundamental and substantive dispute over how to assess applications for patents on incremental innovations in pharmaceuticals (e.g., alternative molecular forms, additional formulations, new uses). INPI's examination guidelines adopt permissive criteria that lead examiners to approve many of these applications. The formal defense of and logic behind this approach is to encourage incremental innovation. The INPI and its parent ministry, the Ministry of Development, Industry, and Foreign Trade (MDIC), maintain that encouraging and rewarding incremental innovation is the key job of a patent system in a developing country. Were patents restricted to radical innovations, INPI would be granting them almost exclusively to foreign applicants. Granting patents on incremental innovations, in contrast, rewards Brazilian innovators.[26] The reasoning is captured well by INPI president Jorge Ávila's testimony to the Brazilian Congress:

> The [Brazilian] firms that have developed innovative capacities demonstrate the need to retain the patentability of incremental innovations, because it is not possible for a new actor in the scenario of innovation to immediately become

---

24 The new approach was announced in RDC 45. Available at http://www.anvisa.gov.br/medicamentos/intelectual/perguntas.htm. Reference to "INPI's boycott" comes from personal communication with the director of ANVISA's patent office (July 4, 2008).

25 Referring to the passage in RDC-45 where ANVISA explains that its analysis is based on application of the patentability criteria established in the LPI, the PGF concludes that ANVISA is acting beyond its legally mandated domain (PGF 2009, 7, paragraphs 31–2).

26 Note that there is also a practical motivation to a relaxed examination system, and that is simply the huge backlog of applications INPI has.

a radical innovator. The entryway to the system of innovation is incremental innovation.[27]

ANVISA's examination, in contrast, is informed by a more critical perspective on incremental innovation in pharmaceuticals. ANVISA maintains that most polymorphs and selection patents are obvious from the original molecules and therefore lack inventiveness, for example, and that second uses lack novelty.[28] ANVISA does not deny the significant amount of research that might go into discovering and developing polymorphic forms of and second uses for existing molecules, but holds that many of these can – and often should – be denied patents by applying patentability criteria rigorously.

The divergent perspectives on incremental innovations are illustrated by looking in more detail at the substantive issues in the conflict between INPI and ANVISA. Silva (2008) provides a detailed analysis of the Prior Consent process, examining every patent application received by ANVISA from 2001–2006. Her work reveals a sharp decline in cases of Prior Consent being issued, from a high of 121 in 2004 to only 51 by 2006 (Silva 2008, 61). The study also examines ANVISA's intermediate reports made after preliminary examinations, revealing that ANVISA began to systematically request more details from applicants after 2004 (Silva 2008, 60). Most interestingly, in examining these reports, Miranda Silva distinguishes according to the substantive concerns expressed by ANVISA. She examines 442 patents that ANVISA did not approve on first exam, but rather sent back to INPI to transmit to the applicants for additional information, and she classifies them according to the reason given by ANVISA. From that total, I have removed the purely procedural issues (e.g., missed deadlines, improper translation, filing irregularities). Of the remaining substantive cases, issues that are directly related to incremental innovations (e.g., degree of novelty, degree of inventiveness, whether the innovation amounts to a therapeutic use) accounted for 45.6 percent of the concerns expressed by ANVISA (see Figure 6.1).[29] Thus, at the same time that the Brazil's innovation strategy was put into a higher gear, not only did ANVISA's strict application of patentability criteria become more rigorous, but the health agency's skepticism regarding incremental innovations became a central theme of its interactions with INPI. And this skepticism, in turn, generated further opposition from INPI.

---

27 Congressional hearings, July 3, 2008 (transcript, 4).

28 According to ANVISA, treating second uses as inventions, which is what is needed to justify a patent, implies that something can be invented multiple times. In Congress, responding to INPI President Jorge Ávila's defense of second use patents, the director of ANVISA's patent team exclaimed, "he invents a molecule and, when he thinks he has a new use, he invents it again. The day he manages to explain that to me, perhaps we'll no longer have so much disagreement on this topic" (Congressional hearings, July 3, 2008, transcript, 60).

29 This is a conservative estimate. Insufficient description of the invention, a concern that is inherently about the breadth of the patents' claims but may also be about inventiveness and incremental innovation, accounts for another 36.4 percent of the substantive cases.

Figure 6.1. ANVISA's concerns

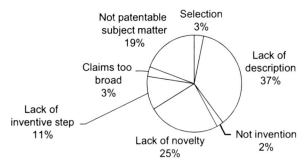

Source: Author's elaboration, based on data in Miranda Silva (2008, 63–7).

To summarize, the preceding analysis suggests that, even prior to the formal elimination of ANVISA's role in 2011, the Prior Consent system functioned much differently than designed, and much less effectively than many observers maintain. INPI and ANVISA did not "collaborate" (Deere 2008); and far from "forcing" (Drahos 2008) coordination between health and patent offices, INPI was able to ignore ANVISA when doing so fit its purposes. The obvious question, then, is why this celebrated, TRIPS-compatible, health-oriented patent policy was so difficult to implement and sustain in Brazil?

The Politics of Incremental Pharmaceutical Innovation in Brazil: Bureaucratic Isolation and Coalitional Erosion

In this section I explain why Prior Consent generated so much conflict and was so difficult to implement. To do so, I focus on ANVISA's inability to mobilize sufficient support for its role in patent examination, both from within the state and from key societal actors.

Bureaucratic isolation

One source of fragility of the coalition for health-oriented patent examination was the isolation of the principal state actors responsible for executing the policy. The inconsistent and somewhat confusing reaction within the rest of government to the conflict between INPI and ANVISA is telling.

In December 2008 the government's Interministerial Group on Intellectual Property (GIPI) declared a "consensus" position against issuing patents on most incremental pharmaceutical innovations. In doing so, it was supporting ANVISA and reproaching INPI, but the "consensus" was not so much a ruling or directive as a statement of opinion. INPI ignored the GIPI, declaring that it would not alter its examination practices without a change in the LPI itself. The GIPI itself is an intragovernmental forum for discussion and not a policymaking body, so it lacks the ability to enforce its consensus.[30] Yet the MDIC, INPI's parent ministry, could certainly bring the patent office in line. And if the MDIC would not force INPI to change its practices, the Casa Civil (essentially the Brazilian president's "chief of staff") could do so. My interviews suggest that what is lacking from the "consensus" is support at the highest level of the executive branch.[31] Ultimately, actions speak louder than words, and the fact that the government does not intervene to enforce the GIPI's resolution causes one to interpret claims of "consensus" with some skepticism. Or as one legislator sympathetic to ANVISA disbelievingly put it, "there is 'consensus' and there is 'consensus.'"

To understand the government's reluctance to reign in INPI, it is important to emphasize how much Brazilian government agencies across the board have been re-geared to promote innovation. A principal objective of economic policy in Brazil is to increase innovation, with patents used as an indicator of progress. The centerpiece of the new approach is the 2004 Innovation Law, which, among other things, facilitates patenting of publicly funded research and aims to increase university–industry linkages via licensing.[32] The institutions strengthened by the new innovation policy – and the influential individuals attached to them – are emphatically in favor of incremental innovations and supportive of INPI's posture vis-à-vis pharmaceutical patents. ANVISA's concerns about the injurious effects of extended periods of exclusivity conflict with the government's overriding enthusiasm for incremental innovation. Although GIPI expresses support for ANVISA, the fact of the matter is that no one seems ready to challenge INPI, which is regarded as an important actor in Brazil's new innovation policy.[33] With everyone committed to encouraging incremental innovation as a means of enhancing the Brazilian economy's international competitiveness, there is an instinctive aversion to policies and practices that appear to go against the grain. To be opposed to incremental innovation – of any sort – simply does not resonate within a government dedicated to increasing incremental innovation.

ANVISA's isolation must also be understood in the context of the Ministry of Health itself. Although the MS itself is a large and powerful ministry in the Brazilian executive, ANVISA is a small part of the MS – and the patent examination team (COOPI) is a tiny and marginal part of ANVISA.[34] While INPI is acting "normally" and doing what

---

30 Interview with Márcio Heidi Suguieda, MDIC and general coordinator of GIPI (Brasilia, 8 June 2009).

31 I conducted multiple interviews in May 2008, April 2009 and June 2009, in Brasilia and Rio de Janeiro, with legislators in the Chamber of Deputies and officials in MDIC, MS, INPI, and ANVISA.

32 The Brazilian law is modeled on the US Bayh–Dole Act. In addition to the Innovation Law, other relevant policies include R&D tax credits and a set of sectoral-specific innovation plans. I am not discussing Brazilian innovation policy in detail here. See Cruz and de Mello (2006); Octaviani (2008); Doctor (2009); Shadlen (2011).

33 INPI had countless directors in the years after the LPI came into effect in 1997, but in 2006 Jorge Ávila, a civil engineer with a doctorate in health and pharmaceutical development, became president. Ávila's directorship has coincided with a government decision to invest in the growth and modernization of INPI as a dimension of the emerging innovation strategy, though some of these changes preceded Ávila's assumption of the presidency.

34 As of 2008, COOPI was still not integrated into ANVISA's data information system.

patent offices do – granting patents – and in doing so, gaining presence and recognition in the international patent community,[35] participation in patent examination is not the sort of thing that health ministries ordinarily do. ANVISA's atypical and unnatural role – even one written into the reformed LPI – makes it difficult to protect and defend. MS officials (and frankly ANVISA officials) are not socialized into thinking about patents – it is not something in their professional toolkits. While they may support the outcome of reducing "trivial" patents and minimizing the extensions of patent terms, they are on unfamiliar and uncomfortable ground fighting on behalf of these goals. Or, to put it differently, ANVISA's patent examination team appears to have sympathizers within the government, but not necessarily advocates.[36]

Not only did the executive not intervene on behalf of ANVISA directly, it also failed to facilitate congressional efforts to do so. In addition to the bill mentioned above that would restrict ANVISA's role in patent examination, another proposal would formally restrict INPI by declaring second use and polymorphs unpatentable subject matter in Brazil. While the former bill is blocked by opposition from legislators from the ruling Workers' Party (PT), the latter was written and sponsored by PT deputies and received easier treatment in relevant PT-dominated commissions. Yet the PT legislators themselves await signals of approval from the executive, signals that have not been forthcoming. While the GIPI expressed disapproval of patents on polymorphs and second uses and, presumably, would like to see INPI alter its examination guidelines to adopt a more restrictive stance, the executive does appear to support an outright, statutory ban on such patents.

Coalitional erosion

Outside of government, ANVISA received the most solid and active support from health-oriented civil society groups. Prominent organizations such as the Brazilian Interdisciplinary Aids Association (ABIA) and the Working Group of Intellectual Property of the Brazilian Network for the Integration of Peoples (GTPI/REBRIP) were steadfast in their support for ANVISA's role in patent examination and their anger with INPI's practices. These actors played critical and indispensable roles in supporting Prior Consent (and other elements of Brazil's health-oriented patent policies).

Yet, the benefits of the support received from civil society were not enough to compensate for the lack of support ANVISA received from another key actor in Brazilian society, namely, the local pharmo-chemical and pharmaceutical sectors. The Brazilian pharmaceutical industry supported Prior Consent when the measure was announced in 1999, yet when the bill was introduced in 2008 that would effectively eliminate ANVISA's role in patent examination, local industry did not

---

35 In 2007, INPI was conferred status as "international search authority" in WIPO's Patent Cooperation Treaty.

36 The most outspoken – and, at times, sole – supporter of Prior Consent in the Brazilian government is the National AIDS Program.

Table 6.1. Research and development

	2000		2005	
	Expenditures (thousands of Rs)	Turnover*	Expenditures (thousands of Rs)	Turnover*
Pharmo-chemicals	2007.37	.0066	8902.21	.0161
Pharmaceuticals	1268.77	.0142	4135.57	.02527

*Turnover is calculated as R&D expenditures as a share of sales.
Source: PINTEC (2000, 2005).

express opposition to the proposed change. To the contrary, while COOPI submitted a detailed rebuttal of the bill (Ministério de Saúde 2008) and met with legislators in the Chamber of Deputies in Brasilia, the local firms and sectoral associations that participated in the legislative process expressed support for restricting ANVISA's role, aligned in this regard with firms from the transnational sector (INTERFARMA).[37] Likewise, in the hearings for a bill that would prohibit incremental innovations in pharmaceuticals, local industry's testimony was nearly identical to INPI's and the transnational sector's, expressing principled opposition to unwarranted patents, but emphatic that policy and practice should not rule out patents on incremental innovations.[38] Indeed, my interviews with officials from associations representing Brazilian pharmaceutical and pharmo-chemical firms reveal these associations' growing unease with the Prior Consent rule. The unease, if not always manifest in terms of outright opposition, is expressed in the form of unwillingness to actively and publicly mobilize in support of Prior Consent.[39]

ANVISA's inability to retain local industry's active support is rooted in the latter's growing interests in and capabilities for incremental innovation. Table 6.1 provides data on average per-firm expenditures on R&D and average amounts of R&D as a share of gross receipts in the pharmo-chemical and pharmaceutical sectors. From 2000 to 2005, R&D turnover increased by 144 percent in pharmo-chemicals and 77 percent in pharmaceuticals, while R&D expenditures increased by 344 percent in pharmo-chemicals and 226 percent in pharmaceuticals. The levels are low, but the growth is unmistakable, and it is growth that underpins actors' changing policy preferences.[40]

---

37 Personal communication with the director of ANVISA's patent office (September 5, 2008); interview with the rapporteur of the bill in Congress (Brasilia, June 9, 2009).

38 Interview with the bill's rapporteur (Brasilia, June 9, 2009).

39 One actor of local industry that has most consistently supported Prior Consent is the association of generics producers. These firms are hurt most directly by "evergreening," and their own business strategies are based less on incremental innovations. That said, the divisions are not clear and changes are afoot in this sector as well, as the "generic" firms in this sector are increasingly fused with transnational and Brazilian firms that retain strong interests in patenting incremental innovations.

40 Hasenclever and Paranhos (2009) and Ryan (2010) provide additional data on these changes.

Figure 6.2. Brazilian patent applications (pharmo-chemicals and pharmaceuticals)

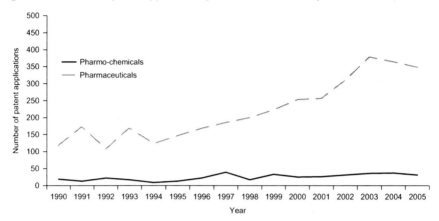

Source: Author's elaboration, based on INPI data.

The pharmaceutical sector's investments have coincided with the emergence of new innovative capabilities, as measured by Brazilian pharmaceutical patent applications. I use IPC categories to map technology classes of Brazilian patent applications, and I use pharmo-chemicals and pharmaceuticals as proxies for radical and incremental innovations, respectively (Schmoch 2008).[41] Though imperfect, this classification system provides a rough distinction between innovations that consist of molecules and compounds and those that consist of adapting and transforming such molecules and compounds.[42] Figure 6.2 presents the data: while there is little change as regards pharmo-chemical applications, the growth in pharmaceutical applications is unmistakable. While radical pharmaceutical innovation remains largely out of the reach of Brazilian firms and scientists, local actors are acquiring increased capabilities to innovate incrementally. Indeed, the data suggest that local firms do not just harbor aspirations for incremental innovations, but many of them already possess such capabilities.[43]

Because a strong bias against patents on incremental innovations would lead to many of Brazilian firms' own applications being rejected, they are inclined to oppose

41 The principal three-digit IPC categories are C07 (organic fine chemicals) and A61 (pharmaceuticals). The WIPO concordance is based on classifications at four digits (e.g., C07D, A61K), but the Brazilian data used here is at three digits.

42 Use of these indicators overstates the extent of radical innovations, since some of the pharmo-chemical patents are, upon closer examination, incremental. To minimize this error, the WIPO concordance does not include pharmo-chemical patents that have a secondary listing as pharmaceuticals, a step I am unable to take with the Brazilian data. Note that the bias goes in just one direction, for the pharmaceutical patents are almost entirely incremental.

43 One way of interpreting the different rates of growth in the pharmaceutical vs. pharmo-chemical applications is that the amount of capability and skill development required to move from imitating to innovating incrementally is less than what is required to move from innovating incrementally to innovating radically. Brazilian industry has made the first transition, but remains far from being able to accomplish radical innovations on a systematic basis.

ANVISA's role in patent examination. No one defends frivolous patents or favors unwarranted extensions of existing patents: in countless public forums, newspaper columns, hearings in Congress and virtually every venue conceivable, the condemnation of patents on trivial modifications that extend terms of exclusion is articulated by local and transnational firms alike.[44] Yet, these principled aversions contribute little to determining actors' actual political positions, precisely because they are shared by nearly everyone. In practice, few if any actors regard their own innovations as "trivial."

The question is if actors want the bias to be in favor or against the granting of patents on incremental innovations in pharmaceuticals as a matter of policy. A bias in favor will disadvantage local firms relative to foreign firms, for notwithstanding Brazilian actors' increased capabilities for incremental innovation suggested in Figure 6.2, they are still far behind the leading, transnational firms in this regard. Yet a systematic bias against granting patents on incremental pharmaceutical innovations will disadvantage local firms in an absolute sense, since incremental innovations are just about the only innovations most can expect to achieve. The empirical question is which set of risks and opportunities mobilize local industry politically. My analysis of the political activities of firms and trade associations in the Brazilian pharmaceutical sector suggests that fear of absolute losses incurred by ANVISA's overly restrictive approach to patenting incremental innovations prevails.[45]

A useful way to think about the politics of Prior Consent is to consider INPI and ANVISA as representing two alternative – and polarized – approaches to pharmaceutical patents. As indicated above, INPI's approach yields a wide scope of patentability and ANVISA's approach yields a narrow scope. The transnational sector and health activists are comfortable aligning themselves with INPI and ANVISA, respectively, but many Brazilian firms appear to be uncomfortable with either. Rather, Brazilian pharmaceutical and pharmo-chemical firms are critical of both positions – INPI's looseness that permits evergreening and ANVISA's rigidity that frustrates their own patenting activities. In the absence of a third approach, however, a middle road that grants patents on incremental innovations but has rigid examination guidelines and procedures to preemptively deny nondeserving applications, local firms appear to prefer INPI to ANVISA.[46]

To be clear, the position of the pharmaceutical sector in Brazil is not one of unity: many individuals and firms within the pharmaceutical sector remain adamantly

44 For example, http://www.inovacao.unicamp.br/report/noticias/index.php?cod=468

45 Cassier and Correa (2007) also point to the opposition of local pharmaceutical firms and scientific researchers to legislative initiatives that limit opportunities for pharmaceutical patenting.

46 The problem, of course, is that this middle road, as sensible as it sounds, is difficult to realize. Both INPI and ANVISA claim that this is what they do, but the significant amount of substantive conflict over patent applications suggests they must not both be doing this. Indeed, the problem is in determining which applications are deserving vs. nondeserving, and, again, this is a political choice, not simply a technical evaluation.

opposed to INPI's practices and supportive of ANVISA's approach, and many are also opposed to ANVISA's approach and supportive of INPI's practices. The emergence of new capabilities in the sector has not created actors with uniform interests in support of one side or the other, but rather has created internal divisions that, in turn, paralyze the sector as a political actor. In fact, at one point the trade association of pharmo-chemical producers (ABIFINA) adopted, after considerable internal debate and with some members abstaining and dissenting, a statement in support of ANVISA, only to then decide not to publicize it.[47]

Interestingly, the conflict over Prior Consent itself radicalized ANVISA and pushed local industry more into INPI's camp. After all, from industry's perspective, an outright prohibition on some types of incremental innovations (e.g., polymorphs and second uses) is more alarming than rigorous scrutiny of each application, as the former essentially equates incremental innovation with triviality. When legislators proposed this outright ban, ANVISA's original response was lukewarm, arguing that it was not necessary to change the law but rather enforce the existing law to assure that ANVISA could discharge its functions. Yet with INPI "boycotting" the system and GIPI unable to back up its "consensus," ANVISA since came to support the more prohibitive (and, from industry's perspective, draconian) legislation.

Finally, it is worth contrasting the Brazilian pharmaceutical industry's contrasting dispositions vis-à-vis Prior Consent and the governments' policy on compulsory licenses. The latter policy threatens minimal losses, as the compulsory licenses (threatened and, in one instance, issued) have targeted essential medicines that are patented by non-Brazilian firms.[48] Compulsory licenses also promise potential benefits in terms of possibilities of becoming suppliers of pharmo-chemical inputs to the Brazilian state-owned labs that will make the medicines.[49] In contrast, a restrictive policy on patenting incremental innovations appears to threaten significant losses.

Conclusion

Since the introduction of TRIPS, tens of thousands of pages of books and articles have been dedicated to discussions of "policy space" and the rights and abilities of countries to tailor their patent systems to suit national needs and objectives. The case study of the politics of pharmaceutical patent examination in Brazil illustrates the political challenges to implementing health-oriented, TRIPS-compatible patent

---

47 I learned about this statement and the events related to its "adoption" in personal communication with a member of ABIFINA. The former director of COOPI evidently was not aware of the association's "support." See the interview with Luis Carlos Wanderley Lima in *Intellectual Property Watch*, cited earlier in note 19.

48 Specifically, the targeted drugs have been antiretrovirals for treating HIV/AIDS.

49 Indeed, a key step in eliciting private industry's support was a reform of the compulsory licensing provisions in 2003 that specified private actors could supply the government with inputs without jeopardizing the noncommercial and public use character of the licenses (see Shadlen 2009, 48).

policies. In particular, I have drawn attention to two conditions that make the social and political coalition for health-focused patent examination extremely fragile: the isolation within the state apparatus of those officials responsible for executing the policy, and the ambivalent interests and political motivations of potentially key constituencies in the Brazilian pharmaceutical industry.

The analysis in this chapter complements the literature's prevailing emphasis on international pressures as determinants of how developing countries utilize their remaining policy space (see also Deere 2008). To be sure, Brazil has come under intense international pressures on account of the Prior Consent rule, but other aspects of Brazil's patent system, such as compulsory licensing, have come under equally persistent pressures. The results of these external pressures differ across policy instruments, because of the different constellations of interests in state and society that I analyze in this chapter.

Given that one of the explanatory factors in the Brazilian case is the isolation of the officials responsible for executing the policy, it might be that a different institutional design would allow Brazil to achieve a different outcome. Related to this, Reichman (in this volume) makes a strong call for more interministerial coordination to help integrate the activities of diverse government branches with an interest in IP policy (health, justice, competition, development, trade, and so on). Yet Brazil has an interministerial group that is designed to do precisely this. Likewise, it has been suggested, that one way to overcome the interagency conflict between ANVISA and INPI would simply be to move ANVISA's patent examiners into INPI. After all, in India, the policy to minimize patents on incremental pharmaceutical innovations does not depend on dual examination, but rather requires that the patent office itself engage in rigorous application of India's stringent patentability criteria. In the simplest terms, examiners in India's equivalent to INPI are expected to treat patent applications similarly to the way ANVISA's examiners do. As simple as it sounds, advocating this for Brazil would seem to be confusing cause and effect, for if ANVISA's examiners were operating within INPI, they almost certainly would not be allowed to examine patents as rigorously as they did from 2001–2011 when Prior Consent was in effect. Indeed, ANVISA's examiners could only get away with strict and rigorous examination of patents because they were isolated. There is something that permits rigorous patent examination and makes a systematic bias against patents on incremental innovations so much more durable in one country than another, but that something is probably not institutional design.

The broader implications of this analysis for knowledge governance are not comforting. Brazil is a leader in protecting developing countries' rights and prerogatives to tailor national patent regimes to national needs. In multilateral forums (e.g., WTO, WIPO and WHO) and bilateral settings (e.g., terminated negotiations over a hemispheric trade agreement), Brazil has been adamant and unbending in its defense of countries' rights to exploit their TRIPS flexibilities. Moreover, as developing countries go, Brazil is atypically large and economically diversified, precisely the sort of country that should be able to overcome international pressures to implement harmonized IP rules. The fact that, for all these efforts, Brazil struggled to implement and sustain this health-oriented intervention is a cause for concern. To be sure, in smaller and less economically diversified countries with less growth of domestic innovative capabilities, such measures may generate less fear among domestic pharmaceutical producers – but countries with such characteristics are also likely to be more dependent (economically and politically) on demanding OECD countries and thus less likely to resist external pressures to forego their right to use TRIPS flexibilities.

References

All web addresses last accessed August 2011.

Amin, Tahir. 2012. "Re-visiting the Patents and Access to Medicines Dichotomy: An Evaluation of TRIPS Implementation and Public Health Safeguards in Developing Countries." In O. Aginam, J. Harrington and P. Yu (eds), *Global Governance of HIV/AIDS: Intellectual Property and Access to Essential Medicines*. Cheltenham: E. Elgar. Forthcoming.

Basheer, Shamnad. 2005. "Limiting the Patentability of Pharmaceutical Inventions and Micro-Organisims: A TRIPS Compatibility Review." IPI working paper.

Basso, Maristela. 2006. "Intervention of Health Authorities in Patent Examination: The Brazilian Practice of the Prior Consent." *International Journal of Intellectual Property Management* 1: 54–74.

Beas Rodrigues, Edson and Bryan Murphy. 2006. "Brazil's Prior Consent Law: A Dialogue Between Brazil and the United States Over Where the TRIPS Agreement Currently Sets the Balance Between the Protection of Pharmaceutical Patents and Access to Medicines." *Albany Law Journal of Science and Technology* 16: 423–56.

Cassier, Maurice and Marilena Correa. 2007. "Intellectual Property and Public Health: Copying of HIV/Aids Drugs by Brazilian Public and Private Pharmaceutical Laboratories." *RECIIS Eletronical Journal in Communication, Information and Innovation in Health* 1: 83–90.

Chang, Ha-Joon. 2002. *Kicking Away the Ladder: Development Strategy in Historical Perspective*. London: Anthem Press.

CIPR. 2002. *Integrating Intellectual Property Rights and Development Policy*. London: Commission on Intellectual Property Rights.

Correa, Carlos. 2007. "Guidelines for the Examination of Pharmaceutical Patents: Developing a Public Health Perspective." WHO-ICTSD-UNCTAD working paper. Available at http://www.iprsonline.org/resources/docs/Correa_Patentability Guidelines.pdf

_____. 2000. *Intellectual Property Rights, the WTO and Developing Countries: The TRIPS Agreement and Policy Options*. London and New York: Zed Books.

Cruz, Carlos H de Brito and Luiz de Mello. 2006. "Boosting Innovation Performance in Brazil." OECD, Economics Department Working Paper No. 532.

Deere, Carolyn. 2008. *The Implementation Game: The TRIPS Agreement and the Global Politics of Intellectual Property Reform in Developing Countries*. Oxford: Oxford University Press.

Doctor, Mahrukh. 2009. "Furthering Industrial Development in Brazil: Globalization and the national innovation system." Paper prepared for the Latin American Studies Association, Rio de Janeiro, June.

Drahos, Peter. 2008. "'Trust Me': Patent Offices in Developing Countries." *American Journal of Law and Medicine* 34: 151–74.

_____. 1995. "Global Property Rights in Information: The Story of TRIPS at the GATT." *Prometheus* 13 (1): 6–19.

Gallagher, Kevin P. (ed.) 2005. *Putting Development First: The Importance of Policy Space in the WTO and International Financial Institutions*. London: Zed Books.

GSK. 2007. "Evergreening." GlaxoSmithKline Briefings. Available at http://www.gsk.com/policies/GSK-and-evergreening.pdf

Hall, Peter A. and David Soskice (eds) 2001. *Varieties of Capitalism: The Institutional Foundations of Comparative Advantage.* Oxford: Oxford University Press.

Hasenclever, Lia and Julia Paranhos. 2009. "The Development of the Pharmaceutical Industry in Brazil and India: Technological Capability and Industrial Development." Unpublished manuscript, Economics Innovation Research Group, Economics Institute, Federal University of Rio de Janeiro.

Helfer, Laurence R., Karen J. Alter and M. Florencia Guerzovich. 2009. "Islands of Effective International Adjudication: Constructing an Intellectual Property Rule of Law in the Andean Community." *American Journal of International Law* 103 (1): 1–47.

Homedes, N. and A. Ugalde. 2005. "Multisource Drug Policies in Latin America: Survey of 10 Countries." *Bulletin of the World Health Organization* 83: 64–70.

Howard, Leighton. 2007. "Use of Patents in Drug Lifecycle Management." *Journal of Generic Medicines* 4: 230–36.

ICC. 2005. "The Importance of Incremental Innovation for Development." Submission to the World Health Organization's Commission on Intellectual Property Rights, Innovation and Public Health (CIPIH). Available at http://www.who.int/intellectualproperty/submissions/SubmissionsInternationalChamberofCommerce.pdf

Kunisawa, Viviane Yumy Mitsuuchi. 2009. "Patenting Pharmaceutical Inventions on Second Medical Uses in Brazil." *Journal of World Intellectual Property* 12 (4): 297–316.

Machlup, Fritz and Edith Penrose. 1950. "The Patent Controversy in the Nineteenth Century." *Journal of Economic History* 10: 1–29.

Matthews, Duncan. 2002. *Globalising Intellectual Property Rights: The TRIPs Agreement.* London: Routledge.

May, Christopher. 2007. "The Hypocrisy of Forgetfulness: The Contemporary Significance of Early Innovations in Intellectual Property." *Review of International Political Economy* 14 (1): 1–25.

———. 2000. *A Global Political Economy of Intellectual Property Rights: The New Enclosures?* London and New York: Routledge.

Ministério de Saúde. 2008. "Nota Técnica: Dispõe sobre alteração do artigo 229-C, da Lei 9.279, de 14.05.1996, e dá outras providências." On file with the author.

Octaviani, Alessandro. 2008. "Biotechnology in Brazil: Promoting Open Innovation." In Lea Shaver (ed.), *Access to Knowledge in Brazil: New Research on Intellectual Property, Innovation and Development,* 127–61. New Haven, CT: Information Society Project at Yale Law School.

PGF (Procuradoria-Geral Federal). 2009. "Atribuições INPI & ANVISA." Parecer 210/PGF/AE/2009.

Rathod, Sandeep Kanak. 2010. "Ever-Greening: A Status Check in Selected Countries." *Journal of Generic Medicines* 7 (3): 227–42.

Reichman, Jerome H. 1997. "From Free Riders to Fair Followers: Global Competition under the TRIPs Agreement." *New York University Journal of International Law and Politics* 29: 11–93.

Rosman, Eduardo Colonna. 2004. "O Limite Normativo de Agencia Nacional de Vigilancia Sanitaria – ANVISA." *Revista da ABPI* 71.

Ryan, Michael. 1998. *Knowledge Diplomacy: Global Competition and the Politics of Intellectual Property.* Washington DC: Brookings Institution Press.

———. 2010. "Patent Incentives, Technology Markets, and Public-Private Bio-Medical Innovation Networks in Brazil." *World Development* 38: 1082–93.

Schertenleib, Denis. n.d. "Patent Lifecycle Management: Strategies for Originators and Tactics for Generics." Available at http://www.cabinet-hirsch.com/document files/PATENT LIFE CYCLE MANAGEMENT.ppt

Schiff, Eric. 1971. *Industrialization without National Patents.* Princeton: Princeton University Press.

Schmoch, Ulrich. 2008. "Concept of a Technology Classification for Country Comparisons." Final report to the World Intellectual Property Organization (WIPO). Available at http://www.wipo.int/export/sites/www/ipstats/en/statistics/patents/pdf/wipo_ipc_technology.pdf

Sell, Susan K. 2003. *Private Power, Public Law: The Globalization of Intellectual Property Rights.* London: Cambridge University Press.

Shadlen, Kenneth C. 2005. "Exchanging Development for Market Access? Deep Integration and Industrial Policy under Multilateral and Regional-Bilateral Trade Agreements." *Review of International Political Economy* 12 (5): 750–75.

———. 2009. "The Politics of Patents and Drugs in Brazil and Mexico: The Industrial Bases of Health Policies." *Comparative Politics* 42 (1): 41–58.

———. 2011. "The Political Contradictions of Incremental Innovation: Lessons from Pharmaceutical Patent Examination in Brazil." *Politics & Society* 39 (2): 143–74.

Silva, Helen Miranda. 2008. "Avaliação da análise dos pedidos de patentes farmacêuticas feita pela Anvisa no cumprimento do mandato legal da anuência prévia." Master's thesis, National School of Public Health, Rio de Janeiro, Brazil.

Souza, Marcela Trigo de. 2008. "Should Brazil Allow Patents on Second Medical Uses?" *Revista da ABPI* 93: 53–67.

UNDP. 2003. *Making Global Trade Work for People.* London: Earthscan.

Watal, Jayashree. 2000. *Intellectual Property Rights in the World Trade Organization: The Way Forward for Developing Countries.* New Delhi: Oxford University Press.

WHO. 2002. "Network for Monitoring the Impact of Globalization and TRIPS on Access to Medicines." Health Economics and Drugs, EDM Series No. 11, WHO/EDM/PAR/2002.1.

Part III

GOING FORWARD: TOWARDS A KNOWLEDGE GOVERNANCE RESEARCH AGENDA

Chapter 7

VARIETIES OF LATIN AMERICAN PATENT OFFICES: COMPARATIVE STUDY OF PRACTICES AND PROCEDURES

Ana Célia Castro

Federal University of Rio de Janeiro

Ana María Pacón

Universidad Catolica del Peru

Mônica Desidério

Federal University of Rio de Janeiro

1. Introduction

The lack of soundness of the patents granted in an environment prone to uncertainty can be detrimental to the generation and transfer of technology and, potentially, could

This chapter is based on a paper that is part of a network research project developed by MINDS/ IMDE (Multidisciplinary Institute for Development and Strategies/Instituto Multidisciplinar de Desenvolvimento e Estratégias), sponsored by the Ford Foundation, under the coordination of Ana Célia Castro. We sought to incorporate the products of the research project, undertaken by Ana Célia Castro, Ana María Pacón (Universidad Catolica del Peru), Annalisa Primi (OECD), Leandro Malavota (INPI), Allan Rocha (UFRRJ), Márcia Nunes de Barros (Federal Justice Department), Vânia Lindoso (Fiocruz) and, in memoriam, Leonardo Justino (INPI). This version was developed by Ana Célia Castro (director of the Graduate Program of Public Policy, Strategies and Development at the Institute of Economics at the Federal University of Rio de Janeiro (PPED/IE/UFRJ), director of the Interdisciplinary Institute on Development and Strategies MINDS-IMDES, and vice director of the National Institute for Science and Technology in Public Policies, Strategies and Development – INCT-PPED), Ana María Pacón and Mônica Desidério (INCT in Neglected Diseases and PPED/IE/UFRJ). We thank Guilherme Rodrigues Lima for the data organization on patent offices' statistics and its comments. We also thank the Ford Foundation for supporting this research. We wish to honor the memory of the researcher Leonardo Justino, who worked in the Brazilian INPI, was part of the research team and unfortunately is no longer among us, having passed away in 2009.

disturb the technological catching-up processes of developing countries. This conceptual flaw is the reason for the statement that a better definition of the criteria for novelty, inventive activity and utility are among the priorities for a possible positive agenda for patent examinations. Thus, developing countries are concerned with the possibility that TRIPS harmonization would limit their ability to contest patent protection restrictions and also the incorporation of their companies in the relevant international innovation networks. The idea of descriptive sufficiency also deserves some attention. It is self-evident that, in the case of developing countries at least, it would seem advantageous to draw the greatest possible amount of information from the process of granting patent privileges.

In this context, it can be useful to reveal the nature of the research for precedence and examination processes for patents, verifying the extent of the research universe, the interpretation accorded to each criterion and the organization of the interaction between the depositing company and the patent office. It is hoped to ascertain the manner in which each of these offices determines the scope of the patents granted. But on the other hand, it is possible to conjecture that some patent offices, in Latin America or elsewhere, do not enroll in examination processes for granting patents, taking into consideration patent examination done abroad.

In open economies, intellectual property (IP) becomes a key issue in knowledge generation and technology diffusion. In such a context, effective intellectual property governance appears to be a necessary step for catching up. The "technology gap" of Latin America is well known, so her lagging behind in patenting and in IP governance capacities should not be surprising. In Southeast Asia, the number of residents' patents is growing at a higher rate than that of nonresidents, while in Latin America and the Caribbean, nonresidents' patenting leads the scene. In this scenario, patenting systems are a powerful tool in the hands of foreign companies: commercialization of foreign products is facilitated, while in most of the cases, local technological capabilities are inadequately protected.

This chapter aims to compare the practices and procedures of different Latin American patent offices – Brazil, Peru and Mexico – and assumes the following starting points:

1. Intellectual property represents the broadest knowledge regulatory system in the current post-TRIPS world.
2. Access to knowledge, and the ways its intellectual property is enforced or not, constitutes the cornerstone for the dynamism of contemporary capitalist economies and assumes particular importance in the intermediate stages of national development.
3. However, through the analysis of the national patent offices' practices and procedures, and its institutional framing, it is possible to reveal relevant differences between them, allowing the concept of "varieties of patent offices."[1]

---

1   As far as this particular appropriation of the concept of varieties is concerned, as a biological metaphor, we are referring to the patent offices as a particular *species* which shares a socially constructed normative isomorphism after TRIPS (Agreement on Trade-Related Aspects of Intellectual Property Rights), but also reveals national particular uniqueness, which is the aim of this project to reveal.

The article proposes the following hypothesis:

1. In spite of a process of normative isomorphism (see DiMaggio and Powell 1991) instituted by TRIPS, patent offices have their own institutional cultures and histories worth studying.
2. This institutional culture is transformed over time but incorporates conflicting tendencies – of the historical moment, of political economic direction and the Patent Office Directory approach.
3. Aside from the patent offices' historical and institutional specificities, the country's legal framework and its normative functioning constitute another element of differentiation that should be taken into consideration. In other words, the juridical order, especially by way of the jurisprudence resulting from its decisions on patent conflicts, is an actor in the constitution of patent regimes.
4. The role of national diplomacy in the global forum (or in global governance institutions), notably at WIPO (World Intellectual Property Organization) and WTO (World Trade Organization), constitutes another relevant aspect in understanding the current patent regime (however, this will not be an object of analysis in this text).[2]
5. And, finally: (a) in spite of the fact that the process of analyzing and issuing patents follows a relatively similar international norm that is, moreover, (b) converging with the introduction of a set of automation tools developed by the European Patent Office (EPTOS – Electronic Patent and Trademark Office System)[3] and (c) which follows in the same direction as the greater internationalization of search processes and the evident project in databases, one can still assert that there is ample variety among patent offices, and patent offices contain a high degree of autonomy and differentiate themselves by their capacity to undertake the patent exam and by their "rate of patent issue."

As will be pointed out in this article, national patent offices, responsible for implementing legal–institutional frameworks for intellectual property at the national level (especially in the case of industrial property), are singular and varied organizations. Moreover, patent examiners hold a high level of discretionary power, in spite of the uniformity observed in patent exams, for example, between the Brazilian INPI, the Peruvian INDECOPI and the Mexican patent office (IMPI).

---

2 In the Brazilian case, one must also note GIPI (Interministrial Group on Intellectual Property), which discusses the direction of the government's intellectual property policies as well as its participation in international forums. The Brazilian government, one could say, keeps a relatively eclectic position toward intellectual property, apparently respecting conflicts of interest within the state and guaranteeing the institutional autonomy of each one of these spheres, notably INPI, the Ministry of Culture, the Ministry of Health, as well as agencies such as ANVISA.

3 In practice, these tools configure a uniform system established in different offices with consistent behaviors, though with specific requirements for each one of these offices.

One of the few studies conducted about patent examiners, in this case on USPTO (United States Patent and Trademark Office), states that "The key insight from our qualitative analysis is that 'there may be as many patent offices as patent examiners'" (Cockburn, Kortum and Stern 2002).

In a contrary perspective, Peter Drahos' (2010) "The Global Governance of Knowledge" focuses on the interaction among patent offices and sees an "invisible" process of harmonization as a consequence of TRIPS implementation. However, although we generally agree with the existence of harmonization processes as a tendency, a closer look inside Drahos' book can show different results:

> Patent offices have a tremendous de facto power over the interpretation of patent standards because they have to establish practicable routines for the day-to-day application of these standards... One exercise in which the three offices examined some hypothetical cases involving the patentability of DNA fragments showed the offices getting to roughly similar results but for different reasons. Another study which looked at actual results for non-PCT applications for 1990–95 that had been granted in the US and the EPO found "significant disharmony" of outcomes across the offices. JPO in particular had rejected 7,024 patents that had been granted by the USPTO and EPO. The study was not able to explain what accounted for these differences of outcome but it suggests that even where patent offices converge in the same standards, there is no guarantee that a common interpretation of the standards will follow. (Drahos 2010, 51–2)[4]

We may state that (1) the relationship between patents granted as a share of applications in different national patent offices varies according to three patterns – around 50 percent, around 25 percent and around 75 percent – and this relates to the existence and the quality of the patent exam, (2) the rate of patents issued by patent examiners in different Latin American patent offices varies, depending upon the patent office's institutional culture and political orientation, which changes over time and is not independent from the government's economic and technological policies,; the type of patents that he or she analyzes, the examiner's tenure – in other words, how long he or she has worked at the patent office – the examiner's training and, finally, the individual examiner's beliefs regarding the public importance of issuing patents.

Together with the changes in the microbehavior of actors, also partly pushed by the emergence of the new technological paradigms, there has been an emerging willingness in the public sector and in the government to look at IP as a tool for knowledge governance, inducing a more coordinated approach towards IP with the science, technology and innovation strategy of the country, and in line with the policies to support industrial development. The use of patents to protect relevant advances in

---

4 The article mentioned is Jensen et al. (2005).

scientific and technological applications with industrial utility is supported by a series of instruments of the national technology policy, such as a series of demand-oriented subsidies and grants for supporting the firm during the filing process. Intellectual property systems are a complex governing arena whose operational mechanisms are not easily understood. Effective IP governance requires proper infrastructure, institutions and prepared actors, as well as suitable legal architecture and a proactive attitude in the international arena.

The increasingly rejected principle of "one size fits all" finds a fascinating example here in which, notwithstanding the whole infrastructure created to reinforce convergence, the solutions found continue to exhibit varied national traits. In this way, the conceptual perspective under development, which treats intellectual property as a dimension of knowledge governance, but not the only one, and patent offices as an element of the property regime of knowledge assets, but not the only one, seems to shed more light on the varied ecology that regulates knowledge production, circulation, protection and appropriation.

We have organized this chapter in five sections: after the introduction, we present a set of statistics on the relationship between patent applications and grants issued in different groups of countries. A short history follows of three patent offices, namely, Brazilian (INPI), Peruvian (INDECOPI) and Mexican (IMPI) and their institutional structures, with general statistics about their operation. The fifth part of this work presents some methodological concerns on the fieldwork, which consisted of interviews with patent examiners, and its results to INPI Brazil, INDECOPI Peru and IMPI Mexico. Finally, our conclusions will reexamine the hypotheses in light of the case studies.

2. Stylized Facts and Some Measures

Statistics published by the WIPO website are the primary source for the following figures. In order to study differences and common patterns as far as granting patents is concerned, the patent offices of different countries were divided into two groups and two periods (1979 to 1994 and 1994 to 2009, pre- and post-TRIPS). The discussion follows after the presentation of the Figures.

Group 1: United States (USPTO), European Patent Office (EPO), China, Japan (JPO), Germany, Korea

In the pre-TRIPS period, especially until 1990, Japan and the United States were dominant – Japan in terms of applications and the United States in terms of patents granted. In the post-TRIPS period, the presence of China becomes predominant in terms of applications but Japan and the United States still represent around 30 percent of the total of applications and grants. In 2008, China represents more than 40 percent of patents granted while the participation of the United States and Japan are around 20 percent of the patents granted in this group of countries.

Figure 7.1. Applications and grants of Group 1 (1979–1994 and 1995–2008)

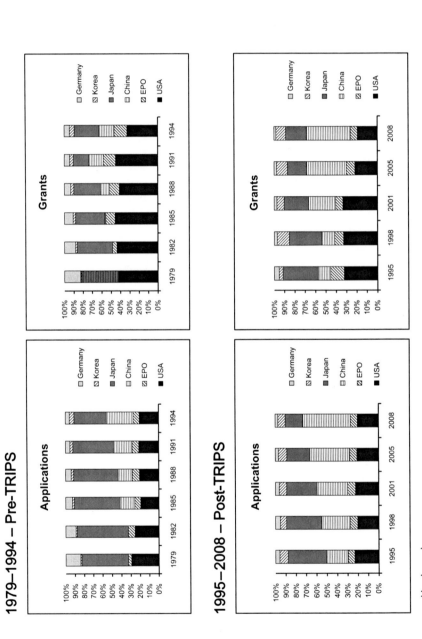

Source: WIPO, prepared by the authors.

Group 2: Argentina, Brazil, Chile, Colombia, Mexico and Peru

Figure 7.2 shows the participation of the six selected countries from Latin America. Due to the lack of data in some years, especially from Argentina, the information might be distorted.

In the first period, we can see that Colombia, Chile and Peru keep a small share both in applications and grants. Colombia has, on average, 3.3 percent of shares in applications and 4.3 percent in grants, while Peru has 1.7 percent in applications and 2.6 percent in grants and Chile has an average of 4.9 percent in both applications and grants.

Brazil starts with around 40 percent in applications and jumps up to more than 55 percent in 1985, due to the lack of data from Argentina, but later loses its share, ending with a little more than 30 percent. In grants, although more volatile, Brazil also has a rise in its share until 1985, which then falls back to end with an average of 40 percent. Mexico starts with around 25 percent in applications, and this number keeps rising until the end of the period, culminating at 49.5 percent of the total. The share of Mexico in grants is also quite volatile, having decreased until 1985 and then increasing until 1994, with an average of 25.6 percent. Lastly, Argentina has a little more than 20 percent of applications at the start of the period, and it is not shown in the next years due to the shortage of data, but in the last year, the participation is 3.5 percent. In relation to its grants, Argentina starts with a high percentage of 36 percent, which later decreases, ending up with an average of 22.6 percent.

In the period after TRIPS, we have the same results. Colombia, Chile and Peru remain with a low percentage of applications (on average 3.5 percent, 3 percent and 3.2 percent respectively). Mexico's figures keep rising, starting with 46 percent and ending with 79 percent, partially due to the lack of data from the other countries. Brazil, due to several reasons analyzed afterwards, falls from 35 percent to a little less than 20 percent. Finally Argentina, in the two years where it is shown in the graphic, has percentages of 13 percent and 20 percent, but due to the absence of figures for the next years, it is not possible to establish a trend. As far as grants are concerned, the figures of the countries are quite variable. We should highlight Mexico, which despite the falling of 2001 has had a strong participation in the post-TRIPS period.

Patent granted as a percentage of patent application

This graph shows the average of the relation between grants and applications for each country of Group 1 in the two periods, before TRIPS and after TRIPS (this number was reached by calculating the ratio between grants and applications for every year and then the average for the period). The behavior of the countries was quite variable. The United States, Germany and Spain had lower averages post-TRIPS than pre-TRIPS. In EPO, China, Japan and Korea, this relation is higher in the second period compared with the first. With the exception of Spain, all the countries in both periods have a rate of patent issue below 50 percent. China, Japan and Germany belong to the group around 25 percent.

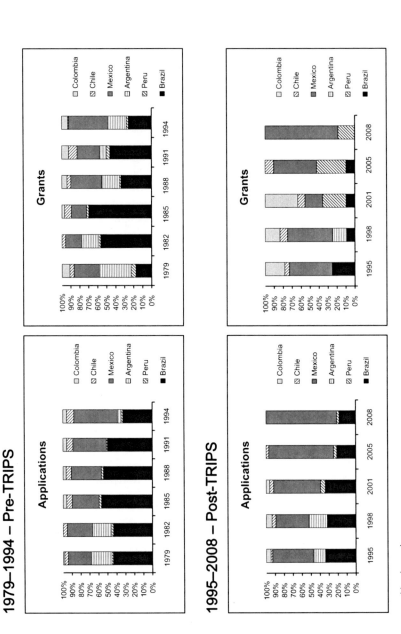

Figure 7.2. Applications and grants by countries as a share of the total applications and grants of Group 2 (1979–1994 and 1995–2008)

Source: WIPO, prepared by the authors.

Figure 7.3. Group 1 – Averages of the relationships between patents granted and patent application in the same year, in two periods – pre- and post-TRIPS

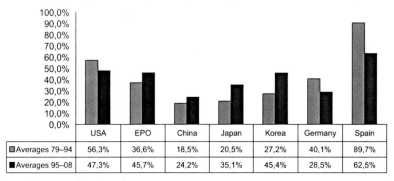

	USA	EPO	China	Japan	Korea	Germany	Spain
▨ Averages 79–94	56,3%	36,6%	18,5%	20,5%	27,2%	40,1%	89,7%
■ Averages 95–08	47,3%	45,7%	24,2%	35,1%	45,4%	28,5%	62,5%

Source: WIPO, prepared by the authors.

Figure 7.4. Group 2 – Averages of the relationships between patents granted and patent applications in the same year, in two periods – pre- and post-TRIPS

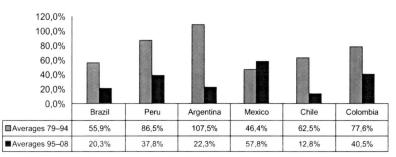

	Brazil	Peru	Argentina	Mexico	Chile	Colombia
▨ Averages 79–94	55,9%	86,5%	107,5%	46,4%	62,5%	77,6%
■ Averages 95–08	20,3%	37,8%	22,3%	57,8%	12,8%	40,5%

Source: WIPO, prepared by the authors.

All countries from the second group had experienced a significant drop in the averages of patents granted over patent applications in the post-TRIPS period, with the exception of Mexico. Taking only this period into consideration, Colombia, Mexico and Peru belong to the around 50 percent pattern, whereas Brazil, Argentina and Chile are part of the group around 25 percent. The average between patents granted and patent application has dropped by more than 80 percent in Argentina between the first and second periods. It is probable that these results are a consequence of whether the patent exam is done domestically or abroad.

Actually, although it is not possible to prove, we could have four different patterns instead of three, defined by the combination of two-by-two variables – instead of relying on the rate of patenting: countries that do or do not do the patent exam (or rely on patent exams done abroad), countries that have a higher (more than 50 percent) or lower (less than 50 percent) rate of patenting. Let us take the case of Brazil: the patent exam is done in-house and Brazil has a relatively low rate of patenting.

Figures 3 and 4 assume that the relationship between patents granted and patent applications in the same year and the averages of all years of the two different periods,

Figure 7.5. Relationship between patents granted and patent applications taking into account a four-year backlog (averages of all years in two different periods – pre- and post-TRIPS)

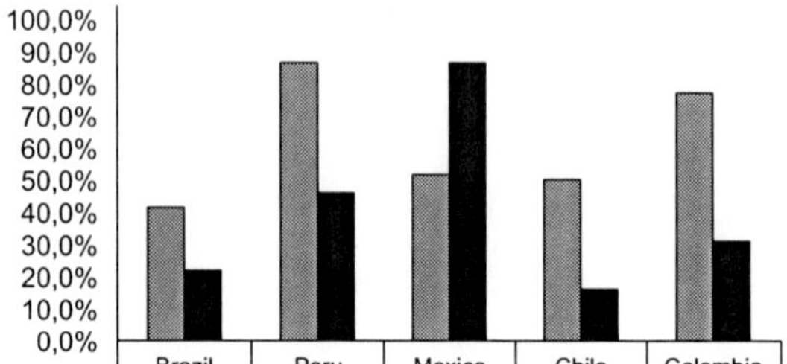

	Brazil	Peru	Mexico	Chile	Colombia
▨ Averages 79–94	42,2%	86,5%	52,9%	50,6%	77,9%
■ Averages 95–04	22,7%	46,4%	87,0%	16,8%	31,5%

pre- and post-TRIPS, would normalize the known existence of a backlog between applications and grants. Figure 7.5 takes into consideration the average of four years of backlog (between different classes of patents) and compares applications in the year t-4 with grants issued in the t period.

As far as the final conclusions are concerned, and for the post-TRIPS period, Brazil and Chile remain in the same around 25 percent group, now with the presence of Colombia. Peru keeps its position in the around 50 percent pattern, whereas Mexico shows a major difference, entering in the group of around 75 percent (where Spain leads). As we will see in the country case analysis, the IMPI relies on patent exams done by EPO.[5]

3. Brief History of the Patent Office (Institutional Approach) and Actual Structure

3.1. INPI – Brazil. The legal–institutional framework of patents in Brazil: Historical milestones[6]

The use of the patent system as an instrument of rewarding and incentivizing inventive activity is quite an old practice in Brazil. There is evidence of exclusive inventors' rights since colonial times, with the oldest record being from 1707.[7] The transfer of the Portuguese court to Brazil in 1808 required the Portuguese state to build a structural apparatus – political, institutional, legal and economical – whose groundwork addressed the need to engender the conditions and opportunities for the modernization of the means of wealth generation, after the mold of contemporary standards

---

5 We did the same exercise for the three groups of countries, but the differences were not significant as the averages "normalize" the series taken into consideration.

6 This part of the text was written by Leandro Malavota and constitutes an important piece of historical research connected to his master and doctoral thesis (Malavota 2011).

7 This concerns a royal act that bans the use by third parties, except by way of previously established payments to the inventor (in this case, four hundred thousand *réis*) of a "machine to make water go up as long a distance as one wishes…" (Cruz Filho 1983, 7).

in Europe.[8] Exclusively in terms of stimulating and protecting inventive activity, a set of measures was introduced that basically consisted of the regulation and systematization of the issue of trademarks and patents to inventors and those who introduced foreign industries, after the example of what already existed in England, France and the United States.

This patent-concession structure was maintained until the 1880s, when legislation suffered substantial changes, more attuned to the principles that at that time undergirded patent protection in Europe's main powers and in the United States.[9] Spurred by issues raised at many international debates and by the Paris Convention, the first international treaty on patents, ratified in 1883, the Brazilian patent-protection system was restructured with various notable changes, including the discontinuation of the practice of a test (except for food, chemical and pharmaceutical products). At century's end, the logic of patent protection in Brazil shifted from an emphasis on merit to an emphasis on the guarantee of the individual right to property. It is important to note that Brazil was the fourth country in the world to have a legal framework for industrial protection, preceded only by England ("Statute of Monopolies," made into law in 1623), the United States (1790) and France (1791) (see INPI 2007).

Another important aspect to be highlighted is that Brazilian law, until 1882, allowed the coexistence of two parallel "systems," that of awards and that of monopoly. Though these served the same purpose – to spur invention – they were endowed with different impulses: the first was grounded on the dissemination and advancement of technological information, insofar as it inhibited secrets, preventing a private appropriation of knowledge, which once "bought" by the state, immediately became a public good, the latter was based upon appropriation, allowing the privileged party to exclude third parties from exploitation of the new market created by the invention, the exclusivity of the latter would be guaranteed by maintaining secrecy during the patent's duration, upon whose expiration, however, technical information would be published in order to allow others to freely explore the patented object. To protect the inventor, the structure that reigned in Brazil during almost the entirety of the 1800s, therefore, blended elements of distinct natures, constituting a singular system that was compatible with the country's level of economic development at the time.[10]

The first official body to oversee patents and trademarks was established in 1923 by Decree 16254 and was named the Industrial Property General Administration (Diretoria General de Propriedade Industrial), which underwent a number of changes in form and linkages to distinct departments until it became the current INPI.

---

8 We can cite as other relevant economic measures the tax exemption of foreign trade with allied nations, the rollback of legal restrictions to the development of manufacturing activities, the creation of the Royal Committee of Commerce, Agriculture, Factories, and Navigation, the establishment of the Bank of Brazil, etc.

9 Law 3229, October 14, 1882.

10 The two systems were applied according to the specificities of each case, with the choice of which to apply based on the highest level of service to the public good.

Starting in the mid-1960s, a process became established in the legal arena to review legislation on industrial property, which was only consolidated in 1971 with the passage of a new statute.[11] This statute was defined by its extreme rigidity in terms of criteria, deadlines and conditions for issuing and enjoying patent and trademark privileges.[12] With this, the government sought to build a framework that both stimulated productive activity and defended the protection of domestic private enterprise from external competition, especially in industries that were considered essential. By doing so, it sought to lessen private appropriation's negative effects on knowledge, taking advantage of flexibility in the mechanisms of the treaty that, at that point in time, internationally regulated patents, the Paris Convention.

As far as institutional reforms were concerned, DNPI, the official agency for patents and trademarks, closed, and a new type of organization took its place. The National Institute of Industrial Property (INPI) was thus formed by General Emilio Garrastazu Médici's government (1969–1974), by Law 5648, on 11 December 1970, emerging as an independent federal agency linked to the Ministry of Industry and Trade. When it was created, three roles stood out as essential among the functions assigned to it, which in turn became its key activities: issuing the privileges afforded by invention patents and trademarks (a role inherited from its predecessor, DNPI), control and regulation of technological trade between Brazil and other nations, and making technological information available and disseminating it. Regulating the trade in technology between Brazil and abroad was done through two general lines of action: control and supervision over technology contracts and assistance to domestic enterprises to achieve the best conditions for negotiating and using imported technology. Such interventions became possible with potent tools the law granted the federal agency, including the screening of contracts containing technology transfers.[13]

---

11 These were the legislatives initiatives, promoted by the executive branch, to reformulate industrial property legislation in the above-mentioned period: Executive Order 254, 28 February 1967 (under President Castelo Branco), Executive Order 1005, 21 October 1969 (under the Military Junta), Law 5772, 21 December 1971 (under President Médici).

12 We highlight among Law 5772/71's mechanisms the following: a 15-year limit on patents from the date of application, a requirement of local exploration, stringent novelty criteria, and the exclusion of chemical, pharmaceutical and food products from patent protection.

13 The contractual *screening* consisted of the appraisal and valuation of technology transfer contracts established between Brazil and other nations, with INPI withholding the power to veto or modify its terms. Such action was based on the following goals: selecting foreign technologies according to the priorities outlined in the National Development Plan, 1972/74 (PND) and the Basic Plan for Scientific and Technological Development (PBDCT), eliminating restrictive contractual clauses, evaluating the value of acquired technologies, always seeking to reduce the costs of importation, establishing contracts involving objects of industrial property as a priority, to the detriment of negotiations based on *trade secrets*, etc.

Another role assigned to INPI was the promotion of the absorption, adaptation and development of new technologies domestically, guaranteeing the enjoyment of accumulated information and disseminating it widely to industrial or research sectors. In this sense, the agency became responsible for building a database on patented technology to make sources of detailed information on technology available, in order to provide technical support to different areas of industry and science, in addition to supporting the agency's own technical staff's operations (contract examiners, patent examiners, etc.).

Nevertheless, the dawn of the twenty-first century seems to point toward a distinct stage in the government's approach to intellectual property, one in which industrial property, tied to a policy of incentivizing industrial innovation and technological achievement, is once again conceived as a strategic element within a greater development project. At this moment of political redefinition, governmental conditions and initiatives suggest a revalorization of the role of the patent and trademark office in operative, functional and political terms. Patent offices became part of the knowledge governance structure. This, however, is a process still underway.

INPI in the recent context

The current Law on Industrial Property, LPI 9279, was approved in 1996 and entered into effect in 1997. It was designed to adjust the legal framework to the requirements of the "Agreement on Trade-Related Aspects of Intellectual Property Rights" (TRIPS), far earlier than the final deadline allowed by the World Trade Organization (WTO). One important aspect of the law was that it allowed pharmaceutical and food products to be patented, in compliance with the agreement.

INPI is a federal agency affiliated with the Ministry of Development, Industry and Trade (MDIC) and is endowed with the power to enforce the rules that regulate intellectual property. INPI oversees assets such as trademarks, patents, records of technology transfer contracts and franchises, software, industrial design, the topography of integrated circuits, traditional knowledge and geographic indications, in accordance with the Law on Industrial Property and Software.

Despite an inconsistent history of research and development and the lack of a coherent policy of industrial and technological development, the country has always been a pioneer in the early adoption of intellectual property frameworks. This points to two situations: the isolated approach to intellectual property, divorced from efforts toward industrial and technological development, and the availability of a basic legal framework for "protection" that did not necessarily lend itself to a high level of understanding of the uses of the intellectual property system or, as a result, the proliferation of inventions.

Current INPI performance indicators reflect the restructuring process underway. In 2004, the time between filing and registering a trademark was 5 years and 9 years for a patent. In 2007, the benchmarks achieved were 2 years for trademarks and 7.5 years for patents. One of the agency's goals is to reduce the time to issue a patent to 4 years, a standard considered to be adequate internationally. One of the obstacles to this goal is the number of patent examiners in relation to the number of applications each year at INPI (INPI 2007).

More specifically, INPI had several important achievements: increased legal standing in the high courts, approval as an International Search Authority (ISA) and International Preliminary Examining Authority (IPEA) by the WIPO, and the establishment of the Academy of Intellectual Property, side by side with the launch in 2007 of the professional masters in intellectual property and innovation.

Organizational structure

Since 2004, INPI has been structured by units connected to the Presidency and Administrations:

Units connected to the Presidency:
>Vice Presidency
>Presidential Cabinet
>Federal Attorney's Office, which is divided into the Judicial
>>Office of Civil Litigation and the Judicial Office of Legal Counsel
>Ombudsman's Office
>Internal Review
>Office of General Budget and Planning,
>General Administration, which includes the Office of Human Resources, the
>>Office of Information and Modernization, and the Office of Administration

Administrations:
>Patents Administration (DIRPA)[14]
>Trademarks Administration (DIRMA)[15]

---

14 The Patents Administration is responsible for analyzing, deciding, and issuing patent-related privileges by law, whose rights are guaranteed constitutionally. In accordance with INPI's internal policies, DIRPA attempts to (1) coordinate, supervise, track and promote the implementation of projects, agreements and treaties concerning patents, (2) analyze, decide, and issue patent privileges according to current law, (3) participate in coordinated activities between INPI and other agencies, companies and entities, with a view toward more Brazilian participation in the intellectual property protection systems, (4) technically monitor proposals for projects, agreements, and treaties concerning patents, and (5) perfect practices and develop operational standards for the analysis and issuing of patents.

15 Article 74 of the current Law of Industrial Property states that the function of the Trademarks Administration is to (1) coordinate, supervise, track and promote the implementation of projects, agreements, and treaties concerning trademarks, (2) analyze, decide and grant trademarks and trademark petitions according to current law, (3) participate in coordinated activities between INPI and other agencies, companies and entities, with a view toward more Brazilian participation in the intellectual property protection systems, (4) technically monitor proposals for projects, agreements and treaties concerning trademarks, and (5) perfect practices and develop operational standards for examining and issuing trademarks.

Technological Information and Coordination Administration (DART)[16]
Technology Transfers and Other Records Administration (DIRTEC)

3.2. INDECOPI – Peru[17]

The protection of intellectual property rights in Peru is part of a comprehensive political reform process that occurred in the economic and social context of the last two decades. The Peruvian government reduced barriers to trade and investment, state intervention in the production and distribution of goods and services, and regulation of economic activity. The government prioritized the reestablishment of the political order, controlling inflation and implementing free market policies.

Currently, its emphasis is on competitive markets in the private sector, on international trade and on macroeconomic discipline. Peru adopted structural reforms to connect its economy with the rest of the world, stabilize its macroeconomic situation, deregulate business practices and allow markets to allocate more resources. While in general the government recognizes the need to intensify reforms, and the reform process continues to enjoy positive public support, the obstacle to building a broader, more integrated and collaborative engagement with development remains.

The National Institute for the Defense of Competition and Protection of Intellectual Property (INDECOPI) was founded in 1992 to create a market-economy culture in which all parties, consumers and suppliers, can safely participate, with the responsibility of promoting competition, protecting the consumer and guaranteeing property rights. The main difference with the Brazilian INPI is the coexistence, in the same institution, of both the defense of the competition board and the judiciary body for litigation in intellectual property rights. As we have seen in the second section of this chapter, the INDECOPI importance in terms of patenting in Latin America countries is not significant. On the other hand, it is a very well organized patent office, as will be pointed out later.

---

16 Technological Information and Coordination Administration (Diretoria de Articulação e Informação Tecnológica – DART). This administration was created in 2004 in the midst of the institute's restructuring, and according to internal policies, its functions are (1) to create, maintain and perfect the means to promote greater Brazilian participation in intellectual property protection systems and to disseminate INPI's mission to the Brazilian society, (2) to promote the coordination of activities of the constituent Administrations in universities, research institutions, federal, state, and regional development agencies, companies and other public and private bodies dedicated to research, technological development, and technological and innovation training activities, (3) to coordinate activities related to the promotion and advancement of innovation and the resulting protection of intellectual property, (4) to implement, under the supervision of INPI's president and in coordination with the other administrations, collaboration with agencies abroad or with international bodies concerned with the protection of intellectual property, (5) to coordinate the documentation and circulation of technological information, (6) to establish partnerships with regional development and technological promotion programs, and (7) to coordinate INPI's service to the needs of micro-, small-, and medium-sized firms.

17 INDECOPI is a younger institution, and the actual research had concentrated on interviews with patent examiners, not on its history.

The consolidation of these activities under the aegis of one institution brought the following advantages: (1) unified institutional positioning, (2) reduction in administrative costs and (3) a common direction in matters of economic competition.

INDECOPI's structure

INDECOPI's organization structure is divided into three important sections:

- Governing Council, the administration's highest body, led by a president responsible for representing the institution, establishing general policies, managing the institution's image and taking the lead in its communication and promotion. The council is supported by an advisory council made up of members from the public and private sectors.
- Executive bodies in charge of managing the standards that regulate the protection of competition, intellectual property and consumer rights.
- Administration, charged with managing the institution's resources, serving as support to the work done by the other bodies.

Above the executive bodies, one finds the Court of Defense of Competition and Protection to Intellectual Property, with the authority to hear appeals and to rule as a last resort for cases that were not resolved at the district court level.

The New Technologies and Inventions Administration (DIN) operates under the area of intellectual property, with the purpose of issuing patents for inventions, utility models, protection certificates, industrial designs, certificates for new vegetable varieties, traditional knowledge of indigenous peoples and integrated circuits. It also offers technological information-retrieval services, supplies complete patent documents, and so on.

3.3. MEXICO: IMPI trajectory and structure

In 1820 the Spanish Court issued the first patent in Mexico, and in 1832, the first Mexican Law for Intellectual Property was published. From that time until the end of the nineteenth century, the Mexican law was changed to accomplish administrative and political demands, with a focus on attracting foreign technologies and stimulating their dissemination and assimilation throughout the country.

In 1890 a new law regarding inventions and improvement established what *materials* are patentable, determined that a patent was valid for 20 years after it was issued and applied sanctions to patents which had not been explored. It also defined a system of oppositions in which any interested person/company could demand that the patent not be issued until two months after its publication.

In 1903 Mexico signed the Convention of Paris and issued a law for patents of invention, which established the types of patents: invention, industrial model or design, improvement patent. Compared to Brazil, the agreement to the convention was signed twenty years later.

In 1942 the first law which combined patents and trademarks was issued. The novelty exam was made mandatory for patents, and if a patent was not explored after three years of being issued, anyone could ask for a license for the right to use it.

In 1976 the law for inventions and trademarks defined areas that were not subject to patenting, such as varieties of vegetables, biotechnological procedures, chemical products, nuclear energy, among others. It also made it mandatory to register contracts for technology transfer.

In 1991 the law for fostering and protection of industrial property defined the creation of IMPI (Mexican Institute for Industrial Property), which was to occur in 1993, and established other areas subject to patenting, the possibility to patent models of utility and the concept of industrial secrets.

In 1994 the Law on Industrial Property clearly established which areas were patentable, and which were not, defined the requisites of absolute novelty and the novelty exam for issuing models of utility and industrial design. It also determined that IMPI had an administrative authority regarding first-instance litigations.

IMPI accepts applications for patent protection for all products, processes or uses created by human beings that can transform matter or energy that exists in nature, so that it can be used by people in order to satisfy specific needs, as long as the products, processes and uses comply with the requirements of novelty, invention and industrial application. Scientific theories, mathematical methods, vegetal and animal derivatives, discoveries of natural substances and commercial or medical treatment methods are not patentable.

A patent will have a nonrenewable term of 20 years from the date of filing and will be subject to payment of the corresponding fees. The registration of utility models will have a nonrenewable term of 10 years from the date of filing and will be subject to payment of the corresponding fees. The registration of industrial designs will have a nonrenewable term of 15 years from the date of filing and will be subject to payment of the corresponding fees. There is no protection term for trade secrets. The layout design of integrated circuits can be registered if it features original blueprints for layout designs and microchips. The registration of blueprints will have a nonrenewable term of 10 years from the date of filing and will be subject to payment of the corresponding fees.

4. Interviews in Three Different Latin American Patent Offices

4.1. Some methodological concerns: Tacit and explicit knowledge in patent office decision processes[18]

As far as the field research depends on interviews with patent examiners, it is important to take into account some methodological concerns. There are a series of elements of quantitative and qualitative orders in a study assessing patent offices,

---

18 We thank Cláudia Chamas for writing these methodological concerns and for her advice during the elaboration of the case studies. However, the authors are responsible for the ideas expressed in the article.

elements that are relevant to the comprehension of the decision-process history and its effect. From the quantitative aspect, it seems obvious that historical patent data – including the resident/nonresident ratio, among others – should be studied. On the other hand, qualitative data requires a special methodology for assimilation. This proves somewhat harder. Interviews naturally constitute the central element of the methodological structure. However, interviews may become complex issues when trying to resolve the conundrum of the distinct periods of an institution's existence. In this context, the selection of interviewees becomes important and demands the sound prior knowledge of the research team. Focusing interviews on people having former strategic and key posts is fundamental, but might be inadequate. Gathering an institution's past from its technicians, collaborators, clients and other participants helps restore combined dispersed and balkanized knowledge. Two major challenges stand out: preparing personalized interviews and choosing the correct sources. Another issue helps to understand the perception process of the institutional activity as seen by its technicians, managers and others. This consists of prior knowledge – by means of data, documents and secondary sources – of the milestones, historical decisions and the major impediments experienced by the patent office. It should be stressed that much may have been lost over time because institutions of developing countries frequently do not have the structures required for recording institutional legacy. Some of the documents may be stored confidentially, adding to other hindrances.

The use of interviews assumes that it is possible to gather part – although admittedly not all – of the relevant information. There is a tacit component that may never come to light. Regrettably, human memory is rather unreliable. Certain facts are simply forgotten. The researchers in applied social sciences made use of a few resources to correct these lapses. However, there are other reasons that explain the tacit aspect inherent to gathering information concerning the decision processes of strategic government agencies: (1) the actors are not always willing to disclose certain information for a series of possible reasons, (2) the actors are not always fully aware of the institutional reasons for their former actions because many simply fulfilled duties imposed by the senior management.

Therefore, it is apparent that the research should consider this tacit aspect as being inherent in any research assessing patent offices and as forming one of the probable limitations without, however, impairing the study or rendering it unfeasible. The researcher must encounter new sources of information, mainly beyond the direct context of the patent office, enabling some well-founded inferences forming an accurate picture based on reliable data and analysis.

4.2. Institutional culture, differences according to generation and patent type and the role of training and education: Findings

As is well known, the quality of the patents issued by different offices and the greater (or lesser) level of legal security they bring, can have positive (or negative) consequences for the transfer of technology according to each case and may disturb developing nations' process of catching up. If this is true, a better definition of the criteria of novelty, inventiveness and utility are among the priorities of a positive agenda for patent analysis.

As a result, and according to interviews that were carried out, the patent examiner must (1) evaluate if the application is clear and well written, (2) restrict the scope of the claim of the patent document – as the patent claimant will always wish to broaden it, (3) verify the degree of innovation of the patent claimed and (4) guarantee the descriptive sufficiency in a way that a competitor with reasonable knowledge of the field is able to reproduce the invention, while the party claiming the patent will prefer to conceal more than reveal his or her product or process.

It can be useful in this context to disclose the nature of research for antecedents and the process of patent analysis, examining the range of research, the interpretation of each criterion and the interaction between the company filing and the patent office. How each office determines the scope of a patent that is issued is a matter of analysis.

Intellectual property becomes a key question in generating knowledge and circulating technologies in open economies. In such a context, the effective governance of intellectual property is a crucial step for the technological outfitting of more-developed countries. Latin American countries' technological gap is well known (though it does not occur in all fields of knowledge) so that their delay in patenting and managing the issue of patents is not surprising. In this scenario, the patent system appears to be a tool in the hands of multinational companies, the commercialization of products is made easier, while local technological capacity does not necessarily generate value (see also Drahos 2010).

The tacit components are frequently related to issues of a political nature. This leads to some pertinent questions: Is the external influence of practices deeply ingrained in developed countries' patent offices relevant to decision-making processes of patent offices in developing countries? How relevant and to what extent? Is the external influence relevant to the development of norms for patent examination by the patent office? Does the training of patent office examiners from developing countries by patent office examiners of developed countries have consequences? What would be the optimal method for developing the internal capacity for examination and issuing patents in a way that avoids simply copying standards inappropriate to the local context?

As a result, our research considered these concerns and this tacit aspect as inherent to any research assessing patent offices and as one of the probable limitations without, however, impairing or rendering the study unfeasible.

Twelve interviews were conducted with Brazilian INPI's patent examiners, fifteen with INDECOPI's patent examiners and fifteen in Mexican IMPI. In each country's case, interviewees were divided into three groups, or "generations": (1) more senior patent examiners, (2) examiners who have been in the position for around five years, and (3) a third generation that joined the institutions most recently. In the Brazilian case, the first generation was labeled "generation PNUD" because of the training process that had occurred, which we will discuss later. The second generation took the civil service exam between 1998 and 2004, and, finally, the third generation was admitted through more recent exams. Another criterion for the selection of interviewees was the diversity of the class of patents they examine.

4.3. Comparative findings

The same questionnaire (interview script) was used in the three countries. The questions referred to the interviewee's history, how he or she entered the institution, his or her academic and professional training profile prior to the position, how he or she handled and examined a patent application, the perception of institutional policies and the degree of autonomy in making decisions. We sought to choose examiners from different technical areas and with different experiences.

Brazil – INPI: All of the interviews were held at INPI at different times during the course of 2008 and 2009.
Peru – INDECOPI: The interviews were held September 1–5, 2008 and January 20–23, 2009. The first series of interviews were held before the patent office's reorganization by Law 1033, which brought up interesting questions on whether the new organization had produced a change in the procedures followed in patent examinations.
Mexico – IMPI: The interviews were held at IMPI in September 2010.

Brazil: Pathway into INPI and examiner background

An overwhelming majority of the patent examiners interviewed joined the agency through the civil service exam. For Brazilian patent examiners, joining the ranks of this career happened by chance. The public exam attracts professionals from technical areas, though these professionals are not necessarily familiar with the field of intellectual property prior to taking it. Although at the very beginning of the INPI history, patent examiners first worked as outside, contracted patent examiners, this arrangement has become rare or even nonexistent in recent years. The work environment was declared very pleasant, the senior colleagues were cooperative, and their experience was duly passed on without conflicts.

The examiners' backgrounds varied according to their "generation." The majority had degrees from the best universities, generally public ones, such as UFRJ (Federal University of Rio de Janeiro) and UFF (Federal Fluminense University), but also from renowned private universities such as PUC (Pontifical Catholic University).

The first generation, here called "generation PNUD," joined in the 1970s and was trained by foreign experts, mainly Germans, with courses taken in Brazil and abroad. Professionals from the areas of civil, electrical and mechanical engineering dominated among the examiners interviewed in this generation, partly because pharmaceutical patents were not issued and chemical patents were only in their infancy.

The second generation, which joined INPI between 1998 and 20014, has a more varied training background. This generation's training process happened within INPI itself through a mostly practical training process supervised by more senior examiners who passed on their experiences and knowledge.

Finally, the most recent generation possessed strong academic credentials before recruitment, frequently including graduate studies at the master's and doctoral levels.

They were also subject to an internal training process within INPI. The areas of their training are quite diverse and the examiners are encouraged to periodically attend courses at home and abroad.[19]

Peru: Pathway into DIN

In Peru, joining the ranks of the patent-examiner career happened by chance. The public exam attracted professionals from technical areas, though these professionals were not necessarily familiar with the field of intellectual property prior to taking it. In the Peruvian case, it could happen that the patent examiners first worked as outside, contracted patent examiners.

However, the majority of interviewed examiners joined DIN (previously OIN) through a civil service exam. In only one case was no exam taken; a position opened and the examiner learned about it through an employee. Interviews were held, and the position was awarded.

The examiners interviewed came out of the University of San Marcos, the Agrarian University, the University of Lima and the National Engineering University. These are considered serious universities with adequate levels of quality and requirements, retaining a certain prestige in Peru. Only one patent examiner studied abroad and has a master's degree.

In most cases, at the moment they joined DIN, knowledge about intellectual property in general, and patents specifically, was nil. Although in almost all cases, they knew INDECOPI through its consumer-rights work, the interviewers did not know that it was also the agency responsible for managing and registering the different kinds of intellectual property. There were three exceptions: in two cases, this last fact was known as a result of a general university-level course and in the third case, the person had worked at an office specialized in patent-research services.

The entirety of the interviewed examiners agreed that DIN's work environment was remarkable and that they had received support and information from colleagues when they began working there. In general, examiners were surprised by the level of organization found in a public agency of that kind.

Mexico: Pathway into IMPI and examiner background

As in the Brazilian case, the majority of the patent examiners interviewed joined the agency through the civil service exam. The examiners' backgrounds varied according to the area they belong to. The patent examiners in the chemical, biotech and pharmacy departments have an academic background and carried out their MSc or PhD research at the University before they joined IMPI. The patent examiners in the electrical and mechanical departments have an undergraduate degree and are not linked to academic research.

---

19 INPI has sought to train its professionals in a multidisciplinary perspective.

According to Mexican law, the civil service exam may be applied to one or two job positions, and in the Mexican case, there have been two major exams when the patent examiners recently joined the institution as means of an expansion of activities. Many other exams were for positions that were vacant because the patent examiner retired or left the institution to attend to an increasing demand in some specific area – usually biotech or pharmacy (we will come to this point again in training and capacity building).

As in the Peruvian and Brazilian cases, joining the ranks of this career happened by chance in the Mexican case. Some patent examiners mentioned the lack of opportunities in the academic field and the possibility of a job where knowledge challenges were expected to be a constant, despite the bureaucratic activity. In most cases, patent examiners were not familiar with the field of intellectual property prior to entering it. In the Mexican case, there are no contracted patent examiners.

Mexican patent examiners emphasized the pleasant and cooperative work environment, and the receptiveness of more senior patent examiners when they joined the institution. As a matter of fact, there is a formal practice that each patent examiner is tutored by a senior examiner during his/her first year in the institution as a means of training on the job, besides the formal one-month capacity-building period, which we will come to in the next session.

Brazil: Training and courses at home and abroad

As was pointed out before, the first generation of examiners received training as a result of an agreement established between INPI and PNUD. The so-called "PNUD Project" was a result of a partnership between INPI's first administration, led by President Thedim Lobo from 1970 to 1973, and the United Nations' Development Program. The partnership's goal was to train a permanent technical staff to perform patent classification, research and analysis, with an initial deadline of five years. Although it was supposed to begin in April 1973, the initial program was not implemented. The project was only implemented starting in 1977. UFRJ participated in this effort through COPPE (Engineering Graduate Programs).

The account given by the first generation's examiners is that the training they received was very important in understanding the mission they were to perform. This group of informants presented, on average, a solid and extensive understanding of the public importance of the process of patent issuing and of the importance of the technology transfer contracts that prevailed at the time.

Having worked at INPI longer, they had enjoyed the opportunity to take part in several courses abroad, financed by WIPO, EPO, USPTO and JPO. In more recent times, INPI itself has organized training courses for the Latin American region and these examiners have participated as students and instructors.[20]

Later, in 2006 and 2007, a new training and research program was conceived, organized and implemented based on a partnership between INPI, CCJE (Center for

---

20 INPI's role in regional training and collaboration between Latin American offices was highlighted by the Peruvians.

Law and Economic Sciences at Federal University of Rio de Janeiro) and the Institute of Economics at the same university: the Research Laboratory on Innovation and Intellectual Property Management. This interdisciplinary program proved to be a pioneering effort combining training activities and research in intellectual property. As a result, it stimulated academic production by both students and professors who had not necessarily been acquainted with intellectual property's relevant themes, but already had solid foundations in the subjects of innovation and development.

The Research Lab on Innovation and Intellectual Property Management contains a non-degree postgraduate course (Institute of Economics) and research activities organized by the Center for Law and Economic Sciences (CCJE), spread over eight thematic groupings.[21] These groups, which combined instructors and course participants, also defined the scope of the disciplines taught. Some of the program's former students, who were patent examiners, were interviewed. Their vision, compared with patent examiners who did not take the course, was broader and more consistent. Without a doubt, differences in worldviews affect the quality of patent examination work.

The lab was responsible for the management and creation of two new graduate programs with significant potential, which can be attributed in some measure to the initial program's success. In 2007 INPI created the Academy of Intellectual Property and Development.[22] That year it also received CAPES' approval and authorization to establish the Professional Master's Degree in Intellectual Property and Development. In 2008, the Institute of Economics created the Graduate Program in Public Policy, Strategies, and Development. Within this program, a concentration in innovation, intellectual property, and development was established offering academic master's and doctoral programs, perhaps the only interdisciplinary doctorate in intellectual property of its kind in Latin America.

As can be discerned from the discussion above, patent examiners' training processes proved to be an extremely relevant factor, whether to differentiate between different generations or to improve the quality of the work performed. On the other hand, training is not restricted, or should not restrict itself, to patent examination. Training encompasses a range of possibilities that extends from professional qualification prior to joining the institution – which was revealed to be inversely related to seniority, in other words, younger staff were generally better qualified technically or academically, while older employees better understood patents' public role – to multidisciplinary courses that allow patent examiners to broaden their perspectives.

21 In addition to teaching activities, the lab was organized into eight research groups: (1) Globalization of the Intellectual Property System, (2) Management of Intellectual Property, Technical Standards, and Technology Trade, (3) Structure and Trade on the International Technology Market, (4) Micro, Small and Medium-Sized Firms' Access to Technological Information, (5) Intellectual Property in Biotechnology and Pharmaceutical Industries, (6) Intellectual Property in Information Technology and Military Technologies, (7) Promotion of Geographic Indication and Protection of Traditional Knowledge, (8) Protection and Infraction of Copyright.

22 In recent years, with the organization of the Intellectual Property Academy, a great part of training activities was done in-house.

Peru: INDECOPI – Training and courses at home and abroad

There is no specific training program at DIN for examiners who join the agency. Examiners learn on their own through each case they receive. Nor is a senior examiner assigned to guide the new examiners through the first few months. In practice, the technical director and the examiners perform this function in some ways. Some examiners take the online courses WIPO offers of their own accord.

Otherwise, every year a number of courses abroad are financed, mainly by WIPO, EPO, OEPM, USPTO and JPO. However, these courses are isolated and are not part of a general training program. In the majority of cases, these are standard basic- or intermediate-level courses. Additionally, participation by DIN staff in these courses is random and dependent on the amount of technical assistance INDECOPI receives in a given year. On the other hand, participation in a course abroad by an examiner follows a handful of general criteria that are not systematized in any internal guidelines (seniority in DIN, area of expertise, participation in previous training courses), and in many instances, these courses are used as a kind of bonus to the examiner. One of interviewees expressed that although these courses are meant for patent examiners, on occasion the Peruvian government sends other technicians (not examiners) to participate in the training program abroad. External examiners participate in these courses rarely and only when a position cannot be filled by an in-house examiner.

There is also – although less and less – general training or courses on specific subjects held at INDECOPI by foreign examiners who work in the world's larger patent offices (EPO, OEPM). These courses are usually scheduled every two years, though the last visit was in 2006. Usually, the instructors have a great deal of work experience and discuss how a specific technical problem is handled at his/her office. The advantage of these courses is that the entire DIN staff can participate without losing work time. The disadvantage is the pressure made to follow his/her office's standards, without regard to the distinct legislation and/or level of local industrial development. In this sense, South-South Cooperation, for instance, with Brazilian INPI, is especially important. This type of course depends on DIN's request, when international technical assistance allows it.

Moreover, as pointed out by the INDECOPI staff, the South-South collaboration undertaken by the Brazilian INPI is very much welcome as the standards and realities are more similar to those of Peru and other Latin American countries. In any case, these types of courses are not offered at the rate that Latin American patent offices would like.

Mexico: IMPI – Training and courses at home and abroad

When the patent examiner joins the institution, he/she is submitted to a one-month capacity-building program, developed and led by senior IMPI patent examiners. After this period, he/she is assigned to a senior patent examiner as his/her tutor for a minimum period of one year. This tutor must not only perform the training on the job activities, but also check all the patent-claim exams this new examiner does.

Despite the geographic and economic proximity with the United States, Mexican IMPI presents a major cooperation in capacity building with EPO. Most Mexican patent examiners have attended more than one training period at EPO, and the senior ones have been trained according to this office's examination criteria. Therefore, Mexican IMPI procedures have been strongly influenced by the EPO perspective. Patent examiners have also been trained by WIPO, besides USPTO and Japanese patent offices, but the influence of and cooperation with EPO must be specially referred to.

There is also a common practice of distance education (mainly related to WIPO programs) and special programs led by EPO, USPTO and also WIPO professionals that are carried out in Mexican IMPI. This type of training offers a major opportunity for IMPI examiners to discuss their procedures and challenges and is welcomed by Mexican professionals, while the programs abroad offer the opportunity to meet patent examiners and practices from other countries.

Mexican patent examiners claim, however, that in the last two years, due to economic restrictions and to the world financial crises, international training has diminished, but they still have teleconference meetings, mainly with EPO specialists, for discussing specific points, mainly referring to the biotech, chemical and pharmacy areas.

The Mexican patent office also has a central position in training and consulting with smaller Caribbean countries, similar to the one of Brazilian INPI for South American. But apparently, there is hardly any cooperation or connection between them.

As can be discerned from the discussion above, patent examiners' training proved to be an extremely relevant factor, not only to improve the quality of the work they performed, but mainly to determine the patentability criteria which will be referred to in the next session.

Brazil: Patentability criteria

The patent examination procedure begins with the receipt of a patent application that has already been subject to a formal preliminary exam. Applications are classified according to the patent's object. The first stage consists in evaluating the patent's claims and composition. Several of the interviewed patent examiners said that this first stage results in a higher number of returned applications so that applicants can improve their claims and work on the composition. In many cases, applications do not return to the patent office since, depending on the backlog and type of patent examined (e.g., information technology), the application simply loses its novelty or its purpose.

Once the application's claims and composition are evaluated, a research strategy is developed consisting of choosing databases. This stage has been made easier by improvements in the access to and databases themselves. The fulfillment of patent requirements (novelty, non-obviousness or the inventive step, industrial utility and descriptive sufficiency) is then evaluated. A technical opinion is issued with the patent approval, the application's rejection or a report on further requirements.

In spite of the fact that the process is the same, here begin the differences between examiners and patent offices. The Andean Community, for example, with financial support from WIPO, published in 2003, and confirmed in 2004, the Andean Patent Manual, which established a practical guide for examining patents and regularized processes in the Andean region. Among the manual's advantages were its suitability to standards already in effect, the community's jurisprudence and what was practiced at national agencies. Another advantage was that it established what could and could not be patented.

A clear example of this was the ban on second-use and polymorph patents. However, the Free Trade Agreement signed by Peru's government with the United States (one of the documents was signed exactly at the time of the second stage of interviews) changed some of the conditions that had been previously established by the Andean Community, such as the case of second use. Despite it being not necessarily a falsifiable statement, a few informants stated that they continued to deny second-use patents, claiming the lack of, or only a reduced, inventive step.

Unlike the Peruvian case, several interviewers at INPI complained of the lack of exam guidelines, with the exception of the area of biotechnology. Another specific complaint was the lack of clarity regarding what is and what is not patentable. There are several problems concerning the concession of patents that generate anxiety for an examiner, especially in the case of second use and polymorphs. Legal instability is created as a result. Here space exists for an individual examiner's own criteria. Another controversial issue, which has given rise to important litigation in the case of pharmaceutical patents, is the attempt to extend patent duration based on the pipeline mechanism.[23]

Interviewers also highlighted that younger examiners tend to be, as far as the exam is concerned, more rigorous and stringent, whether because of the greater use of technology they deploy or because their training has reinforced this requirement.

In INPI's case, and this is of extreme relevance, the examiner's own rate of patent appears to vary greatly and is, normally low, around 25 percent, with considerable variation according to patent class. Data presented in the second part of this article supports this statement. However, the most common reason for this result is the lack of clarity in patent applications.[24]

In general, Brazilian informants considered the patent exam to be rigorous. However, when asked if obtaining a patent is difficult, the typical answer is that obtaining a patent is not difficult. This contradicts both the idea that the exam is extremely rigorous and the finding that each examiner has a low rate of issuing patents, which seems to be the case. One explanation that would reconcile this apparent paradox is the general lack of non-obviousness or the inventive step in patent applications.

---

23 The pipeline issued retroactive patents for pharmaceuticals in Brazil. The duration would be from the patent's original issue date and not its issue date in Brazil. This led to litigation increasingly eliminated by the Superior Court of Justice's second division, whose decisions, initially, had granted extensions to patent durations, but now systematically rejects and denies all claims.

24 We recognize that sufficient empirical evidence does not exist yet to confirm or deny this proposition. Nevertheless, we state it here as a general observation.

Definitely no pressure exists for patent examiners to issue patents. The pressure is to perform the exam in time and fulfill the quotas set by the agencies, which in the majority of cases are extremely difficult to reach.

Nor did the examiners report conflicts with applicants. In reality, patent conflicts are resolved by INPI at another stage. Perhaps this is a fundamental difference between the Brazilian and the Peruvian patent offices.

Peru: Patentability criteria

With the financial support of WIPO, the Andean Community, published the Andean Patent Manual in 2003 (second edition in 2004). The purpose of this document was, on the one hand, to provide a practical patent examination guide and, on the other hand, to reconcile processes and practices in patent proceedings in the Andean region. It was developed on the foundation of Andean norms, community jurisprudence and the practices of national offices. Experts from WIPO, EPO, IMPI and the corresponding Andean offices participated in its development. Therefore, the manual contains, among other things, guidelines on the criteria and standards to be followed in examining a patent application. DIN examiners normally use the manual.

When a patent application is first submitted, the examiner checks it for the minimum requirement in order to assign it a presentation date. Afterwards, the application undergoes an examination for the formal requirements. Many applications are not sufficiently clear. In general, the problem is translation, and the necessary explanations are requested of the applicant. Once these are made (if not, the application is considered abandoned), the claimed invention is examined for its fulfillment of patentability criteria. The first step is to perform a search of antecedents. Technical documents close to the invention in question are sought and then immediately compared with the application document. During the search, previous searches performed by EPO and USPTO weigh considerably. On occasion, additional antecedents are sought but generally, examiners use documents already identified by the above-mentioned offices.

Of the requirements for patentability (novelty, non-obviousness or the inventive step, industrial application), every examiner interviewed concluded that the most difficult criterion is that of non-obviousness or the inventive step.[25]

In order to judge whether an application features an inventive step or non-obviousness, the claimed invention must be obvious to an expert in the field or have an unexpected effect if it contains a technical advantage. In other words, technical differences should not be suggested by its antecedents. On this point, several of the examiners interviewed considered that the newer examiners were stricter and more rigorous in judging whether an application fulfilled this requirement. The patent application must be reproducible in some industry as far as industrial application is concerned.

---

25 In relation to novelty, a photographic innovation applies; all that is required for a previous document is to contain one characteristic, however trivial, also to be contained in the patent application, for the basis of novelty to be destroyed.

If an application presents problems in any of the patentability criteria, a report is written and issued to the applicant. After the applicant's response, a decision is made to issue or reject the patent. Reports written by outside examiners are reviewed by senior examiners. Discrepancies between them are discussed and a reconciled report is usually issued.

According to each interviewed examiner's perception, the rate at which each examiner issues patents is approximately 50 percent. However, it is generally recognized that in many cases, the reason for rejection is due to the lack of clarity in the patent application.

Applicants may check the status of their applications through INDECOPI's website (www.indecopi.gob.pe), though it continues to be common to visit INDECOPI's headquarters to check the status and consult personally with examiners regarding obstacles that may arise in the process.

All of the examiners who were interviewed thought that in comparison with other patent offices in the region, DIN's examination of patent applications is rigorous. However, the majority expressed that being issued a patent was not difficult if an applicant followed the criteria set by the office. This conclusion contrasts with the opinion of some of the informants in the sense that one cannot predict the criteria followed, neither by outside and in-house examiners, nor between examiners in general. It was thought that there should be a greater internal coordination of criteria. Monthly organization meetings have been held due to organizational changes and changes in patent law in Peru, introduced as a result of the Free Trade Agreement with the United States.

All of the examiners denied any outside pressure to complete patent exams. The only pressure that exists is to complete exams within deadlines and fulfill the performance quotas set by the administration.

The relationship between examiners and applicants (or their legal representatives) was not congenial in the past. Applicants regarded examiners as the enemy. This attitude has been changing, although occasionally, attorneys' offices ask for an examiner to be reassigned because they do not agree with the patentability criteria applied, which reflects the fact that DIN's criteria are not applied uniformly.

Mexico: Patentability criteria

As in the Brazilian case, the patent examination procedure begins with receiving a patent application that has already been subject to a formal preliminary exam. Applications are classified according to the patent's object. The first stage then consists in evaluating the patents' claims and composition. Several of the interviewed examiners said that this first stage results in a higher number of returned applications so that applicants can improve their claims and work on the composition. In many cases, applications do not return to the patent office since, depending on the backlog and type of patent examined (for example, information technology), the application simply loses its novelty or its purpose.

Once the application's claims and composition are evaluated, the patent claims are informally divided into two groups: if the claim has already been approved by a European office and cites the international research reports (*reporte de busca internacional*), the IMPI patent examiners do not conduct research, but analyze if the patent object is in accordance with Mexican law, and the patent claim is approved. If the patent claim has been approved by USPTO, on the contrary, the patent examiner will conduct a research of databases (normally free-of-charge databases) before analyzing it. Fulfillment of patent requirements (novelty, non-obviousness or the inventive step, industrial utility and descriptive sufficiency) are considered in the analysis. A technical opinion is issued with the patent approval, the application's rejection or a report on further requirements.

According to Mexican law, since 2005 a patent examiner can issue only four requirements per patent claim (two related to formal aspects and two related to the analysis itself).

Special attention must be given to patent claims applied by Mexican companies, universities or research centers. According to patent examiners from all areas of IMPI, approximately 50 percent of these applications are denied in the formal-aspects exam. The rate of patenting for these applications is very low, and therefore IMPI carries out a varied number of strategies to improve the patent rating of Mexican inventions.

IMPI has a cooperative relation with law firms, in order to clarify criteria and diminish problems in patent analysis. It also helps universities through training programs and free consultancy services for researchers and research centers throughout the country. Besides these activities, it offers free attendance to patent claimants at IMPI offices so that they can formulate their claims appropriately.

IMPI patent examiners also mention the lack of a formal exam guideline (mainly in the biotech area, as did Brazilian patent examiners), which is partially worked out by the extremely cooperative environment they have.

At this point, we may repeat similarities among the three agencies, as already mentioned: (1) lack of clarity in applications, (2) translation problems, (3) poorly composed patents, mainly by nationals, (3) increasing use of previous EPO and USPTO searches (except in the Mexican case) and (4) of the requirements to issue patents, without a doubt the most difficult to ascertain is the existence of non-obviousness or the inventive step. The Mexican case also points out that there is a common attempt to enlarge the claims in relation to what has already been approved by other patent offices.

It is not as clear as it seems to be in the Brazilian and Peruvian cases that the Mexican younger generations are more strict in patent analysis – the interviews indicate that the difference in the rate of patenting is more due to personal aspects, since the access to international not-free-of-charge databases still represents a problem for Mexican examiners.

As well as in the Brazilian and Peruvian cases, the project estimates a personal rate of 50 percent (which in the Brazilian case, is lower), with considerable variation according to patent type. Data presented in the second part of this article supports this statement. However, the most common reason for these rates is the lack of clarity in patent applications, more than the patent examiners' strictness. We recognize that sufficient empirical evidence does not exist yet to confirm or deny this proposition. Nevertheless, we state it here as a general observation.

In general, the three offices' informants considered the patent exam to be rigorous. However, when asked if obtaining a patent is difficult, the typical answer is that it is not. This contradicts both the idea that the exam is extremely rigorous and the finding that each examiner has a low rate of issuing patents, which seems to be the case. One explanation that would reconcile this apparent paradox is the general lack of non-obviousness or the inventive step in applications. In the Mexican case, the European influence in patent-analysis criteria is also a possible reason for denying many applications that have been approved by USPTO, besides the problems already mentioned with applications originated by Mexican companies or universities.

Definitively, no pressure exists for patent examiners to issue patents, according to patent examiners from the three offices. The main pressure is to perform the exam in time and fulfill the quotas set by the agencies, which in the majority of cases are extremely difficult to reach.

In the Mexican case, a highly cooperative relationship has been mentioned to exist between IMPI and patent applicants, although law firms seem to be not so satisfied.

As well as INDECOPI, the Mexican agency also issues legal decisions, but up to the time of the interviews, this does not represent pressure. We mentioned the importance of judiciary power in Brazil, mainly in biotech-related sectors, and there seems to be a tendency that the Mexican case will evolve to a situation similar to the Brazilian case.

Brazil: Continuity of institutional policy

Some of the interviewed examiners noted institutional changes in INPI's last two administrations. In general, these changes have been regarded as positive: the increase in the number of examiners,; improvements in the career pathway, greater concern with training and qualification, establishment of the Academy on Intellectual Property, the reduction in the backlog of trademarks and some patent classes, greater administrative efficiency, concern with upgrading the agency's infrastructure, and, with the exception of biotechnology, chemistry and pharmaceuticals, where most disagreements occur, there is a consensus on the improvement of patent-examination processes. However, a few subjects point to a relaxation of "rigor" in the exams, despite resistance by the more senior staff.

Another interesting result related to institutional changes and continuity was that INPI's institutional culture is more influenced by EPO than by USPTO. On the other hand, a significant number of examiners declared that TRIPS had exerted little influence on the patent-exam process itself, which can be tested by the data presented in the second section.

Peru: Continuity of institutional policy

Changes in INDECOPI's administration, as well as in DIN itself, have been limited to administrative or institutional changes. These have no implicated changes in the patentability criteria, the examination of patent applications or in the procedures of opposing or rejecting applications in general. Due to the high level of technicality in DIN's work, it is difficult for INDECOPI to influence its work (as it has succeeded in other areas operating under its aegis). The change in INDECOPI's administration can be better understood by its level of understanding of matters relating to intellectual property and, therefore, the allocation of resources to DIN.

Based on the interviews, we found that DIN's work environment is pleasant, examiners cooperate well together, the agency operates independently, the examiners' decisions on a claimed invention's patentability follow technical criteria, there is a certain stability and continuity among the examiners who work at DIN and changes in INDECOPI's leadership have not affected DIN's daily efforts.

Mexico: Continuity of institutional policy

Mexican patent examiners mention a continuity of institutional policy, which it is considered to be one of the main reasons for the expansion of IMPI, also in the fields referred to by Brazilian interviewees: the increase in the number of examiners, improvements in the career pathway, maintenance of the concern with training and qualification, the reduction in the backlog of trademarks and some patent types, greater administrative efficiency, concern with upgrading the agency's infrastructure, and, with the exception of biotechnology, chemistry and pharmaceuticals, where most disagreements occur, there is consensus on the improvement of patent-examination processes.

As has already been mentioned, and similar to the Brazilian case, IMPI is more influenced by EPO than by USPTO. On the other hand, a significant number of examiners declared that TRIPS exerted little influence on the patent exam process itself, what can be tested by the data presented in the second section.

Brazil: Main problems found

The main problem found is the physical infrastructure and the high level of backlog in patent examinations. The interviewed examiners noted that the ongoing need for technological upgrades, given the acceleration of progress in the state of technology, has been a difficult issue to solve. The generalist style of examiners hampers the solution of specific problems in leading-edge technological subareas.

There is also a need to regularize criteria and to create greater internal coordination among departments. No proper context exists to discuss the different criteria for patent examination and concession.

Peru: Main problems found

Some problems were detected or expressed openly by examiners. The following can be highlighted:

> lack of training. DIN has not developed a comprehensive training program for new examiners who have no experience with patent examinations. A training program combining job training and theoretical coursework could be very useful.

Nor is there a program for examiners who already work at the agency. Participation in studies abroad is, for the most part, random, although general criteria for participation exist. Moreover, invitations from international or foreign donors depend (except in the case of regional programs where all Latin American countries are invited) on the amount of technical assistance INDECOPI receives for matters of intellectual property. Training workshops inside DIN with foreign examiners are sporadic, concern specific issues that present themselves over time and depend on international aid.

Outside, contracted examiners are limited to the infrequent workshops at DIN and do not enjoy access to courses abroad, even though their work is not, at its heart, different from senior assistants or examiners. The only difference is that outside examiners' reports are submitted for approval by regular examiners.

We have recently learned that INDECOPI is in the process of developing a school to offer training in the subjects with which the institution concerns itself. A course to train patent examiners is being considered among the courses the school will offer.

Lack of criteria uniformity and internal cohesion. Though technical directors should ensure the uniformity of criteria used in patent examination, there is no space at the institutional level to regularly discuss the criteria the agency is applying to patent applications. As a result, examiners do not always follow the same patentability criteria for a given application. However, this need is being addressed, in a way, through regular newsletters the technical directors send to examiners summarizing the facts of a case and explaining how similar cases should be handled.

Language skills. Patent examination is limited in many instances because examiners lack knowledge of foreign languages, finding antecedents principally in English, German and French. This prevents the state of the technology from being suitably determined. Perhaps this was what led a foreign expert to conclude a report on DIN by saying that the agency protected more inventions than Germany.

Inadequate infrastructure. DIN has had to move its offices within INDECOPI's installations several times. Some examiners expressed that DIN's infrastructure was not ideal and that they have always worked in extreme conditions. For example, outside examiners had a room set up to perform searches and examine patent applications assigned to them. Now, with the Internet allowing remote access to databases, they no longer enjoy any physical space within the agency.

Mexico: Main problems found

The main problem found in the Mexican agency, as well as in the Brazilian agency, is the physical infrastructure and the high level of backlog in patent examinations. The interviewed examiners noted that the ongoing need for technological upgrades, given the acceleration of progress in the state of technology, has been a difficult issue to solve. In opposition to the Brazilian case, there is prevalence of a specialist rather than a generalist style of examiner, which helps solve specific problems in leading-edge technology subareas.

Also contrary to the Brazilian case, there is a growing concern regarding the discussion of homogeneity of criteria for patent examination and concession.

Concluding Remarks

How different are Latin American patent offices, and why does this matter?

First of all, the Latin American patent offices differ in their institutional framework – built on a longer (in the case of Brazil) or shorter (in the Peruvian case) historical process. They are subject to their own judiciary order and their principles subject to public interest. Competition policy is a second, but independent, dimension of the regulation of intellectual property, more present in the case of Peru as part of the INDECOPI activities, and less in the case of Mexico. Industrial and innovation policies are behind the role of intellectual protection, as well as the presence of state in governing the economy.

Different levels of industrial development and the size of the patent office affect the rate of doing the patent exam in-house or relying on the patent exam done abroad and, by consequence, affect the rate of patents issued pre- or post-TRIPS agreement. TRIPS, contrary to the common sense, did not affect the patent exam in most of the countries. Harmonization was much more a matter of technical procedure than a matter of institutional culture.

It is useful to return to the beginning of this article. It has been stated that the lack of soundness for the patents granted can be detrimental to the generation and transfer of technology and, potentially, can disturb the technological catching-up processes of developing countries.

A better definition of the criteria for novelty, inventive activity and utility are among the priorities for a possible positive agenda for patent examinations. The idea of descriptive sufficiency also deserves attention. Patent examiners seem aware of the advantage to draw the greatest possible amount of information from the process of granting patent privileges.

Better patents are a positive instrument to foster innovation and development. Patent examiners are civil servants concerned with the importance of their role in granting privileges and monopolistic power. Capacity building, not only related to the technological frontier, but mainly rooted in an interdisciplinary approach, is a crucial dimension as far as a solid institutional culture is concerned.

References

All web addresses last accessed August 2012.

Cockburn, I. M., S. Kortum and S. Stern. 2002. "Are all Patent Examiners Equal? The Impact of Examiner Characteristics on Patent Statistics and Litigation Outcomes." NBER Working Paper No. 8980. Available at http://www.nber.org/papers/w8980

DiMaggio, P. J. and W. W. Powell (eds). 1991. *The New Institutionalism in Organizational Analysis.* Chicago: University of Chicago Press.

Drahos, P. 2010. *The Global Governance of Knowledge. Patent Offices and their Clients.* Cambridge: Cambridge University Press.

Cruz Filho, M. F. 1983. *Patentes e Marcas: o Brasil na Convenção de Paris – Um Século de Participação (1983–1993).* Rio de Janeiro: INPI.

INPI. 2002. "A História da tecnologia Brasileira Contada por Patentes." Realização Instituto Tecnológico Inovador. Rio de Janeiro: INPI.

Jensen, P. H., A. Palangkaraya and E. Webster. 2005. "Patent Allocation Outcomes across the Trilateral Patent Offices." Intellectual Property Research Institute of Australia Working Paper No. 5/05.

Malatova, L. M. 2011. "Inovar, Modernizar, Civilizar: Considerações sobre o Sistema de Patentes no Brasil (1809 – 1882)." Doctorate thesis. Available at http://www.historia.uff.br/stricto/teses/Tese-2011_Leandro_Malavota-S

Chapter 8

AN INTEROPERABILITY PRINCIPLE FOR KNOWLEDGE CREATION AND GOVERNANCE: THE ROLE OF EMERGING INSTITUTIONS

John Wilbanks
Creative Commons

Carolina Rossini
Harvard Law School

This study examines the relationships among funders, research institutions, and the "units" of knowledge creation and local knowledge governance, which are hosted inside research institutions. Our goal is to uncover the knowledge spaces where commons-based approaches, peer production and modes of network-mediated innovation have – and have not – emerged and to examine the conditions under which these approaches either flourish or are discouraged. Our rationale is that the emergence of novel, democratized and distributed knowledge governance represent a meaningful complement to more traditional systems, with the potential to create new public knowledge goods accessible to a global civil society and spur innovation in previously unforeseen ways.

The first section of this chapter is an introduction to distributed knowledge creation and open systems for knowledge transactions (including but not limited to copyrighted and patented knowledge-embedded products; see Blackler 1995).

The second section contains a case study of the complex and interlocking system of relationships governing knowledge-embedded products in the field of genomics, as well as some experimental interventions to adjust these relationships with the goal of maximizing either the total knowledge output or the value captured from the knowledge products. Although we have focused our case study on genomics, which offers a rich set of varied knowledge products and cases for study, the rationale we present in this discussion is also applicable to a variety of areas, from educational resources to alternative energy related technology.

The third section examines the role of national innovation policy in particular, and the specific relationships that research institutions have with public policy and governmental funders, including the role of government and policy mandates (either towards enclosure or openness) as regards knowledge-embedded products. We have chosen to focus on the role of universities because their upstream role in the innovation ecosystem can influence downstream governance of knowledge through creation of cooperation arrangements, the strategic retention of rights and/or publication and distribution of knowledge products.

Finally, we make a series of provisional recommendations for policymakers, funders and research-institution leadership that might decrease transaction costs for knowledge products, increase the incentive for collaborative knowledge production and reuse and increase the odds of novel methods of knowledge creation distribution and transfer emerging from an increasingly connected world.

Introduction

Before the advent of the Internet and the Web, the study of knowledge and its creation was primarily the province of the epistemologist. From a pragmatic perspective, knowledge was created through the interactions of the professors and the students, the texts and the experiments, and was captured through the process of writing. A small number of these writings were preserved for posterity as journal articles, theses or textbooks, and a smaller number became classics of knowledge (Garfield 2005). These classics were heavily cited, reprinted, translated, summarized in review articles, embedded into standard textbooks and more.

However, the revolution in digital technologies and networked communications brings the concerns of the philosopher to a much broader audience. The modern governance of knowledge in institutions covers a complex ecosystem of government, funders, universities, professors, students, textbooks, network-accessed content, software, research tools, research methods and more. The idea of the "article" or the "book" or the "thesis" as a canonical unit of knowledge, preserved and reprinted without constant and often significant changes is rapidly finding parallel competition by the ability of the network to facilitate rapid, distributed and incrementally created knowledge structures like wikis and free/*libre* open-source software.[1]

Almost parallel to this emergence of ecosystem-based knowledge creation sits the research institution and the research funder. Institutions retain specific roles, rights and privileges that govern knowledge production, transfer and exploitation. They are both generator of knowledge at scale and purchaser of knowledge at scale (e.g.,

---

1 See "It's The Customer, Not The Container" debate at the Society for Scholarly Publishing's Scholarly Kitchen site. Available at http://scholarlykitchen.sspnet.org/2009/09/24/johnwil banks-its-the-customer-not-the-container/. Unless otherwise stated, all web addressed in this chapter were last accessed in August 2012.

through library and textbook acquisition). They are often subject to policy mandates of government, legislative commandments and funder terms and conditions. Many institutions have evolved bureaucratic infrastructures for inbound and outbound knowledge governance via the technology transfer office and sponsored research office. But the institution and its infrastructure have existed to date in almost a separate world from the network-based, peer-produced-and-governed world.[2]

This infrastructure now exists inside a different information and innovation ecology driven by the Internet. The interconnection of institutions – companies, universities, NGOs and more – creates a potential world in which a more standardized set of knowledge transactions yields great overall knowledge creation as well as financial opportunity. And in this new ecology, network-driven distribution of knowledge creation is only one challenge to institutions accustomed to playing key roles in the knowledge governance process. Other challenges include changes to technology transfer, intellectual property licensing, data policies and faculty incentives. But universities in particular hold the promise of serving as "public spaces" in which individual knowledge creation via distributed systems is noted and rewarded, as well as engaging in purposeful and systematic knowledge distribution via both formal and informal transaction channels.[3]

Governments and private funders of knowledge creation have begun to recognize these changes and to look for leverage points at which they might intervene in favor of more open and cooperative knowledge governance. Thus, we see movements in favor of open access to research outputs and educational resources towards taxpayer-funded research,[4] private research foundations enforcing a sharing regime on research institutions in exchange for research funding.[5] However, we also see the impact of US pre-Internet legislation on knowledge governance systems across the world as countries eager to create national knowledge-driven innovation systems akin to that in the United States, which can come into both real and perceived conflict with the sharing regimes under experimentation.[6]

In this chapter, we attempt to "see the ocean in a grain of sand" by examining two new forms of knowledge governance (distributed-individual and open-institutional), performing a short case study of knowledge governance creation in the genomic

---

2 There are some very notable exceptions to this general rule, such as MIT's Open Courseware Initiative – see http://ocw.mit.edu. However, of all educational institutions, those exceptions form a very small percentage.

3 It should be noted that there is significant movement by universities to adopt local policies and technologies, typically based on the library system, to facilitate public access to journal articles and e-theses developed on campus. See the Registry of Open Access Repositories at http://roar.eprints.org/ for a lengthy list of such university policies.

4 See US National Institutes of Health Public Access Policy. Available at http://publicaccess.nih.gov/

5 See Wellcome Trust Open Access Policy, http://www.wellcome.ac.uk/About-us/Policy/Spotlight-issues/Open-access/index.htm

6 Legislation similar to Bayh–Dole from Brazil in 2003 and 2004 and South Africa in 2009 and 2010 are clear examples.

sciences sector and looking at the role of the university in particular as a knowledge broker in the networked society.

1. Distributed Innovation, Open Innovation and Knowledge Governance

In a distributed, networked context, knowledge can be created without a central authority assigning tasks and without the maximalist approach to intellectual property associated with traditional forms of innovation diffusion and exploitation. Rather, the communities are formed by many different individuals, participating for very different sets of reasons and incentives (Moglen 1999), who self-organize around challenges and tasks. This type of knowledge creation has been named "distributed innovation" (see, e.g., Lakhani, Karim and Pnaetta 2007) and is most easily seen in peer-produced systems like the Wikipedia online encyclopedia and the Linux operating system, both of which are built for "free" by thousands of individuals, connected by the Internet.

Distributed innovation (DI) examines the power we see in Wikipedia and Linux development, in which a collected set of individuals each donate individual actions to a collective work which then "snap together" into a coherent group through standard technical systems, digital networks,[7] and a community-born set of norms and rules.[8] This is a novel ecosystem for knowledge creation and presents both challenges and opportunities for the traditional, print-based knowledge-governance systems still common in academia. DI brings a significant increase in individual empowerment to participate directly in knowledge governance through membership in multiple distributed knowledge communities as part of the move to network forms of knowledge product creation.

However, as easy as it is to recognize distributed knowledge creation when we look at Wikipedia or GNU/Linux or some initiatives on open educational resources,[9] it is incredibly difficult to "program" distributed innovation. Participants in knowledge

---

7 See Wikipedia Meta Wiki, "Wiki Is Not Paper." Available at http://meta.wikimedia.org/wiki/Wiki_is_not_paper

8 Similarly, you find that "[c]ooperation in peer-production processes is usually maintained by some combination of technical architecture, social norms, legal rules, and a technically backed hierarchy that is validated by social norms" (Benkler 2006, 104).

9 Open educational resources are "teaching, learning and research resources that reside in the public domain or have been released under an intellectual property license that permits their free use or repurposing by others. In this sense, OER includes learning content, software tools to develop, use and distribute any kind of content, and implementation resources such as open licenses. From the Cape Town Open Education Declaration: 'These resources include openly licensed course materials, lesson plans, textbooks, games, software and other materials that support teaching and learning. They contribute to making education more accessible, especially where money for learning materials is scarce. They also nourish the kind of participatory culture of learning, creating, sharing and cooperation that rapidly changing knowledge societies need'" (Rossini 2010, 17).

creation must agree on a standard method to publish knowledge, and there must be significant infrastructure to support the evolution, distribution, storage, search, retrieval and verification of knowledge created. As this kind of agreement is hard to achieve, it is far easier to note examples of distributed knowledge creation than it is to spark the creation of a new one ex-ante.

These requirements are not new to the network: all of them conform closely to the way that scholars have operated since the creation of the scholarly journal in 1665.[10] The article and the book are standard knowledge "containers" and are governed through a set of gating functions. Peer review verifies, publishers distribute, libraries store, retrieve and serve out the knowledge in journals and books. Edits to the scholarly canon are made via new papers, corrigenda, and outright repudiation of previous studies.[11] In this context, we can actually view scholarly publishing as a predecessor to the wiki approach – the culture of knowledge advancing, edit by edit.

On top of this innate synchrony with the concepts of distributed knowledge creation, institutions have tried to make elements of distributed innovation and digital systems part of their daily lives. The technical infrastructures inside the libraries have made the leap to digital portals, web-based catalogs and more, but the new systems are primarily focused on the movement of the traditional units of knowledge in their digital forms rather than encouraging a rapid, decentralized knowledge governance process (Rossini 2009). Component elements of peer-produced systems often appear at universities spontaneously or are funded by government research programs, but as yet have not linked up to transform the system at a broad level outside of specific domains of research.[12]

So why then has distributed innovation in knowledge creation not taken root in academics the way it has in encyclopedias and software? One key reason is the lingering effect of the technology of paper in which academic scholarship

---

10 In 1662 the newly formed "Royal Society of London for Improving Natural Knowledge" was granted a charter to publish by King Charles II and on 6 March 1665 the first issue of *Philosophical Transactions* was published under the visionary editorship of Henry Oldenburg, who was also the secretary of the society. The first volumes of what is now the world's oldest scientific journal in continuous publication were very different from today's journal, but in essence, it served the same function, namely, to inform the fellows of the society and other interested readers of the latest scientific discoveries. As such, *Philosophical Transactions* established the important principles of scientific priority and peer review, which have become the central foundations of scientific journals ever since. See http://rstl.royalsociety publishing.org/

11 A timely example of this would be the January 2010 decision by the *Lancet*, a venerable British journal, to withdraw a long-criticized and controversial study linking autism to vaccines.

12 This is easiest to see in the life sciences, where the Open WetWare wiki system for laboratories and protocols has swept through the field of "synthetic biology" very quickly and where government-funded efforts to create ontologies and open data systems is the international norm. Newer research disciplines like synthetic biology and disciplines with large, rare data generation centers (like high-energy physics and astronomy) anecdotally appear to be more amenable to novel forms of knowledge governance.

developed.[13] The print culture is embedded deeply into academia and represents a major blocking agent to the adoption of distributed innovation. Rewards, incentives and metrics for academic professionals are deeply tied to print-based metrics like citations, references and impact factors. The existing systems of knowledge governance and credit allocation are not well aligned with a distributed knowledge creation environment, and the kind of authority rewarded in academia (typically resulting from award of advanced degrees) is not always the same kind of authority rewarded in a distributed knowledge system.

An institution or group of institutions wanting to enable true distributed knowledge governance would face a sociotechnical set of challenges to implementation, from the difficulty of rewarding participation in peer production of knowledge, the difficulty of defining knowledge into forms that work on wikis and other new modes of knowledge creation and distribution, on the complexity of curating data and databases and on the limitations of library capability in the long-term storage and preservation of data – to name but a few.

There is a key lesson for educational institutions aiming for distributed knowledge creation to draw from the technical world: the idea of interoperability. Interoperability allows unrelated systems to communicate and function in ways unexpected by their designers. The idea of interoperability as something that scales from technology to knowledge itself has emerged alongside the rise of the digital commons in culture and software. In this view, it is not only computer networks that must interoperate, but intellectual property rights and semantic understanding, so that distributed peer production of knowledge can make the leap from an encyclopedia into the sciences and other research disciplines.

Thus, to expand the idea of interoperability from technology to knowledge, it is worth examining where the choice to "separate concerns" in the early design of the Internet itself enabled the emergence of distributed innovation and knowledge construction.[14] Separating concerns is a subtle concept, but a very powerful one. It runs through the worlds of distributed innovation and peer production, from the human level – edits to one article within Wikipedia do not affect other articles inside Wikipedia – to the

---

13 This insight comes from conversations by the authors with Jean-Claude Guédon.

14 "Let me try to explain to you, what to my taste is characteristic for all intelligent thinking. It is, that one is willing to study in depth an aspect of one's subject matter in isolation for the sake of its own consistency, all the time knowing that one is occupying oneself only with one of the aspects. We know that a program must be correct and we can study it from that viewpoint only; we also know that it should be efficient and we can study its efficiency on another day, so to speak. In another mood we may ask ourselves whether, and if so: why, the program is desirable. But nothing is gained – on the contrary! – by tackling these various aspects simultaneously. It is what I sometimes have called 'the separation of concerns,' which, even if not perfectly possible, is yet the only available technique for effective ordering of one's thoughts, that I know of. This is what I mean by 'focusing one's attention upon some aspect': it does not mean ignoring the other aspects, it is just doing justice to the fact that from this aspect's point of view, the other is irrelevant. It is being one- and multiple-track minded simultaneously" (Dijkstra 1982, 60–66).

technical level, in which one can simply install a piece of software on a computer without a deep knowledge of the levels of software already in operation.[15]

The technical separation of concerns that allowed the creation of Wikipedia was the necessary first step towards the development of an online encyclopedia, but was not sufficient.[16] Since Wikipedia is a collective creative work, it has requirements that fall outside the scope of the technical standard systems that form the network – in particular, copyright. Added to the stack of standards for technical knowledge creation are the foundational legal tools of copyleft and open-source software licenses,[17, 18] which guarantee the legal interoperability of the code on top of the technical interoperability. The invention of the public copyright license was essential to remove the legal uncertainty around the collective creation of software code: everyone's contributions not only snapped together technically, but worked through the shared license to snap together legally. Wikipedia rights were first secured through the GNU Free Documentation License and are now secured through the Creative

---

15 The implementation of separation of concerns increases the "modularity" of software systems, technical networks, online encyclopedias and more. The knowledge product is built into a cohesive whole out of a set of disparate parts or modules. This approach allows for many different knowledge creators to work on a similar task without deep personal interaction, while still knowing that the knowledge created (whether wiki articles into an encyclopedia, or a web browser) will "snap together" if everyone involved follows the community and technical standards.

16 In a cultural knowledge product like Wikipedia, the technical stack of infrastructure is embedded and invisible to the end user. Wikipedia exists at one level because of the existence of the Internet itself, because the creator of wiki software did not have to ask permission of the creators of the Web for permission to run software on it, just as Tim Berners-Lee did not have to ask permission of the creators of the Internet to release the Web to run on it, and so on. The technical design of the Internet separates the issues of how to move information around from the issues of how to run applications and to present information. The system is designed from the beginning to allow for technologies that were not yet imaginable by the creators to flourish, for unintended uses to be enabled by default. Wikipedia sits atop this structure, technically, as do the end-user interfaces on users' computers, cell phones and other network access points.

17 "Copyleft uses copyright law, but flips it over to serve the opposite of its usual purpose: instead of a means of privatizing software, it becomes a means of keeping software free. The central idea of copyleft is that we give everyone permission to run the program, copy the program, modify the program and distribute modified versions – but not permission to add restrictions of their own. For an effective copyleft, modified versions must also be free" (Stallman n.d.).

18 "An open-source license is a copyright license for computer software that makes the source code available under terms that allow for modification and redistribution without having to pay the original author. Such licenses may have additional restrictions such as a requirement to preserve the name of the authors and the copyright statement within the code. One popular (and sometimes considered normative) set of open-source software licenses are those approved by the Open Source Initiative (OSI) based on their Open Source Definition (OSD)." See http://en.wikipedia.org/wiki/Open-source_license

Commons Attribution – Share Alike.[19] The application of a standardized permissive copyright license guarantees the rights of users to copy, distribute and modify the knowledge inside Wikipedia without asking permission of other individual users, or of the "leaders" of Wikipedia.

Wikipedia has an effective, if nontechnical, "semantic" amount of modularization, which is derived from the very format of the encyclopedia. One can insert random gibberish into a Wikipedia page without damaging the rest of the language on the page, and an editor or any user can quickly remove the offending language, again without interfering with the ability of a reader to see and use "traditional" knowledge-processing systems (e.g., the brain) to understand the content. The standard MediaWiki technical format renders content in a harmonious form, and embeds content versioning similar to software code versioning systems.

As institutions move towards a public role in distributed innovation, it will be vital to implement something akin to the technical separation of concerns into the governance of knowledge creation and distribution. It is a framework with a major role in existing distributed knowledge governance processes, and it carries deep implications for academia: it promises to transform the role of the individual inside academia by allowing more and greater access to knowledge, faster publishing and correction, more democratic peer review, at the same time that it may also allow less traditional actors to enter the knowledge governance systems, as editors, readers, critics and, hopefully at least occasionally, new partners.

However, the distributed systems of innovation we have been discussing disdain the larger institutions inside which the traditional actors of knowledge governance sit, and which play an enormous role in the exercise of intellectual property rights beyond the copyrighted creative work or software. The institution in this context is much more similar to a corporate firm than a collection of individuals and thus needs its own theory of innovation to evolve into something more modern and network friendly. There is another new theory of knowledge governance, known as "open innovation," which is more closely associated with the firm as governor than the individual or the collective of individuals who provides some ideas for the university.

The open innovation theory builds on the observation that an institution sits in an ecosystem of empowered individuals and other institutions, but that in a pre-network world, the transaction costs of accessing the innovations of those actors was too high to justify. Thus, the institution develops its own internal knowledge creation and governance systems (technology transfer offices, tenure and review boards, etc.). In a network culture, there is the opportunity to connect more and more of those smart people to an institution's mission: to contribute to internal projects from the outside, to take a project that fails to gather internal support forward using outside funding, to generate novel projects outside and "spin into" new internal projects. All of this becomes possible as the transaction costs involved in the knowledge movement required drop.

---

19 See http://www.gnu.org/copyleft/fdl.html and http://creativecommons.org/licenses/by-sa/
   3.0/us/

Open innovation builds on the idea of knowledge "leakage" from the firm or institution to the outside world, which is an informal kind of governance.[20] This leakage comes from many sources depending on the kind of institutions. It could be publication, via scholarly journal, by patent, by conference presentation, informal conversation or more currently, via blog post or wiki edit. The core insight of open innovation is the ability to use the world outside an institution to generate internally useful knowledge – and the core dependency of open innovation in turn is the need to make the flow of knowledge in and out of an institution a purposeful thing, not a random process.

Another relevant element of open innovation theory is the importance of the business model. A world of purposeful information flow in and out of institutions is at odds with many of the business structures of the last 50 years – especially intellectual property rights. Copyrights govern the copying, distribution and reuse of the documents containing actionable knowledge, from software to scholarship. Trade secrets and knowledge leakage on the public web are completely at odds with one another. And patents prevent institutions from acting on useful knowledge, even if the action would be far afield from the business concerns of the patent owner. Business models incorporate these knowledge "properties" as assets to be protected and build infrastructures of lawyers and compliance offices precisely to prevent their flow out and usage in the external world. Thus, the business model often forms a block to the institution's adoption of an open-innovation-based knowledge governance model, even if the ideas and theories of open innovation are attractive to the management and leaders of the institution.

Network-mediated knowledge governance in the university, then, sits inside a complicated context. Institutions must deal with changes in technology, pedagogy, incentive structures, libraries, intellectual property rights, business models and more if they are to fully engage in either distributed innovation or open innovation models – or, ideally, both. It is clear that making open systems simple and scalable turns out to be a complex affair. And the standardization of the network is, so far, a technocratic one. It enables the emergence of the open innovation paradigm but does not yet enable the horizontal spread of open innovation, because each institution must develop its own unique strategy for knowledge governance (and rights to use the knowledge) needed for each situation.

---

20 "Recent scholarship has argued that the comparative success of the Silicon Valley high-technology industrial district and failure of Route 128 outside of Boston, resulted from different patterns of interfirm employee mobility which, in turn, led to differing patterns of industrial organization: network organization as opposed to traditional vertical integration. The cause of the different patterns of employee mobility is said to be cultural differences between California and Massachusetts. This chapter offers a different causal analysis. After reviewing the new economic geography's emphasis on interfirm knowledge transfers as an agglomeration economy, I focus on the critical role of employee mobility – the vehicle for interfirm knowledge transfers – in facilitating second-stage agglomeration economies: those that allow the district to transcend its original product cycle and reinvent itself" (Gilson 1998).

In both the distributed and open cases of network-mediated knowledge governance briefly explored above, we saw the impact of interoperability as a baseline philosophy. Standard technical systems combine with standard knowledge formats to create open, generative solutions to problems. We also saw how the concept of interoperability applies from the pure technical "stacks" of standards to the legal realm via public licenses for knowledge products. We also saw that the existing paradigm cases of distribution and openness like Wikipedia and GNU/Linux exist outside traditional, "top down" approaches to knowledge governance – echoes of John Perry Barlow's famous declaration of independence of cyberspace,[21] and David Clark's famous summation:

> We reject: kings, presidents and voting.
> We believe in: rough consensus and running code. (Clark 1992)

Yet, interoperability, the basis for all of this emergent knowledge governance, is a choice. Like all choices, it can be undone, as Lessig has repeatedly warned. Interoperability can decay through slow changes to technical standards, government regulation and consumer choice – as in the emergence of "semiclosed" ecosystems of social networks like Facebook in which the interoperability is only enabled inside a walled garden (Zittrain 2006). The choice of licensing can also affect the downstream interoperability of a knowledge system, with even "open" licenses having negative impacts on knowledge integration and diffusion as unintended "environmental" consequences of an attempt to foster a sharing culture.[22]

2. Case Study: Genomics

Genomics is the study of the genomes of organisms. The field includes intensive efforts to determine the entire DNA sequence of organisms and fine-scale genetic mapping efforts. The field also includes studies of intragenomic phenomena and other interactions between loci and alleles within the genome[23] and the techniques of

---

21 "Governments of the Industrial World, you weary giants of flesh and steel, I come from Cyberspace, the new home of Mind. On behalf of the future, I ask you of the past to leave us alone. You are not welcome among us. You have no sovereignty where we gather." See http://homes.eff.org/~barlow/Declaration-Final.html

22 "...a possible unintended consequence in the long run is the possibility of creating systems of data sharing that have embedded within them the seeds of license incompatibility – seeds that once planted may mature into future interoperability problems that were not only unanticipated and unintended, but that are also too complex to solve or even to understand completely. These problems may undermine the very goals of public data sharing and artificially limit data exchange and collaboration between communities – not for justifiable technical or scientific constraints, but merely for license incompatibility reasons. There is evidence that such problems have already arisen throughout the open data community and may become more severe unless we take steps to address them at an early stage through developing a workable policy consensus." Science Commons "Comments on the Open Database License Proposed by Open Data Commons." Available at http://sciencecommons. org/resources/readingroom/comments-on-odbl/

23 See http://en.wikipedia.org/wiki/Genomics

sequencing, genome mapping, data storage and bioinformatic analyses. The wide range of genomics outputs means that the entire range of intellectual property rights come into play, and its relative youth as a field provides an ideal case study for knowledge governance systems in development and transition.

The Human Genome Project (HGP), a massive intergovernmental effort to sequence the human genome, can be studied through the lens of three knowledge products – narratives, data and tools – that are at the core of knowledge governance in both industrial and academic genomics. This analysis will focus on the IP rights associated with the knowledge products, provide a short overview of the HGP, examine the changes in knowledge governance that developed over the course of the HGP and close with the trends currently in play in post-HGP genomics.

2.1. Intellectual property rights and knowledge products

Copyrights, which govern the right of users to make and distribute copies of creative works, attach to narratives like journal articles, conference proceedings, posters, blogs, wikis and other narrative forms of communication, as well as to bioinformatics and cheminformatics software. Copyright protection is typically transferred from the author to the publisher of information in communication systems that predate the Internet (especially journal articles) and the copyright is used by the publisher to extract revenues from subscribers. For software, there is a broad range of licensing options from classic open-source models (more and more prevalent in bioinformatics) to very closed models, heavily protected by copyright licenses and charging high fees per seat.

Copyrights also factor into data and database protection: although raw "facts" like gene sequences are typically held to be noncreative works and thus not subject to copyright, varying levels of protection are allowed on the collective database itself depending on the national location of the database. US law allows a very limited copyright on the elements of the database that represent "selection and arrangement" (Carroll 2009), while the United Kingdom and some other countries allow a stronger "sweat of the brow" copyright over a database that rewards the act of collection itself. In the European Union, a law was written specifically for database protection that creates a "sui generis" right akin to copyright, which governs databases whose servers are located in the European Union.[24]

Patents, which govern the rights to exclude others from practicing an invention, attach to innovations like isolated gene sequences,[25] genetically modified sequences,

---

24 Directive 96/9/EC of the European Parliament and of the Council of 11 March 1996 on the legal protection of databases. Available at http://eur-lex.europa.eu/LexUriServ/ LexUriServ.do?uri=CELEX:31996L0009:EN:HTML

25 The possibility of patent of isolated genetic sequences is currently under debate in American courts in the case ACLU v. Myriad. ACLU is seeking invalidity on claims affirming that isolated genetic sequences are unpatentable subject matter. See more at http://www.genengnews. com/news/bnitem.aspx?name=54504126&source=genwire. Nowadays, there are more than 50,000 USA patents in genetic sequences. See http://dnapatents.georgetown.edu/

disease mechanisms of action, engineered tools like stem cells, mice, drug compounds, among others. Patents are considered to be a critical element of the business of genomics and proteomics and can bring great wealth to owners if the patent turns out to be a critical element of a drug or diagnostic that is taken to market.

Trade secret is also a powerful force in genomics and proteomics. Before publication, most academic research is held in secret, as is most corporate research before a project either leads to a patent or to abandonment.

In the context of knowledge governance, the natural contours defined by the use of intellectual property give further focus to our study. Those contours create a path to understanding genomics and proteomics more generally and also cast light on the broader biotech field itself. From pricing pressures in scholarly publishing,[26] to the impact of a natural public domain data status,[27] to the impact of community norms,[28] legislative and judicial changes on research tools,[29] our study of tools, narratives and data provides a lens onto cooperation across most of the key actors and segments of the industry.

The role of copyright on papers fits into a complex ecosystem of knowledge governance, which ties together many of the stakeholders in more "traditional" scientific knowledge transfer. "Tools" are a key knowledge-embedded product in genomics, whether or not the inventor seeks a patent, and withholding of unpatented tools plays a critical role in the informal knowledge governance of the sector (Walsh, Cho and Cohen 2007). The relative disharmony of database copyright treatment will be examined later in the case study as it affects knowledge governance, but so far has been avoided through the aggressive use of the public domain as a legal treatment for data.

---

26 "The term "serials crisis" has become a common shorthand to describe the chronic subscription cost increases of many scholarly journals. The prices of these institutional or library subscriptions have been rising much faster than the Consumer Price Index for several decades, while the funds available to libraries have remained static or have declined in real terms. As a result, academic and research libraries have regularly canceled serial subscriptions to accommodate price increases of the remaining current subscriptions." See http://en.wikipedia.org/wiki/Serials_crisis

27 "Information that is created by or for the US government on this site is within the public domain. Public domain information on the National Library of Medicine (NLM) Web pages may be freely distributed and copied. However, it is requested that in any subsequent use of this work, NLM be given appropriate acknowledgment." See http://www.ncbi.nlm.nih.gov/About/disclaimer.html

28 "The 'Bermuda Rules' may sound like standards for lawn tennis, but in fact they are guidelines for releasing human sequence data. Established in February 1996 at a Bermuda meeting of heads of the biggest labs in the publicly funded genome project, the rules instruct competitors in this cutthroat field to give away the fruits of their research for free" (Marshall 2001, 1192).

29 "Fundamentally, Bayh-Dole shifted the incentive structure that governed the research and development path of federally funded tools by allowing institutions to own tools resulting from federally sponsored research and to exclusively license those tools" (Boettiger and Bennett 2006).

2.2. Human Genome Project and data governance

Completed in 2003, the Human Genome Project was a 13 year, three billion dollar project coordinated by the US Department of Energy and the National Institutes of Health. During the early years of the HGP, the Wellcome Trust (UK) became a major partner; additional contributions came from Japan, France, Germany, China and others. Project goals were to identify all the approximately 20,000–25,000 genes in human DNA, determine the sequences of the three billion chemical base pairs that make up human DNA, store this information in databases, improve tools for data analysis, transfer related technologies to the private sector and address the ethical, legal, and social issues (ELSI) that may arise from the project.[30]

While the entire project raised issues of knowledge governance, we will first examine the issues related to the datasets and databases created in the HGP, because the data governance regimes that emerged from the HGP served as the basis for setting norms for the development of common-based practices in the genomics field that last far beyond the HGP itself.

As a globally distributed project, the HGP was forced early on to grapple with the issues of legal and technical interoperability, data acquisition and distribution, and scientific traditions of priority, publication and citation. It was also a deeply asymmetric project – it was understood that a limited group of people could contribute since there was a lack of capacity and infrastructure. This limited funding to large sequence centers at major, well-known and powerful universities. Not many had the scientists, the labs or the machines to develop the study – a marked characteristic of differentiation when you compare the HGP with open source projects, where there is a democratization of means. Knowledge governance leading data *from the few to the many* would be required to facilitate an open system's later emergence.

However, after some time into the project development, the sponsors of the project – the governments and private funders – realized that the public data deposits were falling behind the rate of publicly funded data production. Worse, a private competitor (Celera) was rapidly accelerating the creation of a closed whole-genome sequence. The government and funder reaction was to send the key scientific leadership away to Bermuda (later to Fort Lauderdale, FL) to work out the problem among themselves.[31] The basis was scientific, not legal, and deeply tied to the innate asymmetry of funding and the knowledge governance obligations it created:

> [I]f genome centers restrict their data and get preferential access to it, then some members of the community will no longer support monopolistic funding models (in which large centers sequence one genome after another

---

30 See Human Genome Project home page, http://www.ornl.gov/sci/techresources/Human_ Genome/home.shtml

31 A detailed analysis of this is well beyond the scope of this chapter, but Sir John Sulston's book *The Common Thread* contains a first-hand, lively and knowledgeable account of the events.

without peer review of each project). Instead, they will demand the right to compete with these empires, especially for the most scientifically desirable genomes. Other scientists, especially bioinformaticians, will seek to relocate to the centers to gain the advantage of early data access. Data restrictions will therefore promote factionalization where we should be seeking efficiencies of scale, and centralization where we should be promoting diversity. (Salzberg et al. 2003)

The resulting 1996 agreement is widely known as the Bermuda Rules. This landmark agreement is not a legal construct, contract, license, or otherwise binding in a court of law. It simply represented the norms of the HGP sequencing community. And the rules are simple. First, take care of the backlog by releasing, immediately, all DNA strands longer than 1,000 units; second, all new data goes on the web and into the public domain within 24 hours of coming off the machine.

Within this open governance regime the sequencing centers developed a strong competitive streak, which drove more and more data into the public domain, faster. One key requirement in the success of the Bermuda Rules was, in exchange for access, the application of a scientific publication norm, the centers depositing retained certain rights of first publication. But this again was a norm, not a legal requirement. Violators were in the realm of scientific publication and community judgment, not the courts.

There was great expectation that the impact of the release of the genome data would be that genomics companies would dominate the new face of drug discovery and development,[32] which faded as it became clear that data on its own was not sufficient to provide the knowledge required to understand diseases or discover drugs. The publication of the complete human genome in the public domain also had a significant governance impact on companies whose business was to use trade secrets to protect their data products, and companies such as Celera were unable to continue

---

32 Derek Lowe, who was there, wrote the following on the genomics craze: "[M]ost of the stuff you heard, at least in press releases and the like, ran to 'Genomatronic Corp. announces that it has now filed patent applications (a whopping load of patent applications) on another huge, important swath of the vital human genome (remember, there's only one!), and reminds the industry that its back walkway is open on Tuesdays and Thursdays for Big Pharma to come crawling up it.' Over at Megapharm, Inc., their opposite number, the fear was quite real that the Genomatronics of the world actually were staking out all the deposits of gold, and that all the drug targets in the world were going to end up owned by someone else – like those other big drug companies that were daily announcing huge deals with Genomatronic et al.… It was easy for panic to set in. How much of the genome could possibly be left by now? We'd better do a deal while there's something to buy! After all, when you got down to it, these folks were right – there's only one human genome, and we're only going to read it for the first time once, and all the drug targets that will ever exist are in there – right? So why would you sit there and watch the competition walk off with all the good stuff? Right?" See http://pipeline.corante.com/archives/2009/01/19/ten_years_after_the_genomics_frenzy.php

a business model based on expensive subscriptions for data that was available on the web in the public domain.[33]

Another key aspect of the HGP was the systematic investment in the technical infrastructure to distribute the sequences, a combined effort of the various governments involved, that included nightly sequence harmonization across the various data repositories. The emergence of the US National Center for Biotechnology Information (NCBI) was essential to the success of the project, demonstrating that technical accessibility is part of knowledge governance as well, and also developing some of the early integration of technology access with policy access – the NCBI not only clearly marks government data as public domain, but will not accept data whose depositors request controls based on intellectual property into its molecular databases.[34] Knowledge in this context must therefore also be studied with an eye towards technical architectures and their impact on governance.

The norms that emerged from the HGP were the inspiration for the norm-setting process of its successor, the "HapMap" project of human genetic variation,[35] and many of the same technical infrastructures were expanded to include the variation data alongside the genome. However, as opposed to the origins of the HGP, when the HapMap was born, the open source movement was a well-developed and -studied movement. The founders were inspired by open source to adopt an "open click-wrap" data license that tried to regulate publication processes and intervene in the exploration (more precisely – the abuse) of patents that may have emerged from the HapMap outputs.[36]

This licensing approach was abandoned for an unregulated environment running under the Bermuda Rules after a few years of operations. The fear of patent enclosure had been ameliorated by the dedication of so much data to the public domain, so

---

33 Specifically within the United States , over the past ten years, companies like Celera, Incyte, Human Genome Sciences, Millennium and more have exited the foundational data market, with Celera the most extreme example – abandoning the database market entirely by depositing their private genome sequence directly into Entrez. This is a reflection both of changing market conditions and of the growing economic power and value of the unregulated open systems. Merck, one of the world's largest pharmaceutical companies, added to this growth by the deposition of the Merck Gene Index into the Entrez system, which was a strategy to establish precompetitive gene sequences to avoid widespread gene patent "thickets," but had the secondary consequences of increasing market power in an unregulated-open space and creating market standardization around the Entrez technology platform as well as the public domain.

34 "NCBI itself places no restrictions on the use or distribution of the data contained therein. Nor do we accept data when the submitter has requested restrictions on reuse or redistribution." See http://www.ncbi.nlm.nih.gov/About/disclaimer.html

35 Whereas the Human Genome Project set out to map the DNA that is common to us all and makes us human, the HapMap project set out to map the individual genetic variations that make us individuals.

36 "More Than Two Years After Its Inception, Int 1 HapMap Project Defines Data-Release Policies." See GenomeWeb, December 18, 2003. Available at http://www.genomeweb.com/dxpgx/more-two-years-after-its-inception-int-l-hapmap-project-defines-data-release-pol

the patent aspects of the contract were felt unnecessary, and the unintended *knowledge governance impact* of the contract was that the HapMap data could not be integrated into the HGP data without creating legal contamination. Thus, the contract was lifted and the norms moved into place instead (Science 2004).

The HGP is in many ways a paradigmatic case of the shift in knowledge governance from privacy and withholding to open sharing. The perfect mixture of policy, funding, norms, law and technical infrastructure came together to open up the genome to all – when an alternative outcome could have easily occurred. The genome is now fundamentally open data, legally and technically.[37] Its entirety can be downloaded without registration and redistributed. It can be annotated, visualized and built upon. It leverages standard data formats, data repositories, software tools and more. And we see the long-term environmental impact of "conserving" the genome in a realm where the knowledge governance of genome data was run by the scientists, not the courts, in the explosion of downstream knowledge products emerging from the HGP and its successors.

From the genome as a foundational base, we see many distributed efforts emerging, as we might expect from an open source or wiki approach. Distributed annotation systems emerged to mark up the genes on the genome (Dowell et al. 2001), and an entire new field – synthetic biology – erupted, using the information gleaned in the genome sequence to create standard biological "parts" to be used in biological programming systems (Elowitz and Leiber 2000). Yet, to achieve this, the HGP represented a years-long investment in fundamental data generation with an unclear outcome and required the creation of significant funding streams to support technical distribution systems. Scientists had to come together and develop new norms and ethics for knowledge governance and distribution, not to mention standards for annotation and reuse as well as software tools and systems that made the genome useful, accessible and interoperable.

2.3. Governance of narratives and tools

Although we have focused on data so far, we can also contemplate the outputs of the Human Genome Project as they formed narratives and tools. The HGP yielded thousands of these knowledge products and a concurrent explosion of startup companies in genomics and proteomics, which peaked in the genomics "bubble" of the late 1990s. After the end of the genomics bubble, genomics companies trended away from data and towards "platforms" typically based on tools: massive-scale sequencing, cloning expertise and functional genomics.

What each of these companies has in common is a foundation in the academic literature, which is where the vast majority of theoretical research was published,

---

37 There is a knowledge utilization issue related to gene patents that is both real and significant, but sits outside the scope of this short case study. Readers wanting more information on this topic are encouraged to examine the excellent work of many scholars, in particular Cook-Deegan (1994).

and in academic laboratories, where many tools were first developed before being "polished" inside corporate structures for sale. Each of these classes of knowledge products underwent significant and sweeping changes over the 13-year history of the HGP. We will first examine the changes in governance over narratives as the publishing industry adapted to the Internet and then the changes in invention governance in the face of a changing legislative and judicial context.

Over the same time period as the HGP, scientific scholarly publishers saw in the Internet an increase in their ability to leverage technology. Similar to the music and movie industries, a small but dominant group of publishers (e.g., Elsevier, Nature, Springer, Wiley-Blackwell and others) explored models in which their traditional methods of selling physical copies of narrative scholarly content gave way to new business models of renting access to content via copyright licenses.

Unlike music, however, profits exploded in science and technology publishing. Combined with practices like "price bundling," in which university subscribers were forced to subscribe to less-popular journals in order to access the most desirable titles, and by a powerful reliance on copyrights enforcement, the overall cost of access to scientific narratives outpaced the cost of living increase by 600 percent over the course of the biotech industry, from the beginning through the bubble and into the present day.[38] In reaction to this pricing crisis, the open access movement evolved into a fully empowered active system in the narrative space,[39, 40] opening space for new open-business models and for institutional mandates for "author self-archiving."

Production and distribution of narratives exists at a different cycle than data and tools, because the narrative endures two completely separate cycles of production: knowledge generation in the lab and article production. The former is less our concern here but can take years, and if the experiment "fails," the narrative is frequently not developed out of laboratory notebooks into an article at all. The emergence of blogs and wikis may eventually have a powerful role in capturing these "failed" narratives, but as yet have had little impact.

The article-production cycle is shrinking with the advent of the digital journal. Where it may once have taken a year or more to get an article from submission into a print media journal sent via mails, the cycles can now be as short as a few weeks as in

---

38 See American Library Association, Economics of Scholarly Publishing, http://www.ala.org/ala/mgrps/divs/acrl/issues/scholarlycomm/scholarlycommunicationtoolkit/librarians/librarianeconomics.cfm

39 "By 'open access' to this literature, we mean its free availability on the public Internet, permitting any users to read, download, copy, distribute, print, search or link to the full texts of these articles, crawl them for indexing, pass them as data to software or use them for any other lawful purpose, without financial, legal or technical barriers other than those inseparable from gaining access to the Internet itself. The only constraint on reproduction and distribution, and the only role for copyright in this domain, should be to give authors control over the integrity of their work and the right to be properly acknowledged and cited." See Budapest Open Access Initiative, http://www.soros.org/openaccess/read.shtml

40 See Open Access Overview, http://www.earlham.edu/~peters/fos/overview.htm

the case of PLoS One.[41] The entire production cycle is much more efficient, although journals with high rejection rates continue to demonstrate the longest production cycle. The defining factor in these long cycles is the peer review process, which can be aided by technology but remains inherently slow, as it is mediated by the social networks of a discipline. Distribution of the narrative has undergone similar transformations as other digital media, with the ability to email PDFs of papers, post copies of preprint articles and hyperlink articles into websites, emails and more. The ability of individuals to circulate their work marks a major change in knowledge distribution. Thus, we see echoed in the narrative governance the importance of the technologies as a dimension of knowledge governance.

A key inflection point towards openness in narrative governance came when the US government flexed its market power as a funder of research, and implemented a mandate that all taxpayer-funded health research should be available under open access terms.[42] Deposits of scientific research skyrocketed in response.[43] Another key point in the open access market came in late 2008, when Springer purchased the open access publisher BioMed Central, whose revenues approached US$15 million per year (Oransky 2008). Both of these occurred against, again, a technical backdrop in which governments created technical repositories to host open narrative content, just as with open data for the HGP.

The governance of tools in genomics underwent a similar transformation over the life of the HGP. Tools were also dramatically affected by changes in knowledge governance via changes in the IP environment. Court cases allowing the patenting of modified genes,[44] and legislation encouraging universities to acquire and license patents on government-funded research,[45] paralleled the genomics bubble with a

---

41 PLoS ONE is an open-access, "online only" scientific journal from the Public Library of Science. It covers primary research from any discipline within science and medicine. All submissions go through a rigorous, internal and external prepublication peer review, but are not excluded on the basis of lack of perceived importance or adherence to a scientific field. The PLoS ONE online platform has postpublication user discussion and rating features. See http://www.plosone.org/home.action

42 "The NIH Public Access Policy ensures that the public has access to the published results of NIH -unded research. It requires scientists to submit final peer-reviewed journal manuscripts that arise from NIH funds to the digital archive PubMed Central upon acceptance for publication. To help advance science and improve human health, the Policy requires that these papers are accessible to the public on PubMed Central no later than 12 months after publication." See NIH Public Access home page, http://publicaccess.nih.gov/

43 NIMHS statistics are representative, see http://www.nihms.nih.gov/stats/

44 *Diamond v. Chakrabarty*, 447 U.S. 303 (1980) was a United States Supreme Court case dealing with whether genetically modified microorganisms can be patented.

45 The Bayh–Dole Act, or University and Small Business Patent Procedures Act, is United States legislation dealing with intellectual property arising from federal government-funded research. Adopted in 1980, Bayh–Dole is codified in 35 USC § 200–212[1], and implemented by 37 CFR 401[2]. Among other things, it gave US universities, small businesses and nonprofits intellectual property control of their tools and other intellectual property that resulted from such funding. See http://en.wikipedia.org/wiki/Bayh–Dole_Act

dramatic increase in the number of patents filed by universities on biology (Jensen and Murray 2005) .

Biological tools can range from simple biological materials that can be generated from standard protocols (similar to recipes in the kitchen) and everyday lab materials to complex living systems like genetically modified mice. Some biological materials are breakthrough products on their own, like the first human stem cell lines, and can take years to develop in the first instance, though their living nature allows them to be "cultured" and grown again and again after the first successful cycle.

The importance of biological materials has grown over the last fifteen years, as research tools like genetically modified mice and stem cells became critical to replicating published research, but access to those materials was (and is) frequently blocked by patent rights and by competitive withholding by scientists, research institutions, companies and other stakeholders.[46] Strikingly, policies that echo the data and narrative deposit requirements have been slow to emerge and difficult to implement – a 1998 working group of the US National Institutes of Health recommended open and precompetitive access to research tools generated with taxpayer funds, but that recommendation has never been associated with mandates, metrics or other systems that would encourage a transition to a true governance policy for tools (whether patented or not).[47]

While there is no centralized repository for tools like the NCBI for data and narratives, the market for tools is also affected by the establishment of biological resource centers (BRCs) into which funders sometimes mandate the deposit of knowledge products developed under funded research. Tool distribution tends to follow publication (and depending on the perceived economic value of the tool, patent applications) and again differs depending on the kind of tool, the existence of BRCs in that class of tool, facilitating distribution on behalf of the scientist, and the popularity of the material.[48] Distributing and governing tools is inherently more expensive than data and narratives, as the tools are nondigital assets.

---

46   The market for research tools is hard to characterize in a general fashion and tends to be related more to the individual tool, like a method for generating human stem cells, than to a broader perspective economically. Plasmids tend to be traded without recourse to economics or patents, while genetically engineered mice almost always include patent licenses.

47   See the report of the National Institutes of Health (NIH) Working Group on Research Tools, presented to the Advisory Committee to the Director, June 4, 1998.

48   Other tools in this context are laboratory robots, which are essential to the data production cycle. Such robots include microarrays for rapid analysis of gene expression, high-throughput genetic sequencers, flow-assisted cell sorters and more. These tools are commodities available from catalogues at varying price levels (even on eBay) or as services from genomics core facilities to produce data on demand at levels previously unthinkable. The only restrictions on data production capacity where these machines exist is funding and the ability to utilize the data. Distribution of the generated data tends to depend on technical capacity and class of data – if the NCBI system accepts deposit of a class of data, distribution of that data tends to be dominated by NCBI. Otherwise, there is a wide range of knowledge governance behavior ranging from posting of data files on laboratory websites to "email me to ask for the data" to outright withholding.

2.4. Knowledge governance trends

Policy trends in genomic and proteomic research unambiguously favor openness and unregulated access. The most notable policy trend in publishing narratives for genomics and proteomics is the powerful shift towards open access to research articles symbolized by the public-access policies implemented by the US government (NIH most obviously) and endorsed by governments and institutions across Europe, in Australia and elsewhere.[49] The original policy direction of a few funders is now echoed by private foundations and research universities.[50]

A similar set of trends is also evident in foundational data, which tends to be created as a "big science" collaborative project, and in which the funds to disseminate data are part of the funding contract. The success of the HGP and related projects has created an expectation of data sharing of what we might call "foundational" information to serve as a basis of future experimentation.[51] At the smaller scale, the experimental data generated in laboratories is subject to less formal policy requirements though the expectations of scientist and funder, informal and formal, are tilted towards sharing, with NIH grant proposals requiring the submission of data-sharing plans. However, optimism for open data must be tempered with the reality of data sharing, which is difficult, expensive and often unsatisfying when the repository is not the NCBI.

Research tools like stem cells and plasmids are subject to completely voluntary sharing policies under the NIH system, and though some private research foundations do both mandate and fund the sharing of tools, this is the exception rather than the rule. The counterbalancing trend is brought by the continuing reliance on innovation-systems legislation as an influence for universities to patent research tools. Innovation legislation (such as the Bayh–Dole Act in the United States) is also occasionally brought into play in the sharing of data from which patentable tools might be drawn.

---

49 See http://www.earlham.edu/~peters/fos/newsletter/01-02-10.htm#2009

50 "Autism Speaks, the nation's largest autism advocacy organization, announced that effective December 3, 2008, all researchers who receive an Autism Speaks grant will be required to deposit any resulting peer-reviewed research papers in the PubMed Central online archive, which will make the articles available to the public within 12 months of journal publication. This new policy will make the results of Autism Speaks-funded research easily accessible – at no charge – to individuals with autism, families and other advocates, as well as interested researchers. Autism Speaks is the first US-based nonprofit advocacy organization to institute this public access requirement." See http://www.earlham.edu/~peters/fos/2008/11/autism-speaks-adopts-oa-mandate.html. The Registry of Open Access Repositories lists 204 institutional policies on open access at the time of writing. See http://www.eprints.org/openaccess/policysignup/

51 By foundational, we mean data that is standardized and common – the genome would be an example, as would be the height of Mount Everest – that takes an enormous amount of funding to create and can serve as the foundation for much other research. This is a term of the authors' invention, to distinguish it from the kinds of data generated in a laboratory by the perturbation of a system.

However, the lack of standardization in contracts and technology means that very high percentages of tool-sharing requests result in denial.[52]

Another market aspect of genomics and proteomics is the market for research funds, which is dominated by the pursuit of NIH "R01" grants, the oldest and most common type of government-funded research in the world of biotech within the United States. In addition to R01 funding, researchers also compete for funds from private research foundations (frequently focused on specific diseases, but including some large research foundations like the Howard Hughes Medical Institute and the Wellcome Trust). Competition for grants is intense and leads to some instincts towards data- and tools-withholding, while placing an enormous pressure on the researcher to publish narrative in "high quality" journals.

2.5. Genomics: Early conclusions

From this necessarily brief study, we can draw some conclusions about knowledge governance and its changes in reaction to the emergence of the technical revolutions of biotechnology/digital communications and the legal–social revolutions of the distributed creation of knowledge.

First, each knowledge product carries its own set of informal and formal governance regimes that affect distribution and transfer. Intellectual property rights are one of the factors here, but competitive withholding (either for academic advancement or corporate value) has a major impact as well. Second, the infrastructure and incentives for distribution and reuse are complex yet essential. Data is of little value if there is no infrastructure to make it comprehensible, and tools represent a valuable commodity for hoarding under the current knowledge governance system. And third, in order to achieve real changes in knowledge governance regimes, a coalition of funders, research institutions, knowledge publishers, governments, and technical infrastructure providers seems essential.

3. National Innovation Policy

The three conclusions noted above hint at the direct role in the stimulation of innovation that knowledge governance must play. But although innovation policy has become a core element of policymaking in both the developed and developing world as countries engage in the information society process and compete in the globalized world, there is little "network-centric" knowledge governance included as part of the process. Instead – looking to the example of the United States and later Asian countries and as a answer

---

52 "In the university-to-university setting, estimates range from delays of over a month for between 11 percent and 16 percent of requests, 'a substantial delay in a fast-moving field,' to estimates that there are routine delays of over 6 months for 20 percent of requests and over 2 months for 42 percent of requests. Studies also show increasing rates of outright denial of requests, and of abandonment of 'promising research projects' because materials are not received. In the commercial–university arena, with no standardized agreements at all, most observers believe the situation is worse. Commercial–academic denial rates are estimated to be nearly twice those in the academic–academic context (33 percent to 18 percent)." See "Empirical Data About Materials Transfer Problems," Science Commons. Available at http://sciencecommons.org/projects/licensing/empirical-data-about-materials-transfer/

to the OECD's call related to the technology transfer of publicly funded research – countries of the North and South have implemented national legislation and public policies based in large part on the expansion and management of intellectual property. These trends are specifically intended to emulate the success of the United States in innovation, in a traditional innovation context, but may have significant and potentially toxic effects on emerging, distributed or open-knowledge-governance regimes.

Kenneth Shadlen argues that "National patent regimes influence trajectories of industrial development and governments' capacities to address humanitarian concerns. As pillars of national systems of innovation, patent regimes drive technological change and shape trajectories of knowledge creation and knowledge diffusion" (Shadlen 2008). The "traditional innovation belief is that Intellectual Property should serve as the primary measurement of innovation, as a proxy for knowledge creation and governance, and also act as the primary safeguard to attract investment in research and development, and not just as a promoter of diffusion."[53]

The policies around traditional innovation focus on institutions, mainly universities and companies, as the key bridge between design and manufacturing. This focus reflects the experiences of the US Bayh–Dole legislation and implementation. Countries as diverse as Brazil, China, South Korea, India, Japan, France and Finland have implemented variations on the Bayh–Dole legislation into their innovation laws and policy arrangements (Graff 2001).

The US Patent and Trademark Law Amendment Act 96-517 of 1980, the formal name of the Bayh–Dole Act, is the legal framework for the transfer of university generated, federally funded inventions to the commercial market place. Bayh–Dole "swept away the patchwork of individual agency-controlled IPAs and instituted a uniform federal patent policy for universities and small businesses under which they obtained the rights to any patents resulting from grants or contracts funded by any federal agency."[54]

---

53 Research and development is considered the fundamental step in what economists call innovation of product and process to market, while diffusion is just related to the incorporation of existing technology to satisfy necessities of cost reduction, standardization of products and process and manufacturing efficiency.

54 This opinion is not uniform among authors that discuss the Bayh–Dole effects, since the Bayh–Dole, as determined in its Section 202, was first intended to regulate universities, small businesses and nonprofits, as will be seen further in the paper. Jordan J. Baruch, assistant attorney general, during its testimonies, as quoted by Eisenberg, affirmed that: "The Bayh–Dole bill was only a partial solution that did nothing to unify patent policy across agencies; indeed, if the right of large contractors were still to be governed by the inconsistent practices and policies of the various agencies, a new set of statutory rules applicable only to nonprofit institutions and small business would merely add a twenty-seventh policy to the twenty-six inconsistent sets of rules and regulations already an the books" (Eisenberg 1996, 1694). The concern was to avoid market power concentration and promote widespread commercialization of inventions and the flourishing of new companies (start-ups), since large business are generally pictured as "short-sighted, risk-averse, and predatory, more likely to suppress new technologies than to adopt them" (Eisenberg 1996, 1696). This problem finished in 1984, when an amendment, endorsing President Regan's memorandum previously sent to the head of the agencies, extended the authorization of title retention to large business.

Under this 1980 law, as amended, the title to inventions made with government support is provided to the contractor if that contractor is a national small business (and after 1984, also large business), university or another nonprofit institution such as a hospital or research institution.[55] The legislation is intended to use patent ownership as an incentive for private-sector development and commercialization of federally funded research and development (R&D).

The influence of Bayh–Dole is so great that it is worth examining its terms closely. In section 200, the act establishes as objectives for the use of the patent system to (1) promote the utilization of inventions arising from federally supported research or development, (2) encourage maximum participation of small business firms in federally supported research and development efforts (3) promote collaboration between commercial concerns and nonprofit organizations, including universities, (4) ensure that inventions made by nonprofit organizations and small business firms are used in a manner to promote free competition and enterprise without unduly encumbering future research and discovery, (5) promote the commercialization and public availability of inventions made in the United States by United States industry and labor, (6) ensure that the government obtains sufficient rights in federally supported inventions to meet the needs of the government and protect the public against nonuse or unreasonable use of inventions, and (7) minimize the costs of administering policies in this area.

With the passage of the Bayh–Dole Act, universities began to develop and strengthen their internal expertise to engage in the patenting and licensing of inventions, through the establishment of entirely new technology transfer offices, building teams with legal, business and scientific backgrounds. The Association of University Technology Managers (AUTM) shows that its membership increased from 113 members in 1979, to 691 in 1989 and to 2,178 in 1999. The table below from the 2006 AUTM Licensing Survey shows how many universities per year, since the 1970s, started their Technology Transfer Program, which usually implies the organization

---

55   35. USC part II. ch. 18: 202: "Disposition of rights: (a) Each nonprofit organization or small business firm may, within a reasonable time after disclosure as required by paragraph (c)(1) of this section, elect to retain title to any subject invention." The section follows to established exceptions to the rule by saying: "Provided, however, that a funding agreement may provide otherwise (i) when the contractor is not located in the United States or does not have a place of business located in the United States or is subject to the control of a foreign government, (ii) in exceptional circumstances when it is determined by the agency that restriction or elimination of the right to retain title to any subject invention will better promote the policy and objectives of this chapter, (iii) when it is determined by a Government authority which is authorized by statute or Executive order to conduct foreign intelligence or counter-intelligence activities that the restriction or elimination of the right to retain title to any subject invention is necessary to protect the security of such activities or, (iv) when the funding agreement includes the operation of a Government-owned, contractor-operated facility of the Department of Energy primarily dedicated to that Department's naval nuclear propulsion or weapons related programs and all funding agreement limitations under this subparagraph on the contractor's right to elect title to a subject invention are limited to inventions occurring under the above two programs of the Department of Energy..."

of a Transfer Technology Office (TTO). AUTM's report also shows that TTO staff levels are steadily increasing.[56] Creating and commercializing intellectual property has become one of the most important institutional objectives in various academic settings, a change usually credited to Bayh–Dole and traditional innovation.

It is important to juxtapose the centrality in traditional innovation of the institution as a closed entity, gaining and licensing intellectual property, against the role of the institution (company or university) in the Chesbrough open innovation paradigm,[57] as well as against the role of the university as the host of a set of individuals participating in distributed innovation systems across traditional academic lines. The national innovation systems are set up to favor the traditional role, bolstered by academic incentives, high transaction costs for change and general inertia towards organizational innovation.

In the traditional innovation context, an important role is played by research universities that are positioned in a relational context with the government and the industry. This context is explained as a process in which a university adds industry-like responsibilities to its core mission of generation and dissemination of knowledge through education and scholarly research, in order to engage with the government and industry in the promotion of economic development (Etzkowitz and Brisolla 1999). Inside this relation, the inherent tension of the academia–industry relationship, and in particular the role of patenting, has been the focus of significant analysis and discussion, particularly within the academic community (Eisenberg 1996; Rai 1999; Kieff 2001) .

Facing the challenges of national development and the goal of independent participation in the global economy, Brazil, for instance, developed a national innovation system (NIS) internalizing these innovation theories. Its NIS emulates foreign laws, such as the US Bayh–Dole University and Small Business Patent Act of 1980, as well as the French Loi Sur L'innovation et la Recherche of 1999. The main results were the NIS of 2003 and the Innovation Law of 2004 – among other norms related to tax incentives – both finalized and structured under the Luis Inacio Lula da Silva ("Lula") administration in Brazil. Under the NIS, Brazil created priority areas such as biotechnology, pharmaceuticals (medicines and vaccines), biomass, information technology and software among others and developed the *fundos setoriais* ("sectoral funds") under the Ministry of Science and Technology budget to foster the expansion of research and its translation into commercially valuable goods and services. There is particular privilege for private–public partnerships, which receive tax incentives and other benefits. A parallel was recently developed under the coordination of the Development, Commerce and International

---

56 See in general: AUTM, FY 2006 AUTM Licensing Survey (2006). Available at http://www. autm.net/events/file/AUTM_06_US LSS_FNL.pdf

57 "Open innovation is the use of purposive inflows and outflows of knowledge to accelerate internal innovation, and expand the markets for external use of innovation, respectively. [This paradigm] assumes that firms can and should use external ideas as well as internal ideas, and internal and external paths to market, as they look to advance their technology" (Chesbrough 2006).

Trade Ministry, called the Productive Development Plan (PDP) of 2008 that is not yet fully coordinated with the NIS under the work of interministerial commissions. All of these laws recognize the interconnections and interdependence between the knowledge institutions of industry, academia and government.

However, none of these industrial policies have taken into consideration nontraditional knowledge governance arrangements like the open and distributed ones discussed in Section 1. In the rush to emulate Bayh–Dole, many key elements of emerging, network-centric innovation policy, including new approaches to the patent system, remain unexamined by Brazilian policymakers.

Bayh–Dole was designed over 30 years ago, before the network transformed our daily life. Bayh–Dole systems assume significant social, financial, legal and institutional infrastructure to take innovations out of the academic–nonprofit worlds to manufacture and marketing. Such legislation has the potential to significantly imbalance intellectual property regimes in countries that implement a variation of it. Bayh–Dole will require localization and adjustment to local knowledge governance realities if it is to work in Brazil as it has arguably worked in the United States.[58] Bayh–Dole "porting" is even more complex when one notes that developing nations in general do not present the cultural knowledge exploitation ecosystem inside which the Bayh–Dole functions in the United States, such as a strong private equity market, technology transfer community or an entrepreneurial support system.

There is also a significant set of interlocking factors that can affect the effectiveness of Bayh–Dole-like legislation in a localizing country. Bilateral agreements and national legislation can inhibit the effectiveness of innovation policy by creating strong incentives for South-to-North knowledge transfer innovation expropriation (especially if there is no local infrastructure to exploit local innovations). Other factors can retard innovation by making local forms of cultural or scientific business innovations difficult via expansive use of contract restrictions, anticircumvention TPM (technological protection measures) laws or expropriation of traditional knowledge.

The university has a real role to play here, as a "public space." The university represents a well-placed actor to foster and host arrangements of networked knowledge creation and distribution, adding to the triangle or helix of university–industry–government a

---

58 "The Bayh-Dole Act has been seen as particularly successful in meeting its objectives. However, while the legislation provides a general framework to promote expanded utilization of the results of federally funded research and development, questions are being raised as to the adequacy of current arrangements. Most agree that closer cooperation among industry, government, and academia can augment funding sources (both in the private and public sectors), increase technology transfer, stimulate more innovation (beyond invention), lead to new products and processes, and expand markets. However, others point out that collaboration may provide an increased opportunity for conflict of interest, redirection of research, less openness in sharing of scientific discovery and a greater emphasis on applied rather than basic research. Additional concerns have been expressed, particularly in relation to the pharmaceutical and biotechnology industries, that the government and the public are not receiving benefits commensurate with the federal contribution to the initial research and development" (Schacht 2006).

fourth and empowered actor, the networked universe of individual user-innovators. Through the application of "commons" techniques like open licenses and through the use of cyber-infrastructure, the university can create a public space not just for its internal clients (students and faculty) but also public spaces in which the collected set of users on the network can connect through open educational resources and materials to the formerly closed industry–university–government innovation system.

For this, the university will have to develop a sufficiently complex internal policy of knowledge governance to allow the open and distributed knowledge models to emerge, concepts that bring together some important themes such as user reinvention, the economics of open source, open licensing, technologies of cooperation and collective action and cyber-infrastructure for national and international collaboration and access to and transfer of knowledge. Also, the university will need interlocking governmental policies that support infrastructure development for nontraditional innovation and a legislative and judicial compromise to bar the expansion of the intellectual property rights, while industry will need to develop business models that can exploit innovation of every form, including those based on nontraditional approaches to intellectual property.

Conclusions

The world of knowledge creation, distribution and governance sits at a crossroads where the potential of new network-driven systems hits the reality of traditional institutionally mediated knowledge governance. This is particularly the case in areas, such as science, that require more infrastructure and tools than are available from the consumer and commercial Internet. Infrastructure brings institutions to the table, and institutions bring many traditional roles of knowledge governance into the conversation, which interact uneasily, at best, with network systems and cultures.

There are few, if any, "easy answers" to the questions of what an institution, a government, a funder or an individual should do in the short term. But there are early lessons to draw from the successes in knowledge access, formation and distribution outside the traditional system that provide clues.

First, the principle of interoperability should not be confined to technology, but instead should inform decisions ranging from policy to intellectual property to institutional arrangements and forward. Legal implications can reach through software to touch technology, content, knowledge products and more – and interoperability as a design principle represents "good taste" in knowledge governance, as it both empowers those with the current capacity to participate in innovation and those who have not yet acquired that capacity. Practicing this principle of interoperability and separation of concerns means that we do not merely create infrastructure that serves today's knowledge problem, but that it can be extended and built upon to serve many knowledge problems in the future, most of which we cannot yet see. The leading expression to be followed here is *design it so it can attain interoperability*.

Second, the role of democratized access to infrastructure is essential. Open systems, be they legal, technical or policy, that are not designed with interoperable infrastructure in mind are likely to yield unintended consequences. We saw this in the case study with the HapMap license, which blocked database integration as a side effect of attempting to enforce patent openness. By violating the separation of concerns, an open-knowledge-governance attempt in patents resulted in a non-interoperable governance reality in data. Thus, policy and governance should not only tend towards open infrastructure, but also contemplate the "environmental impact" of specific decisions on the availability of infrastructure.

References

All web addresses last accessed August 2012.

Benkler, Y. 2006. *The Wealth of Networks*. New Haven, CT: Yale University Press.
Blackler, F. 1995. "Knowledge, Knowledge Work and Organizations: An Overview and Interpretation." *Organization Studies* 16: 1021–46.
Boettiger, S. and A. Bennett. 2006. "Bayh-Dole: If we knew then what we know now." *Nature Biotechnology* 24: 320–23.
Carroll, M. 2009. "Copyright in Databases." Available at http://carrollogos.blogspot.com/2009/02/copyright-in-databases.html
Chesbrough, H. 2006. *Open Innovation: Researching a New Paradigm*. Available at http://www.openinnovation.net/
Clark, D. 1992. "A Cloudy Crystal Ball – Visions of the Future." Available at http://xys.ccert.edu.cn/reference/future_ietf_92.pdf
Cook-Deegan, R. 1994. *The Gene Wars: Science, Politics, and the Human Genome*. New York and London: W. W. Norton & Co.
Dijkstra, E. W. 1982. "On the role of scientific thought." In E. W. Dijkstra, *Selected Writings on Computing: A Personal Perspective*, 60–66. New York: Springer-Verlag.
Dowell R. D., R. M. Jokerst, A. Day, S. R. Eddy and L. Stein. 2001. "The distributed annotation system." *BMC Bioinformatics* 2 (7).
Eisenberg, R. S. 1996. "Public Research and Private Development: patents and technology transfer in Government-Sponsored Research." *Virginia Law Review* 82 (8): 1663–1727.
Elowitz M. B. and S. Leibler. 2000. "A synthetic oscillatory network of transcriptional regulators." *Nature* 403: 335–8.
Etzkowitz, H. and S. Brisolla. 1999. "Failure and success: The fate of industrial policy in Latin America and South East Asia." *Research Policy* 28 (4): 337–50.
Garfield, E. 2005. "The Agony and the Ecstasy: The History and Meaning of the Journal Impact Factor." Available at http://garfield.library.upenn.edu/papers/jifchicago2005.pdf
Gilson, R. J. 1998. "The Legal Infrastructure of High Technology Industrial Districts: Silicon Valley, Route 128, and Covenants Not to Compete." Stanford Law School, John M. Olin Program in Law and Economics, Working Paper No. 163. Available at http://ssrn.com/abstract=124508 or doi:10.2139/ssrn.124508
Jensen, K., and F. Murray. 2005. "Intellectual Property Landscape of the Human Genome." *Science* 310 (14): 239–40.
Kieff, F. S. 2001. "Facilitating Scientific Research: Intellectual Property Rights and the Norms of Science – A Response to Rai and Eisenberg." *Northwester University Law Review* 95 (2): 691–705.
Graff, G. D. 2001. "Echoes of Bayh-Dole? A survey of IP and technology transfer policies in emerging and developing economies." In A. Krattiger, R. T. Mahoney, L. Nelsen, J. A. Thompson and A. B. Bennett (eds), *Intellectual Property Management in Health and Agricultural Innovation: A Handbook of Best Practices*, 169–195. Oxford: MIH/Davis, CA: PIPRA.

Lakhani, K. R. and J. A. Panetta. 2007. "The Principles of Distributed Innovation." *Innovations: Technology, Governance, Globalization* 2 (3): 97–112 .

Marshall, E. 2001. "Bermuda Rules: Community Spirit, With Teeth." *Science* 291 (5507): 1192.

Moglen, E. 1999. "Anarchism Triumphant: Free Software and the Death of Copyright." *First Monday*. Available at http://emoglen.law.columbia.edu/my_pubs/anarchism.html

Oransky, I. 2008. "Open access publisher BioMed Central sold to Springer." *Scientific American*, October 7, 2008.

Rai, A. K. 1999. "Regulating Scientific Research: Intellectual Property Rights and the Norms of Science." Duke Law Faculty Scholarship Paper No. 451. Available at http://scholarship.law.duke.edu/faculty_scholarship/451

Rossini, C. 2010. "The State and Challenges of Open Educational Resources in Brazil." Available at http://www.soros.org/initiatives/information/focus/access/articles_publications/publications/oer-brazil-20100101

———. 2009. "The Need for a Knowledge Web for Scholarship." Available at http://publius.cc/need_knowledge_web_scholarship/020509

Salzberg, S., E. Birney, S. Eddy and O. White. 2003. "Unrestricted Free Access Works and Must Continue." *Nature* 422 (24): 801.

Schacht, W. 2006. "The Bayh-Dole Act: Selected Issues in Patent Policy and the Commercialization of Technology Congressional research Services." Available at http://italy.usembassy.gov/pdf/other/RL32076.pdf

Science. 2004. "Netwatch: HapMap Lifts Data Restrictions." *Science* 306 (5705): 2167.

Shadlen, K. 2008. "Revolution, Reform and Reinforcement: Latin America Responses to the Globalization of Intellectual Property." Working paper presented at the European Consortium for Political Research.

Stallman, R. n.d. "The GNU Project." Available at http://www.gnu.org/gnu/thegnuproject.html

Walsh, J. P., C. Cho and W. M. Cohen. 2007. "Where Excludability Matters: Material v. Intellectual Property in Academic Biomedical Research." Georgia Institute of Technology School of Public Policy Working Paper No. 20. Available at http://smartech.gatech.edu/xmlui/bitstream/handle/1853/23810/wp20.pdf ?sequence=1

Zittrain, J. L. 2006. "The Generative Internet." University of Oxford Faculty of Law Legal Studies Research Paper Series, Working Paper No. 28.

Chapter 9

THE SEARCH FOR
ALTERNATIVES TO PATENTS
IN THE TWENTY-FIRST CENTURY

Luigi Palombi
Australian National University

Introduction

During the mid-nineteenth century, a debate took place in Europe and Great Britain about the merits of patent monopolies.[1] At its height, the Netherlands repealed its patent law,[2] Switzerland refused to enact one[3] (see Schiff 1971), German economists voted to abolish patent monopolies (see Seckelmann 2001),[4] and there was a

---

This chapter brings together ideas that were first formulated in the author's book, *Gene Cartels Biotech Patents in the Age of Free Trade* (Cheltenham: E. Elgar, 2009).

1 "The privileges granted to inventors by patent laws are prohibitions on other men, and the history of inventions accordingly teems with accounts of trifling improvements patented, that have put a stop, for a long period, to other similar and much greater improvements. It teems also with accounts of improvements carried into effect the instant some patents had expired. The privileges have stifled more inventions than they promoted, and have cause more brilliant schemes to be put aside than they the want of them could ever have induced men to conceal. Every patent is a prohibition against improvements in a particular direction, except by the patentee, for a certain number of years; and, however, beneficial that may be to him who receives the privilege, the community cannot be benefited by it... On all inventors it is especially a prohibition to exercise their faculties; and in proportion as they are more numerous than one, it is an impediment to the general advancement, with which it is the duty of the Legislature not to interfere, and which the claimers of privileges pretend at least to have at heart." Editorial, *Economist*, February 1, 1851.
2 The Netherlands repealed its first patent law (proclaimed in 1817) in 1869. It did not reintroduce a patent law until 1912.
3 It was not until 1888 (The Federal Law on the Protection of Inventions, July 29, 1888) that Switzerland first adopted a national patent law. Even so, says Schiff, "[it was] probably... the most incomplete and selective patent law ever enacted in modern times" (1971, 93). Not until 1907 did Switzerland fully embrace the patent monopoly.
4 The Association of German Economists (Verein deutscher Volkswirte). Reported in the *National-Zeitung*, March 18, 1863.

succession of inquiries into the workings of the British patent system, the last in 1872, recommending the length of the British patent monopoly be halved from 14 years to 7 years (see Palombi 2009).

Alternatives to patent monopolies were also mooted. John Stuart Mill, a British economist, proposed that inventors be given "pecuniary rewards." Although supportive of patent monopolies, in his treatise *Principles of Political Economy* he suggested that in lieu of patents, "a small temporary tax, imposed for the inventors benefit, on all persons making use of the invention" would suffice. In France, Michel Chevalier, an economist and one of France's leading exponents of free trade, agreed. And in Switzerland, the creation of a statutory fund from which inventors would be paid a reward, more like one-off prizes rather than royalty streams paid over time, was considered (see Ritter 2004).

The turning point, however, came with the first international patent convention held in Vienna in August 1873 (see Palombi 2009). This was the event that stemmed the antipatent tide in Europe. By 1883, the convention's resolutions had been incorporated into the world's first international intellectual property treaty, the Paris Convention for the Protection of Industrial Property, and by 1893, the United International Bureaux for the Protection of Intellectual Property, the forerunner to the World Intellectual Property Organization (WIPO), was established in Berne, Switzerland. Today 153 countries, as members of the World Trade Organization (WTO), have patent laws that meet the minimum standards prescribed by the Agreement of Trade Related Aspects of Intellectual Property Rights (TRIPS).

The result: at no other time in the history of intellectual property rights have laws which facilitate their enforcement been as uniform as they are today. That said, it would be a mistake to assume that the road to this point has been smooth, just as it would be a mistake to believe that patents are the principal inducers of technological development.

Nonetheless, during the twentieth century, political leaders questioned the effectiveness of patent monopolies. In a letter to Congress, President Roosevelt advocated the nonexclusive licensing of all US patents in an attempt to neutralize the danger that patents and corporate power posed to the national security of the United States.[5] In fact, many of the criticisms that had been leveled at patent monopolies in the nineteenth century (see Machlup and Penrose 1950) were raised again in the twentieth century (see Diggins 1955; Machlup 1961) just as they are again being raised today (see Drahos and Brathwaite 2002; Dutfield 2003; Jaffe and Learner 2004; Drahos 2005; Boldrin and Levine 2008; Bessen and Meurer 2008; Burk and Lemley 2009; Palombi 2009). This leads to the question: Are patent monopolies the most efficient and effective form of encouraging innovation and capacity building?

This is a relevant question given that in the past 20 to 30 years, as the scope of patentable subject matter has expanded, the world's patent systems have come under increasing pressure in an attempt to meet the demands of their users, significant among these being large multinational corporations. The emerging evidence suggests that patent systems are

5 President Franklin D. Roosevelt's message on 29 April 1938 to the US Congress on "Curbing Monopolies."

unable to process patent applications efficiently while at the same time maintaining patent quality.[6] Consequently, the European Patent Office (EPO), the United States Patent and Trade Mark Office (USPTO) and the Japanese Patent Office (JPO) are now looking to create "patent superhighways" as a way of defraying patent costs, reducing the burgeoning backlog of patent applications and improving the quality of patent monopolies.[7]

The quandary for the "patent community" (see Drahos 1999),[8] as patent offices expand the scope of patentable subject matter, thereby stretching the traditional boundaries of patentability and, perhaps, even exceeding them in response to "customer demands," is that they are compounding the cause of the problems, not solving them (see Gold et al. 2008). Patent applications on a "patent superhighway" are like cars on vehicular freeways. Initially they allow cars to travel rapidly but inevitably, as the number of cars increases, speeds begin to drop. Eventually, as the freeways reach their carrying capacity, speeds slow to the point that a backlog or traffic jam results. Only this time, there are many more cars travelling at a much slower speed.

The underlying objective of the "patent community" is growing patent revenue. For users, patent monopolies provide them with the ability to extract monopoly profits. For patent attorneys, who draft and prosecute patent monopolies for their clients, they provide them with the ability to earn substantial revenues. Finally, for patent offices, patent applications and granted patent fees provide them with revenues that make them

---

6 In September 2008 at the AIPPI Congress held in the United States in Boston, MA, Alison Brimlow, president of the European Patent Office, was reported to have said that the great increase in the number of patent applications, the long pendency and the uncertainty that this creates is a problem for the world's patent systems. "Action urged to reform patent system" (*Managing Intellectual Property*, September 15, 2008). See also "Landmark study reports breakdown in biotech patent system" (*FierceBiotech*, September 10, 2008). In October 2009 at a congress held in London and organized by The Chartered Institute of Patent Attorneys, the title of which was "The IP System under Attack," Ian Fletcher, the United Kingdom's IPO chief executive, said that there was a "growing global consensus" over the creation of international work-sharing arrangements to clear the backlog of pending patent applications. "UK IPO head pushed work-sharing" (*Managing Intellectual Property*, October 5, 2009).

7 "Blueprint Laid Out for Work-sharing among Five IP Offices" (European Patent Office Press Release, October 31, 2008). "The heads of the five offices recognize the trend toward greater globalization and seek to minimize the resultant redundancy of patent searches and examinations. They also share a concern for the growing number of pending patent applications and the prolonged pendency period; and they acknowledge that delays in granting patents hinder the promotion of innovation, which is an intrinsic function of the patent system. To tackle this global phenomenon in an efficient manner, the IP5 offices have agreed to collaborate in moving forward with a work-sharing initiative." "EPO and US speed up patent-granting process" (*Managing Intellectual Property*, March 17, 2008).

8 The term "patent community" was coined by Peter Drahos, a professor of intellectual property law at the Australian National University in Canberra and the Queen Mary Institute of Intellectual Property Research in London. He defines the "patent community" to include "patent attorneys and lawyers, patent administrators, and other specialists who play a part in the exploitation, administration and enforcement of the patent system. They form a community by virtue of their technical expertise and general pro-patent values. Regular users of the patent system (like the pharmaceutical companies) might also be said to be part of this community."

financially self-sufficient government agencies (see Lawson 2008). So the incentive to expand the market for patent monopolies is self-evident. The flip side is that as the marginal cost eventually exceeds the marginal revenue, profits (per unit of production) begin to fall (see Moir 2009).

Patent statistics indicate that over the past 30 years, there has been a significant growth in patent applications and granted patent monopolies. Not only have gene-related patents significantly increased, but so, too, have patents for business methods and computer software. Today there are tens of thousands of granted patents for these so-called "inventions," but little anecdotal evidence to suggest that there will be a slowing down in patent applications in the future. Controversy continues to rage over their legality,[9] because, arguably, these patent monopolies transgress the prohibition of the patenting of "natural phenomena, mathematical formula and abstract ideas."[10] The problem is that they raise social, economic and political issues – issues which must be taken into account if an appropriate balance between the needs of the inventor and those of the greater society is to be achieved (see Heller and Eisenberg 1998).

For example, the patenting of isolated biological materials by biotechnology and pharmaceutical companies and universities and agencies of developed countries has encroached and continues to encroach on medical and scientific research by depriving scientists of the ability to use these biological materials freely. The materials are identical or substantially identical to those that exist in nature, yet they have been patented on specious grounds.[11] Once granted, patent monopolies limit the ability of

---

9 The US Supreme Court has granted *certiorari* in *Bilksi and Warsaw v. Kappos*. The appeal is pending. Numerous Amicus Curiae briefs were filed in September and October 2009 arguing for and against the legality of the patent for a business method.

10 Justices Breyer, Souter and Stevens in their dissent in *Laboratory Corporation of America Holdings v. Metabolite Laboratories, Inc.* 126 S. Ct. 2921 (2006) explained the nature of a principle of US patent law that "excludes from patent protection…laws of nature, natural phenomena and abstract ideas." They confirmed: "this principle finds its roots in both English and American law," and said that its justification "does not lie in any claim that 'laws of nature' are obvious, or that their discovery is easy, or that they are not useful… [T]o the contrary, research into such matters may be costly and time consuming; monetary incentives may matter; and the fruits of those incentives and that research may prove of great benefit to the human race [but even so] the reason for the exclusion is that sometimes too much patent protection can impede rather than 'promote the Progress of Science and useful Arts.'"

11 "…the important point is that patent offices maintain that the DNA sequences claimed in patents are not natural phenomena. Instead, they…take the view that extracting the genetic information encoded by a DNA sequence is not just a matter of gaining scientific knowledge about a natural phenomenon: it involves the use of cloning techniques to create an artificial molecule in such a way that it includes much the same genetic information as is to be found in the natural phenomenon. And what is held to be important here is that the scientific knowledge concerning the genetic information has been discovered through the creation of the artificial molecule. That is to say, without isolating and cloning a gene, it is not possible to identify the sequence of bases of which it is comprised. Hence, patent offices have concluded, the genetic information is essentially part of an 'invention', a molecule which is human handiwork, and can be patented as such" (see Nuffield Council on Bioethics 2002, at 3.11, 3.21).

scientists to develop alternative diagnostics, treatments and cures of human disease – in effect, the patent owners of the genes and proteins control their use in research, clinical and industrial applications. Increasingly, they also deprive developing countries of an equitable share of the economic benefits derivable from their natural resources (see Dutfield 1996; Te Pareake Mead, Ratuva 2007). This has become particularly evident as pharmaceutical and biotechnology companies have refocused their new drug research toward natural biological materials (see Koehn and Carter 2006; Newman and Cragg 2007). One consequence of this push has been the reaction from developing countries, which have become protective of their natural biological resources, wary of the possibility of having to pay a high price for the patented drugs which may be developed from those very resources (see Hammond 2009).

Thus, patents in the twenty-first century are at least as problematic as they have been in the past and probably more so, given the ever expanding scope of patentability, the development in the twentieth century of human rights law (see Hestermeyer 2007),[12] and the continued economic development in the twentieth and twenty-first centuries of countries that were subject to European colonization in the past. It is possible, therefore, that rather than encouraging innovation and building capacity, patent monopolies have the opposite effect. Accordingly, not only is there a need to explore alternatives to patent monopolies in the twenty-first century, there is a need to reevaluate their very relevance (see Moir 2008).

Patents for Chemical Substances (Medicines): A Retrospective Analysis of the Anglo-American Patent Systems in the Nineteenth and Twentieth Centuries

During World War I, German-owned patents were confiscated throughout the world, and it was in the United States that the single most significant transfer of "enemy" IP rights occurred. After military hostilities had ceased, but before the Treaty of Versailles had been finalized, some 10,000 US patents, trademarks and copyrights, and plant, equipment and other physical and financial assets owned by German companies and individuals in the United States were compulsorily acquired by the US government and placed into US hands (see Palombi 2009). It was characterized as an act of wartime retaliation, but the manner in which this policy was implemented betrays that characterization.

The objective was not only to compensate the United States, a country that had been at war with Germany for only 18 months, it was to reverse the unexpected economic consequences which the control of US patents had given to German chemical companies. Unlike the German patent law of 1877, US patent law did not prohibit patents for chemical substances. Therefore, the scope of US patent monopolies was

---

12 The controversy of HIV/AIDS drug pricing and the impact this had on developing countries is one example of how the patent system failed to assist in dealing with a humanitarian disaster.

broad enough to cover any existing chemical processes or those that could be invented. Any process that resulted in the production of a patented chemical substance infringed a US chemical patent. As a result, it was impossible to invent around these patents. This restriction then enabled German chemical companies to successfully suppress the development of a US chemical industry (see Vaughan 1919), ironically achieving in the United States the doomsday scenario that German industrialist Ernst Siemens was determined to avoid in Germany (see Kronstein and Till 1947).[13]

On February 1917, two months prior to the US declaring war on Germany, Dr F. E. Stewart, a pharmacist, wrote in a letter to a US government committee that was investigating the impact of these patents:

> It becomes evident that patent law as now interpreted and applied does not promote progress in the arts of chemistry, pharmacy and drug therapeutics as carried on in the United States; in fact it is a very serious hindrance…to science… because it does not stimulate original research on the part of would-be inventors in this country. Neither does it build up United States industries. (Sayre 1919)

It should come as no surprise that it was a pharmacist who raised the alarm. Synthetic chemicals were the revolutionary products of state-of-the-art processes. By 1914 the US textile industry not only needed a constant supply of new synthetic dyes (see Chandler 1992) to keep its factories in production and its products competitive, but hospitals and pharmacies in the United States also needed a steady supply of new state-of-the-art medicines to keep Americans healthy.[14] Unfortunately, with the vast majority of these chemical products manufactured in Germany, wartime shortages highlighted just how vulnerable the United States had become without a capacity to produce them domestically. By 1919, it had become a matter of national security that a US chemical

---

13 "Today [German] industry is developing rapidly; and as a result monopolization of inventions and abuse of rights will inevitably expose large segments of industry to serious injury. The government must protect industry against these dangers. From abroad another danger may arise. Inventive work is far more developed in England, United States and France than in Germany. Up to the present the number of patents taken out in Germany by foreigners has been small because the scope of protection given to the inventor has been insufficient. New legislation will lead to a substantial increase of foreign patentees. We shall experience a wave of foreign – particularly American – patent applications. These patents will not be taken out in order to protect industrial plants established or to be established in Germany; they will be taken out to monopolize production abroad. These articles will be imported into this country. Such a danger must be met. It is not enough to provide that foreign patentees be required to submit evidence that they have established a plant in Germany. Such evidence may be mere shadow; they can merely keep a small domestic production going to maintain their patents." Speech made by Ernst von Siemens in 1876 to an expert committee that was drafting the first national German patent law.

14 These included drugs such as aspirin, an analgesic, and salvarsan, the world's first nonmercury antisyphilitic. In 1916, the US patents for salvarsan and neosalvarsan alone earned the US importer, Herman Metz, a gross revenue of US$970,000 and a net profit of US$430,000.

and pharmaceutical industry be established, and what better way of achieving this than to confiscate the assets of those that had deliberately suppressed it.

The United States, however, was not alone. The British government had preempted their nation's own vulnerability and had been determined to stop it. Rallying against what was described as "an abuse" of the British patent system perpetrated by "powerful foreign syndicates" (see G. Schuster 1909), Lloyd George MP, at the time the president of the British Board of Trade, oversaw the passing of a new patent law in 1907.[15] This law required the working of British patents in Britain (see E. J. Schuster 1913).[16] It also made it easier for British manufacturers to seek compulsory licenses for any British patent that was not worked in Britain. Unfortunately, in the 7 years prior to World War I, although the law had encouraged more direct foreign investment into Britain, it failed to protect the country from the effects of a wartime embargo on chemical exports imposed by the German Imperial government. In 1919 British lawmakers acknowledged that merely requiring the working of British patents was not enough. There was a need, for the purpose of promoting a domestic chemical production capacity, to also bring British patent law in line with German patent law.[17]

Thus, by 1920 German chemical companies had been stripped, by various means, of the legal power, which patents provided, to suppress chemical industrialization in either the United States or Britain. On the one hand, the US government simply created an American-owned capacity by confiscating German-owned US assets and transferring them to US companies (see Palombi 2009; Steen 2001). On the other, the British government sowed the seeds of a British-owned capacity by restricting the ability of German patent owners to continue value-added production outside of Britain thereby constraining the British invention of new chemical processes. This policy was further reinforced by the Safeguarding of Industries Act, 1921 which imposed significant duties on imported chemicals (see Thomas 1958). As a result, Britain's pharmaceutical production, negligible in 1919, was £15 million by 1924 and £19 million by 1935 (see Thomas 1958).

Despite the policy's apparent success, by 1949 its continued effectiveness was in doubt. First, the ban had been undermined by the drafting practices of British patent attorneys. According to this practice, every conceivable method or process for the manufacture of a specific chemical was claimed in a chemical patent, so that the chemical substance itself, for all intents and purposes, was also patented (see UK Board of Trade 1947).[18] Secondly, the British pharmaceutical industry (Association of the British Pharmaceutical

15 UK Patents and Designs Act, 1907.

16 In 1911, German patent law was amended to introduce a requirement that German patents be worked in Germany. It was a tit-for-tat response to the UK Patents and Designs Act, 1907.

17 S.38A(1) was inserted into the UK Patents and Designs Act, 1907. This excluded from patentability "any substances prepared or produced by chemical processes or intended for food or medicine" unless "prepared or produced by special methods or processes of manufacture described and claimed."

18 The Swan Committee noted that the ban had been easily circumvented by "the drafting... [of claims] to cover all conceivable methods of manufacture...[so that] the substance itself and not the process of manufacture" was patented.

Industry, ABPI) now considered the ban to be discriminatory.[19] This marked a significant shift in opinion, particularly when a review of the British patent system 18 years earlier found the ban to "have been of considerable value in encouraging the development of the British chemical industry" (see UK Board of Trade 1931).[20] What had changed in the intervening period was the focus of British pharmaceutical companies, which, in seeking greater profits, had shifted their sales attention to foreign markets, particularly the United States.[21] Accordingly, they now sought the same broad patent protections in Britain as their US competitors enjoyed in the United States.[22]

This shift in opinion also coincided with the establishment of the National Health Service (NHS),[23] under which prescription medicines would be free. This presented the newly elected Labour government with a dilemma: How to keep the cost of prescription medicines down when broad patent protection for chemicals restricted generic drug competition? The answer, apparently, was provided by the very same report that recommended the repeal of the ban on the patenting of chemical substances.[24] The point was that, whether the government liked it or not, the price of prescription medicines could rise significantly unless something else was done to induce a competitive price effect. While one option for the government was to impose a stricter ban on the patenting of chemical substances to close the loopholes that had been opened by patent attorneys, there was no guarantee that other loopholes would not be found, effectively neutralizing the new stricter ban. If that were to happen, then the government would be in the invidious position of not having any effective mechanism to control the price of these medicines. Instead, the government accepted the report's other recommendation, namely, to strengthen compulsory licensing and crown use and use these as price control mechanisms.[25] In effect, the government was

---

19 The Swan Committee received submissions from the ABPI suggesting: "the real invention lies in the discovery of a new substance, with new and useful properties, and that the process of manufacture often involves little novelty in itself."

20 The committee's report referred favorably to a speech made by Sir William Pearce MP, a Liberal, in the House of Commons and himself a chemical manufacturer who said that the law was a "great improvement" because patentability "depends upon the process rather than the actual substance itself." *Hansard*, UK House of Commons, July 28, 1919, 118 (1), 860.

21 The larger of these included Burroughs Wellcome, Glaxo Laboratories, The British Drug Houses and Evans Medical Supplies.

22 Investment in R&D may have also been a factor since new drugs and markets depended on the discovery of antibiotics, then the new wonder drugs. According to the ABPI, British pharmaceutical companies invested £2.5 million in 1949, that is about 2.5 percent of gross output, whereas the US pharmaceutical industry invested nearly 5 percent. See Thomas (1958, 347).

23 William Beverage was a noted economist and social advocate. His report, *Social Insurance and Allied Services*, published in 1942, revolutionized government thinking and led to the creation of the welfare state in Britain. This report led to the establishment of the National Health Service.

24 UK Board of Trade, chaired by K. R. Swan, 1945–47. It produced two interim reports in 1945 and 1946 and a final report in 1947.

25 Crown use provides the ability of government agencies to effectively ignore patents.

forced to concede that the ban on the patenting of chemical substances was no longer effective. Therefore, there was nothing more to be done in that regard other than to repeal it.

Unfortunately for the British Ministry of Health, the marketing ingenuity of pharmaceutical companies undermined the scheme.[26] Within ten years the NHS budget had ballooned to £70 million.[27] By 1959, two inquiries had been ordered by the British Ministry of Health into the cost of the NHS.[28] Even the introduction of the Voluntary Price Regulation Scheme in 1957 seemed not to have made any significant difference,[29, 30] leading to a third inquiry in 1965.[31] Once again British pharmaceutical companies, through their industry association, resisted any suggestion for a comprehensive pharmaceutical price control scheme.[32] They fought back, arguing for even more changes to Britain's patent law. This time, however, their objective was not only the removal of compulsory licensing as it applied to pharmaceuticals but,

26 "The joke among doctors' wives today is that when they want to do shopping in town they leave their husbands to have lunch with a drug firm. The following invitation came to my notice last week. It says: 'Bayer Products Ltd. have pleasure in inviting Dr. – to the showing of a new film-strip on rheumatoid arthritis. Any medical colleagues will also be welcome. At the Green Dragon, N.21, on Wednesday and Thursday, 8th July and 9th July. Cocktails, 12.45; Film. 1 p.m., lunch, 1.20 p.m.' A doctor whom I know, who went to one of these shows – rather a cynical man – said, 'We were expecting some pep pills at cocktail time.' But no, there was an adequate supply of gin. The film was not a film at all, but a few cheap lantern slides. The lunchers were well supplied with wine, and another cynical doctor said, 'The most important things given out were leaflets telling us what drugs to prescribe' – all made by the firm, to recompense it for the lunch." Edith Summerskill MP, *Hansard*, House of Commons, July 15, 1959, 609, 419–548, 421.
27 *Hansard*, House of Commons, July 15, 1959, 609, 420.
28 In 1953, the British minister for health appointed Prof. Guillebaud to chair a Committee of Inquiry "[t]o review the present and prospective cost of the National Health Service; to suggest means, whether by modifications in organisation or otherwise, of ensuring the most effective control and efficient use of such Exchequer funds as may be made available; to advise how, in view of the burdens on the Exchequer, a rising charge upon it can be avoided while providing for the maintenance of an adequate Service; and to make recommendation." In 1959 another Committee of Inquiry, this time chaired by Sir Henry Hinchcliffe, submitted a report on the "Cost of Prescribing" to the UK minister for health.
29 The objective of the VPRS (which still operates today as the Pharmaceutical Price Regulation Scheme) was to induce the pharmaceutical companies to set reasonable prices by allowing new medicines a 3-year window during which there was no price control. After that time, the price would be established between the Ministry of Health and the respective pharmaceutical company. The problem, as its name suggests, was that it was voluntary. The other problem was that the ABPI did not fully support it.
30 In the first year of operation, price reductions for 300 medicines were achieved, but the saving to the British government was, at £350,000, insignificant.
31 This inquiry was chaired by Lord Sainsbury and was directed to the "Relationship of the Pharmaceutical Industry with the National Health Service."
32 Australia, on the other hand, had already established the Pharmaceutical Benefits Scheme. It is still in operation today and is considered to be the gold standard. See Neville for a comprehensive account of its history.

consistent with a draft European Patent Convention released in 1963,[33] to extend the term of a British patent from 16 to 20 years.

Understandably, the Sainsbury Committee dismissed these arguments, not only because the committee's key objective was to reduce the cost of the NHS, but also because the British pharmaceutical industry had, since the end of World War II, become increasingly owned or controlled by foreign interests.[34] The committee was, therefore, skeptical of the association's ability to represent British interests and, in fact, to make submissions that were in the best interests of British people. Indeed, these submissions, had they been adopted, were unlikely to produce any downward effect on the price of prescription medicines. If anything, they would do precisely the opposite.

In its report (see UK Committee of Inquiry 1967), presented to the British government in 1967, the committee expressed the view that the existing patent term of 16 years was "too long" and that "a shorter period of complete protection" would suffice. Turning to the argument that there was a need for strong patent laws in order to "induce adequate research and development and innovation in the pharmaceutical industry," the committee's retort was to recommend "a shorter period of monopoly for the patentee followed by a right to receive royalties under a licence of right." As for the criticism that compulsory licensing was ineffective because it had been "little used," the committee blamed the British Patent Office's "inefficient" administration, which, it said, "seemed to have discouraged or delayed potential licensees." In fact, rather than recommending the repeal of compulsory licensing, as the British pharmaceutical industry had urged it to do, the committee recommended the British government take measures to retain and encourage it.

Despite recommendations that could reasonably have been expected to help curtail the rising cost of the NHS, the British Labour government of Harold Wilson did a most surprising thing. It ignored them. More than that, just as Lord Sainsbury was about to present the committee's report to the British minister for health, the government appointed another committee of inquiry,[35] this time to investigate the British patent system itself. The chair of this committee was Sir Maurice Banks, a retired executive from British Petroleum.

The end result of the Banks Committee's inquiry was a report (see UK Committee of Inquiry 1970) presented to the newly elected Tory government of Edward Heath in 1970. And whereas the Sainsbury Committee's report contradicted the British pharmaceutical companies, the Banks Committee's report was consistent with its stated position. The report made three principle recommendations. First, that nongovernment compulsory licensing be abolished. Next, that "pharmaceutical substances...continue

---

33 The committee was chaired by Kurt Haertel, who served as the president of the German Patent Office between 1963 and 1975.

34 According to data presented, American pharmaceutical companies supplied 49 percent, the Swiss supplied 14 percent and other European countries supplied 10 percent of drugs in Britain.

35 The Banks Committee was established by Mr Douglas Jay, president of the British Board of Trade, on May 10, 1967.

to be patentable." Finally, that the term of a British patent be extended from 16 to 20 years.

It would seem, therefore, that by 1970 neither a left- nor a right-wing political party in Britain was interested in bringing down the costs of the NHS through the use of the patent system. In the space of 50 years, the political pendulum in respect of patents had swung 180 degrees. Patents were no longer something to be carefully monitored. Rather, they were something to be promoted because they "encouraged innovation." The British pharmaceutical companies had won their fight and now they were on the same footing as their American counterparts.

However, a survey conducted in 1971 (see Teeling-Smith 1974) into the prescribing habits of British doctors made some interesting findings. The first was that of the total cost of prescribed medicines, 94 percent could be attributed to those that were either patented or, if no longer patented, sold under their registered trademark. The second was that since 1949, the number of prescribed patented or trademarked medicines had risen from 16 percent to 80 percent. The third was that, despite the fact that 20 percent of the prescriptions were for generic medicines, when they were dispensed, only 6 percent were dispensed as generic medicines. Finally, and most importantly, even if the remaining 74 percent patented or trademarked medicines had been prescribed and dispensed as generic medicines, the savings to the NHS would have been "very modest." The explanation given was as follows:

> For the great majority of preparations the same single ingredient or combination of ingredients is available only as the original branded preparation. In these cases, either as a result of patent protection or because of the small market potential and limited profit margin, no one has introduced a cheaper competitive formulation consisting of the same active ingredient or ingredients. (Teeling-Smith 1974, 65)

Quite possibly, and being in possession of similar data, the British government may have simply decided that it was an exercise in futility to attempt to change the prescribing habits of the British medical profession, especially when, even if it were possible, the end result in reducing the cost of NHS would have been marginal. Likewise, for the government to have implemented policies to encourage the use of compulsory licensing, when, as the Sainsbury Committee had confirmed, there was very little evidence of its use, which, of course, explained the lack of generic alternatives to patented or trademarked medicines, may have seemed equally futile. But as superficially attractive these reasons are in providing some explanation for the sudden about-face, in fact, there were other considerations that were pivotal.

These had to do with the Wilson government's decision to have Britain join the European Economic Community (EEC). Joining the EEC was now the principal objective of Harold Wilson and his government. Not only was it seen as an achievement that would help to secure his government's reelection, but it was also seen as an essential step forward in securing Britain's economic future (see Young 2002). Unfortunately, the report by the Sainsbury Committee presented the government with a problem.

Although its principle focus was on finding a way to reduce the cost of the NHS, it had made recommendations that were antagonistic to the British pharmaceutical industry, now a powerful political lobbying force in Britain in the field of patent law. Furthermore, and more to the point, these recommendations ran counter to the draft European Patent Convention (see Oudemans 1963), which by 1967 was progressing through diplomatic channels towards a multilateral resolution. Therefore, it was an imperative for the Wilson government to find a solution to the problem created by the Sainsbury Committee's patent law recommendations and that solution came in the form of the recommendations made by the Banks Committee.[36]

Alas, the Wilson government lost the election in 1970 to Edward Heath, which was quite ironic really because it was Heath who, as a member of the Macmillan government, oversaw Britain's failed attempt to join the EEC in 1960.[37] Heath, then, was presented with a fait accompli.

By the end of 1973, Britain, Denmark and Ireland had become members of the EEC, and the final diplomatic meeting to settle the terms of the European Patent Convention (EPC) had taken place. Under these terms, the EPC was to become operational in 1978, and among its key provisions was the requirement that all EPC countries provide patent laws that (1) extended patent protection for 20 years and (2) covered "any inventions," namely, all technologies without discrimination.[38] This, of course, suited the British pharmaceutical industry, although the transition for the Italian pharmaceutical industry was somewhat rocky (see Scherer 2000).[39]

As a consequence, Britain passed a new patents law in 1977.[40] This was the most significant amendment to its patent law since 1852, when a patent law

---

36 The Banks Committee was established in May 1967 to "examine and report with recommendation upon the British patent system and patent law, in the light of the increasing need for international collaboration in patent matters." That its establishment coincided with the Wilson government's announcement that Britain would make a second attempt to join the EEC suggests a link between the two. More to the point, however, were the terms of reference, which Douglas Jay, the president of the British Board of Trade, provided in July 1967. Specifically, the Banks Committee was directed to examine, report and make recommendations with respect to "the desirability of harmonizing national patent laws and the degree of protection obtained by the same invention in different countries." This term was aimed squarely at the Sainsbury Report's patent law recommendations, which, if implemented, rather than harmonize Britain's patent laws with its neighbors, would have led to a clash. Clearly, by May 1967 the minister for health, if he had not received a copy of the Sainsbury Report, was aware of what to expect.

37 Britain's application was vetoed by French president Charles de Gaulle in January 1963.

38 Although art. 52(1) EPC was subsequently amended in 2000 and the words "in all fields of technology" were inserted, these words simply clarified the requirement to grant patents for "all inventions." After all, how can something be an "invention" if it is not a technology? The insertion was made merely to bring the EPC into line with TRIPS.

39 Italy had become a major supplier of generic medicines and it took a decision of its Constitutional Court in 1978 to confirm that it was no longer permissible to ban the patenting of pharmaceutical substances.

40 UK Patents Act, 1977.

establishing the British Patent Office was passed,[41] and, before that, 1623, when the Statute of Monopolies, a law that banned all monopolies except for a few, one of these being for a "manner of new manufacture",[42] sowed the seed for the Anglo-American patent systems. Quite suddenly, nearly 400 years of British patent law jurisprudence appeared to have been made redundant. Not only did the primary threshold of patentability change from something that was a "manner of new manufacture" to something that was an "invention," undefined under the EPC other than by reference to excluded subject matter,[43] but the grant of patent monopolies was not solely a matter for the British Patent Office. It was now also a matter for the European Patent Office, an intergovernmental European agency situated in Munich. To make the position even clearer to the European national courts that the EPO was not to be ignored, the EPC and the domestic patent laws of EPC countries required national courts to take judicial notice of EPO policy. And as understandable as that policy is, especially when the harmonization of patent laws across Europe is a central objective of the EPC, the evidence, after thirty years is not positive.

Within 10 years a schism had developed between the EPO and the British courts over what were "inventions" within the meaning of art. 52 (1) EPC.[44] The word was undefined, and while that may have been convenient in reaching an agreement over the text of the EPC in 1973, soon there were serious problems. For the national courts, which retained their exclusive right to determine validity, the language of art. 52 EPC was problematic. Was the word "inventions" to be defined by reference only to the list of excluded subject matter? Was anything that came within the excluded subject matter not patentable subject matter? Was it possible for something not to come within any of the excluded subject matter and still not be patentable within art. 52 (1) EPC?

---

41 UK Patent Law Amendment Act, 1852.

42 Section 6 of the Statute of Monopolies, 1623: "That any Declaration before-mentioned shall not extend to any Letters Patents and Grants of Privilege for the Term of Fourteen Years or under, hereafter to be made, of the sole Working or Making of any Manner of new Manufactures within this Realm, to the true and first Inventor and Inventors of such Manufactures, which others at the Time of Making such Letters Patents and Grants shall not use, so also they be not contrary to the Law, nor mischievous to the state, by raising Prices of Commodities at home, or Hurt of Trade, or generally inconvenient: The said Fourteen Years to be accounted from the Date of the first Letters Patents, or Grant of such Privilege hereafter to be made, but that the same shall be of such Force as they should be, if this Act had never been made, and of none other."

43 Excluded subject matter includes discoveries (art. 52(2)(a) EPC), methods for doing business and computer programs (art. 52(2)(c) EPC).

44 The original 1973 version of art. 52 (1) EPC states: "European patents shall be granted for any inventions which are susceptible of industrial application, which are new and which involve an inventive step." The current version states: "European patents shall be granted for any inventions, in all fields of technology, provided that they are new, involve an inventive step and are susceptible of industrial application."

As it turned out, it was the breakthroughs made in the field of biotechnology from the early 1970s that first began to expose what were, as Lord Justice Mustill described them,[45] "the deep flaws…in the current regime."[46]

In *Genentech Inc's Patent* (1989) RPC 147 the British Court of Appeal held that an isolated protein, human tissue plasminogen activator (t-PA),[47] produced by recombinant technology was not an "invention."[48] It also held the patent granted by the British Patent Office to be invalid.[49] What was particularly interesting about the decision is how both judges, at the invitation of the lawyers for the parties, referred back to their old patent-law jurisprudence to come to a conclusion about whether there was an "invention" disclosed in this patent under the new patent law. Applying the old law they held:

> Whatever discovery has been made, irrespective of section 1(2), a patentee may not claim as "inventive" artifacts or processes owing nothing to what he has done.[50]

This was the crux of the matter, for if learning the amino-acid sequence of an isolated protein was a discovery, then the physical embodiment of that sequence, the protein itself, was not an artifact created by the inventor.

This, however, was not how the EPO interpreted the EPC. The EPO's examiners and appellate officers had mostly come from European patent offices, particularly the German Patent Office. Therefore, having a technical rather than a legal background, they approached the issue in quite a different way (see Pila 2005b).

---

45 Lord Justice Mustill was a Lord Justice of Appeal between 1985 and 1992, when he was appointed Lord of Appeal in Ordinary in the House of Lords where, as a member of its Judicial Committee, he was, in effect, a member of Britain's highest court of appeal. He retired in 1997. On October 1, 2009, the Supreme Court of the United Kingdom took over that role.

46 *Genentech Inc's Patent* [1989] RPC 147, 259 lines 28–39; 259 line 52–260 line 3.

47 t-PA is a protein produced and used by the human body in the process of dissolving blood clots. In large quantities, t-PA became available as a therapeutic agent and this was a useful development for human health. However, before t-PA could be produced by recombinant technology, it was first necessary to identify the human gene that coded for t-PA. It was generally known that all proteins consisted of amino acids, but the complete amino acid sequence of t-PA was not known. The patent disclosed the DNA sequence of the t-PA gene and the complete amino acid sequence of t-PA.

48 Claim 1, the primary claim of the patent, defined the scope of the monopoly as "recombinant human tissue plasminogen activator essentially free of other protein of human origin." Claim 3 defined the scope of the monopoly as "human tissue plasminogen activator as produced by recombinant DNA technology."

49 GB 2,119,804: "Human tissue plasminogen activator pharmaceutical compositions containing it, processes for making it, and DNA and transformed cell intermediates therefore" (application filed 5 May 1982 and published November 23, 1983). Inventors: D. V. Goeddel, W. J. Kohr, D. Pennica, G. A. Vehar.

50 Lord Justice Purchas quoting Mr Jacob Q. C. for Wellcome in *Genentech Inc's Patent* [1989] RPC 147 at 12.10.

Instead of focusing on whether isolated t-PA, as a biological material derived from the human body, was an "invention" and whether the biotechnological processes employed in its synthesis (distinct from the genetic sequence of the human gene which coded for the protein) were themselves sufficiently novel and inventive to be patentable inventions, they instead focused on the "chemical" structure of the protein. The issue for them was not so much from where the protein had been derived, but whether the protein, as a chemical, was itself novel. In other words, had the protein's amino-acid sequence been published (or how difficult would it have been to deduce its amino-acid sequence on the basis of what was published about the protein itself)?[51] There were other patentability issues, such as whether the chemical had been sufficiently described, but all of these issues were resolved on the basis of an assumption: that an isolated biological material derived from a human being (being no different in any material way, apart from being isolated) was nothing more than a chemical. And as chemicals could be "inventions", that was the end of the controversy.[52] Consequently, when the equivalent European patent was reviewed by the EPO,[53] its patentability was determined only by reference to its compliance with technical thresholds such as novelty, inventive step and sufficiency.[54]

There were also practical consequences of these disparate approaches. Whereas the British patent was revoked by the British courts, the European patent was maintained by the EPO. This was an entirely unsatisfactory state of affairs. First, it created uncertainty for European patent applicants and their patent attorneys. Secondly, it exposed a serious flaw in the European patent system, namely that a European patent was not a single legal document but a bundle of national European patents granted by the EPO and each revocable by the relevant national European court applying the domestic patent law in its jurisdiction.[55]

Thus, while the European patent system facilitated the grant of a European patent by reducing the cost to the patent applicant by charging only one set of application

---

51 There are 20 naturally occurring amino acids. These are the building blocks of all natural proteins. The amino acid sequence for t-PA is inextricably associated with the human gene for t-PA, which itself is made of nucleic acids or DNA. Thus the amino-acid sequence of t-PA has a direct relationship to that part of the human genome which carries the instructions which enable cellular mechanisms within or outside of the human body to synthesize it.

52 See note 11 earlier in this chapter.

53 EP 0093619 "Human tissue plasminogen activator pharmaceutical compositions containing it, processes for making it, and DNA and transformed cell intermediates therefore" (application filed 5 May 1982 and published November 9, 1983). Inventors: D. V. Goeddel, W. J. Kohr, D. Pennica, G. A. Vehar.

54 Decision of the EPO Technical Board of Appeal T 0923/92 – 3.3.4 (November 8, 1995).

55 This patchwork of national patents stitched together under the banner of a "European patent" was not part of the original proposal. The original draft in 1963 proposed a single European-wide patent. By 1973, when the final draft was approved at a diplomatic conference, it had been modified to accommodate concerns about the sovereign rights of nations to control the creation of property under their domestic laws.

fees and by reducing the examination process to a single examiner, it created the opportunity for differences of opinion to arise over the validity of the same patent and patent claims, not only between the EPO and a single national court, but also between the various national courts themselves. Therefore, it was possible for the EPO to grant a European patent and for there to be different courts revoking different claims for different reasons, while the EPO's own appellate bodies made their own rulings, which applied across all of the designated EPC countries to which the patent applied.[56]

These differences of opinion, which only multiplied with time, strained relations between the British judiciary and the EPO. Within 5 years, another major biotechnology patent, this time over a recombinant hepatitis B virus particle,[57] produced an identically dysfunctional result. Once again the EPO maintained the validity of the patent, whereas the British House of Lords revoked it.[58] And while the biotechnology patent for another human protein, erythropoietin, granted in 1984, was upheld as valid by the EPO, between 2001 and 2004, three British courts each came to different conclusions over its validity and whether it had been infringed. At first instance before the Patents Court, the patent's validity was confirmed and it was found to have been infringed.[59] On appeal, the Court of Appeal agreed on its validity, but disagreed that it had been infringed.[60] Finally, on a further appeal, the House of Lords held two key process claims invalid and the remaining patent claims not infringed.[61] If that was not bad enough, the House of Lords took the opportunity to criticise some of the EPO's reasoning.[62] Their Lordships remarked about "being a little puzzled" by the differences in the molecular structure which the EPO found to exist between the artificially synthesized erythropoietin and natural erythropoietin.[63] And even if it were to be assumed that there was a difference, which their Lordships found not to be the case, they held that such a difference did not justify the conclusion reached by the EPO that the relevant

---

56 "Smother of invention: European companies are suffering from an ineffective patent system," *Economist*, July 23, 2009. "In 1997 the European Patent Office (EPO) gave a patent to Massachusetts General Hospital for its use of nitric oxide to treat bronchoconstriction, a method often used for 'blue baby' syndrome. Three gas companies – America's Air Products, France's Air Liquide and Germany's Westfalen Gas – appealed against the grant of the patent. Mass General and its Swedish licensee, AGA, then launched actions for infringement in the Netherlands, France and Germany. In 2000 a Dutch court said the patent was partially valid, in 2003 a French court said its validity was questionable and in the same year a German court judged it valid. Then in 2004 the EPO revoked the patent entirely."

57 EP 0182442.

58 *Biogen Inc. v. Medeva PLC* [1997] RPC 1.

59 *Kirin-Amgen, Inc. v Hoechst Marion Roussel Ltd and others* [2002] RPC 1.

60 *Kirin-Amgen, Inc. v Hoechst Marion Roussel Ltd and others* [2003] RPC 31.

61 *Kirin-Amgen, Inc. v Hoechst Marion Roussel Ltd and others* [2005] All ER 667.

62 Ibid., at paragraphs 92–5.

63 The EPO distinguished between the two proteins on the basis of a small difference in the molecular structure of the artificially synthesized protein (which did not enhance, improve or modify its performance in the human body) and found this modification to be a "technical feature" of the two processes, which were the "inventions."

process claims were valid.[64] In their opinion, the two process claims were invalid for the simple reason that the end product was a protein which was not "new."[65]

These cases are only three out of a number of cases illustrating the problems that biotechnology has created for the European patent system. Just as controversial are patents for computer software and business methods (Pila 2005a, 2005b).[66] Like gene patents, these kinds of patents have contributed to a truly bewildering situation (see Fink 2004), hardly being the epitome of efficiency which the drafters of the EPC had originally envisioned in 1963.[67] Of course, the problems created by disparate decisions between the EPO and European national courts and between the European national courts themselves has been acknowledged by the European Union and a solution, in the form of a single European patent with a single European patent court, is an option that is currently being considered. Even so, it is unlikely to be implemented soon (see Van Pottelsberghe 2009).[68]

---

64 "The first requirement is that the product must be new and that a difference in the method of manufacturing an identical product does not make it new. It is only if the product is different but the difference cannot in practice be satisfactorily defined by reference to its composition etc that a definition by process of manufacture is allowed." Ibid., per Lord Hoffmann, paragraph 98.

65 "The result is that I would allow TKT's appeal and revoke the patent on the ground that claim 19 is insufficient (section 72(1)(c)) and claim 26 is anticipated (section 72(1)(a)). Standing back from the detail, it is clear that Amgen have got themselves into difficulties because, having invented a perfectly good and ground-breaking process for making EPO and its analogues, they were determined to try to patent the protein itself, notwithstanding that, even when isolated, it was not new. Hence the patenting of the two product-by-process claims which have failed, one because the last-minute amendment to distinguish the product from the natural EPO turned out to based upon the *false premise that all uEPO had the same molecular weight* and the other because *the factual basis on which the European Patent Office allowed it turned out to be wrong*." Ibid., per Lord Hoffmann, paragraph 109 (emphasis added).

66 EPO Press release, "Patentability of methods of doing business," (August 18, 2000). Available at http://www.epo.org/about-us/press/releases/archive/2000/18082000.html

67 According to Bruno Van Pottelsberghe, the EPO's chief economist between 2005 and 2007, a European patent can cost between four to ten times as much to get than an equivalent patent in the United States, Japan, China or South Korea.

68 "The obstacles are still high. Surrendering their veto over patents would be a substantial loss of sovereignty for the EU's members. In some areas, such as genes, software and stem cell research, the question of what qualifies for protection is controversial. Language is another big difficulty. Most countries still insist that any patent must be translated into their language to apply on their soil. In 2008 the burden was reduced somewhat by the London Agreement, under which countries can waive the right to have patents translated into their national language. But only 14 countries have agreed to do so. The EPO has only three official languages: English, French and German. Spain is particularly aggrieved at this. The fuss over language may conceal other motives. Less innovative countries are unlikely to back a strong European patent, since their governments fear that companies which rely on imitation would lose market share to more inventive foreigners. National patent offices do not want to give up power and money. They, and the EPO itself, are worried that a unified process with a lower cost to companies would result in lower revenues. For the same reason, legal firms and translators have also fought against harmonisation" (Van Pottelsberghe 2009).

The European patent system, however, is not the only patent system in crisis (see Jaffe and Learner 2004; Drahos 2005; Boldrin and Levine 2008; Bessen and Meurer 2008; Burk and Lemley 2009; Palombi 2009). For the past five years, the US Congress has been considering a raft of proposed changes to the US patent system,[69] one calling for the US patent system to move from a first-to-invent to a first-to-file.[70] Other reforms seek to improve the quality of US patents and the ability of the courts to effectively remove poor-quality patents from the system. The report to the US Congress says:

> The legislation is designed to establish a more efficient and streamlined patent system that will improve patent quality and limit unnecessary and counterproductive litigation costs.[71]

Despite the report's optimistic slant, it cannot be ignored that issues such as poor patent quality, lengthening patent pendency and very expensive patent litigation, have been repeatedly raised over the past 150 years.[72] All attempts to eradicate these chronic problems have failed. In spite of the fact that since the mid-nineteenth century, the cost of applying for patents has been significantly reduced, formalities streamlined, minimal international enforcement standards harmonized and cooperation between patent offices around the world improved, serious concerns remain about the ability of patent systems to cope with the challenges that a burgeoning demand for patent monopolies produce. Moreover, measures introduced to mitigate against the effect of so-called "patent abuses," particularly compulsory licensing and crown use, have also been ineffective.[73] In point of fact, about the only measures that have been effective are the drastic actions taken by the British and United States governments during World War I to establish domestic chemical industries in their countries.

Beyond these issues are the social challenges that patent monopolies pose. Patents have intruded on human rights. Access to medicines (see Abbott 2005; Correa 2006; Krikorian 2008; 'tHoen 2009), the unfair exploitation of indigenous traditional and scientific knowledge (see Gupta and Balasubrahmanyam 1998; Greene 2004; Gorman et al. 2006) and the bioprospecting of the natural biological resources of developing

---

69   "The need to update our patent laws has been meticulously documented in eight hearings before the United States Senate Committee on the Judiciary, in addition to reports written by the Federal Trade Commission and the National Academy of Sciences, hearings before the House of Representatives Judiciary Committee's Subcommittee on the Internet, Intellectual Property, and the Courts, and a plethora of academic commentary." Report 111-18 from the Committee on the Judiciary to the US Congress, May 12, 2009.

70   The US Patent Reform Act of 2009 is the latest version (Bill S. 515) that includes this proposal.

71   Burk and Lemley (2009, 3).

72   In the case of the British patent system, these very same concerns were considered during the 1851 parliamentary inquiry, the 1862–64 Royal Commission and the parliamentary inquiry in 1870–71.

73   In the 106-year history of the Australian patent system, only three compulsory licenses have been applied for, and none have been granted. There is no evidence of crown use ever being applied.

countries (see Abbott 2008; Shanker 2005) have cast a shadow over the credibility and social utility of patent systems.

So is there a future for patents? Are there alternatives that might be more appropriate? Or, has the time come to reopen the nineteenth-century debate about whether patents are needed at all?

Alternatives to Patent Monopolies: Their Abolition

One of the most notable comments about patent monopolies was made by Fritz Machlup in 1958.[74] He wrote of the United States patent system:

> If we did not have a patent system, it would be irresponsible, on the basis of our present knowledge of its economic consequences, to recommend instituting one. But since we have had a patent system for a long time, it would be irresponsible, on the basis of our present knowledge, to recommend abolishing it.[75]

Since Machlup undertook his famous review of the US patent system, there have been significant developments in patent systems around the world, and while there remains scant empirical data to support the proposition that patents are a necessary (or unnecessary) inducement to innovation, the time may be right to reassess the entire rationale for patents. Just like then, "factual data of various kinds" sufficient to enable "a team of well-trained economic researchers and analysts…to reach competent conclusions on questions of patent reform" is missing,[76] and given that economists seem unable or unwilling to provide the necessary data (or governments are not interested to have them carry out the research), does society stand idle and ignore the consequences? Would it be "irresponsible…to recommend abolishing" patent monopolies in the twenty-first century?

Across the world, calls for patent law reform have continued unabated, and these have encouraged proposals to ameliorate some of the economic and social problems attributed to patent monopolies (see Merges 2001; Gold 2003; Drahos 2004; Ebersole et al. 2005; Verbeure et al. 2006; van Zimmerman et al. 2006; Learner et al. 2007; Soini et al. 2008; Leveque and Meniere 2008; Hope 2008). The creation of sui generis intellectual property rights,[77] the adoption of international treaties and agreements directed towards facilitating intellectual property administration and making enforcement easier,[78] and the progression of patentable subject matter into prohibited

---

74 "An Economic Review of the Patent System." Study of the Subcommittee on Patents, Trademarks, and Copyrights of the Committee on the Judiciary, United States Senate, 85th Congress, Study No. 15. Washington DC: US Government Printing Office.

75 Ibid., 84.

76 Ibid.

77 US Plant Patent Act, 1930, International Convention for the Protection of New Varieties of Plants, 1961 and US Semiconductor Chip Protection Act, 1984.

78 Paris Convention, 1883; Strasbourg Convention, 1963; Patent Cooperation Treaty, 1970; European Patent Convention, 1973; Budapest Treaty, 1977; TRIPS, 1995; and the Patent Law Treaty, 2000.

territory has made the world obese with patent and patent-like monopolies.[79] Patent terms have been extended to 20 years, and 25 years for pharmaceutical substances, and the ability of governments to employ compulsory licensing has been curtailed. Yet, have rates of innovation risen?

Certainly in the case of new drug discovery, the emerging data suggests not. Two accomplished researchers at the National Cancer Institute in the United States have written:

> Although combinatorial chemistry techniques have succeeded as methods of optimizing structures and have, in fact, been used in the optimization of many recently approved agents, we are able to identify only one *de novo* combinatorial compound approved as a drug in this 25 plus year time frame.[80]

Their study of drug development between 1981 and 2006 identified the antitumor compound sorafenib as the only "new chemical entity reported in the public domain" to come from combinatorial chemistry,[81] a technique that enables large numbers of chemical analogues to be synthesized simultaneously.[82] From this data the researchers concluded:

> …a multidisciplinary approach to drug discovery, involving the generation of *truly novel molecular diversity* from natural product sources, combined with total and combinatorial synthetic methodologies, and including the manipulation of biosynthetic pathways (so-called combinatorial biosynthesis), provides the best solution to *the current productivity crisis* facing the scientific community engaged in drug discovery and development. (Newman and Cragg 2007, 476; emphasis added)

Researchers Jesse Li and John Vederas from the Department of Chemistry at the University of Alberta maintain that their data confirms that "currently there is a substantial decline in new drug approvals" (see Li and Vederas 2009). Peaking in 1987 with 80 new drugs approved by the United States Food and Drug Administration (FDA), with the trend pointing downward ever since, in 2007 only 20 new drugs were approved. Even more troubling in the search for new drugs is the shift in focus away from natural products. They argue this runs contrary to the evidence. In 1990, nearly 80 percent of new drugs were derived from natural products.

According to Newman, Cragg, Li and Vederas, the best prospects for the development of new drugs is for pharmaceutical companies to return to the past – to their very beginnings – when new drugs came from natural products. However, while Newman and Cragg (2007) are content to suggest that the answer simply lies with that, Li and Vederas (2009) suggest there is more to it. First, they point to the demise of the "blockbuster drugs"

---

79 The European Biotechnology Directive, 1998.
80 Newman and Cragg, 2007, 461.
81 Sorafenib (Nexavar 1) is manufactured by Bayer. It received FDA approval in 2005.
82 For an explanation see "Combinational Chemistry: A Strategy for the Future." Available at http://www.netsci.org/Science/Combichem/feature02.html

model,[83] which a decade ago provided pharmaceutical companies with "double-digit sales growth."[84] Key to the success of this model are drug patents, some of which have already expired and some which are due to expire shortly. Next is the impact of extensive litigation related to drug failure or anticompetitive marketing practices.[85] Finally, there is the purchase by large pharmaceutical companies of smaller pharmaceutical companies. Apart from the cost of such acquisitions, this activity has contributed to a shift away from in-house research and toward the acquisition of target companies whose research shows potential. A further effect has been the concentration within the pharmaceutical sector, reducing both market and research competition within that sector.[86]

Thus, even with the strongest and most uniform patent laws in history, new drug discovery is in decline. This implies that strong patent protection is not a prerequisite for new drugs. In fact, what history demonstrates is quite the opposite: that new drug development flourished at a time when patent protection for chemical substances was either nonexistent or much weaker and certainly much less uniform than it is today. We know, for instance, that between 1877 and 1968, German patent law expressly excluded chemical substances from patent protection. The same was true in France and Italy until 1978. Between 1919 and 1949, Britain followed suit. And most interestingly, both Novartis and Hoffman La Roche, two of the world's largest pharmaceutical companies, started business in Switzerland before the first national Swiss patent law was passed in 1888.

It was during this time that the world's first wave of modern medicines, such as aspirin, heroin, salvarsan and penicillin, to name but a few, were developed. Not only was it legally impossible to patent penicillin itself, it was considered unethical (see Palombi 2009). Although the first medicinal insulin made from animal pancreases was manufactured under license in Britain, the Medical Research Council eventually ignored British patents for the process (see Li 2003). More recently, Indian pharmaceutical company Cipla developed Triomune, an antiretroviral HIV/AIDS drug, by combining three drugs that were patented, but not in India. This is because until 2005, it was impossible to patent

---

83 Blockbuster drugs are defined as drugs with sales in excess of US$1 billion in annual sales.

84 In 2007, 58 percent of Pfizer's worldwide sales revenue of US$44 billion was produced by only eight drugs.

85 The authors cite the case of Vioxx. The potential to increase the risk of heart attack and stroke in patients prescribed this drug caused Merck, its manufacturer, to set aside US$970 million for legal fees alone. The potential compensation claim, reached via a class action settlement in the United States, is US$4.85 billion.

   In January 2009, the Federal Trade Commission and the State of California sued three US generic pharmaceutical companies and Solvay, a European pharmaceutical company, for anticompetition violations. The essence of the complaint is that the companies colluded to stall the marketing of a generic drug in the United States. The generic manufacturers had sought to revoke a patent for the drug. An out-of-court settlement between them and Solvay resulted in the revocation suits being dismissed. However, the generic manufacturers received some US$200 million from Solvay and also agreed to delay the marketing of the generic version until 2015. See FTC and State of *California v. Watson, Par, Paddock and Solvay* CV 09-00598 (US District Court for the Central District of California).

86 The examples they give are Pfizer's acquisition of Wyeth for US$68 billion and Merck's acquisition of Shering-Plough for US$41 billion.

chemical substances in India. Cipla also made Triomune available at a price that was affordable to people from developing countries. At US$600 per year, reduced to US$1 per day for Médecins Sans Frontières, it was much less than the US$10,000 per year it would otherwise have cost. Cipla's drug innovation did not stop there. It also developed Duovir-N, Duovir, Viraday and Efavir, each drug useful in the treatment of AIDS; and while it is true that these used otherwise patented ingredients, Cipla's innovation came in developing a drug that combined two or more of the active ingredients into one, simplifying the dosage regime and improving AIDS treatment. In fact, Viraday not only contained ingredients that treated HIV, but because of the way it had been formulated (which is less toxic than if the ingredients are taken separately), it could be taken together with a tuberculosis medicine, something that was not possible before then.

Anecdotal evidence also suggests that strong patent protection may be hampering new drug development. Take, for instance, Alzheimer's, a degenerative illness that leads to dementia and eventually death. Currently there is no cure, but the cause has been attributed to the accumulation in the brain of beta-amyloid and tau proteins. This, in turn, has led to many patents for these proteins and the genes that code for them. The result, according to one Alzheimer researcher is "a complex thicket of intertwined patents on genes, tests, reagents, research tools, and compounds."[87] This patent thicket acts as a barrier to drug innovation because of "the fear…that once there is real money being made on an Alzheimer's treatment the lawyers will descend on the company that brought it to market and significantly reduce the profitability of the treatment through lawsuits."[88]

Drugs aside, there is even more anecdotal evidence that patents are hampering the development of genetic diagnostic tests. Perhaps the most publicized in recent times concerns the genetic test for the breast- and ovarian-cancer gene mutations, BRCA 1 and BRCA 2. Patents for the gene mutations and the proteins that they code for, as well as the use of these materials in any manner of medical or scientific application, including but not limited to diagnostic tests, have been the subject of intense international criticism and opposition (see Matthjis 2006). The result in Europe for Myriad, the

---

87 Corante, weblog *In the Pipeline*, July 23, 2008. See comment 5 "AD Researcher." The researcher states, "The conflicting and overlapping patents cover the production and use of antibodies that recognize amyloidogenic fragments of A-beta, mutations in A-beta that may lead to excess production of A-beta fragments, mutations in the secretase enzymes that process A-beta, the whole genes encoding these proteins, the measurement of A-beta itself by any means, and all of the standard animal models of AD (some of which probably were made using technology that infringed other patents). There are also a number of broad 'Ariad-style' patents that attempt to cover the entire field. Most, if not all, have highly overlapping claims and include claims for discovering and developing drugs. Our patent attorneys simply threw in the towel when trying to map out a strategy for gaining clear rights to practice any of these inventions. The conclusion was that the first company to hit the market with a successful anti-amyloid drug could be in litigation for years. Not being a patent attorney, its difficult to properly evaluate whether this conclusion is true, but it certainly held back development of a potential AD treatment." Available at http://pipeline. corante.com/archives/2008/07/23/patents_stopping_an_alzheimers_wonder_drug.php

88 Ibid.

original (and principal) patent owner, has been unsatisfactory. Although the validity of the main BRCA 1 gene patent has been upheld by the EPO, the EPO's appellate tribunal has reduced the scope of the patent monopoly to an unintelligible and possibly unenforceable state.[89] In Australia, a second attempt by the exclusive licensee of all four BRCA 1 and 2 patents to enforce its patent rights resulted in a Senate inquiry.[90] The reaction, especially by genetic counselors and clinicians, was to criticize the company for disregarding the impact that such a policy would have on the management of the needs of patients, most of whom are women. Evidence taken during this inquiry, some of which was confidential, confirms that patent owners of human genes (the claims are over the isolated form of the genes, not the genes in the human body) do seek to enforce their patents against clinicians and, indeed, that patents for the BRCA 1 and 2 genes and the Long QT gene (which is linked to life-threatening heart arrhythmias) have interfered with medical research in Australia.[91] This evidence, of course, is merely the tip of the iceberg, as most of the policy decisions made in this respect remain confidential and out of the public domain. However, occasionally some of this kind of information slips out. For instance, a newspaper article about the impact of a patent for a gene linked to Dravet syndrome, an especially severe form of epilepsy,[92] provided details of how 50 percent more genetic testing would be performed on infants if there were no patent for the gene and the genetic test.[93] The Australian Senate inquiry has been urged by the Cancer Council of Australia, the peak cancer research body, to recommend to the Australian government that patents for isolated genes that are identical or substantially identical to those that exist in nature be banned. Professor Ian Olver, its Chief Executive Office, gave evidence about the growing importance of genetic information in the development of new anticancer drugs. He said:

> In the next couple of decades the genetic sequence of, say, a cancer will be the most important aspect of it, now that we can measure multiple genes, so the pattern of your cancer's genes will tell you what type of cancer you have, what targeted treatments you should have and what the prognosis or the aggressiveness of the cancer is. The whole thing will be determined by your genetic sequence. Looking down a microscope will not be an issue anymore; it will be the genetic pattern of the changed genes.[94]

89 "Europe to pay royalties for cancer gene," *Nature* 456 (December 4, 2008): 556.
90 The motion establishing the Australian Senate inquiry was passed on November 11, 2008. The first hearing was on March 19, 2009. The Senate committee appointed to undertake the inquiry has received over 75 submissions and heard evidence over five days. It is due to report to the Australian parliament on November 26, 2009. Full details are available at http://www.aph.gov.au/Senate/committee/clac_ctte/gene_patents/index.htm
91 Evidence of Dr Du Sart, August 4, 2008 (in camera); Prof. Bowtell and Dr Mitchell, August 4, 2008. *Hansard* transcript, CA 114–15.
92 "Sick babies denied treatment in DNA row." *Sydney Morning Herald*, November 29, 2008.
93 According to Dr Deepak Gill, the head of neurology, Westmead Children's Hospital, Sydney, Australia.
94 Senate Community Affairs Committee, Gene Patents: Hearing. *Hansard*, August 5, 2009, CA 8.

The effect of patent thickets in the field of biomedical research was predicted by Michael Heller and Rebecca Eisenberg more than 10 years ago. In their seminal paper (published in *Science* 1998), they theorized that patents granted too early in the process of innovation could be used by patent owners to increase the cost of downstream research and frustrate the commercial exploitation of the end products of that research. This effect would be multiplied if the end products were composed of many components, each of which was patented. Despite the kind of anecdotal evidence from scientists mentioned in this paper, there remains a degree of skepticism about the "tragedy of the anticommons," the term coined by Heller and Eisenberg to describe this effect. Some reports have attempted to dismiss it due to a lack of empirical data that confirms it. In the Australian context, one such report (see Australian Law Reform Commission 2004) by the Australian Law Reform Commission (after it had conducted a one-and-a-half-year inquiry into gene patents), stated:

> There is no clear evidence of any adverse impact, as yet, on access to medical genetic testing, the quality of such testing, or clinical research and development.[95]

If there was "no clear evidence" as the ALRC found, it is possible, especially in light of the more recent evidence presented at the Australian Senate's inquiry, that the ALRC simply failed to find it or, as is more likely the case, was not really interested in finding it. The simple truth is that this kind of evidence is difficult to obtain. Much of it is deliberately suppressed by scientists, themselves fearful of jeopardizing their research funding and careers. But in the case of the ALRC, the constituency of the advisory board provided the answer – the board was made up of intellectual property lawyers, patent attorneys or academics (whose published views were pro-patent). Indeed, the lawyers and patent attorneys were employed by firms that acted for companies that patented genes. The apparent conflict of interest aside, the ALRC simply did not have the power to protect witnesses, as did the Senate inquiry and this may also help to explain why it was unable to find "clear evidence" of the adverse impact which gene patents were having on Australian biomedical research and clinical services.

Still, the issue remains: what to do about gene patents and gene testing patents? This is an issue that has been problematic ever since the first gene patents were granted about 30 years ago. In the latest draft report on the issue,[96] and soon to be released in a final form, the US Secretary's Advisory Committee on Genetics, Health, and Society (SACGHS) has recommended the "creation of an exemption from liability for infringement of patent claims on genes for anyone making, using, ordering, offering for sale, or selling a test developed under the patent for patient care purposes."[97] A more convoluted and narrow exemption could not have been thought up, and it raises the question: How can an independent committee made up of experts in the

---

95 Ibid., 503 (20.72).
96 Final draft report of the SACGHS, September 17, 2009.
97 Ibid., 61.

fields of intellectual property law and the relevant sciences conclude that a human gene is an "invention" and therefore legally entitled to patent protection? Is not the patent system only about protecting "inventions" and not discoveries?

In evidence given to the Australian Senate inquiry, a number of key Australian scientists stated that virtually any competent geneticist would be capable of making a genetic test using currently available materials and testing technologies once the gene sequence is known. And the fact still remains that a gene sequence is not something that anyone invented.

The correct answer, to be blunt, would have been to recommend that gene patents be banned and that the inventive-step threshold on the use of genes be properly enforced so that obvious applications of genetic materials, such as in diagnostics, would also be excluded from patentability. Of course, such a recommendation is inconsistent with the demands of the US biotechnology industry.

Even more surprising, however, is an admission by the SACGHS about the prospect of patent pools and other nonexclusive licensing models to ameliorate the negative impact of gene patents. The report states:

> The Committee also concluded that patents and licensing practices pose significant challenges to the development of multiplex testing and clinical whole genome sequencing, with patent pools and clearinghouses an *uncertain solution* to these challenges.[98]

This brings the discussion back to this question: If the patent system is so problematic and nonexclusive licensing models do not provide a mechanism that works, would it not be better to do away with patents all together?

Once again, the SACGHS seems sympathetic to this idea, for although it makes a passing reference to patents "stimulat[ing] private investment in genetic research and genetic test development,"[99] it reaches the conclusion that:

> ...patents provide limited benefits in promoting the development of genetic tests and involve costs in terms of the quality of genetic testing and patient access to genetic testing.[100]

The Committee explains that much of the funding for genetic research comes from the public purse and this provides "independent incentives to conduct research,"[101] Moreover, "many laboratories are willing and able to invest in developing genetic testing services even when they have no patent protection."[102]

---

98 Ibid., 60, emphasis added.
99 Ibid., 61.
100 Ibid.
101 Ibid.
102 Ibid.

That it has taken some 30 years for this conclusion to be expressed, unequivocally and in writing, is perhaps a reflection that opinions about the privatization of science, especially when it is funded by the public purse, have changed. Many of the promises made about biotechnology during the heady days of the 1980s when Genentech (see Hughes 2001) was floated on the New York Stock Exchange, undoubtedly providing the impetus for the Bayh–Dole Act (see So et al. 2008),[103] and which spurred the genetic gold rush that followed have, on reflection, failed to materialize. For instance, there is still no vaccine against hepatitis C virus infection, even though back in 1988 when Chiron, the worldwide patentee, applied for its patents, it was adamant that it would only take some routine experimentation for an efficacious human vaccine to be developed. As for gene therapies that would treat a multitude of diseases and illnesses, the cold, hard reality is that despite showing some promise in animal trials, none as yet have been shown to treat or eradicate human illnesses.

Gene patents, however, are not the only cause for concern. Computer software and business methods are the next in line for similar attention. And it would seem, if the vast number of amicus curiae briefs filed in the US Supreme Court in the case of *In re Bilksi* is any indication,[104] that the same kinds of concerns being raised with respect to biotechnology are also being raised with respect to business methods.[105]

Economic Empirical Data: What Difference Does It Make?

Fritz Machlup's reticence to recommend that the United States not have a patent system was due to his training as an economist and the conviction that empirical data was a necessary prerequisite, which is quite surprising when most of the significant changes to the patent systems in the past 150 years have been made without any empirical evidence to show that they were even necessary. Take, for example, the extension of patent terms. For hundreds of years, they were either 14 or 15 years. Today these are 20 years and, in the case of pharmaceutical substances, up to 25 years. What empirical evidence was produced during the TRIPS negotiations to show that there was a need to extend patent protection at a multilateral level from what they were to 20 years? The answer: none. Indeed, that they started at 14 years had nothing more to do with the fact that the period of apprenticeship in seventeenth century Britain was 7 years, and so it was multiplied by 2, quite arbitrarily, to reach the period of 14 years.

---

103 The purpose of the legislation, which was sponsored by US senators Birch Bayh and Bob Dole, was to enable universities and academics to retain ownership of the intellectual property developed through the receipt of public funds. For an excellent critique of the Bayh–Dole Act see Leaf (2005). As for the application of Bayh–Dole style legislation in developing countries see So et al. (2008).

104 *Bernard Bilski and Rand Warsaw v. Kappos*, US Supreme Court Action No. 08-964.

105 See, for instance, the AC brief filed by 11 US law professors and the AARP (October 2, 2009).

The fact that patent monopolies still exist is because, although they are protectionist economic tools, they have, over time, been spun into "socially reforming" tools. That transformation, however, is a recent phenomenon. It occurred after World War II and only through the efforts of the pharmaceutical industry, which warned policymakers that unless full patent protection was extended to all chemicals regardless of their use, the new drug pipeline would dry up. Supposedly, so the argument goes, without strong patent protection, the incentive to invest capital in new drug discovery would be absent. This is a socially beneficial result that outweighs the negative effects that monopolies exert on society in other ways, such as in the form of high prices for goods and services. Thus, it is better to have patent monopolies than not. This is the mantra of proponents of patents that is repeatedly bandied about whenever there is a perceived threat to the sanctity of their beliefs,[106] yet, just as in the past, there is not a shred of economic data that can verify it. And, in fact, as a number of scientists have confirmed that, even with the strongest and most uniform patent laws in history, the new drug pipeline has dried up. However, it has been an effective weapon that, as is amply demonstrated by the recent experience in the United States, has brought the patent reform process in that country almost to a grinding halt.

In 1984 a report was presented to the Australian government by the Industrial Property Advisory Committee (IPAC).[107] The report was the result of a review of the Australian patent system instigated in 1979 by the Australian government in office then. By the time the report was presented, the government had changed. The political pendulum had swung from the right wing to the left wing. Five years later, the present Australian patent law was making its way through the Australian parliament,[108] and the left-wing government minister responsible for the legislation referred back to the IPAC report. He needed to explain away a difference of opinion between the majority of the committee, made up of patent attorneys, patent bureaucrats, patent lawyers and patent licensing executives, and the minority, a single academic economist. The sole economist expressed the view that the majority had ignored the economic data,[109] which showed that 92 percent of all patents granted in Australia were owned by foreign organizations. His conclusion, based on this and other economic data, was that there was no real evidence to support the continuing grant of patent monopolies. The majority disagreed. The minister resolved the schism this way:

IPAC's report did not wholeheartedly embrace the patent system, but it by no means rejected it. Some view the system as some kind of mysterious sacrament which has to be observed if we are to proceed along the path to economic heaven.

---

106 "Some view the [patent] system as some kind of mysterious sacrament which has to be observed if we are to proceed along the path to economic heaven." Statement made by The Hon. Barry Jones MP, minister for science and technology, June 1, 1989 in the Australian Parliament during the second reading of the Patents Bill, 1989.

107 IPAC, Patents, Innovation and Competition in Australia (August 29, 1984). Presented to the minister for science and technology, the Hon. Barry Jones.

108 Patents Act, 1990.

109 Prof. Don Lamberton, University of Queensland.

The Committee took a more pragmatic view. Faced with conflicting opinions on economic questions, IPAC recognised that it is imperative that Australia continue to operate a patent system and to participate in the international patent system.[110]

Much like Machlup, and despite the economic evidence which questioned its worth to the country's economy, the Australian government persisted with the patent system simply because the status quo favored its retention rather than its annihilation.

The Australian parliament in due course passed the legislation in 1990, one of the objectives being to improve Australian technological innovation. According to the relevant minister, meeting this objective required the Australian patent system "to make it harder to get a 16-year standard patent."[111] This statement was, no doubt, prompted by the economic data that showed the vast majority of Australian patents were being granted to foreigners.

Despite that compromise leading to the decision to retain the Australian patent system, during 2009 the Australian patent office, IP Australia, issued no less than six consultation papers aimed at reforming Australian patent law. In one of these, entitled, "Getting the balance right," the paper explained that the need for the review was brought about by the inventive-step threshold being much lower than that of its major trading partners. As a consequence, it is presently much easier to "get a 20-year patent" in Australia than elsewhere. Incidentally, 25 years later, 92 percent of Australian patents are still granted to foreigners. Interestingly, the paper blames the Australian courts for the apparent failure of the legislation to meet its stated objective and suggests that the time has come, yet again, for parliament to remedy the situation through the use of a stricter legislative test.

Monopolies in the Age of Free Trade

Despite the words of Cordell Hull and the establishment of the International Monetary Fund, the World Bank and the United Nations – three of the world's most significant institutions – the world has not reached a state of economic détente. This failure, in part, explains why the world's patent systems have dramatically expanded their technological footprints, eroding more and more of the public domain in the process. Indeed, since World War II the public domain has shrunk in spite of the technological innovation and development that the world has witnessed. While it is true that significant inventions such as the steam engine, light bulb, telephone and radio were in themselves like superhighways that directed innovation at faster speeds and which took technologies into areas that were, prior to their development, thought impossible, the

---

110 The Hon. Barry Jones MP, *Hansard* (Australian House of Representatives), Second Reading Patents Bill, 1989 (June 1, 1989).

111 Ibid.

fact remains that alongside these advancements, protectionist political and economic policies have played, and continue to play, an important role in encouraging the erosion of the public domain.

That patent systems were actually antithetical to free trade was well recognized in the United Kingdom and in Europe in the mid-nineteenth century; and had it not been for a global recession in 1873 and the American promotion of patents, the future for patents would have seemed rather bleak. Believing in "man's natural property in his own original ideas," Americans perceived the "many complaints and criticisms… directed against patent laws" to have been caused by a "misapprehension of the true principles of the law" (see Howson and Howson 1872). Yet it was the protection of German industry which was the primary motive behind Bismarck's decision to establish a national patent system in Germany, and it was, ironically, America's inability to foresee how Germany could exploit the "generosity" of the US patent system that enabled German industry to use it like a Trojan horse and suppress the development of an American chemical industry prior to World War I. Consequently, amid shortages of needed medicines, chemicals, dyes and other products, Americans learned just how their much lauded patent system was used by German chemical companies during peacetime to deliberately undermine both the US national security and economy during war. This was a powerful lesson and Americans learned that lesson well; and so began to use their newly found political and economic postwar power to develop policies that would protect their own nation and economy against all contingencies in the future. Their free-trade rhetoric was used in much the way that German economist Friedrich List accused the British of doing in the nineteenth century, to mask their own protectionist objectives. The American withdrawal in 1950 of support for the International Trade Organization (ITO), the last piece in Cordell Hull's free-trade paradigm, made that perfectly clear. An offensive strategy was henceforth built upon the premise of technological superiority – a superiority that would enable American companies, through the mutual recognition of patents and other intellectual property, to gain a competitive advantage. Thus, in the latter half of the twentieth century, intellectual property laws legitimated a policy of domestic protection by characterizing as unfair trade the manufactured goods made in countries that did not respect or enforce intellectual property to American standards. Naturally, the implications of this strategy for European manufacturers was understood by the EEC, which then set about countering the American challenge. Applying the motto "If you can't beat 'em, join 'em," much of the work of Kurt Haertel during the 1960s and early 1970s was focused on providing Europe with a centralized mechanism for the creation and enforcement of patents. The European Patent Convention thus provided Europe with the EPO, a substantial organization that could compete with the USPTO to generate European patents for Europeans. Clearly, European policymakers knew that they had to encourage their industries to patent as much technology as possible if Europe was to have any reasonable chance of beating the Americans at their own game. The competitiveness between these two substantial economic regions then laid the groundwork for an economic war for technological supremacy.

The lie, of course, was that this would be achieved in the spirit of free trade, and with the GATT failing to acknowledge the role that intellectual property could play in erecting trade barriers, there was little that could be done to stop their proliferation. Inevitably, Stanley Cohen and Herbert Boyer's breakthrough opened the doors to the exploitation of a new technology, but in the heat of this economic war, and with technological supremacy being its objective, the patent systems in the United States and Europe ignored a fundamental principle – that patents are about products of man and not products of nature, mathematical formula or abstract ideas.

The ability of a foreign patent owner to exercise absolute control over the use of a patented technology in any country that has a patent system is a conduit through which the economic policies of foreign countries can be implemented within the host country. Whether those policies are directed to encouraging skilled workers and artisans to emigrate from one country to another or to create barriers to such emigration as they were in the past, or whether they are directed towards protecting economies from the effects of "unfair" competition as they are now, a case can be made that patents, rather than being the harbingers of innovation, are merely the instruments of a protectionist agenda. That inventors have benefited from patent monopolies is merely incidental to, and not a primary objective of, patent systems. Therefore, patents facilitate extraterritorial control of technology in countries that are net importers of technology, and this is one of the reasons why Switzerland in the nineteenth century repeatedly ignored Germany's demands that it adopt a national patent system and why India in 1970 passed a patent law that specifically excluded "substances intended for use, or capable of being used, as food or as medicine or drug" as inventions.[112] Indeed, that is the very reason why Germany did not allow the patenting of chemical substances between 1877 and 1968 and why Italy (along with other European countries) did not allow patents on pharmaceutical substances until 1978. Moreover, until 1978, the United Kingdom pursued a policy of compulsory licensing that could be applied in various ways, and between 1919 and 1949 also excluded the patenting of chemical substances.

This, of course, does not explain why countries that are net importers of technology have continued to embrace the patent system. Perhaps they believe that technological innovation needs to be encouraged; or they believe that the costs imposed by the patent system are less than the benefits that it provides; or they believe that they must retain it simply because, in the past, someone thought that granting monopoly rights was a good idea; or maybe they have accepted that without a patent system, the markets of net exporting technology countries will be closed to them. Whatever the reason, the current orthodoxy promotes the view that higher productive capacity and employment are generated by technological development – something to be encouraged. Of course there are many ways to encourage innovation. The fact that technological innovation occurred for thousands of years before anyone had heard of letters patent or *privilegi* may have simply been due

---

112 Section 5(1)(a) Patents Act, 1970 (India).

to necessity. But as Eric Shift's famous study on Switzerland and the Netherlands showed, the lack of a patent system did not stifle their industrialization during the late nineteenth century. Furthermore, Christine McLeod and Alessandro Nuvolari found that at the height of the United Kingdom's economic domination of world trade in the mid-nineteenth century, about 40 percent of significant inventions were not patented (see MacLeod and Nuvolari 2006). In fact, it was the appropriation of thousands of German and other "enemy" patents, trademarks and copyrights by American governments in World War I and World War II that facilitated the establishment of key chemical, pharmaceutical and defense industries in the United States.

That patents continue to be part of the armory that protects the American economy from "unfair competition" is demonstrably clear. On February 6, 2008 a group of US trade unions that included the Communications Workers of America, the International Brotherhood of Teamsters, United Steelworkers and Patent Office Professional Association wrote to the US Senate expressing their "deep concern" that the patent-reform proposals contained in s. 1145, Patent Reform Bill, 2007 "could undermine the competitiveness of US industry and put our members' jobs at risk." The proposed legislation sought to bring US patent law in line with the patent law of other countries, but instead of supporting the creation of a level playing field, the trade unions complained that the legislation would increase "the likelihood of American inventions being stolen by our international competitors" and this would have the negative effect of "inhibiting sorely needed new investment in domestic manufacturing." In rather an apocalyptic crescendo, the trade unions' letter concluded that the legislation would only "contribute" to the loss of American jobs, devastating "scores of communities" across America.

Even prior to the trade unions' letter, John Sullivan, the General Counsel of the US Department of Commerce, admitted that the first-to-file patent system, one of the proposed reforms that would bring the US patent system into line with the rest of the world, had "potential benefits" to the United States. Yet in a letter to Howard Berman, the chairman of the Subcommittee on Courts, the Internet, and Intellectual Property of the Committee on the Judiciary in the House of Representatives, on May 16, 2007, he wrote that the department did "not support immediate conversion to first-to-file via this legislation." One might have believed, judging by these letters, that the proposed legislation was detrimental to American competitiveness. In truth, it was merely the extension of a process of internationalization that was initiated by the United States in 1873.[113]

---

113 US concerns over the antipatent movement in Europe prompted the US government of President Ulysses Grant to ask the Austro-Hungarian Empire, which was to host a World Trade Fair in Vienna in 1873, to invite governments to send representatives for what was to be the first international patent convention. The Austro-Hungarian government agreed, and so in August 1873, delegates from all over the world met to discuss how to improve international cooperation with respect to intellectual property.

It would seem that the US trade unions were touting the same message as Pfizer and the American software industry in the 1970s (Gorlin 1985),[114] that the so-called "unprecedented decline" of the US international trade position was caused by the theft of "American inventions by…international competitors." Not only was this accusation now blatantly untrue and unfairly inculpatory, but it overlooked that fact that it is the sovereign right of all countries, subject to their own constitutions and to the international treaties to which they have subscribed, to make whatever laws they wish. In this respect, it is a matter for their governments, subject to these caveats, to decide what is and what is not property or intellectual property within their sovereign domains. Indeed, the unions ignored the fact that since 1995, when the WTO was established, TRIPS, one of the core agreements of the WTO and now applicable in 153 countries, specifically provides minimum legal standards for the creation and enforcement of all forms of intellectual property, including patents. Thus, for more than a decade these uniform standards, to which the United States subscribes, has operated to counter the very threat that the trade unions were now afraid of. Since TRIPS, Free Trade Agreements, which the United States has since negotiated with many countries, have raised these standards of intellectual property protections even more.

Moreover, their letter overlooked a key issue: many American companies are no longer owned or controlled by Americans but have become subsidiaries or associates of multinational corporations headquartered in other countries. For instance Novartis and F. Hoffman La Roche, both Swiss pharmaceutical giants, have been building significant business portfolios in the United States in the biotechnology, agriculture and pharmaceutical sectors.[115] Consequently, many American subsidiaries, or associates of companies like them, owe no particular allegiance to the United States, let alone to US workers, particularly as their foreign-based managements are not predisposed to making investment and production decisions with the US economy or workers in mind. Predictably, and properly, their focus is on maximizing profits and, accordingly, their responsibility to shareholders means that if in order to achieve this objective

---

114 Provided to the author by Peter Drahos through private correspondence. According to Jacques Gorlin, "There is mounting recognition that improved protection for software can be achieved by moving the IP (copyright) protection issue into the international trade regime. A number of trade associations have begun specifically to promote the inclusion of the issue in the MTN [Multinational Trade Negotiations]. These associations, in views already presented to the Office of the US Trade Representative, seek: (1) strengthen copyright enforcement in the developing countries in order to deal with the piracy of computer software in such countries as Singapore, Taiwan, Korea and Brazil and in the Arab countries of the Persian Gulf. These LDCs are centers of piracy because they either do not have adequate copyright legislation that meets the minimal standards contained in Berne or Universal Copyright Conventions, or, if they do, do not undertake adequate enforcement measures that are generally found in the industrialised countries…"

115 Novartis fully acquired Chiron Corporation in 2005, and La Roche fully acquired Genentech in 2008.

the company is required to move production away from the United States to lower-manufacturing-cost countries, then this is precisely what happens. Put bluntly, at the time of their letter, many significant "American inventions" were probably no longer owned or controlled by Americans.

Finally, in accusing other countries of patent piracy, what the unions were clearly unaware of was the history of the actions of past American governments that led to the confiscation of the intellectual property and other property of foreigners, which directly resulted in the advancement of the US economy; and while these foreigners were the nationals of countries that were considered to be enemies at the time, they were nonetheless private companies and individuals that were not directly involved in military hostilities against the United States. As a result, the rationale used by the United States to justify the confiscation of "enemy" property appeared insincere and convenient in hindsight. Indeed, if patents are personal property that belong not to a state, but to individuals, then on what possible basis could the American government have justified the confiscation of that property? Surely, a more appropriate response would have been to invalidate American patents, thereby enabling anyone to work the technology or property that was previously subject to those patents. It may be that such legislative action would have been just as unfair and inequitable to the former patent owner as confiscation, but if the rationale for this action was – as indeed it was – to overcome the effects of wartime shortages of essential medicines and commodities in the United States, then would it not have been better to simply open the market up, rather than transfer patent monopolies to fledgling American chemical companies?

Arguably, the reason why these American patents were not invalidated, but were confiscated to be kept intact and then sold to Americans for prices well below their true value, was that the patent monopolies that came with them could then be used to inhibit the postwar reentry into the US market of the foreign companies and individuals. American policymakers knew well that it was better to maintain these monopolies so that they could be used to protect their own postwar economy and their new owners, the American owners, in their home market. Furthermore, the intention was to then use the US market and the anticipated productive capacity of the US economy as a springboard upon which to compete with the former owners in their previous international markets. In this respect, the United States was not alone in acting in this capricious manner towards foreign "enemies." Other Allied Powers used the Treaty of Versailles to confiscate patents, many of which were also ultimately transferred to US and UK companies. As a result, the German chemical and pharmaceutical industries lost significant shares of their international markets to US or UK interests. One might argue that this was a form of wartime reparation, but the German companies involved did not start World War I, nor did they generally facilitate it.

However, if one accepts that patents are not merely private property, but are also instruments of state-sanctioned economic war, then perhaps the Allied action was justified. In fact, when one remembers that German chemical and pharmaceutical companies deliberately embarked upon a commercial strategy well before World War I that used US patent laws to suppress US production and employment, perhaps then the United States and other Allied Powers were arguably justified, on the grounds of national security alone, to do what they did.

Plainly the postwar American efforts to globalize their industries have produced economic and political policies that have favored the freer movement of goods and services, especially useful when production is based in the United States or the technology is owned or controlled by the United States; but today the effects of these policies are starting to undermine American workers as more and more manufacturing (and also research and development) moves offshore. Unsurprisingly, views within the United States are starting to shift away from the rhetoric of "free trade" and back towards "protectionism." Gene Sperling, a former aide to US president William Clinton, was quoted by the *Wall Street Journal* on November 21, 2007 as saying:

> Even those of us who are supportive of the open-market policies of the '90s have to take seriously that the large inflow of workers from China and India digesting American jobs is placing downward pressure on wages. That doesn't mean the answer is closing up shop in globalization, but it can't just mean business as usual either.

Globalization, however, is not as recent a phenomenon as Sperling suggests. Since World War II, American policymakers have understood that the United States has had much more to gain by exporting its domestic excess productive capacity. Not only did this bring employment to American workers, particularly in the early decades after World War II, but as American companies established factories in countries that had lower costs of production than in the United States, they were able to reduce prices of manufactured goods to American consumers while maximizing profits that were ultimately repatriated back to the United States to the benefit of American shareholders and taxpayers. In the drive for cheaper labor and production costs, American companies have invested billions throughout the world and in so doing have succeeded not only in meeting their own investment criteria but have, through these investments, significantly contributed to the industrialization of many developed and developing countries.

The change in emphasis in the United States away from manufacturing, particularly since the 1990s, has been facilitated with the help of various international trade agreements, such as the North American Free Trade Agreement (NAFTA), which came into effect on January 1, 1994. Through the effect of these kinds of agreements, the United States has ensured that international intellectual property protections have been raised to acceptable US standards. Unfortunately, this change in economic emphasis has also accelerated the redirection of capital away from traditional manufacturing industries in the United States and both toward new technologies such as biotechnology and toward manufacturing in lower-cost countries. These newer technologies are not as labor-intensive as manufacturing, and the capital inflows into these industries have funded a closer, much more collaborative, relationship with American universities. Even by 1970, American policymakers could anticipate this, and the Bayh–Dole Act was one of the principal instruments through which this policy was eventually brought into effect.

Evidently, as America's internal capacity to generate income through manufacturing has diminished, it has been necessary to find a replacement source of income, and one way to do this has been through an economic rent charged on those that use American intellectual property. That rent, being income in the form of patent, trademark and copyright royalties (in other words, state-sanctioned monopolies), is absolutely vital to the American economy today (just as it is to Japan and increasingly to members of the European Community). Of course, it was foreseeable that without adequate rent-collection measures, this strategy would be undermined by counterfeiters; so by the late 1980s, it had become essential that the world adopt minimum intellectual property protections – that is those acceptable to the United States, Japan and the European Community. This, of course, required the legal enforcement of those protections, and TRIPS, as previously discussed, was a result. Soon this economic rent will become significant to India and China as they are transformed from being net producers of manufactured goods into net producers of new technology and other intellectual property.

Essentially, what this means is that for the past 40 years, American economic policy has deliberately sacrificed the traditional manufacturing working classes of the US Midwest for a new paradigm – one that has significantly contributed to the income and wealth of the western coast states of Washington and California in particular, where America's IT and biotechnology industries established themselves. While the benefits to these states and industries have been enormous, the cost in terms of social dislocation in the Midwest has certainly been devastating. The result has seen a predictable political shift; on October 4, 2007 the *Wall Street Journal* reported that "by a nearly two-to-one margin, Republican voters believe free trade is bad for the US economy." That change in popular opinion among Republican voters has been encouraged in states like Ohio that have "lost more than 200,000 manufacturing jobs...since Nafta was implemented."[116]

Perhaps until now this gamble has paid off for the United States, given lower levels of inflation and the inflows of foreign capital through its stock markets, but for the American workers who have been caught in the crossfire, other than through the lower prices that they have been paying for consumer goods made in other countries using or applying American-owned intellectual property, the personal cost has been high.

The creation of more and more intellectual property has regrettably fueled the idea that this new economic paradigm, assuming a satisfactory enforcement system is in place internationally, is sustainable. And with dulled memories or deficient knowledge, politicians and policymakers have accepted this, not only in the United States, but throughout the world. Following the lead of the United States, Europe and Japan followed suit, which explains, for instance, why patents on chemical substances were permitted in Germany in 1968 and why in 1978 Italy was forced, through its

---

116 "Candidates Rebuked For Attacks on NAFTA," *Financial Times*, February 28, 2008.

membership of the European Patent Convention, to remove the ban on the patenting of pharmaceuticals. Even India, which in 1970 passed a patent law that prohibited the patenting of pharmaceutical substances, complied with its obligations under TRIPS to remove this ban in 2005.

And this expansion of intellectual property is regrettable, too, because much of it has been created in biotechnology and IT through patents that do not deserve merit because they are not "inventions." The expansion of the patent domain into these fields has often only been made possible by ignoring the historical fact that in 1623 the English Parliament acknowledged that it would be ultimately detrimental to the economy for monopolies to be allowed unless for a very limited time and in respect to something that was an "invention." That the American courts have aided and abetted the distortion of the patent system through the enforcement of American patents for innovations that are not "inventions," and that they have been supported in Europe and Japan and, ultimately, by many other countries in similar ways, suggests that the time has come for the world to reconsider whether a patent system today is operating as it should.

Presently, the patent systems of the world are incapable of adequately assessing whether the patentability criteria which are set under art. 27.1 TRIPS are being satisfied. The explosion in the number of patents has stretched the resources of patent offices everywhere. Many now struggle to employ the numbers of patent examiners needed to properly make these assessments. Moreover, the cost of enforcement of patents is, as it has always been, incredibly high and inefficient. The economic cost of that inefficiency has been felt not only by patent owners who are trying to enforce their property claims around the world in different courts, but by the users of technology who may be paying an unnecessarily high price because no one can afford to challenge the validity of what is possibly an invalid patent. Often the breadth of the patent monopolies is so wide that they claim as inventions the speculative use of the technology that is the subject of the patent; for example, patents that claim the use of isolated biological materials in vaccines, when all that the patent discloses is the genetic and amino acid sequence of that material and the use of that material in a rudimentary diagnostic assay. The impact of such overreaching and greedy activity is mostly unmeasured, but some would intuitively argue that it must be the case that it acts as a dampener on medical and scientific research, especially when the nexus between that research and commerce is as close as it is today. Surely it is obvious that if the ultimate objective of medical and scientific research is the achievement of a patent, then it must follow that if the field of research is already claimed by other patents, then the research that would have happened if that were not so, *will now not happen*. Beyond these issues, today the vast majority of the world's patents are owned or controlled by companies that do not necessarily bear any allegiance to any particular country or any particular people. Fundamentally, this was never the purpose of patents.

The assumption that without the world's patent systems, the necessary investment in new technologies would evaporate or would be inadequate must be challenged; and if it is found that there is a need for some form of incentive, then adequate measures should be put in place to ensure that these incentives are not abused. Frankly, the time has come for the world, as a global community, to seriously question whether the patent system is all that it purports to be.

That the patent systems of the world are still facing the same sorts of criticisms that the English patent system faced in the 1850s and 1860s surely suggests that the world's patent systems are not and never can be optimal.

Winston Churchill said that "the farther backward you can look, the farther forward you can see," and yet, as we seek solutions to the problems inherent in the workings of the world's modern patent systems, we seem unable to grasp this simple wisdom. If we cast our minds back to England 150 years ago, the British patent system was the subject of serious criticism; indeed, by 1872 the House of Lords had passed a bill that would have, if the House of Commons had followed suit, reduced the patent term to 7 years. The British parliamentary committee that scrutinized the British patent system between 1862 and 1864 examined a number of issues that are today, once more, the subject of the very same criticisms and concerns as expressed at that time. First there was the issue of patent quality, which was said to have led to patents of dubious validity. Next there was the issue of the lack of a proper system of pre-grant patent examination, also contributing to dubious and overlapping patents. Finally, there was the issue of the inefficiency and cost of the post-grant judicial scrutiny of granted patents that, it was believed, acted as a disincentive to the removal of invalid patents.

Nineteenth-century Americans, on the other hand, believed that the US patent system, which had preliminary examination and "less expensive" litigation, provided the right balance between the rights of the inventor to a patent monopoly and the rights of the state, which would be free to make use of the invention at the expiration of that monopoly. So it was the United States that was determined to arrest the trend that threatened Europe's patent systems. The process of internationalization encouraged further reforms in the British patent system and in other European countries and slowly led to the establishment of the WIPO and facilitated dialogue at an international level, which also led to additional reforms and innovations within the patent systems of the world. The Patent Cooperation Treaty in particular was to provide inventors with a simple and efficient system of applying for patents around the world through a single patent application filed with the patent office of their choice; and today the unprecedented cooperation between patent offices is leading to the establishment of patent "superhighways" in an attempt to further reduce the cost of patent examination and increase the productivity of the patent systems.[117] Whether this experiment will provide a permanent solution is yet to be seen.

In the meantime, in spite of all the developments, the patent communities are really no closer to resolving these persistent problems (Jaffe and Lerner 2004). Whether this is because the patent system is a model that is fundamentally flawed or whether this is because, as those who believe in the patent system argue, it is merely a reflection of the fact that the process of reform has not yet reached its zenith, is a debate or discussion that has yet to happen at an international level.

---

117 "EPO and US speed up patent-granting process," *Managing Intellectual Property*, March 17, 2008.

So far all diplomatic efforts have proceeded on the assumptions that the patent system is a permanent reality; that there is no better system; that if only it could be "improved" and made more "efficient," then perhaps the issue of the lack of patent quality,[118] greater patent productivity,[119] and less patent litigation and expense[120] – a patent utopia – would result.

The problem is that the present controversy over patent-law reform in the United States, which has stalled, and the ad hoc discussions that have taken place across the globe about various aspects of patent law and patent administration have been blind to the fact that the world today is no longer a collection of feudal states that are so independent of each other that they can legitimately ignore how their internal decisions impact their neighbors. This is the point that Cordell Hull was making before the outbreak of World War II, and this is the point of having such organizations as the IMF, the World Bank, the United Nations and the WTO. The world no longer needs to operate under the illusion that the patent systems encourage innovation and improve economic opportunities. We now live in a global community that has been working

---

118 Staff Union of the European Patent Office (SUEPO) position paper, *Quality of Examination at the EPO*, May 2004. Also see US Government Accountability Office report, *Hiring Efforts Are Not Sufficient to Reduce the Patent Application Backlog*, GAO-07-11-2, September 2007. This report states that the GAO undertook the report because of the "increases in the volume and complexity of patent applications have lengthened the amount of time it takes the US Patent and Trademark Office to process them."

119 EU Administrative Council report to the Administrative Council Members of the EU, *Future workload*, CA/144/07, November 23, 2007. The report states "the pressure that follows from b) to h) translates itself into problems for the major patent offices in the world to cope with the ever increasing workload. These problems consist of growing backlogs and insufficient time and resources to examine applications with the necessary thoroughness" 7(17). The problems b) to h) as listed are: b) dramatic growth of the number of patent applications; c) the complexity and volume of applications is increasing; d) much of the growth in patent activity comes from new and emerging technologies, like ICT, nanotechnology and others; e) international patent activity increases, and h) impact on the production. 3(7)–7(16).

120 Statement of Mark B. Myers, senior vice president, Corporate Research and Technology, Xerox Corporation (retired) to the US House of Representatives Committee on the Judiciary, *A Patent System for the 21st Century*, February 15, 2007. He stated: "Since 1980 a series of judicial, legislative, and administrative actions have extended patenting to new technologies (biotechnology) and to technologies previously without or subject to other forms of intellectual property protection (software and business methods), encouraged the emergence of new players (universities), strengthened the position of patent holders vis-à-vis infringers domestically and internationally, relaxed other restraints on the use of patents (antitrust enforcement), and extended their reach upstream from commercial products to scientific research tools and materials. As a result, patents are being more zealously sought, vigorously asserted, and aggressively enforced than ever before. There are many indications that firms in a variety of industries, as well as universities and public institutions, are attaching greater importance to patents and are willing to pay higher costs to acquire, exercise, and defend them. The workload of the US Patent and Trademark Office has increased several-fold in the last few decades, to the point that it is issuing approximately 100 patents every working hour. Meanwhile, the costs of acquiring patents, promoting or securing licenses to patented technology, and prosecuting and defending against infringement allegations in the increasing number of patent suits are rising rapidly."

towards true free trade for over 60 years, and although it is clear that the ultimate goal of no trade barriers of any kind has yet to be achieved, it is also clear that history does not support nor justify the retention of the world's patent systems – systems that are one of the key instruments of economic protectionism. In a free trade world, there is no place for such economic protections, and the global community needs to acknowledge that the patent system sits like the elephant of protectionism in the free trade room.

Watching how the patent system has ultimately intruded upon a field that until recently was sacrosanct – namely, nature – only reinforces the strength of the argument against the retention of the world's patent systems. What this incursion has led to is a proliferation of patents for thousands of biological materials that are not and never were inventions; it has led to an explosion of patents that have reduced the productivity of patent offices throughout the world with respect to the prosecution of legitimate inventions; it has led to the misallocation of capital into the production of therapeutics and diagnostics over human illness and diseases that are expensive and inefficient; it has contributed to undermining social and industrial reforms in the developing countries that have become the manufacturing centers for the owners of intellectual property; it has led to the growing reliance on technology to solve the world's problems by ignoring the problems that unregulated new technologies create; it has distorted the scientific spirit by encouraging scientists to be less open about their research and encouraged only by the promise of wealth; it has produced universities that are no longer citadels of independent research and learning, but components of a commercial world that justifies its actions solely on the basis of profit. Finally, the patent system has contributed to the destruction of the generosity of past generations, generosity that had allowed people to freely borrow information about themselves, their cultures, their technologies and the world around them and contributed to that store of knowledge that the US Supreme Court described as being "free to all men and reserved exclusively to none."[121]

A free culture has been our past, but it will only be our future if we change the path we are on right now.

—Lawrence Lessig

Note

Since writing this chapter there have been three significant developments in patent law in the United States that are relevant. The first is the passage of the American Invents Act (AIA) in 2011. This law significantly reforms US patent law. Apart from changing it from a first-to-invent to a first-to-file system, the AIA also directed the USPTO to undertake a study into the impact of US patent law on secondary genetic tests. That inquiry commenced in February 2012 and is continuing. The second is in regard to the

---

121 *Funk Brothers Seed Co v. Kalo Inoculant Co.* 333 US 127 (1948).

US Supreme Court decision in *Prometheus v. Mayo Clinic* which was delivered on March 20, 2012. In its unanimous decision the court invalidated patent claims to a diagnostic method that involved various steps in determining the correlation of metabolites in the human body in response to the administration of specific drugs in the treatment of specific aliments. According to the court the claims were patent ineligible under s.101 (i.e., lacking patentable subject matter) because they sought to monopolize "a law of nature." The court held:

> If a law of nature is not patentable, then neither is a process reciting a law of nature, unless that process has additional features that provide practical assurance that the process is more than a drafting effort designed to monopolize the law of nature itself. A patent, for example, could not simply recite a law of nature and then add the instruction "apply the law."

And finally the third is the US Supreme Court's decision to grant *certiorari* in *Association for Molecular Pathology et al. v. USPTO and Myriad Genetics*. This case concerns the validity of claims to composition of matter and methods over the BRCA genetic mutations linked to breast and ovarian cancers. The court also ordered that the decision of the Federal Circuit, which reversed the District Court's finding of invalidity and upheld the validity of the composition of matter claims, be vacated and remanded back to the Federal Circuit in light of *Prometheus v. Mayo Clinic*.

References

All web addresses last accessed August 2012.

Abbott, F. M. 2008. "Post-mortem for the Geneva Mini-Ministerial: Where does TRIPS go from here?" International Centre for Trade and Sustainable Development, Information Note No. 7, August.

_____. 2005. "The WTO Medicines Decision: World Pharmaceutical Trade and the Protection of Public Health." *American Journal of International Law* 99 (2): 317–58.

Australian Law Reform Commission Report. 2004. *Genes and Ingenuity: Gene Patenting and Human Health*. Available at http://www.austlii.edu.au/au/other/alrc/publications/reports/99/index.html

Bessen, J. and M. J. Meurer. 2008. *Patent Failure: How Judges, Bureaucrats, and Lawyers Put Innovation at Risk*. Princeton: Princeton University Press.

Boldrin, M. and D. K. Levine. 2008. *Against Intellectual Property*. New York: Cambridge University Press.

Burk, D. L. and M. A. Lemley. 2009. *The Patent Crisis and How the Courts Can Solve It*. Chicago: University of Chicago Press.

Correa, C. M. 2006. "Pharmaceutical inventions: When is the granting of a patent justified?" *International Journal of Intellectual Property Management* 1: 4–21.

Chandler, A. D. 1992 "Organizational Capabilities and the Economic History of the Industrial Enterprise." *Journal of Economic Perspectives* 6 (3): 79–100 (82).

Diggins, B. 1955. "The Patent-Antitrust Problem." *Michigan Law Review* 53 (8): 1093–1118.

Drahos, P. (ed.) 2005. *Death of Patents*. London: Lawtext Publishing and Queen Mary Intellectual Property Law Institute.

_____. 2004. "Towards an International Framework for the Protection of Traditional Group Knowledge and Practice." UNCTAD-Commonwealth Secretariat Workshop.

_____.1999. "Biotechnology Patents, Markets and Morality." *European Intellectual Property Review* 21 (9): 441–4.

Drahos, P. with J. Braithwaite. 2002. *Information Feudalism*. London: Earthscan.

Dutfield, G. 2003. *Intellectual Property Rights and the Life Science Industries*. Hampshire: Ashgate.

_____. 1996. "Beyond Intellectual Property: Towards Traditional Resources Rights for Indigenous Peoples and Local Communities." Ottawa: International Development Research Centre.

Ebersole, T. J., M. C. Guthrie and J. A. Goldstein. 2005. "Patent Pools as a Solution to the Licensing Problems of Diagnostic Genetics." *Intellectual Property and Technology Law Journal* 17 (1): 6–13.

Fink, M. 2004. "Patenting Business Methods in Europe: What Lies Ahead?" *Indiana Law Journal* 79: 299–321.

Gold, E. R. 2003. "Biotechnology patents: Strategies for meeting economic and ethical concerns." *Nature Genetics* (30): 359.

Gold E. R., W. A. Adams, L. Bernier, T. Bubela, D. Castle, G. C. de Langavant, L. M. Cloutier, A. S. Darr, H. Delerue, A. J. Glass, E. Henry, L. Knowles, J. Morin, T. Piper and P. J. D. Smith. 2008. "Toward a New Era of Intellectual Property: From Confrontation to Negotiation – A Report by the International Expert Group on Biotechnology, Innovation and Intellectual Property." Available at http://papers.ssrn.com/sol3/papers.cfm?abstract_id=1260099

Gorlin, J. J. 1985. "A Trade-Based Approach for the International Copyright Protection for Computer Software." Unpublished monograph.

Gorman, J. T., A. D. Griffiths and P. J. Whitehead. 2006. "An Analysis of the Use of Plant Products for Commerce in Remote Aboriginal Communities of Northern Australia." *Economic Botany* 60 (4): 362–73.

Greene, S. 2004. "Indigenous People Incorporated." *Current Anthropology* 45 (2): 211–37.

Gupta, R. K. and L. Balasubrahmanyam. 1998. "The turmeric effect." *World Patent Information* 20: 185–91.

Hammond, E. 2009. "Indonesia fights to change WHO rules on flu vaccines." *Grain*, April. Available at http://www.grain.org/seedling/index.cfm?id=593

Heller, M. A. and R. S. Eisenberg. 1998 "Can Patents Deter Innovation? The Anticommons in Biomedical Research." *Science* 280 (5364): 698–701.

Howson, H. and C. Howson. 1872. *A Brief Inquiry into the Principles, Effect, and Present State of the American Patent System*. Philadelphia: Sherman & Co.

Hestermeyer, H. 2007. *Human Rights and the WTO: The Case of Patents and Access to Medicines*. Oxford: Oxford University Press.

Hope, J. 2008. *Biobazaar: The Open Source Revolution and Biotechnology*. Boston: Harvard University Press.

Hughes, S. S. 2001. "Making Dollars Out of DNA," *Isis* 92: 541–75.

Jaffe, A. B. and J. Learner. 2004. *Innovation And Its Discontents: How Our Broken Patent System Is Endangering Innovation And Progress and What To Do About It*. Princeton: Princeton University Press.

Koehn, F. E. and G. T. Carter. 2006. "The evolving role of natural products in drug discovery." *Nature Reviews Drug Discovery* 4: 206–20.

Krikorian, G. 2008. "The politics of patents: Conditions of implementation of public health policy in Thailand." Paper prepared for the ECPR 2008 Joint Sessions of Workshops Workshop "The Politics of Intellectual Property," Rennes, April 11–16.

Kronstein, H. and I. Till. 1947 "A Reevaluation of the International Patent Convention." *Law and Contemporary Problems* 12 (4): 765–81.

Lawson, C. 2008. "Managerialist influences on granting patents in Australia." *Australian Journal of Administrative Law* 15: 70–99.

Leaf, C. 2005. "The Law of Unintended Consequences." *Fortune*, September 19. Available at http://money.cnn.com/magazines/fortune/fortune_archive/2005/09/19/8272884/index.htm

Learner, J., M. Strojwas and J. Tirole. 2007. "The Design of Patent Pools: The Determinants of Licensing Rules." *RAND Journal of Economics* 38 (3): 610–25.

Leveque, F. and Y. Meniere. 2008. "Technology Standards, Patents and Antitrust." *Competition and Regulation in Network Industries* 9 (1): 29–48. Available at http://papers.ssrn.com/sol3/papers.cfm?abstract_id=1133834

Li, A. 2003. *J. B. Collip and the Development of Medical Research in Canada*. Montreal: McGill-Queen's University Press.

Li, J. W. H. and C. Vederas. 2009. "Drug Discovery and Natural Products: End of an Era or an Endless Frontier?" *Science* 325 (5937): 161–5.

Machlup, F. 1961. "Patents and Inventive Effort." *Science, New Series* 133 (3463): 1463–6.

Machlup, F. and E. Penrose. 1950. "The Patent Controversy in the Nineteenth Century." *Journal of Economic History* 10 (1): 1–29.

MacLeod, C. and A. Nuvolari. 2006. "The Pitfalls of Prosopography: Inventors in the Dictionary of National Biography." *Technology and Culture* 47: 757–76.

Matthjis, G. 2006. "The European opposition against the BRCA gene patents." *Familial Cancer* 5: 95–102.

Merges, R. P. 2001. "Institutions for Intellectual Property Transactions: The Case of Patent Pools." In R. Dreyfuss, D. L. Zimmerman and H. First (eds), *Expanding the Boundaries of Intellectual Property*. Oxford: Oxford University Press.

Mill, J. S. 1848. *The Principles of Political Economy with some of their Applications to Social Philosophy*. London: Longmans, Green and Co.

Moir, H. 2009 "Do Patent Systems Improve Economic Well-Being? An Exploration of the Inventiveness of Business Method Patents." PhD thesis, Australian National University.

———. 2008. "What are the costs and benefits of patent systems?" Centre for the Governance of Knowledge and Development, Australian National University. Available at http://cgkd.anu.edu.au/menus/workingpapers.php

Neville, W. J. 2007. "Healing the Nation: Access to Medicines under the Pharmaceutical Benefits Scheme – The Jurisprudence from History." PhD thesis, Australian National University.

Newman, D. J. and G, M. Cragg. 2007. "Natural Products as Sources of New Drugs over the Last 25 Years." *Journal of Natural Products* 70: 461–77.

Nuffield Council on Bioethics. 2002. "The Ethics of Patenting DNA: A Discussion Paper." Available at http://www.nuffieldbioethics.org/patenting-dna

Oudemans, G. 1963. *The Draft European Patent Convention*. London: Stevens & Sons Ltd.

Palombi, L. 2009. *Gene Cartels Biotech Patents in the Age of Free Trade*. Cheltenham: E. Elgar.

Pila, J. 2005a. "Article 52(2) of the Convention on the Grant of European Patents: What did the framers intend? A study of the travaux preparatoires." Available at http://papers.ssrn.com/sol3/papers.cfm?abstract_id=736064

———. 2005b. "Dispute over the meaning of 'Invention' in Article 52(2) EPC – The Patentability of computer-implemented Inventions in Europe." Available at http://papers.ssrn.com/sol3/papers.cfm?abstract_id=593881

Ritter, D. 2004. "Switzerland's Patent Law History." *Fordham Intellectual Property, Media and Entertainment Law Journal* 14: 463–95.

Sayre, L. E. 1919. "Patent laws in regard to the protection of chemical industry." *Transactions of the Kansas Academy of Science* 30: 39–44 (43).

Schiff, E. 1971. *Industrialization without National Patents: The Netherlands, 1869–1912, Switzerland, 1850–1907*. Princeton: Princeton University Press.

Schuster, E. J. 1913. "Germany." *Journal of the Society of Comparative Legislation* 13 (2): 302–3.

Schuster, G. 1909. "The Patents and Designs Act, 1907." *Economic Journal* 19 (76): 538–51.

Seckelmann, M. 2001. "The Quest for Legal Stability: Patent Protection within the German Empire, 1871–1903." European Business History Association conference paper, Oslo, August 31–September 1, 2001.

Shanker, D. 2005. "Fault Lines in the WTO: An Analysis of the TRIPS Agreement and Developing Countries." PhD thesis, University of Wollongong.

So, A. D., B. N. Sampat, A. K. Rai, R. Cook-Deegan, J. Reichman, R. Weissman and A. Kapczynski. 2008. "Is Bayh-Dole Good for Developing Countries? Lessons from the US Experience." *Plos Biology* 6 (10): 2078–84.

Soini, S., S. Ayme and G. Matthjis. 2008. "Patenting and licensing in genetic testing: Ethical, legal and social issues." *European Journal of Human Genetics* 16 (1): 10–50.

Steen, K. 2001. "Patents, Patriotism, and 'Skilled in the Art': USA v The Chemical Foundation 1923–1926." *Isis* 92: 91–122.

't Hoen, E. F. M. 2009. *The Global Politics of Pharmaceutical Monopoly Power: Drug Patents, Access, Innovation and the Application of the WTO Doha Declaration on TRIPS and Public Health.* The Netherlands: AMB Diemen.

Teeling-Smith, G. 1974. "How doctors prescribe and why." *Postgraduate Medical Journal* 50: 65–7.

Te Pareake Mead, A. and S. Ratuva (eds). 2007. *Pacific Genes and Life Patents.* Call of the Earth (Llamado de la Tierra) and the United Nations University Institute of Advanced Studies.

Thomas, C. J. 1958. "The Pharmaceutical Industry." In Duncan Burn (ed.), *The Structure of British Industry A Symposium,* vol 2. London: Cambridge University Press.

UK Board of Trade. 1947. *Patents and Designs Acts, Final Report of the Departmental Committee.* 1946–47 (Cmd 7206), K. R. Swan (chair).

_____. 1931. *Report of the Departmental Committee on the Patents and Designs Acts and Practice of the Patent Office.* 1930–31 (Cmd 3829), C. H. Sargant (chair).

UK Committee of Inquiry. 1970. *The British Patent System.*1970–71 (Cmd 4407), M. A. L. Banks (chair).

_____. 1967. *Relationship of the Pharmaceutical Industry with the National Health Services.* 1965–67 (Cmd 3410), Lord Sainsbury (chair).

US Subcommittee on Patents, Trademarks, and Copyrights of the Committee on the Judiciary. 1958. *An Economic Review of the Patent System.* United States Senate, 85th Congress, Study No. 15. Washington DC: US Government Printing Office.

Van Pottelsberghe, B. 2009. "Lost Property: The European patent system and why it doesn't work." Available at http://www.bruegel.org/download/parent/312-lost-property-the-european-patent-system-and-why-it-doesnt-work/file/761-lost-property-the-european-patent-system-and-why-it-doesnt-work-english/

Van Zimmeren, E., B. Verbeure, G. Matthijs and G. van Overwalle. 2006. "A clearing house for diagnostic testing: The solution to ensure access to and use of patented genetic inventions." *Bulletin of the World Health Organization* 84: 352–9.

Vaughan, F. W. 1919. "Suppression and non-working of patents, with special reference to the dye and chemical industries." *American Economic Review* 9 (4): 693–700.

Verbeure, B., E. van Zimmeren, G. Matthijs and G. van Overwalle. 2006. "Patent pools and diagnostic testing." *Trends in Biotechnology* 24 (3): 115–20.

Young, J. W. 2002. "Technological Cooperation in Wilson's Strategy for EEC Entry." In O. J. Daddow (ed.), *Harold Wilson and European integration: Britain's Second Application to Join the EEC.* London: Frank Cass Publishers.

Lightning Source UK Ltd.
Milton Keynes UK
UKOW040952011112

201459UK00002B/23/P